ON THE HIGH ROAD The History of Godin Tepe, Iran

PUBLISHED BY ROYAL ONTARIO MUSEUM PRESS
WITH THE GENEROUS SUPPORT OF THE LOUISE HAWLEY STONE CHARITABLE TRUST
AND WITH DONATION FROM THE A. K. JABBARI CHARITABLE TRUST

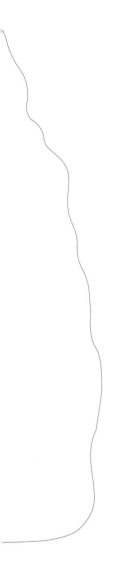

Bibliotheca Iranica

Archaeology, Art and Architecture Series, No. 1

Hilary Gopnik

Mitchell S. Rothman

with contributions by Robert C. Henrickson and Virginia R. Badler

ON THE HIGH ROAD The History of Godin Tepe, Iran

Mazda Publishers in association with the Royal Ontario Museum

To T. Cuyler Young, Jr.

Mazda Publishers, Inc.
Academic publishers since 1980
P.O. Box 2603, Costa Mesa, California 92628 U.S.A.
www.mazdapub.com
A. K. Jabbari, Publisher

Royal Ontario Museum
100 Queen's Park
Toronto, Ontario
M5S 2C6
www.rom.on.ca

The Royal Ontario Museum is an agency of the Ontario Ministry of Culture.

Library of Congress Cataloging-in-Publication Data

On the High Road : The History of Godin Tepe, Iran / edited by Hilary Gopnik and Mitchell S. Rothman.
p. cm. — (Bibliotheca Iranica: Archaeology, Art & Architecture Series ; 1)
Includes bibliographical references and index.
ISBN 13: 978-1-56859-165-0 (alk. paper)
ISBN 10: 1-56859-165-9
1. Godin Tepe (Iran)—History 2. Excavations (Archaeology)—Iran—Godin Tepe. I. Gopnik, Hilary, 1960- II. Rothman, Mitchell S., 1952-
DS262.G6O6 2008
935—dc22
2008020398

Contents

Maps

Plans

Sections

Tables

Key to Architectural Plans

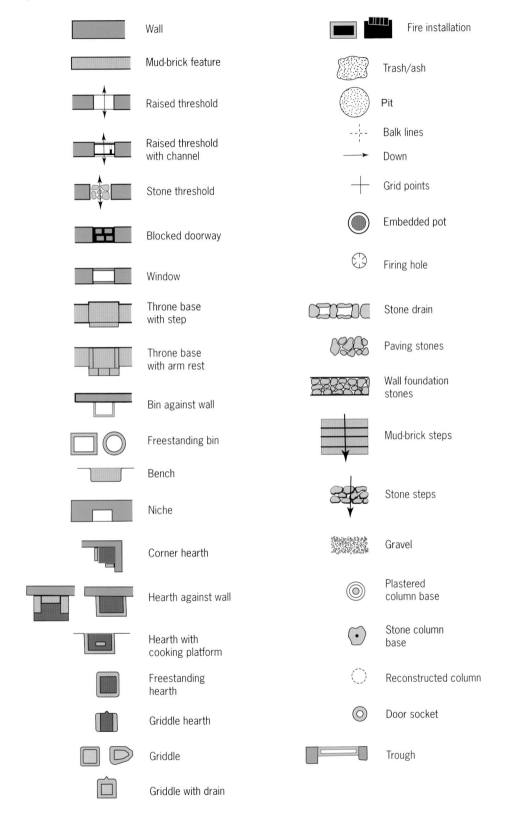

Wall

Mud-brick feature

Raised threshold

Raised threshold with channel

Stone threshold

Blocked doorway

Window

Throne base with step

Throne base with arm rest

Bin against wall

Freestanding bin

Bench

Niche

Corner hearth

Hearth against wall

Hearth with cooking platform

Freestanding hearth

Griddle hearth

Griddle

Griddle with drain

Fire installation

Trash/ash

Pit

Balk lines

Down

Grid points

Embedded pot

Firing hole

Stone drain

Paving stones

Wall foundation stones

Mud-brick steps

Stone steps

Gravel

Plastered column base

Stone column base

Reconstructed column

Door socket

Trough

Preface

Hilary Gopnik

The site of Godin Tepe was excavated by T. Cuyler Young, Jr., under the auspices of the Royal Ontario Museum (ROM) over the course of five field seasons from 1965 to 1973. Thirty-four years later this volume presents for the first time in one place the results of these excavations. Perched on the High Road, the major east-west route through the Zagros Mountains, Godin was an impressive site throughout the 4,000 years that it was occupied. Its excavation was a benchmark in the archaeology of central western Iran, but most of the material from that excavation, much of it now part of the ROM collection, remained essentially unknown to all but a few experts for many years.

Cuyler Young had planned to put out a series of publications about Godin, one for each level at the site, but a full life as an academic and administrator at the ROM, including a stint as the Museum's director from 1985 to 1990, forced him to put his precious Godin on the back burner. After his retirement he made a firm plan with Mitchell Rothman to publish Periods IV and VI, but a series of health problems delayed work on that volume. In 2005, when it became clear that Cuyler's failing health would not permit him to fulfill his goal, his close friend and colleague Lisa Golombek contacted me to see what could be done.

Lisa suggested that the full publication project of a one-volume-per-level classic excavation report presenting all of the data from the site was too unwieldy for anyone other than Cuyler to manage and another plan of attack was needed. As we discussed the glories of Godin and the necessity of making this material available to scholarship, we began to realize that Godin was really too interesting to keep only within the academic community. It should be possible, we reflected, to bring Godin out of the storerooms for a larger audience as well. The problem of the huge quantities of data that an archaeological excavation produces, and that a classic archaeological site report must publish, could now be managed through electronic media, so the print publication could focus on the interpretation of finds instead of just the presentation of data. This volume is what emerged from these discussions.

I recruited Mitchell Rothman to write the chapters on Godin IV and VI, as well as a chapter on the environment of Godin. Virginia Badler agreed to contribute her many years of research on Period VI by collaborating with Mitchell Rothman on the Godin VI chapter. Robert Henrickson, who had completed a dissertation on Godin III, was asked to write a chapter on the material from those levels at the site.

The goal of this publication is to present the most important material from each period of Godin in a style that is accessible to interested readers who are not specialists in archaeology, while at the same time providing scholars with enough raw data and interpretation to give a good overview of each level of the site. We also use the long history of Godin from the Neolithic to the Iron Age to discuss the nature of human societies in the highlands of the ancient Near East. We have tried to use straightforward terminology whenever possible and when technical terms were required we have glossed them. We have used extensive photographic illustration on the principle that a picture is worth a thousand words, particularly to those who are not familiar with the look of a Near Eastern excavation. This volume is accompanied by a Web-based archive on the University of Toronto's T-Space research repository (https://tspace.library.utoronto.ca) that includes all the additional data on Godin in a format that scholars can access much more readily than they could printed data in even the weightiest of published volumes. Field notes, lot sheets, artifact lists, provenience lists, site photographs, and full technical reports are posted on that site for those scholars who require further information on a particular aspect of Godin. Fully referenced versions of the chapters are also available on the T-Space site. We believe that this dual approach to publishing Godin reflects Cuyler Young's lifelong commitment to both scholarship and the museum-going public.

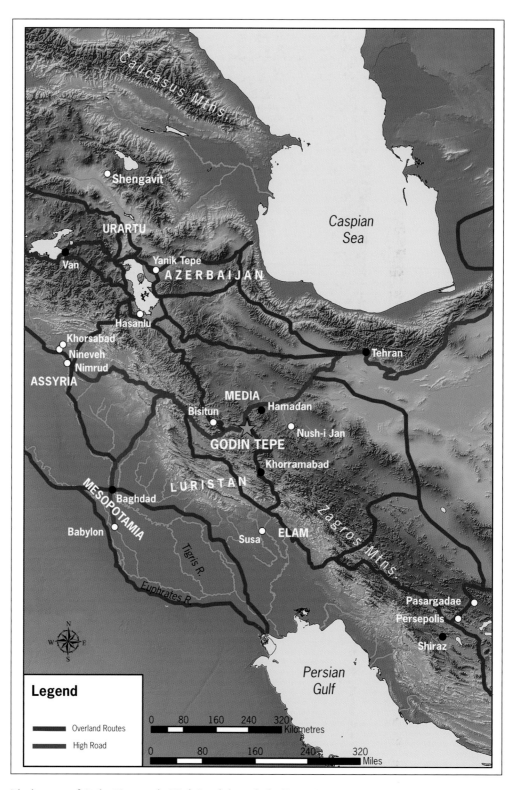

The location of Godin Tepe on the High Road through the Zagros Mountains

Introduction: Godin Tepe on the High Road

Hilary Gopnik

The mound of Godin Tepe towers above the plain of the Kangavar Valley in the Zagros Mountains in central western Iran, like a small volcano rising out of the sea. But Godin is not a natural formation. Its entire mass, covering some 15 hectares (37 acres) at the base and rising some 30 metres high, is composed almost entirely of the remains of people's lives. People chose to make their home in this strategic spot over the course of some 5,000 years, and layer upon layer of debris is all that is left to testify to their existence. The excavation of Godin Tepe, conducted by T. Cuyler Young, Jr., and the Royal Ontario Museum from 1965 to 1973, attempted to recover one small part of the lives of these long-dead people.

Godin Tepe is located directly on the High Road, the main pass from Mesopotamia through the Zagros Mountains to the resources and cultures of the East. This route, which in later periods came to be part of the Silk Road, was the main avenue for trade between East and West. It runs from southern Mesopotamia north along the Diyala River, and then into the Zagros Mountains. It follows mountain passes through the Mahidasht, Kermanshah, and Bisitun plains before arriving at the Kangavar Valley. From the Hellenistic era to modern times, the route would then run northeast over the towering Alvand range through the Asadabad pass, and onto the Iranian plateau. But during the period that Godin was occupied, the road through the Kangavar Valley took the shorter, if narrower and steeper, route through the pass cut by the Gamas Ab River, which flows past Godin and from there to the Asadabad Valley and onto the plateau. Godin stood astride the High Road like a cork in a bottle—the largest, highest, and most easily fortified site between Kermanshah and Hamadan. The history of the people of Godin is intimately connected to the site's location at the crossroads of cultures.

The Kangavar Valley floor provided rich agricultural land for farming, and the foothills of the mountains had abundant pasturage for animal herds. Wet winters and plentiful, snow-fed streams meant that crops could be grown without the large-scale irrigation projects that were needed in the great civilizations of neighbouring Mesopotamia. Throughout the five millennia that people lived at Godin, they grew crops of barley, wheat, fruit, and vegetables on the valley floor and grazed their flocks of sheep, goats, and cattle in the surrounding hill-country. All in all Godin must have been a pleasant place to call home.

Godin Tepe provides the longest continual sequence of occupation excavated in any site in central western Iran, and is among the longest excavated sequences in the entire Near East. Godin was first occupied during the Early Chalcolithic period in the sixth millennium BC and was home to a variety of cultures more or less continuously until the mid-first millennium BC. This long period witnessed many of the great developments in human history, from early farming to the rise of the first states and the advent of empires. The people living at Godin participated directly in all these developments.

The sequence of cultures at Godin has been divided into ten general cultural periods, ranging in date from the late-sixth millennium to the mid-first millennium BC. They are numbered as they were found, from most recent to oldest. Period I was assigned to an Islamic tea house and some modern graves that were located on one side of the mound; the sequence really begins (or ends in terms of the historical sequence) with Godin Period II.

The main excavations at Godin consisted of the clearing of the Period II Iron Age citadel, at the top of the mound, and one very large 750-square-metre trench, called the Deep Sounding, which began in the middle of this building and went more or less straight down for some 11 metres through Periods III and IV to Period VI. Each successive layer of occupation excavated in the Deep Sounding of Godin revealed a unique and significant aspect of life on the High Road of ancient Iran. The earliest of these cultural periods, Periods XI–VII, were recovered only in some small soundings and we know very little about them. They are discussed in this volume in connection with Period VI.

Phase VI:1 (Chapter 4), lying at the bottom of the Deep Sounding, is a remarkable compound of several small, but carefully constructed, buildings enclosed by a thick, curving wall. This compound was built directly over some of the simple houses of the earlier phase VI:2 and is unlike anything that preceded it. When Cuyler Young first uncovered this oval compound, he thought it represented a whole new arrival at the site and gave it a new period name (the missing Period V), but he later came to discover that this compound was only one element in an ongoing Period VI culture. The distinctive objects found in the Godin VI:1 oval compound, including beveled-rim bowls, tablets, and seals, have direct connections to the Uruk period in southern Mesopotamia, hundreds of kilometres away. Uruk was one of the first large cities in the history of the world. It is associated with the development of all the markers of complex states, including writing, monumental art and architecture, and bureaucratic administration. The discovery of the Uruk-related Godin VI:1 oval compound changed the way historians think about the Uruk period and the development of the state.

After the Period VI oval compound was deserted, a seemingly new group of people moved into the area (Chapter 5). They brought with them distinctive grey and white pottery as well as the styles of architecture characteristic of the Early Transcaucasian Culture (ETC), which had already had a long history in regions to the north of Godin. The villagers of the Period IV occupation lived in small houses, but a single larger building containing a lot of animal bone and a raised hearth seems to have been used for communal or ritual feasting. This southernmost extension of the ETC in Iran helps explain how and why this distinctive group of people left their mark on the archaeological landscape for thousands of years.

The Bronze Age town of Period III (Chapter 6) is by far the longest occupation at Godin. This 7-metre-deep deposit of architecture and artifacts spanned a period of some 1,200 years. Even the relatively small portion of the Period III architecture uncovered in the Deep Sounding reveals the day-to-day activities in the most prosperous settlement of the region. Here we get abundant evidence for how people worked, played, and ate in a thriving highland town. In the regional perspective, Godin III was involved in the briefly lived highland confederation of polities that put an end to the Ur III state in Mesopotamia.

The Period III village and much of the surrounding valley were abandoned in the mid-second millennium BC, and for the first extended period of time in 4,000 years, Godin lay vacant. We have no single explanation for this extensive depopulation of the area, but it may be related in some way to the migration of Indo-Europeans, including the Medes and Persians, into ancient Iran. By the time a Median ruler decided to build a citadel-palace on the top of the deserted mound of Godin it was already a hill of ruins more than 20 metres high.

The Period II citadel (Chapter 7) was the largest and wealthiest building at Godin. It was the home of an Iron Age Median ruler who received his subjects in a great columned hall and entertained his guests in a dining-room with elaborate feasts of roast sheep, suckling pig, and a lot of wine. The citadel seems to have been designed originally as a true fort with thick exterior walls and many arrowslots, but through time the arrowslots became filled with debris and nobody bothered to clear them out; the citadel became a place to hold court rather than bear arms. The Near East in the first millennium BC was dominated by the Neo-Assyrian Empire, and the Medes of Godin II were intricately involved in the power relations tied to being vassals to this intimidating state.

Godin Tepe is an exceptional place, not only because of some of the remarkable objects and architecture that were found there, but because it gives us a truly unique view of what life was like in a single location over the course of much of early human history.

1 | History of the Excavations at Godin Tepe

Hilary Gopnik

Godin was altogether a delightful place to excavate.

—T. Cuyler Young, Jr., 2006

In the fall of 1961, T. Cuyler Young, Jr., was a young archaeologist searching the Zagros Mountains of western Iran for a site to call his own. He had been working on the fabulously well preserved site of Hasanlu in northern Iran, and, in spite of the impressive wealth of ancient treasure that was coming out of the trenches at that site, Cuyler chafed at the excavation director's reluctance to dig deeper. Cuyler was writing his PhD dissertation on the Iron Age pottery of Iran, and was trying to sort out a sequence that made sense of the quantities of ceramic sherds that littered the archaeological mounds in western Iran. As he drove through the Zagros Mountains in a continually overheating old Land Rover, he stopped at every ancient mound that could be seen from the road to collect ceramic sherds. At site number 22 in the Kangavar Valley, on a very large mound next to a little village named Godin, Cuyler fell in love. As he "sherded" this 30-metre-high hill of ruins, he looked northwards across the fertile Kangavar Valley to the mountains beyond and, as he recalled in an interview a few weeks before his death in 2006, he thought: "This would be a damn pleasant spot to run an excavation."

Figure 1.1. Photo of Godin Tepe mound in the Kangavar Valley, village of Godin in foreground

T. Cuyler Young, Jr., was born to be a historian of ancient Iran. The son of Presbyterian missionaries stationed in Resht, Iran, Cuyler came into the world on March 30, 1934, only 400 kilometres from the site of Godin Tepe. His parents returned to the United States when Cuyler was just a baby, but when his father, T. Cuyler Young, Sr., was appointed press attaché at the American Embassy in Tehran in 1943, the family moved back to Iran for the duration of the war. Cuyler spoke fondly of his two years as a young teenager in Iran. He was just old enough to be interested in the rich culture of Persia that surrounded him, but young enough not to feel alienated by its strangeness. His father took him to visit the great archaeological site of Persepolis in which the columns of the ancient Persian palaces still soar above the plain, and Cuyler knew right away that he wanted to know more about these people. He went to an English language school but managed to pick up enough Persian from the neighbourhood kids and servants to serve as a substantial base for his study of Persian as an adult. Cuyler credited this early exposure to the language for his ease in dealing with Iranian authorities later in his professional career.

From his roots as a missionary and diplomat, Cuyler's father developed into a prolific and respected scholar of modern Persian language and Iranian culture and history. After the war he was appointed as Professor of Persian Language and Literature at Princeton University, and Cuyler soon followed him there as an undergraduate in Near Eastern Studies. To the end of Cuyler's life, his father clearly still loomed large in his consciousness—he always referred to him in conversation as "Father" rather than "my father"—and it was clear that his decisions were often motivated by what "Father" might think of him. After graduation from Princeton, Cuyler chose to differentiate himself from Young Sr. by taking up the archaeology, instead of the languages, of the Near East. He entered graduate school at the University of Pennsylvania to work with Robert Dyson and explore archaeology.

Cuyler was a complex man. Tall, athletic, and classically handsome, he looked a bit like Gary Cooper playing an archaeologist. He exuded self-confidence and from a young age adopted the hail-fellow-well-met bonhomie of a seasoned traveller. His journals of trips through Iran (always typed on an old manual in the hunt-and-peck style cultivated by men of the period) self-consciously borrow their tone from

Figure 1.2. Cuyler Young at age 11 at Persepolis

the travel journals of such turn-of-the-century travellers as Sir Aurel Stein. He wrote of an American diplomat he met in Tabriz that he "found Thomas a very quiet, reserved, calm sort of fellow—but knowledgeable and sound . . . He needs a little fire. I suspect he lacks imagination and that is something we need in the service these days." (Journal entry, February 25–March 4, 1964). This written by a young man in 1964, the year of Beatlemania and the first Vietnam War protests. Cuyler felt himself to be very much the heir of no-nonsense Mesopotamian archaeologists such as Sir Max Mallowan—the husband of mystery writer Agatha Christie—who believed in getting the job done efficiently, but with some of the same lack of imagination of which Cuyler complained in the American diplomat. But Cuyler was himself too interested in new ideas to fully fit this mould. In spite of claiming an antipathy to the New Archaeology, an intellectual movement of the 1960s that challenged traditional excavation techniques and analyses, Cuyler co-wrote a number of important articles about the impact of population densities on the growth of cities that used many of the approaches advocated by the New Archaeology. He had the manner of a Princeton-educated golden boy, and he often handled difficult situations with a combination of macho bravado and self-confident charm that were impressive when he was on your side and infuriating when he used them against you. At the same time Cuyler would sometimes reveal a vulnerability—the sad look of a hurt child or a catch in his voice—beneath his smooth exterior that could be disarming, and you could never be certain if this was another sally from his arsenal of persuasive tactics, or if it was at these moments that his true character was disclosed.

Figure 1.3. Cuyler Young in 1961 examining a human skull at Hasanlu

At Hasanlu, where he was appointed field director in 1961, Cuyler learned to excavate. Site director Robert Dyson was a great proponent of the "Wheeler" method, a systematic approach to complex sites as developed by the Scottish archaeologist Sir Mortimer Wheeler. Wheeler insisted on careful recording and excavation by stratum. He advocated the use of an excavation grid to keep track of the horizontal position of finds, and unexcavated units, or balks, were left between squares to track the vertical layering created by generation upon generation of superimposed mud-brick architecture. As it turned out though, Hasanlu—an Iron Age citadel that fell to a conflagration so sudden that the inhabitants and all their luxury goods were trapped beneath the burning beams—was such an exceptional site that more time was spent recording finds than digging stratified trenches. Cuyler itched to move to his own site so that he could develop the kind of extended ceramic chronology for western Iran that had been established so usefully in neighbouring Mesopotamia.

Cuyler knew that as the field director at the high-profile site of Hasanlu, he could take his pick of sites to dig. Relations between the Iranian monarchy and the United States were burgeoning in the 1950s and 1960s as the U.S. sought to strengthen its ally against Iran's northern neighbour, the Soviet Union. Iranian archaeology had traditionally been dominated by the French, who had been granted exclusive rights over all archaeological excavation by the Iranian government in 1900. Even when that agreement was nullified in 1930, the French had continued to control many of the important sites. After the Second World War, however, the United States had become a powerful new political presence in Iran, culminating in their orchestration of the 1953 coup that gave Mohammed Reza Shah absolute power over the government of the country. With this new attitude towards the

West, foreign archaeologists were being encouraged to excavate new sites by the Iranian Archaeological Service and the field was open for ambitious new projects. Cuyler had a broad field to choose from, but he also knew that his first directorship would end up colouring his career for many years to come, and he agonized over the decision.

In 1964 Cuyler, with PhD in hand and a brand new job as assistant curator at the Royal Ontario Museum in Toronto, received a Fulbright fellowship that allowed him to spend the year doing research in Iran. He embarked on a series of exploratory surveys of central Iran, ostensibly in order to collect further data for his ceramic chronology, but always in search of a site to call his own. He travelled with Louis Levine, Phil Smith, and David Stronach, exploring new sites but always coming back to Godin Tepe for another look, and seeking confirmation from others for his choice, like a young man introducing his girl to his friends before proposing. He had a list of criteria he had drawn up for what he wanted in a site. His graduate work on the Iron Age was still uppermost in his mind, and any site he dug should have an Iron Age component, preferably one built by the pre-Persian Medes; the Medes had remained an archaeological enigma in spite of their strong presence in the Assyrian and Greek historical sources, and it would be a coup to uncover material evidence for their culture. But he had another, grander goal as well.

The archaeology of Iran had concentrated mainly on the few monumental sites in the south that had been dug by the French and Germans since the 1930s. If he could excavate a single site in central Iran with a long, superimposed series of occupations, it would establish himself, and the newly expanding Royal Ontario Museum, as the go-to source for all future work in Iran. Cuyler recalled his search in a 2006 interview: "If we could establish a firm sequence of cultures, we would have created a database that everyone would have to refer to for the next fifty years." The ceramic sherds he had collected during his scouting visits to Godin indicated that it had been continuously occupied from the fourth millennium BC to about 500 BC.

> I must have gone back there at least eight times over that year. Here was the sequence of sequences. It had what was obviously a sizable Iron III building just below the surface, but I also collected tons of second-millennium painted sherds, and much to my surprise some material that looked like Yanik Tepe in the third millennium, and even more to my surprise some beveled-rim bowls from the southern Mesopotamian Late Uruk in the late fourth millennium.

Cuyler continued to survey and to search: "I was looking to see if there was any site better than Godin. There might be something with an even longer sequence or a better

Figure 1.4. Cuyler Young examining pottery

layout just around the corner or down the next valley." Finally in 1965, with his Fulbright about to run out, he went out one more time with David Stronach. David had been appointed to head the newly founded British Institute of Persian Studies in Tehran in 1961, and Cuyler and he had become fast friends. David's easygoing, impish, Scottish charm complemented Cuyler's American bravado, and being with the two of them together, even years later, was like being Zeppo around Groucho and Harpo. David is one of the few people I have ever met whose eyes *actually* twinkle when he tells a funny story, even when the punch line is at his own expense. I have heard both men recount the story of their travels through the Zagros Mountains that spring on numerous occasions for a variety of audiences. The details of the story change as such tales are apt to do, but it was clearly a joyous trip, and one that helped to define their professional lives. Travelling southwest from Tehran, they entered the Zagros chain via Arak and then headed north to the Malayer Valley. The site of Nush-i Jan stands out as a major prominence in the middle of the Malayer Plain, and although at first glance they thought it might be a natural formation, they soon realized that perched on the top of the natural hill were the mud-brick remains of a sizable settlement. As David Stronach recounted in his 2008 book on Nush-i Jan:

> A glance through the binoculars soon confirmed that the whole summit of the site consisted not of rock but of relatively soft earth in which at least one large animal burrow could be made out. Soft earth in such a situation almost always stems from crumbled mud-brick, and the steep sides of the mound suggested the presence of either well preserved buildings or strong defences.

For the first time Cuyler seriously contemplated shifting allegiances away from Godin. Even the surface remains of Nush-i Jan made it clear that it was an exceptional site. The quantities of mud-brick that littered the mound must have come from some very substantial architecture—a perfectly preserved temple complex as it turned out—and the pottery sherds were of the Iron III date that would put the occupation squarely into the Median period. As Cuyler remembered it forty years later, he looked at David as they drove away from the site and realized that his friend had been smitten by Nush just as he had by Godin four years earlier: "I turned to him and said, 'Hey, that big old pile of bricks over there is all yours. I'm taking Godin.'"

Cuyler applied to the Archaeological Service of Iran for an excavation permit for Godin, and, still wavering like a nervous groom before the wedding, he got one for Haftavan Tepe too, "just in case." Cuyler's permit, in accordance with the agreement that had been in effect in Iran since the 1930s, stated that all artifacts recovered during the excavation would be divided equally between the excavators and the Iranian government. The split occurred at the end of the season in a ritual that marked the season's end at Near Eastern sites throughout the better part of the century. The excavators and the representatives of the archaeological service would meet at the artifact depot and try to come up with an equal division. One cylinder seal might be worth three whole vessels, but a particularly well preserved statue might be worth three cylinder seals. Nobody knew which side would get which pile so it was in everyone's interest to make the division as fairly as possible. When everyone had agreed that the split was even, they tossed a coin and chance decided who got which collection. The Iranian authorities at this point were uninterested in ceramic sherds or scientific samples, so the Godin project was allowed to bring all sherds, which numbered in the tens of thousands by the end of the project, and whatever scientific samples they may have collected, back to the ROM. By 1973, the last full field season of the Godin excavations, the Iranian Archaeological Service, like most antiquities departments around the world, had begun to seriously question the wisdom of exporting their heritage at all, and they started to insist that anything of value be kept in the country. It so happened that it was only in 1973 that the cylinder seals and tablets of Period VI were recovered, and as a result all of these stayed in Iran.

In the fall of 1965, for eight glorious weeks, Cuyler and Louis D. Levine began the first field season at Godin Tepe. Cuyler and Lou had met as graduate students at Penn. Cuyler was the senior of the two and Lou admits to being in awe of him when they were first introduced. During the course of a lifelong friendship and intellectual partnership, Lou, himself a supremely assertive man normally, would always remain just a little deferential in Cuyler's presence. Cuyler and Lou were an unlikely pair. Cuyler, the son of missionaries, and Lou, the son of Jewish immigrants, shared almost nothing in terms of their background or manner. Cuyler's easy confidence was contrasted by Lou's nervous energy. To be in a seminar room with the two of them together was like watching a whippet play with a golden retriever: Lou sitting forward on the edge of his seat, arms in constant gesture, and voice always just a bit louder than a normal seminar pitch, launching into an explanation as he jumped up to retrieve one more book from the shelf, Cuyler sitting back with mandatory cigarette clutched between his thumb and forefinger, brows furrowed listening, then cutting in with his deep sonorous voice in support of Lou's hard-won point. Despite their contrasting styles, they were clearly happy in each other's company and fed off each other's intellectual strengths, often interrupting one another to finish a sentence, as old married couples will do. By 1965, when Cuyler began work at Godin, the two had become close friends, and there was no doubt that Lou, as assistant director, would be an integral part of the project.

Figure 1.5. Cuyler Young (left) and Louis Levine sitting on throne base at Godin

In that first season they opened up two, 5-metre-wide trenches (Operations A and B) on the north face of the mound. Operation A went down some 14 metres, and then as the walls of the trench became too deep for safety, Operation B took up where Operation A

left off, but less deeply cut into the side of the mound. The plan was to dig until they hit virgin soil (the term archaeologists use for the level before human occupation sullied the ground). They would dump the excavated back dirt (relieved of any artifacts that it might have contained) over the edge of the sharply eroded ravine into the stream that ran along the north side of the site, where they could hire a bulldozer to clear it away at the end of the season, ensuring that piles of picked through dirt didn't end up obscuring new parts of the site to dig. As they uncovered level after level of occupational material it became clear that the site would be even more prolific than the surface sherds had suggested. Near the surface was the first millennium BC Iron Age component (Period II) as expected, but the second millennium Bronze Age levels (Period III) were much longer lived than they had dreamed and would make it possible to construct a detailed ceramic sequence for the Iranian Bronze Age. Period IV of the third millennium was also well represented and the pottery had even stronger connections to Yanik Tepe than they had first thought. Below this, Periods V–VII extended the sequence into the Early Chalcolithic of the sixth millennium BC. Somehow, even though the most impressive finds would be excavated in future seasons, the 1965 sounding, coming at the beginning of his career with so much promise before him, was fixed as a golden period in Cuyler's memory: "I had no idea how spectacular it would be.

That 1965 season was the triumph of my professional life."

Back in Toronto at the ROM, Cuyler set out a timetable for the excavation of Godin Tepe. He anticipated completely clearing the large Period II building on the top of the mound and sinking a large 30 metre by 30 metre "Deep Sounding" that would explore the rest of the levels at the site. He calculated that it would take four further field seasons to complete the task, and wrote in his grant proposal to the ROM that he anticipated that by the end of the 1973 field season they would be 12 metres down in the Deep Sounding at Period VI.

On September 7, 1973 Cuyler sat drinking a whiskey on the floor of the Godin V (now known as VI:1) oval compound some 11.5 metres below the surface of the mound: "I have always been very proud that I was able to see into the mound and see where we would be." His

Figure 1.6. Lou Levine (above) in 1965 recording Operation B

prescience, however, came at a cost. In order to meet the tight deadlines he had set for himself, much of the last season of excavation was a race to the finish, and, in spite of everyone's best intentions, detail was inevitably lost.

Sir Max Mallowan and Agatha Christie visited Godin in 1967. As Cuyler showed the great man around, Mallowan slowly picked up sherds and peered down the test trenches without saying a word. Finally he turned to an expectant and uncharacteristically anxious Cuyler and said: "It's a big site, my man. You've got to dig a big hole." That "big hole" would cut down from the very summit of the mound through three successive millennia of occupation. When they arrived in 1967, the plan had been to cut the Deep Sounding between the 1965 Operations A and B in order to incorporate the material from those excavations into the broader exposures. Cuyler ordered the workmen to start laying out the pegs for a grid with this area at its centre so that the square labelled A1 would be the centre of the operation. As they worked, Cuyler began to have second thoughts about his decision to dig here. This big hole would be the only chance to see how people had lived for more than 4,000 years in this lush valley of the Zagros Mountains. If he got it wrong, and the best of the occupation was just under the unexcavated earth right next door, it would be a chance lost forever. He told the workers to take a break, crossed the stream at the base of the mound on the north, and walked into a farmer's field where he could get a complete view of the mound. Sitting on a low stone wall, he peered at the mound before him. "I must have sat there for at least an hour, just trying to guess what was in that damned thing. I decided, 'If we're going to dig it we should do it from the very top.'" He returned to the site and told the workers to move the grid over so that A1 was squarely at the highest point on the mound, just to the west of the 1965 Operation A. If it hadn't been for this last minute change in plans the remarkable Period VI:1 oval compound would never have been discovered. But then we will probably never know what other significant building or artifact still lies buried 10 metres to the east of the Godin Deep Sounding.

The first few seasons at Godin were full of excitement and promise. Cuyler and Lou had assembled a great team of intelligent and able site supervisors who would work right through the four seasons. William Sumner, Carol Kramer, Christopher Hamlin, Irene Winter, and Harvey Weiss, in addition to dozens of students and guest excavators that came through over the four seasons, would all cut their archaeological teeth on the mud-brick debris of Godin, and many would go on to have important careers in Near Eastern Studies in their own right. All in all, Cuyler thought he had made the right choice of sites after all:

Figure 1.7. Excavation of Godin Period III

The climate was great for a Near Eastern, summertime excavation with cool mountain air and sunny days. The view of the Zagros in the distance was breathtaking, Darius' famous monument at Bisitun was right down the road for those who wanted more antiquities, and there was an excellent hotel in Hamadan with a great restaurant and a pool for weekend respites. Godin was altogether a delightful place to excavate.

There were of course some blemishes in this rosy picture of life on an excavation. This was the 1960s, and the younger students and site supervisors, like students everywhere at that time and since, were not always enamoured of Cuyler's autocratic, if charming, directorship. There was a strike by the local workers, ostensibly over working conditions, and a number of the Canadian students decided to support the workers and refuse to supervise their squares. Cuyler laughed at what he felt was their misplaced idealism, negotiated with the workers for a slight raise, and work resumed. Then the Iranian secret police came to visit him. It seemed that they were assembling a dossier on the Godin project. "Why?" Cuyler demanded to know. The secret police, apparently feeling that secrecy was their métier, refused to tell him. After many cups of tea with officials, it was finally revealed that some of the students had taken to going to the local teahouse to smoke opium with the locals. Opium smoking was tolerated by the police as a local custom, but they certainly didn't want young Westerners coming in and spreading the word that Iran was the place to come to smoke dope. "I had to put a stop to that," Cuyler recalled, his tone making it clear that he had laid down the law.

The 1967 and 1969 archaeological excavations themselves proceeded more or less as planned. The Iron Age building at the top of the mound proved to be much larger and more complex than Cuyler had suspected. The distinctive architecture—it appeared to be the antecedent to the ruins at Persepolis and it resembled what was being uncovered by David Stronach at Nush-i Jan—was a sign that Median culture was finally being revealed. The extra work of clearing the whole building seemed worth the effort. The Deep Sounding had uncovered metres of Period III village architecture, which appeared to be never-ending, but preservation was good and the exquisitely painted pottery, which was often lying on floors where it had last been used, had the potential for being the basis for the definitive ceramic chronology for the Iranian Late Bronze Age. Numerous small soundings were dug at the periphery of the mound to try to figure out the limits of occupation for each period, and just about everywhere they put in a trench, there was Godin III material.

By the time they got back to the field in 1971, everybody was just a little fed up with Godin Period III. By season's end they were already more than 7 metres down into the Deep

Sounding and still digging through the now groaningly monotonous Bronze Age village. In mid-season the Deep Sounding had gone far enough into the widening mound that it was possible to step it outwards and create two new squares, A01 and B01, right at the edge of the cliff face. These new squares finally revealed signs of the deeper Period IV deposit, but the architecture was badly eroded and it was impossible to reconstruct a decent plan. Frustration was setting in. Cuyler recalled: "As we dug the Deep Sounding, I got more and more bored. I got sick and tired of the Late Bronze Age and its piles and piles of painted pottery. It would not end! Time was wasting and money was going and I wanted the Uruk stuff!"

There was only one possible course for the 1973 season: Uruk or bust. There was to be a two-pronged plan of attack. First they would sink two more test trenches on the lower terrace of the mound, XYZ and the Brick Kiln Cut (so called because of its location next to an abandoned modern brick kiln), in order to get a complete sequence of the lower levels of occupation, and then they would pick up the pace of excavation in the Deep Sounding. They hired fifteen extra local workers that season, and the mantra became "move dirt." Period VI:1 (then still called Period V) was reached first in the northern ravine-edge square, A01, where the Period IV remains had been so scanty and enigmatic the season before. Cuyler ordered these scrappy Period IV walls to be quickly removed within the first week of the excavation, and lying under them was not only the elusive Uruk-related pottery but also what was clearly the northern end of a finely built, beautifully preserved building, complete with a wide, curving enclosure wall that hinted at more buildings to come. Then, on June 6, two weeks into the season, an Uruk-period numeric tablet was found lying on the floor of this well-preserved room. This changed everything. Suddenly what had been vague hopes of finding a significant occupation that could be related to the Uruk period in southern Mesopotamia, became a certainty. This tablet at this level of the site could change the nature of the understanding not just of central western Iran, but of the spread of the southern Mesopotamian Uruk culture, the period that had seen the rise of the earliest large-scale urban civilization in the world.

Now the quest to move dirt became even more imperative. For the first time since excavation had begun, three supervisors worked side by side excavating material from three different periods of occupation. In square A1 the earliest phases of Period III were still being uncovered, while in square B1 the large western building of Period IV was cleared, while yet another team worked on the Uruk Period VI building in B01. In the meantime a fourth unit, led by a more junior supervisor, was back on the top of the mound finishing the clearance of the southern portion of the Period II citadel.

The field notes from the 1973 season reveal the tension brought on by too much to do in too little time. Claus Breede, the lone photographer, draughtsman, and architect, was in constant demand to photograph features, or to sketch a plan before a building was removed to "go down further." Supervisors complain in the notes of having to hold up excavation while they wait for him. Harvey Weiss, Irene Winter, and Marie Henriette Gates, supervising the digging through level IV, were particularly distressed, as their normally careful excavation techniques—in the previous season Weiss had strenuously, but unsuccessfully, argued for sieving the back dirt—were sacrificed for the sake of reaching that grand building in level VI:1. Short of supervisors, Cuyler asked the representative from the Iranian Archaeological Service to oversee the excavation of the large dump in the magazines of the Period II citadel since it involved no careful recording of stratigraphy. As the able, but inexperienced, government official worked his way back through the magazine and into tower 13, no notes were taken at all, and as a result there is no written record of one of the largest deposits of pottery, animal bone, and charcoal from Period II.

The tops of the walls of the main portions of the Period VI:1 oval compound in squares B1 and A1 were finally reached on August 1, 1973, one month before excavation was scheduled to be completed. The rest of that month would be spent clearing the oval compound as carefully as possible given the short time left. Fortunately for the excavators, if not for the original inhabitants, at least some of the building had been destroyed by a fire and preservation of the mud-brick walls was good. Harvey Weiss now convinced Cuyler that the potential for recovering crucial small finds by sieving the backdirt would be worth the

Figure 1.8. Godin Tepe after excavation

time and effort, and a limited sieving and flotation operation was undertaken. The carefully planned nature of the architecture, and the relatively brief occupation of the building, also meant that there were few surprises or confusing stratigraphic relationships: "The oval was fun to dig because it was so well preserved. We had a good team in there. We were rushed, but we got it done," Cuyler recalled. On September 11, 1973, the last cleaning of the floor of the oval compound was finished, and the excavations at Godin Tepe ended.

When the dust had cleared, and the site was packed up to endure the next three millennia as best it could, it became clear that the Godin Project had accomplished an impressive archaeological feat. The excavators had dug for a total of 471 days and had removed more than 7,000 cubic metres of dirt. They had uncovered substantial occupation of a sequence stretching back 3,000 years and had evidence that the site was actually occupied for some 2,000 years even before that. Cuyler summarized the excavation thirty-four years later: "We dug a big hole with a damned impressive building on the top and bottom of it and a great sequence in between. But still it didn't tell us enough. I still sometimes wish I could go back and dig more."

Postscript to an Excavation

All together, 2,638 objects were registered from the site of Godin, with 1,363 of them kept by the ROM and the remainder staying in Tehran. About 40,000 pottery sherds were packed up and shipped back to the ROM, and during the first three seasons of excavation, before the rush to Period VI in 1973, an additional 100,000-plus body sherds were counted by ware type before they were discarded. Boxes containing 449 scientific samples (carbon, soil, slag, etc.) and 13,000 animal bones were also brought back to Toronto. In addition to all these artifacts, reams and reams of paper records were kept including field notes, sherd-count sheets, lot sheets, carbon-sample sheets, photography records, and object-registry cards, not to mention slides, negatives, contact sheets, architectural plan and section drawings—enough material to fill a small room of filing cabinets.

Despite this accomplishment, Cuyler's goal for the ROM excavations at Godin to serve as the definitive reference for Iranian archaeology never materialized. The quantity of data is impressive, and a little intimidating, which could be one of the reasons that much of it remained untouched in storage at the ROM for more than thirty years. A few graduate students, including myself and contributor Robert Henrickson, completed analyses on some portions of the pottery over the years, but almost all the scientific samples (bone, carbon, slag, soil) sat mouldering in boxes during most of that time, and the pottery and objects from Periods IV–VII remained unpublished. Once the excavations were over, the energy that had kept so many people going back to the site over those five seasons in the 1960s and early 1970s seemed to dissipate. The excellent preliminary reports of the first few seasons gave way to silence.

Cuyler never relinquished his intention to get this material analysed and published. He sent all the bone to an analyst in the United States, but when no results were forthcoming he neglected to follow up on it. He chose the hundred best carbon samples and sent them out to be dated, but the analyst in charge left the lab and the samples were lost. He hired a variety of research assistants and draftspeople to sort through the lot sheets and field notes, and a certain amount of organization, retyping and filing was done, but without the spur of a deadline to meet, of a grant to run out, or of a season to end, these research assistants worked in a void and simply accumulated more paper.

Cuyler himself got caught up in new responsibilities and burdens. He became the director of the Royal Ontario Museum during a tumultuous period in the mid-1980s that witnessed a staff strike and a series of public demonstrations over a controversial exhibit called *Out of Africa*. For the first time in his life, Cuyler's persuasive powers weren't enough to keep the peace, and the job of museum director took its toll on him more than years of gruelling field work ever would. Two weeks before his death, as we sat talking about Godin and the possibility of this book renewing his dream of his cherished Godin seeing the light of day, he looked at me with one of those glimpses of vulnerability that would make you forgive all his moments of arrogance and said, "The biggest regret in my entire life is not having fulfilled my responsibility to publish Godin." We hope that the following chapters in some way finally fulfill the promise of this great site.

Further Reading

Abdi K. "Nationalism, Politics, and the Development of Archaeology in Iran." *American Journal of Archaeology* 105 (2001): 51–76.

Stronach, D., and M. Roaf. *Tepe Nush-I Jan I: The Major Buildings of the Median Settlement.* London: British Institute of Persian Studies, 2007.

Young, T. C. "Population Densities and Early Mesopotamian Urbanism," In *Man, Settlement and Urbanism*, edited by P. J. Ucko et al., 827–842. London: Gerald Duckworth and Co., 1972.

———. *Excavations at Godin Tepe: First Progess Report.* Royal Ontario Museum Occasional Paper 17. Toronto: Royal Ontario Museum, 1969.

———. "The Iranian Migration into the Zagros." *Iran* 5 (1967): 11–34.

———. "A Comparative Ceramic Chronology for Western Iran." *Iran* 3 (1965): 53–85.

Young, T. C., Jr., and L. D. Levine. *Excavations of the Godin Project: Second Progress Report.* Toronto: Royal Ontario Museum, 1974.

2 | Making Sense of the Mound: Archaeological Interpretation at Godin

Hilary Gopnik

We have here a new and exact method for dealing with all those vague ages as yet unfathomed, and for extracting all that is possible about their history. Prehistoric archaeology has made another step toward becoming an exact science. And now the responsibility of those who excavate is tenfold increased, as the extent of their care and exactitude will more than ever restore or ruin the history of the past.

—Sir Flinders Petrie, 1899

Interpreting the results of an archaeological excavation is like putting together a jigsaw puzzle of Monet's *Water Lilies* that is missing all the blue pieces, all the edge pieces, and some pieces that were swept off the table by a stray gust of wind. The assembled puzzle in some sense reflects what must have originally been there, and some of the gaps are either predictable or restorable, but it is impossible not to acknowledge that the holes in the picture are wide and gaping. At the same time, what is left has a beauty and logic of its own that can be appreciated without reference to the complete puzzle. The impact of the abstracted wings of the rampant eagle on a Godin Period III jar (Figure 2.1) stands on its own as a universally beautiful object and a testament to the potter who made it, without any knowledge about the society in which they lived. Even when we can piece together the puzzle itself, however, it is still a huge leap to move from the impressionist painting to the garden at Giverny. And yet, while some contemporary anthropologists would argue that there is no way beyond the daubs of paint that constitute the outward manifestation of societies even for living, observable, human cultures, most archaeologists still search to reconstruct not only the pond, but the frogs in it, the flies on the frogs, and even sometimes the fleas on the flies.

Figure 2.1. Painted eagle on Godin Period III jar

In spite of the apparent difficulty of relating the broken material remains of past human cultures to the vibrant living activities that produced them, archaeologists, by necessity an optimistic breed, have developed a set of techniques over the years to expedite the task. First and foremost the puzzle pieces are sorted, classified, and pieced together so that at least the general configuration of the picture is revealed; next, the predictable gaps are filled in as far as possible; and finally, and most problematically, archaeologists attempt to use some general principles about the relationship between the physical manifestation of human activities, the daubs of paint as it were, and the teeming pond that they represent.

At Godin, where millennia of human activities are represented, each cultural period presents a unique set of interpretive problems, and different tools have been used to try to understand them. The nature of the reconstructions offered about the actual activities that took place at the site differ from period to period, not only because the hilltop settlement of Godin was used in different ways at different times, but because the material left behind, the puzzle pieces, were themselves deposited and sorted in different patterns. The occupants of the latest ancient level at the site, Godin II—archaeologists number their periods as they discover them, from top (latest) to bottom (earliest), and Godin I was a modern Islamic teahouse—seem to have taken anything intact along with them when they peacefully abandoned their citadel/palace. All that remained, apart from the remarkable building itself, were the small broken bits of pottery that had accumulated in some garbage dumps in its backmost rooms. In certain sub-phases of the Bronze Age occupation of the site (Godin III) however, many houses were destroyed suddenly, probably by an earthquake, leaving whole pots, tools in mid-use, and in a few cases the people themselves, lying on the floor. In these houses destroyed some 4,000 years ago, tragically for their owners but fortuitously for the archaeologists trying to reconstruct their way of life today, it is possible to reconstruct in some detail the activities that took place in every room. The puzzle pieces in these two periods are so differently arranged and the gaps so widely spaced that the final picture that emerges is as much a product of the puzzle-making process as it is of the original subject matter. The nature of the remains in one period lead us to talk about the way people lived their daily lives, and in another about the role of ethnic identity, even though we know full well that both are always at play. The upside to this variability is that at least by the end of this book we will have explored many of the facets that made Godin Tepe a unique and fascinating place.

The Formation of an Archaeological Site

Dirt is the medium of archaeology. Most of what we excavate is encased, surrounded, and supported by dirt. An archaeological excavation is really the process of disentangling the source of this matrix so that we can begin to understand how the artifacts and architecture left behind by the long-dead occupants of the site got there. The differences in the processes that create this matrix in different environmental and cultural complexes can be huge, and even at any one site there are many forces at work that produce the final deposits. At Godin and other Near Eastern sites, it is possible to reconstruct at least a general sequence of deposition, destruction, and decay.

As humans move through their environment, they leave bits and pieces of their lives scattered behind them. Occasionally this human detritus is actually left in the place where it was used. In this case archaeologists call it a primary deposit. The occupants of a house destroyed suddenly, because of a natural disaster or an invasion, may leave behind the full contents of their living space, but this "Pompeii" effect is very rare. As it happens, Cuyler

Figure 2.2. Dust storm at Godin

Young and Lou Levine both received their baptism in the archaeology of Iran at one of these rare sites, Hasanlu.

Hasanlu, at the southern end of Lake Urmia, was an Iron Age citadel not unlike Godin Period II in that it was clearly the residence of a wealthy local ruler who lived, or at least received his subjects, in large columned buildings. At that time northern Iran was sandwiched between the two great and growing empires of Assyria and Urartu, and Hasanlu fell victim to one of their skirmishes. The invading Urartians, however, had apparently never learned the time-honoured maxim of every self-respecting marauding force: "First loot, *then* burn." Somebody, either an over-anxious Urartian soldier or a local hero, set fire to the town as the soldiers carried out the best of the treasure, and the tall poplar columns and roof beams must have ignited in a flash, smashing the skulls of inhabitants and invaders alike. Precious goods including gold, silver, ivories, and countless beads and vessels were buried along with their looters, so that Robert Dyson and his crew recovered an almost complete inventory of the original contents of the buildings. Where at Godin a single carnelian bead found in the debris of Period II was carefully registered and photographed, Lou Levine recounts that at Hasanlu beads were registered by the bucketful, and unless a ceramic vessel was complete nobody dreamed of recording it. Cuyler and Lou both once admitted that after excavating at Hasanlu any archaeological material seemed a little flimsy—although they both hastened to add that they would rather have the challenge of digging a deeply stratified site like Godin. Had the citadel of Godin II been destroyed by an invading army instead of having been peacefully abandoned, chances are that it would have been equally replete with precious objects.

Hasanlus are few and far between, but they do remind us of how much of the living culture we are usually missing when we excavate. The majority of archaeological sites, including Godin, have only very limited primary deposits. The earthquakes that suddenly destroyed some of the houses of Godin Period III did create some primary deposits, and in Period VI:1 a lot of artifacts were left on the floor of the oval compound when it was abandoned by its careless or hurried owners. In other phases a few isolated cooking pots were left in place near hearths where a final meal was cooked, and a grinder or two was abandoned in a courtyard, but otherwise little primary occupational material was found at Godin.

Archaeologists usually think of primary deposits in terms of artifacts in use, but the most common source of primary deposits are burials, where objects are placed to accompany the dead and are therefore usually recovered in exactly their context of last "use." Burials are usually by far the best source of intact artifacts, and if you see a perfectly preserved painted ceramic vessel in a museum, you can be pretty certain that it comes from a tomb of some sort. Collectors and looters love burials of course, but archaeologists are usually a little leery of them. They can provide a lot of good information about artifact sequences because they give a good picture of groups of artifacts that were probably made within a very short space of time—although "antiques" do sometimes find their way into a burial group. Archaeologists also use mortuary sites to reconstruct systems of social hierarchies based on factors such as gender, age, and ethnicity. But artifacts found in burials reflect only funerary systems, and it's not always clear how they are mirrored in the living culture. At Godin, the only excavated burials all date to Period III, probably because the people at Godin in other periods disposed of their dead in other ways (by exposure, cremation, or off-site burial mounds), but maybe simply as the result of the vagaries of recovery. Between earthquakes and burials, Godin Period III trumps the rest of the site by far in terms of primary deposits and the consequent preservation of artifacts, as a quick glance at the object photos from each period makes only too obvious.

Secondary deposits contain artifacts that were discarded by the people that used them. If all archaeology is the study of garbage, secondary deposits are the mainstay of the field. Formal dumps, piles of kitchen waste, the remains of cleaning after a single feast, sweepings from a floor, broken pot sherds trampled into a courtyard by animals, a bronze pin dropped behind a bench by a drunken reveller, a large pot sherd stuck into an arrowslot to block the wind: all are examples of the secondary deposits that form the bulk of archaeological remains.

Garbage disposal is one of the fundamental requirements of all societies. Once people are fed and sheltered, they need some way to get rid of their waste. Archaeologists can speak to waste-disposal patterns more than any other single aspect of culture, because even the thriftiest of villagers leave their garbage behind them when they decide to abandon or rebuild a site. Every society has its own restrictions about where and how refuse can be placed, and every culture has different norms about how meticulously to clean up after itself. In Godin Period IV, it seems that people were fairly cavalier about garbage disposal. They apparently had no problem with leaving a quantity of animal bone and broken pots lying on a floor before they resurfaced it. The rich patron of the Godin II citadel would probably have been horrified at such an idea, and all floors were carefully swept before a new floor was laid. Still, the Godin II ruler was casual enough about garbage disposal to allow a very large, and presumably very smelly, garbage dump, which included animal carcasses, food remains, and lots of broken pottery, to accumulate in the back corridor of his palace/citadel, at least in the final days of its occupation.

The problematic thing about secondary deposits is that they are subject to a lot of intentional or unintentional sorting even before they are deposited, and this can seriously skew the interpretation of what went on at the site. When a drunken partygoer or careless child drops a small fragile drinking bowl, for instance, it tends to shatter into many pieces.

Many of the fragments might well remain embedded in a dirt floor even after the morning-after's clean-up. A large, thick-sided jar usually breaks into only a few large pieces, however, and these sherds are likely to be disposed of in an exterior dump. If we find only the floor with the fine drinking-bowl pieces, or only the garbage dump with the larger bits of jars, we will get very different views of the life of the inhabitants. An average household can also expect to go through many more fine drinking vessels than they would heavy-duty storage jars—my own small household has managed to break an entire set of eight wineglasses this year, and our drunken revels have been really quite limited. This means that by counting sherds recovered from secondary deposits, we are really only measuring how many vessels were broken, not how many coexisted when they were whole. It is possible to sort out these pieces of the puzzle and reconstruct what might be missing by carefully recording and measuring the preservation of each sherd and taking into account the nature of the secondary deposits being analysed. But the very careful observation and recording of contexts required to accomplish this are not always possible in the press of a limited excavation season with limited manpower. During the excavation of Godin, every attempt was made to record contexts, but in a few cases, particularly during the last part of the 1973 season when the rush was on to reach Period VI, accuracy was sacrificed to speed, and some of the secondary deposits of Periods IV and II were left without descriptions in the field notes. We may have the ceramic sherds in the storerooms of the ROM, but without the context of the deposit in which they were found, it's almost impossible to figure out where they fit into the puzzle.

Primary and secondary deposits accumulate while a settlement is actively occupied, but most of the real mixing and confusion occurs after everybody has left town. Near Eastern archaeology, like Near Eastern civilization, relies in large part on the properties of mud-brick. Almost all of the buildings at Godin (with the exception of some wattle-and-daub houses in Period IV) were constructed of this cheap and versatile building material. Mud-bricks, fashioned quite simply of available mud mixed with straw and left to dry in the sun, are an unbelievably durable building material. A mud-brick wall can last for hundreds of years, provided that it is carefully plastered every year to keep out the rain. But as soon as a mud-brick building is abandoned, water erosion begins to undermine the tops and bottoms of the walls and the whole thing starts to turn back into the mud from which it came. The usual sequence of decay starts with the roof, normally made of wooden beams covered with reeds and plastered. Wood is a valuable resource in the Near East and wooden beams are often recycled for use in new houses. Even when they are left in place, without careful maintenance the plaster roofs soon leak, and the wet reeds and beams rot in fairly short order. The collapse of a roof is usually the first major destructive event after a house is abandoned. If there were any complete pots on the floor, they are now crushed and their sherds become incorporated into the roof collapse. Once unplastered tops of walls are exposed to rain or snow, they fall inwards, filling the room with mud-brick debris. Further rain, wind, and sun consolidate the debris, which forms a very hard muddy surface, actually protecting the wall bases below. This is when the real disturbances start.

Figure 2.3. Superimposed layers of architecture in the Godin Deep Sounding

A Near Eastern tell is made up of layers of these collapsed mud-brick buildings because each level of collapse forms a solid enough surface to rebuild on, but of course each rebuilding further disturbs the levels beneath it. Animals burrow, foundation trenches are sunk, pits are dug, and wells are sunk, and each time these disturbances happen, the primary and secondary deposits from below are mixed with new construction materials from above. All this decay and disturbance is called a tertiary deposit. Tertiary deposits are the farthest removed form the cultural context in which they were originally used and are generally not very useful for reconstructing past lifeways. Still, since they make up the bulk of the material at the site, they must be untangled in order to identify the more useful primary and secondary deposits. Many of the hours of study, hair-pulling, and argument that go on during the course of a season of excavation concern these tertiary deposits. The stratigraphic section is the archaeologist's primary tool to unmix what has been mixed and make sense out of the pile of mud.

Record Keeping at Godin Tepe

When Cuyler Young began his first field season at Godin Tepe in 1965, he was pretty sure he knew how to record the excavation of a large site. He had been trained under Robert Dyson at the impressive site of Hasanlu and was a true believer in the scientific methods of Sir Mortimer Wheeler, the great British archaeologist whose textbooks had established the basic field techniques for excavating large, complex sites. Wheeler had insisted on the recognition and recording of stratigraphy first and foremost. He had established the grid system of excavation whereby units are dug in squares with an unexcavated divider (balk) between them to keep track of the vertical levels. In theory, as each new cultural level or stratum was reached in the excavation, the excavator would record this in his or her notes, and the artifacts from that day would be registered with that stratum number. Cuyler and Lou unquestioningly adopted this method during their first field season at Godin, and it worked fairly well for the small test trenches (Operations A and B) that they dug in that year.

The field season of 1967 was to be the real start of full-scale excavations at Godin and Cuyler dutifully laid out the 10-metre by 10-metre Wheeler grid, with letters labelling the north-south axes, and numbers the east-west. This grid would define the main excavation units (called operations) for the course of the project. Every sherd or object would be recorded by the operation/square coordinates or test trench letter, with the stratum number written beside it in a circle for clarity. Both Cuyler and Lou Levine recount that as that season progressed, however, they started to feel uneasy about their ability to recognize strata as they dug this complex site, and they started to discuss the possibility of using a finer system of recording material than the operation and stratum. The first refinement to be added was the area, an arbitrary sub-division of the horizontal surface of the operation (grid square), defined by excavators as they went along and recorded in the field notes. Areas, written in triangles to distinguish them from strata, could be half of the square or one corner of a test trench depending on how the excavator chose to define them on that day. Still, even with this greater detail, excavators were frustrated by being forced to lump together into strata material that they weren't sure belonged to exactly the same occupation level. Lou Levine had excavated for a month in Israel, and had seen the locus system in use there, and in his own notes he started to introduce the "lot" as a smaller and better defined unit of excavation than a stratum. Lots were sequentially numbered within each operation (grid square or test trench) and could refer to any distinguishable unit of excavation. A lot could be all the mud-brick debris over a room, the contents of a hearth, a few sherds in an arrowslot, or all the material on a floor. The important thing about a lot was not that it was necessarily stratigraphically or culturally significant, or even consistent from square to square or day to day, but that it was well defined in the field notes (and eventually on specially designed lot recording sheets) and could therefore be referred to in later notes and discussions. Bill Sumner was also in the field that year and Cuyler credits him with suggesting that the lot system be used not only in the notes but also in recording all the sherds and registered objects. Cuyler admits that he was initially very reluctant to break with the Wheeler system, and thought that these lot numbers would be too confusing and complicated to record. In the end Lou and Bill Sumner won out however, and the lot system was finally introduced as the basic recording method at the site in the middle of the 1969 season.

As a result of this evolving recording system, the sherds and objects recorded in 1965 were listed by operation (either A or B) and stratum number; those excavated in 1967 and the first half of 1969 were recorded with grid-square coordinates (A3 for example) or test-trench letters (both still labelled "operation" for the sake of consistency), area numbers in triangles, and stratum numbers in circles. In the last half of 1969 lot numbers—underlined to distinguish them from areas and strata—were added to this system. By 1973 it was realized that the areas and strata had become redundant, and only the operations (grid coordinates or test-trench letters) and the underlined lot numbers remained to record an excavation unit or the material from it. In the 1980s and 1990s, back in Toronto, various researchers converted the earlier area/stratum designations into lot numbers, so that uniform databases could be constructed. As a result, in this publication and the accompanying Web archive all objects are recorded by lot, even when they were excavated before the lot system was introduced.

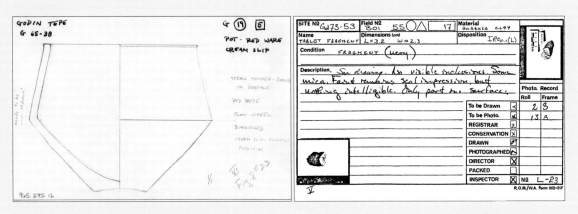

Figure 2.4. Object-registration cards from the 1965 and 1973 seasons showing the changes in recording techniques

Stratigraphy

In the language of post-structuralism, archaeological stratigraphy is often used as a metaphor to invoke the analysis-resistant, multi-layered nature of cultures (Michel Foucault's *Archaeology of Knowledge*, a very dense treatise on epistemology, was originally mistakenly classified as "archaeology" by the Library of Congress). But for the archaeologist the layering that makes up an archaeological site is a source of clarity as it works like a street map to guide an excavator through the processes that formed the site. The single word "unstratified," like "bastard" in a genealogy, is the ultimate dismissive insult in an archaeological report. The first step in the sorting process that precedes almost any archaeological interpretation is an analysis of the stratigraphy of the site.

The basic principle of stratigraphy, first enunciated in the field of geology in the eighteenth century, relies on the fact that the material on the bottom of a pile must have been deposited before that on the top. That basic principle can, and almost always is, violated by subsequent disturbance of the deposit by men digging ditches, animals burrowing, wall foundations being trenched, or wells being sunk. As a graduate student given the task of sorting through Godin Period II, I had a recurring dream that I was back in time in the large central building, and the people around me were methodically digging up dirt and throwing it in piles while I stood by yelling nightmare-like, "No, no stop! You're messing up the stratigraphy!" But, in spite of my subconscious anxiety, archaeologists are generally pretty confident that they can detect such disturbances by noting differences in the texture and content of the intrusion. Careful excavation and recording of the deposits as they are excavated can usually trace the sequence of deposition.

Excavation material is ideally removed in relatively small, square units, and a "balk," an unexcavated wall of dirt, is left between units. A meticulously cleaned and straightened balk is a token of honour for an excavator, because the side of the balk should precisely reflect the levels that were excavated and removed in the square. The unexcavated balk can then be "read" and drawn as a record of the levels dug. The drawing is known as a "stratigraphic section" and forms one of the key records of the excavation. Several formally drawn sections were produced by the draftsperson at Godin and many more "sketch sections," of small units were drawn by excavators in field notes.

These stratigraphic sections work well for small areas, but unless the process of deposition is uniform across the site, which it almost never is, it is very difficult to link the layers in very large units or from separate excavation units. In theory it is possible to create a cross-site section by making sure that all areas are linked with each other on the ground, but the exigencies of working on a large site with a large staff make it very difficult to maintain this ideal. At Godin a master section was kept of the south side of the Deep Sounding (Figure 2.6), but the strata recorded there are difficult to relate to the entire 7,000 cubic metres of deposit of walls, floors, courtyards, animal pens, and garbage dumps that accumulated in this area over the course of 3,000 years. Many strata stopped short of the southern extremity of this huge excavation unit, and most walls do not meet the edge of the square. Levels IV and VI were only partially recorded by this stratigraphic section. The western side of the balk that ran along squares AA1 and AA2 was also drawn consistently through the 1971 season, but in 1973 this balk was removed in order to get a better view of the impressive building of level VI:1, so that anything dug during the last half of that season is not recorded in that section.

The depth and breadth of the millennia of occupation debris that formed the site of Godin forced the excavators into some hard decisions. To maintain strict control over the stratigraphic record by excavating only in small adjacent units would mean sacrificing knowledge of the overall configuration of the site. The problem is badly exacerbated in the earliest levels at the site because of a simple technical difficulty: it is very difficult, if not downright dangerous, to dig a large deep hole in the ground, particularly one with straight sides. More than one archaeologist has been killed by a fall into a deep trench or by the collapse of a trench wall. To mitigate the danger, deep excavations are stepped in so that the walls of the trench are less prone to collapse. This means that by the time workers reach the bottom levels there is a smaller area left to expose. The Deep Sounding at Godin shrunk

Figure 2.5. Cuyler Young recording the stratigraphic section of the Deep Sounding

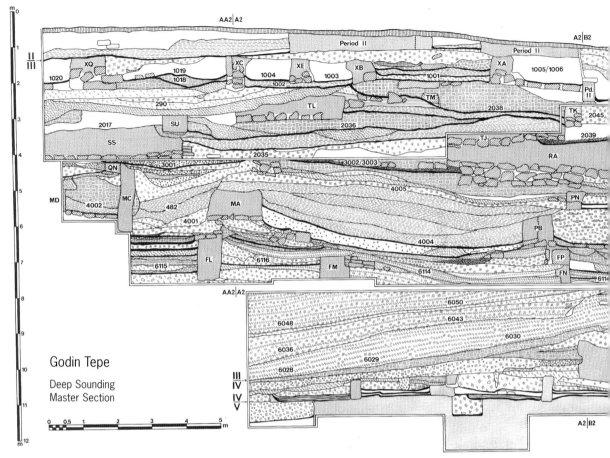

Figure 2.6. Stratigraphic section of Deep Sounding

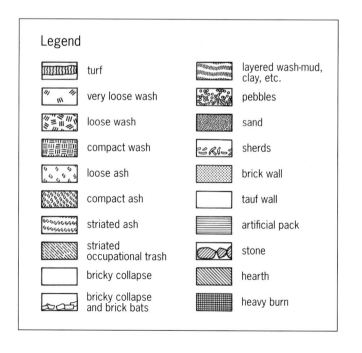

Legend

turf		layered wash-mud, clay, etc.	
very loose wash		pebbles	
loose wash		sand	
compact wash		sherds	
loose ash		brick wall	
compact ash		tauf wall	
striated ash		artificial pack	
striated occupational trash		stone	
bricky collapse		hearth	
bricky collapse and brick bats		heavy burn	

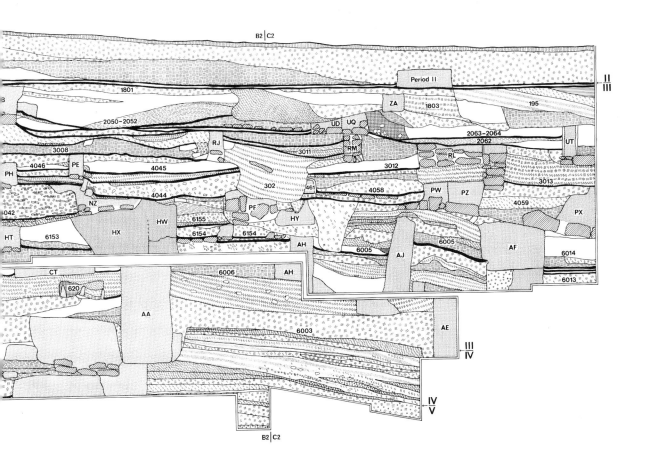

from about 30 metres by 30 metres when it was first laid out to about 25 metres by 20 metres at the Period VI:1 oval compound, 11 metres below.

In order to obtain more information about the deeper levels at the site and to get a better idea of the extent of occupation of each period, the directors at Godin decided to open up a series of smaller exploratory trenches in widely spaced areas of the site. The compact size of these trenches meant that the stratigraphy, or sequence of layers, could be much more easily seen and recorded, but it also meant that it was very difficult to determine the nature of the architecture of the deposit. A small trench tends to cut through portions of walls at odd angles, and it is usually very difficult to interpret what the whole room, let alone the whole building, might have looked like, or even whether it was a stable, a house, or a workshop. In some cases the excavators did not even attempt to record the make-up of the deposits in these soundings. In what Cuyler dubbed "search and destroy" operations the aim was to find out only the gross sequence of occupation by the major phases to determine the extent of any one period's presence across the site. The nature of that occupation was not even on the table.

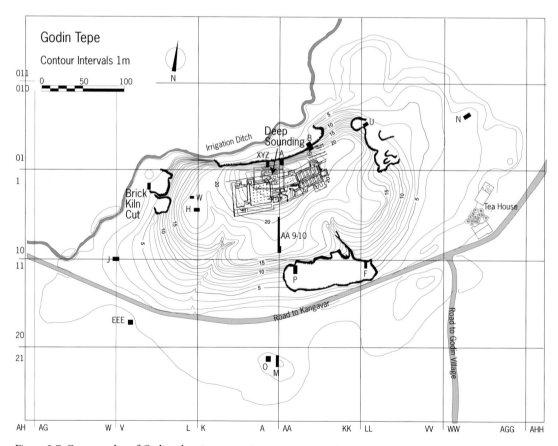

Figure 2.7. Contour plan of Godin, showing excavation areas or operations

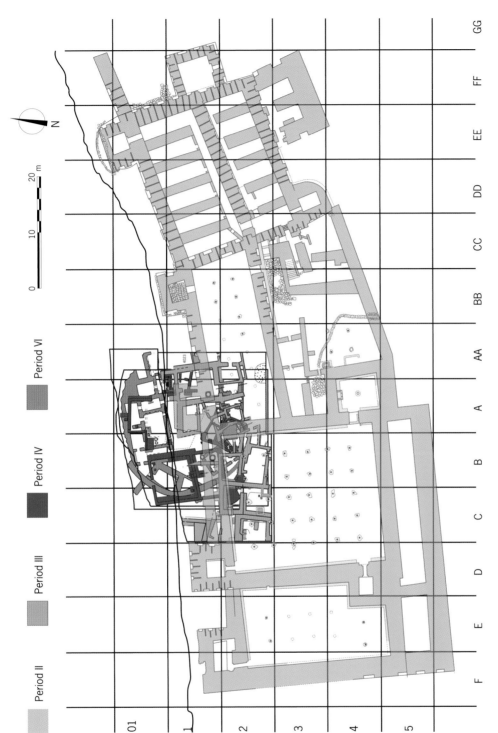

Figure 2.8. Overall plan of architecture at Godin Tepe, showing the major site grid and location of each period within the excavation units at the summit of the site

Archaeological Dating at Godin

Among the most critical first steps in archaeology is to establish a matrix of time and place for the material being analysed. Relative dating compares styles in artifacts at different sites to establish the contemporaneity of distinct levels at these sites. We can then speak of periods or phases across geographical regions. If it is possible to assign an absolute chronological date to even one of these levels (by a coin or a written document, for instance), then we can create a matrix of cross-dates that allows us to construct an approximate chronology for a large region and time frame. But many problems can throw those relative dates off. Sometimes, an artifact of a particular style is passed from one place where it is popular to another where it is unique, or the style may become popular in one area after it has been abandoned in another. Sometimes styles that go out of fashion return, like bell-bottom jeans. In general, relative dating is able to assign a level at a site to only a fairly broad time frame. The broad periods at Godin were all established by comparing the pottery from each level to that from other dated sites. These comparisons are listed and discussed in each chapter.

In 1949, two physicists, James Arnold and Willard Libby, provided archaeologists with a more precise method of dating called radiocarbon or carbon-14 dating. Carbon exists in nature in a number of isotopes or slight variations in atomic weight, including ^{12}C and ^{14}C. As plants photosynthesize, they build up their cells using carbon dioxide in the same proportion that ^{12}C and ^{14}C exist in the atmosphere bound in carbon dioxide molecules. When an organism dies, the ^{14}C starts to decay at a steady rate. By counting the amount of ^{14}C left in a sample, it is possible to give a date within a range of 60 to 200 years for when the organism stopped absorbing ^{14}C. One major problem with these counts is that the quantity of ^{14}C in the earth's atmosphere has fluctuated significantly over the past ten thousand years. Fortunately, scientists have discovered that by measuring the rings of very old trees—a tree lays down one ring a year—and calculating the proportion of carbon present in each ring, they can calibrate the ^{14}C curve to compensate for the changes in levels of ^{14}C. For this publication, we have used the calibrations provided by the OxCal calibration program developed by Bronk Ramsey.

When Godin was excavated, every attempt was made to collect carbon for dating. At that time, because of the techniques used, fairly large samples were needed and burnt wood was really the only good source of enough carbon for dating. Charcoal was collected from all of the levels at the site, and more than two hundred carbon samples were shipped back to the lab at the ROM. In the early 1980s, Cuyler chose the best one hundred of these samples, the largest or those with the most accurate contexts, and sent them to Robert Stuckenrath at the Smithsonian Institution Radiocarbon Laboratory for analysis. Unfortunately, Stuckenrath left that lab, and Cuyler lost track of both him and the precious samples. Stuckenrath has since passed away. The editors of this book tried to track down the samples but to no avail. We did manage to recover the remaining carbon samples in the storage facilities at the ROM. Naomi Miller, of the University of Pennsylvania Museum, examined these samples to identify plant species at Godin (see "Ancient Agricultural Landscape at Godin," p. 59), and we then submitted twenty-one of them for ^{14}C dating. The resulting date ranges for the various periods at Godin are presented in the following chapters.

A complete list of these dates is available in the Godin Web archive at https://tspace.library.utoronto.ca/.

What we get at Godin, then, is one very large excavation unit, called the Deep Sounding (whose nickname at the site was "The Big A"), where the layers of the deposits are sometimes difficult to understand, but where the architecture can be minutely planned, and several smaller units where there is a clearer sequence of layers but almost no recoverable architecture and few clear contexts for any recovered artifacts.

It is very difficult to correlate the actual layers themselves between excavation units in different areas of the site, in this case between the Deep Sounding and the test trenches, but by adding the artifacts found in the levels into the equation it is possible to detect a pattern of occupation across the site, and to relate that pattern to other sites. Information about the stratigraphic layers is combined with the architecture and the artifacts found in them to create the phases and sub-phases that form the basic chronological framework for understanding the vast quantity of material that was uncovered at Godin Tepe. In each of the chapters of this book the writers refer to the stratigraphy of the site, but it is the reconstructed phases and sub-phases that are the real backbone of our understanding of what went on during the thousands of years that the site was occupied. Archaeological phasing is based on the simple principle of stratigraphy combined with the very complex principle of artifact style.

The Meaning of Style

If there is one thing that all archaeologists can agree on, it is that observing the distribution of the style of objects through time and space will reveal something important about the cultures that created them. But there the agreement ends. How to make those observations, what they might mean, and why they are important have been the subject

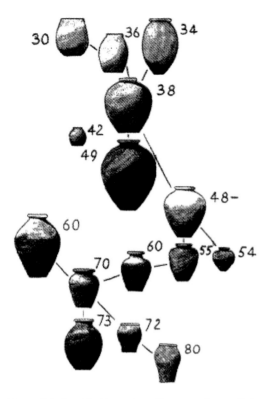

Figure 2.9. Petrie's illustration of pottery change: "The genealogies of some forms of pottery from beginning to end of the whole period"

of intense and sometimes virulent debate for the past century. The notion that man-made objects, such as art or architecture, have distinct styles in different time periods is common in art history and criticism. Art historians are concerned with style inasmuch as it differentiates one artistic tradition from another, but normally they seek the source of that change in the individuals who produced the work. Oddly, archaeology has only recently entered the arena of the art-historical debate about style. Instead, many archaeologists have treated man-made objects as if they belonged to the natural world and have created classification systems that are much more like biological taxonomies than art-historical descriptions.

When in 1899 the great Egyptologist and pioneer of Near Eastern archaeology Sir Flinders Petrie set out to sort through the pottery from a set of tombs in Egypt, he borrowed principles from the then nascent field of evolutionary biology to suggest that ceramic forms would appear, flourish, and then die out slowly. He didn't make reference to the makers of the pots or worry too much about why new forms appeared, but instead treated the objects as though they had a life of their own. He wrote of artifact types appearing, evolving, and degrading, and he charted this course as a genealogical tree.

Petrie's work was uncannily accurate and brilliantly inventive, and he very self-consciously set the stage for much of what was to become scientifically based archaeology: "We have here a new and exact method for dealing with all those vague ages as yet unfathomed," Petrie concluded in his seminal turn-of-the-century article about these tombs. "Prehistoric archaeology has made another step toward becoming an exact science. And now the responsibility of those who excavate is tenfold increased, as the extent of their care and exactitude will more than ever restore or ruin the history of the past." This step towards an exact science, however, also brought an approach to classifying man-made objects that divorced those artifacts from the people who made them.

Archaeology is a relative newcomer as far as academic disciplines go. In the mid-nineteenth century when biologists had already established all of the basic principles of biological taxonomy and chemists had created the periodic table, Near Eastern archaeology, insofar as it existed at all, was little more than a hunt for treasures to add to the collections of the great European museums. By the turn of the century, archaeologists had a lot of catch-up to do. Most of that work was accomplished between the end of the First World War and the beginning of the Second, in the heartland of Mesopotamia between the Tigris and Euphrates rivers. By the 1950s archaeologists had established the basic sequence of Mesopotamian archaeological periodization as a series of phases and sub-phases based on styles of architecture, art and, above all, pottery. This process of comparative stylistic analysis to establish the contemporaneity of sites, called relative dating, was critical to unravelling the history of the Near East. Once the basic sequences had been recognized, key absolute dates, derived from written texts or radiocarbon analysis (see "Archaeological Dating at Godin," p. 36), could be plugged into the grid and a true chronology created.

In 1959 Cuyler Young was a young graduate student at the University of Pennsylvania. The budding close relationship between Iran and the United States had fostered the growth of American-led archaeology in that country, and Cuyler's knowledge of the language and culture of Iran put him in the perfect position to be a major player. Earlier Iranian archaeology had concentrated on the impressive monumental sites of the southwest, such as Susa and Persepolis. It was clear that the archaeological phasing that had been so useful in Mesopotamian archaeology must be extended to Iran as well, particularly to the highland areas of the Zagros Mountains. Cuyler chose pottery style as the basis for creating this new sequence, as had the Mesopotamian archaeologists before him, because pottery is found abundantly in all Near Eastern sites and displays a satisfying pattern of stylistic grouping through both time and space. Cuyler concentrated on the pottery from the first millennium BC and convincingly showed that the material from previously excavated sites, as well as pottery collected from the surface of unexcavated sites, could be arranged into three basic phases (Iron I, II, and III) that succeeded one another through time. Some shapes were continuous from phase to phase, but most changed in some way and the fabric of the pottery, the clay and grits from which the pots were formed, as well as the way the pots were fired in a kiln, changed through time. The main reason Cuyler decided to tackle the huge site of Godin Tepe as his first large-scale excavation was because it looked like a promising place to extend his pottery sequence back through several millennia. The analyses in this book all compare the pottery styles that were recovered in any given period to those from other excavated sites, in part to refine still further the comparative ceramic chronology of western Iran. But the authors also suggest that the pottery of each level reflects something more fundamental about the people that produced it.

Archaeologists have a curious relationship to pottery. It is by far the most abundant artifact type in archaeological deposits, and it forms the basis for most archaeological phasing, but, in part because of its abundance, archaeologists traditionally didn't usually ponder too much about how or why it looks the way it does. They knew from long experience that both the shapes and the fabric of pots change through time and across space, and this patterned distribution is the basis for almost all archaeological chronology, but the reasons for these changes were usually not examined too closely. It was understood that ceramic shifts sometimes have something to do with the replacement and movement of population groups, and the advent of a new pottery style was often interpreted as the arrival of a foreign ethnic group, but the mechanism through which pottery style was associated with culture change was usually glossed over. When styles changed slowly over a period of time, or when it was known from written texts that no new people moved into the area, it was usually assumed that craftspeople adopted or invented new forms or motifs in a casual way and that this new style then fanned outward like a contagion. Like Petrie with his scientific seriation, archaeologists often treated pottery as an independent species capable of evolution, reproduction, genetic drift, and mutation, without reference to the people who produced it.

During precisely the time that Godin Tepe was being excavated in the 1960s and 1970s, some archaeologists began to seriously question the assumptions that had allowed researchers to jump from pottery style to population movements, and to demand that attention be paid to how exactly the connection could be made. As it happens, one important voice in that debate was Carol Kramer, an important member of the Godin excavation team.

For the first few excavation seasons, the Godin crew lived in a local village near the site and, being a gregarious bunch, quickly made friends with the local villagers. Inspired in part by the work of Patty Jo Watson who was studying the architectural patterns of Iranian villages, Carol began to try to make connections between the material culture that surrounded them in the village and the artifacts she was digging up every day on the mound, and she started questioning the villagers about how and why they made particular kinds of pottery or tools. She soon realized that some other archaeologists from around the world were also looking to living, modern societies as models to understand how exactly the cultural patterning that we recover archaeologically might have come about. Informal chats in dig houses in the field and conferences back at home quickly escalated into the development of a new archaeological discipline: ethnoarchaeology.

Carol's interest in ethnoarchaeology eventually burgeoned into a four-month, dedicated study of a small agricultural village in the Kangavar Valley, not far from Godin. Carol lived in the village, now chatting (and taking notes) in a more formal way with the villagers about the nature of their lives. Her study departed from traditional anthropology, which tended to focus on such intangibles as kinship and ritual, by focusing on the material objects that were such an important part of the villagers' everyday lives, and that would be all that would survive for the archaeological future. After fieldwork in Iran was halted by the revolution of 1979, Carol moved her research to India where she studied pottery making in the state of Rajasthan. She used the pots of living potters to do the very kind of statistical analyses that archaeologists were then performing on excavated ceramic assemblages—with some surprising results.

While Carol and her colleagues were busy studying the living cultures that still produced pottery locally, another group of archaeologists were debating the theoretical nature of style change and what it might mean in terms of past cultures. Disciplines can seldom point to one specific article that altered the substance of a debate, but Martin Wobst's 1977 article "Stylistic Behaviour and Information Exchange" served as a catalyst for archaeologists to rethink the nature of style. Wobst argued that style was not simply what was left over when you eliminated the functional components of a vessel, but that style itself played the very important function of communicating information about the user of the artifact to surrounding communities. Instead of being an unintentional result of craft traditions, style could be understood as the deliberate manipulation of the artifact to identify its user as a member of a certain group. Suddenly there seemed to be a way to explain directly why and how pots might reflect people.

Wobst's article became one of the most frequently quoted references in archaeology journals, but it soon became apparent that the importance of information exchange in style went far beyond even what Wobst was claiming. Wobst suggested that the more visible an element of style was, the more likely it was to be used to communicate information, and that exterior decoration was therefore the most likely source for this kind of variation. Many archaeologists assumed, therefore, that shape and size were more likely to reflect functional than stylistic variation. Wobst also said that artifacts that were used in public areas, or when the user was travelling, were more likely to involve information exchange because they were visible to outsiders, and that purely domestic artifacts were therefore unlikely to be heavily influenced by stylistic considerations. The new field of ethnoarchaeology found, instead, that people seemed capable of endowing even the most subtle variations in form with stylistic relevance, and that they did this consistently even for the most mundane cooking pot or mixing bowl.

People from a large variety of societies around the world use objects of specific shapes, sizes and decoration to identify themselves as members of many different kinds of groups, including families, craft guilds, economic classes, ethnic groups, religions, and even specific political parties. Maybe even more importantly, researchers found that self-identification was just as important as signalling group membership to outsiders, and that people preferred to use their own recognizable forms even when a neighbour's pot type might offer functional advantages.

Ian Hodder found that members of the Kalinga ethnic group living in the Philippines identify the potters who made a particular vessel based on the thickness of the pot's rim and the curvature of the lip in addition to the complexity of decoration. The Kalinga living in the Pasil River valley differentiate their pots from those produced by Kalinga of the Tanudan River valley on the basis of a distinctive shoulder, which always occurs on Tanudan-area pots and never occurs on Pasil-area pots. The Lozi of Zambia differentiate themselves from the neighbouring Mbunda through the proportions of their reed baskets, and when the Mbunda make the baskets for sale to the Lozi they use the proportions preferred by the Lozi. Each tribe living in the Baringo district in Kenya uses wooden eating bowls with distinct formal characteristics, including shape and depth, but they all use the same standard form of water jar, which is manufactured in a distant city. I might add that in early-twenty-first-century North America, where most tableware is undecorated, mass-produced, brightly coloured plain wares are purchased and used by a specific group of the middle class (including certain professors of archaeology and I would guess many readers of this book).

Carol Kramer and her colleagues' findings suggested that, contrary to all expectations, cultures didn't necessarily try to optimize the functional characteristics of objects, and that even though pottery was often called by a name that reflected its original function, the same form could be used for a wide variety of other uses and still retain the functional name. In Rajasthan, India, Carol observed the bulk manufacture of water-storage jars (*matkas*) for use as chicken coops, and food-storage bins (*kundias*) as spittoons. Pierre Lemonnier found that in New Guinea whole technological systems ranging from pig traps to bark clothing are identified with specific groups of aborigines in spite of the fact that all groups live in the same demanding environment and are fully aware of one another's technologies. I have personally possessed a series of very beautiful but very dribbly teapots. Clearly the aesthetic qualities of the vessel (and all of the social messages about my personal style that these invoked) were more important to me than the advantages of serving hot tea without spilling.

In nineteenth- and twentieth-century America, coffee pots were almost always tall and skinny, where teapots were short and squat, although both were used to serve hot liquids after a meal. This stylistic pattern was so marked that an informant (well, my sister-in-law) remembers breaking her china coffee pot and being in a serious quandary about what to do with her Melitta coffee filter even though she had a perfectly serviceable teapot that would have held and served coffee just as effectively: "It just seemed kind of gross to pour coffee out of a teapot." She eventually settled on a small metal pot without a spout as the best alternative. This marked stylistic preference may have originated in the eighteenth century when coffee pots first came into wide distribution in Europe. At that time coffee was associated with hot chocolate service and the preparation of hot chocolate had required a tall narrow container to froth the cocoa properly. The form of a coffee pot might be said to be associated with function in an oblique way, but once it became involved in the very dense codes of social food service, a residual functional component became a crucial symbol of the proper use of the vessel for more than two hundred years. So is the shape of a coffee pot the result of function or style or both? And if archaeologists recovered a complete china service of the mid-twentieth century, would they have any chance of being able to reconstruct this peculiar history?

Carol Kramer's insight, that the best route to understanding artifact styles might be to observe them in use in living societies, was the basis for one of the most important sources of information about style for archaeologists and anthropologists. Her colleagues who took up her work after her untimely death have now studied hundreds of societies where ceramics are still locally produced. Essentially they have found that the patterns of distribution and use are much, much more complex than anyone had predicted. Style seems to be so embedded in every aspect of the manufacture and use of an object within a culture that it cannot be easily extracted as a single variable to study. To make matters worse, the objects themselves are actively used to negotiate identity, and so themselves play a role in shaping the very identity they are supposed to be passively reflecting. The scientific optimism of the 1970s, which had looked forward to the formulation of a set of laws of style that could be applied to archaeological cultures, was replaced by the relativist post-structuralism of the 1990s, which argued, using metaphor and dense analogy, that by its very nature culture defied any such strict analytical processes.

There is one source of optimism in all this, though. If ethnoarchaeologists found that patterns of stylistic distribution were specific to individual cultures and depended heavily on all other aspects of that culture, they did universally find such patterns. The one thing that has never been observed (at least not yet) is a culture in which people make and use objects without really caring what they look like or in which the craftspeople make up styles as they work with no reference to a stylistic tradition. It has even been surprisingly difficult to find an instance of people adopting a stylistic trait in a casual way without assigning some kind of meaning to it, even if that meaning can reflect everything from ethnicity to political affiliation to social status to craft guilds. And this casual transmission of cultural traits was something that archaeologists had really assumed would be an important part of stylistic change.

Human beings seem to be uniquely adapted to detecting formal patterns in the world around them and to want to find significance in this patterning. Pottery styles have actually become such an iconic example of this trait that when, in his book *The Selfish Gene*, geneticist Richard Dawkins searched (in what many think was a misplaced inquiry) for the locus of cultural genes, or "memes," he listed pottery styles as one of his prime examples: "Examples of memes are tunes, ideas, catch-phrases, clothes, fashions, ways of making pots or of building arches." I think Carol Kramer would be very happy to know that her cherished Iranian villagers' pots were right up there with advertising jingles as a significant cultural adaptation.

Style at Godin

Archaeologists may not always be able to determine the particular historical or cultural sequence that created a single style, but by searching for stylistic patterns at a variety of levels they will be able to create some reasonable hypotheses about the source of at least some of that variation. It is precisely this kind of fine-tuned analysis that the authors of this book have performed on the pottery from the different levels of the site, with very different results for each cultural period.

In the earliest part of Godin Period VI, herdsmen and farmers living in a small village used hand-formed pottery that they probably made and painted themselves. We don't know a lot about this phase because it was recovered only in the small soundings on the slope of the mound, but we do know that at some point a very large oval enclosure was built on top of some of the small houses of the villagers, and a new form of pottery appeared within its walls. The old handmade bowls still were being used, but they were accompanied by wheel-made unpainted jars and very distinctive coarse bowls (beveled-rim bowls) that were clearly either imports or copies of the pottery made in the distant cities of Mesopotamia and southern Iran. The advent of this new pottery type and architecture seemed to mark such a break from the preceding culture that the excavators originally assigned it a whole new phase number (the missing Phase V). These foreign-looking pots are very crude, certainly no more attractive or durable than the local vessels that preceded them, and it seemed unlikely to anybody that they were being imported for their own sake. Their stylistic origins almost certainly belonged in Mesopotamia but it is not clear if that means that *people* from Mesopotamia brought them there, or if these pottery forms were so closely associated with a newly emerging system of government by an elite class that the local potentates at Godin adopted them to indicate their identity within this system. In Chapter 4 Mitchell Rothman examines these possibilities and uses additional chemical analyses of the actual fabric of the pottery to determine its source.

The distinctive black, incised Early Transcaucasian Culture pots from Godin Period IV are also a new introduction into the area, but they appear more gradually than the lowland-inspired wares in Period VI:1. Here we get a much more classic Petrie-like slow introduction, florescence, and gradual disappearance, but Rothman is able to show that this is not because pots follow a model of genetic reproduction, but because the distinctive ware was introduced by ripples—he suggests that the classic "waves of migration" metaphor does not apply here—of incoming migrants. Small groups of immigrant "scouts" came first, and, when the pasturage looked good and the trade routes were intact, other larger groups with the same ethnicity (as expressed in their pottery and other artifacts) followed on their heels.

Henrickson's study of the exquisitely painted buff and grey ware that dominated the Godin Period III pottery narrows down the field of inquiry. Instead of looking outward to sources for the decoration, Henrickson, in one of the most minutely detailed studies of pottery styles ever produced in Near Eastern archaeology, looked at the painted style of more than 20,000 sherds, to demonstrate that there were not only very distinctive sub-phases in the decorative repertoire, but that the work of individual potters with their quirks and talents could be identified.

The mass-produced unpainted wheel-made pottery of Godin Period II looks, at first glance, like the poor relation of the Godin pottery family. Found almost exclusively in a few large garbage heaps in the backmost corners of the citadel, the thousands of small sherds of bowls and cooking pots, which are all that is left of the assemblage, are not prepossessing. In fact I have to admit that when touring visitors around the Godin collection at the Royal Ontario Museum I feel a degree of embarrassment at having to admit that the many drawers of broken Period II sherds are "mine." Yet it was during this period that Godin probably controlled the most wealth and power of any time in its long history. A quantitative analysis of these bits of broken bowls reveals that they were almost certainly the result of a series of wine-laden feasts, and that it is possible to reconstruct a matching service of cooking, serving, and drinking vessels. These pots were not designed for long life, but for the good life.

If the puzzle pieces at Godin don't always add up to a clear picture of life in the pond, at least we can fill in the gaps to create an impressionist canvas. If you step back and squint a bit, you may even see a frog.

Further Reading

Arnold, P. J. "Working Without a Net: Recent Trends in Ceramic Ethnoarchaeology." *Journal of Archaeological Research* 8 (2000): 105–132.

Bradley, R., and M. Fulford. "Sherd Size in the Analysis of Occupational Debris." *Bulletin of the Institute of Archaeology* 17 (1980): 85–94.

Bronk Ramsey, C. "Development of the Radiocarbon Calibration Program Oxcal." *Radiocarbon* 42 (2000): 199–202.

Dawkins, R. *The Selfish Gene*. New York: Oxford University Press, 1976.

Dietler, M., and J. Herbich. "Tich Matek: The Technology of Luo Pottery Production." *World Archaeology* 21 (1989): 148–169.

Dyson, R. H., Jr., et al. "East of Assyria: The Highland Settlement of Hasanlu." *Expedition* 31 (1989): 3–106.

Dyson, R. H., Jr., and M. D. Danti. *Hasanlu IVB: Burned Building I*. Hasanlu Excavation Reports III. University Museum Monograph. Philadelphia: University of Pennsylvania Museum, in preparation.

Hayden, B., and A. Cannon. "Where the Garbage Goes: Refuse Disposal in the Maya Highlands." *Journal of Anthropological Archaeology* 2 (1983): 117–163.

Hodder, I. *Symbols in Action*. Cambridge: Cambridge University Press, 1982.

Kramer, C. "Pots and People." In *Mountains and Lowlands: Essays in the Archaeology of Greater Mesopotamia*, edited by L. D Levine and T. C. Young, Jr. Malibu: Undena, 1977.

Kramer, C. *Pottery in Rajasthan*. Washington, DC: Smithsonian Institution Press, 1997.

———. *Village Ethnoarchaeology: Rural Iran in Archaeological Perspective*. New York: Academic Press, 1982.

Lemonnier, P. "The Study of Material Culture Today: Toward an Anthropology of Technical Systems." *Journal of Anthropological Archaeology* 5 (1986): 147–186.

Longacre, W. A. "Sources of Ceramic Variability among the Kalinga of Northern Luzon." In *Ceramic Ethnoarchaeology*, edited by W. A. Longacre, 95–111. Tucson: University of Arizona Press, 1991.

———. "Kalinga Pottery: An Ethnoarchaeological Study." In *Pattern of the Past: Studies in Honor of David Clarke*, edited by I. Hodder, G. Isaac, and N. Hammond, 49–66. Cambridge: Cambridge University Press, 1981.

Mcintosh, R. J. "Archaeology and Mud Wall Decay in a West African Village." *World Archaeology* 6 (1974): 154–171.

Orton, C. R., and P. A. Tyers. "Counting Broken Objects: The Statistics of Ceramic Assemblages." *Proceedings of the British Academy* 77 (1992): 163–184.

Petrie, W. M. F. "Sequences in Prehistoric Remains." *The Journal of the Anthropological Institute of Great Britain and Ireland* 29 (1899): 295–301.

Sackett, J. R. "Isochrestism and Style: A Clarification." *Journal of Anthropological Archaeology* 5 (1986): 266–277.

———. "Style and Ethnicity in the Kalahari: A Reply to Wiessner." *American Antiquity* 50 (1985): 154–159.

Schiffer, M. B. *Formation Processes of the Archaeological Record*. Albuquerque: University of New Mexico Press, 1987.

Stark, M. T. "Current Issues in Ceramic Ethnoarchaeology." *Journal of Archaeological Research* 11 (2003): 193–230.

Watson, P. J. *Archaeological Ethnography in Western Iran*. Viking Fund Publications in Anthropology 57. Tucson: University of Arizona Press, 1979.

Wiessner, P. "Style or Isochrestic Variation? A Reply to Sackett." *American Antiquity* 50 (1985): 160–166.

———. "Reconsidering the Behavioural Basis for Style: A Case Study among the Kalahari San." *Journal of Anthropological Archaeology* 3 (1984): 190–234.

Wobst, H. M. "Stylistic Behaviour and Information Exchange." In *For the Director: Essays in Honor of James B. Griffin.*, edited by C. E. Cleland, 317–342. Anthropological Paper no. 61. University of Michigan, Museum of Anthropology, 1977.

3 | The Environment of Godin Tepe

Mitchell S. Rothman

Look at the mountains. See how impassable they are in every direction.
—Xenophon on entering Kurdistan, *Anabasis* IV.1.20

The rich natural environment of Godin Tepe shaped the lives of the people who lived there. The environment influenced the social organization of its successive settlements and structured their residents' relations with other areas. The crops that could be grown, the animals that could be pastured, and the raw materials that could be exploited in the Kangavar Valley, all helped to mould the ancient cultures that made their home at Godin. The constrained passes through the rugged terrain of the central western Zagros Mountains limited travel, but this challenging topography was also the source of Godin's strategic position on one of the only routes from west to east.

Figure 3.1. Godin and local topography of mountains, valley bottom, and tree-lined streams

Geography, Geology, Hydrology, and Climate

The principal societies of the ancient Near East, including Sumer, Babylonia, and Assyria, were based in Mesopotamia, the agriculturally rich basin formed by the run-off of the Tigris and Euphrates rivers. But most of the natural resources including metals, semi-precious stones, and wood that these civilizations needed for their buildings, tools, and luxury goods were obtained from the great mountain ranges that surround Mesopotamia: the Taurus and anti-Taurus Mountains in modern Turkey, and the Zagros Mountains in modern Iran.

Travellers through the central western Zagros Mountains find themselves bracketed by craggy walls of stone as they traverse green, often narrow passes with tree-lined rivers and streams snaking through them. These passes are lined by stony, low-lying hills dotted with the small clumps of oak or pistachio trees, which are all that remain of forests destroyed by human activity. The narrow passes open into wider, cultivated valleys that appear like green carpets surrounded by craggy, snow-capped peaks.

The geology that created this landscape long before humans arrived on the scene was forged when the Arabian tectonic plate pushed against the Iranian continental block. It was this phenomenon that created valley systems running northeast to southwest in the folds of the limestone and chert mountain ranges typical of the Kangavar Valley where Godin is located (Figures 3.3 and 3.4). The degree of folding is most intense south of Kerman-

Figure 3.2. Road through the Zagros Mountains

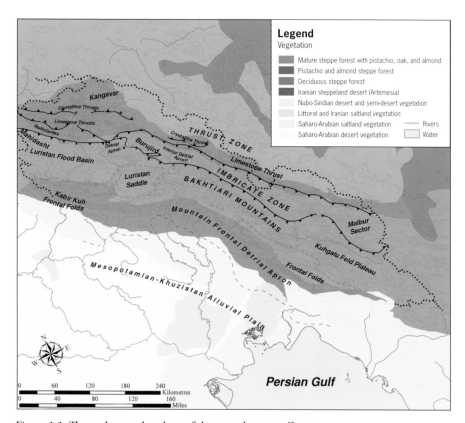

Figure 3.3. The geology and ecology of the central western Zagros

Figure 3.4. The anticline (upward-thrusting fold) formation in the Kuh-i-Kialan, just north of the Kabir Kuh

shah near Khorramabad and from there southeast through the Bakhtiari Mountains and Kuhgalu fold plateau. The least intense folding occurs in the Pusht-i-Kuh fronting on the Iraqi piedmont. The central western Zagros is also a seismically active area where fault lines often run perpendicular to the folded zones, so that great faulted slabs of sediment have been thrust up and over other blocks. However, the process of folding and up-thrusting was not uniform. The peaks in the overthrust Bakhtiari Mountain section are the highest, reaching 4,300 metres (approximately 14,000 feet) above sea level. The other areas of the folded zone tend to peak at 1,800 metres (about 6,000 feet) with valley bottoms at about 900 metres (3,000 feet) above sea level. The high Dasht-i-Kavir desert plateau northeast of the high Zagros ranges averages 1,500 metres (5,000 feet) above sea level. Tangs, almost impassable narrow canyons cutting through the folds and ranges, make movement across the mountains through a limited number of passes very difficult (Figure 3.5).

The width and shape of valley bottoms and the angle of upward folds (anticlines) created by these processes are quite variable, and these variations in shape and size directly affect the wider environment of the region. In one case the angle of anticlines promoted heavy floods that dumped large quantities of silt on the alluvial Mahidasht Plain southwest of Kangavar. This is the richest agricultural zone in the Zagros highlands. The deposit of river-borne alluvium, at places 10 metres deep, on the bottoms of the Kangavar and Mahidasht valleys created rich soil for growing crops. The steep surrounding hills are subject to erosion and are therefore less suitable for agriculture, but they provide excellent pasture for animals.

The run-off from snow and rain in the mountains creates a series of parallel streams, running

Figure 3.5. The Tang-i Chahar in the Bakhtiari area

Figure 3.6. The wide floor of the Kangavar Valley

through valley bottoms down to the Gulf. Run-off from the Kangavar basin yields three streams, the Asadabad, the Kangavar, and the Khorram Rud, which join to form the larger Gamas Ab River flowing through Kangavar into the Mahidasht. Before 5,000 BC runoff from the central Iranian mountain glacier, now gone, supplemented snow run-off. Some folded fronts, such as the Kabir Kuh, function as islands deflecting the streams around them, but water finds its way down to the Shatt al-Arab and the Persian Gulf. The process of folding and up-thrusting that formed the Zagros Mountains created subterranean pockets where water collects and bubbles up to the surface as springs. In some areas today farmers irrigate their fields by means of *qanats*—tunnels that lead water from deep aquifers at the foot of mountains, accessed from the surface by a line of shafts.

The unpredictable year-to-year variability in temperature and rainfall of the central western Zagros Mountains means that in any given year crop yields can be either abundant or scarcely sufficient to provide next year's seed. Mean daily temperatures typically range from 2°C (35.6°F) in January to 27°C (80.6°F) in July at Kermanshah, but vary widely with altitude. The summer months are effectively rainless. From October to May moisture arrives with low fronts moving in from the Mediterranean. The mountains catch much of this precipitation, although the way the fronts hit various folds creates a patchwork of poorly watered and well-watered land in neighbouring valleys. Average rainfall per month at Kermanshah from November to May from 1952 to 1972 was 64 millimetres (2.5 inches), as compared to less than 23 mm (.9 inches) per month during the same period in southern Iraq. In the lowlands of southern Iraq rain-fed agriculture is largely impossible. Even in the highlands, irrigation is often used to supplement rainfall because summer rains are sometimes insufficient. For about three months each winter in Kermanshah snow or frost prevents cultivation, but the remaining nine-month growing season provides ample time to plant and harvest an array of crops. In the higher altitudes there are not enough frost-free days to make agriculture practical, but animal herds can feed in the high pasture during the summer months, so this land is also an essential part of a highland village's ecosystem.

The Environment of Ancient Kangavar

As current evidence for climate change indicates, climate and the natural landscape can change as the result of both natural processes and human activity. Researchers examine the tracks of now-dry river beds and the sedimentation left by the ancient snowline to reconstruct the air temperature and humidity of past environments. They also core into lake beds to find direct evidence for the plant pollens that fell into the lake in successive periods. A new study by Naomi Miller of the burnt wooden beams of Godin buildings and the charcoal found in their hearths has revealed a great deal about the environment in the direct vicinity of Godin (see "Ancient Agricultural Landscape at Godin," p. 59).

Results of these investigations suggest that from 8000 to 4000 BC a steppe forest with oak and pistachio trees was established in the central western Zagros (Figure 3.7).

After 4000 BC—this covers the Godin sequence from early Godin Period VI to Period II —humidity increased from additional precipitation or a drop in temperature, permitting oak to expand at the expense of pistachio trees. A seemingly small rise in temperature of 1–2°C from 5000 to 2000 BC was enough to melt the Iranian glaciers, which increased the ground water available for agriculture. After 2000 BC, the climate approximated that of modern times.

Figure 3.7. This photograph illustrates the typical landscape of the Zagros today. In earlier times the density and size of trees would have been greater (photo courtesy of Naomi Miller).

Naomi Miller's study of the charcoal at Godin identified surprisingly little oak. Either the oak forest was not as abundant around this area as researchers had thought, or the ash, hackberry, and poplar trees that grew along the banks of the river beside Godin provided enough wood for the villagers' needs without having recourse to the more distant oak trees (Figure 3.8).

Figure 3.8. A riparian forest along the Gamas Ab River near Godin

The fragrant artemisia shrubs that dominate the Zagros hillsides today are an indicator of just how extensively the landscape was altered by human beings. *Artemesia* is typical of drier climates, but also of areas that were over-grazed by sheep and goats, which tear young saplings up by the roots. The spread of the drought-tolerant *Artemesia* and various weeds was also probably the result of the degradation of the soil by over-farming. Some salinization in the southern part of the Kangavar plain suggests that at some point improperly drained irrigation works contaminated the land with their salty residue. The people of Godin cut down trees to open fields, to provide fuel for metallurgy, and to construct the roof beams of their houses. Deforestation not only lessens tree density, it leads to the erosion of the thin topsoil of the hillsides whose rocky subsoil supports only the most rugged vegetation. Lake cores indicate that the greatest denudation of trees happened only at the very end of occupation at Godin in the Late Iron Age. We can assume that for the periods covered by this volume, the natural environment was somewhat wetter, the soils deeper, and in general the region was more densely wooded than at the present time.

Environment and Culture

There is no simple relationship between culture and the natural environment. Human culture, especially its technology, changes people's relationships to natural environments, and often human action fundamentally changes nature itself. Many of the core characteristics of any culture, even our modern, technologically sophisticated one, are dependent on elements of the natural environment. People adapt and readapt, and the matrix of culture, technology, and ecology recombine in many, often unforeseen ways.

The high mountains and deep, relatively narrow valleys of central western Iran gave rise to small, localized cultural pockets that were concentrated in its valley systems. The relative isolation of the valleys tended to encourage the formation of independent social and political units, although there were many commonalities between these regional cultures. During those few periods when central governments ruled, the highland societies, protected from military incursions by their inaccessibility, were often the first to break away from the central state.

Over the past few centuries, each of the major physiographic zones of the Zagros Mountains has been occupied by a different blend of ethnic groups, practicing different forms of agriculture and animal raising. Confederations of pastoral nomadic tribes, including the Turkish-speaking Qashqa'i and the Persian-speaking Basseri, pastured their flocks of sheep and goats in Fars to the southeast of the region. The Kuhgalu Plateau was occupied by the Kuhgalu Persian tribes of pastoralists and farmers, and the Bakhtiari Mountains were the domain of Bakhtiari nomadic shepherds and goat herders. Luri tribes farmed the best agricultural land in the southwestern folded zone, and transhumant Kurds made their home in the up-thrust zone north of Kermanshah. The culture areas of the ancient past often followed the same geographic and subsistence patterns as their modern counterparts, since the lives of ancient peoples were in part adapted to the same ecological factors.

Food Producing

People in the Middle East have raised plants and animals for close to 9,500 years. Middle Eastern farmers have made use of a number of different techniques for growing their crops, including gardening and horticulture, slash-and-burn cultivation, and permanently cleared fields. In slash-and-burn agriculture, villagers carve a small niche out of the natural habitat, often a forest or woodland, burn off some trees, and concentrate already existing plants in the clearing. Intensive agriculture, such as is practiced in most of the Western world, involves permanently opening large areas of arable land, and often planting crops that are not native to the area. The one requires fire and digging sticks, the other ploughs, intensive labour for planting and harvesting, and often large storage facilities to store excess produce. In each productive system, labour, technology, investment, control of land, and the farmer's ultimate goals are in play; the same environment can be exploited in different ways, depending on the interplay among these factors.

In the second millennium BC the rich alluvial plains of southern Mesopotamia were fertile ground for planting barley, wheat, and dates. The surviving land contracts, ration lists, and taxation records in which the farmers and landowners recorded their day-to-day transactions reveal a complex system of land use and agricultural practices.

Private landowners produced reliable annual crops for feeding themselves and their families by alternating periods of cultivation and fallow in their grain fields, and by growing low-maintenance date trees on levees

Figure 3.9. Seal impression of a second-millennium-BC Babylonian seed plough

along the irrigation channels. In contrast, the leaders of the centralized institutions of the state and temple needed to produce maximal yields of grain to pay for their burgeoning bureaucracies, armies, and dependent labourers. They used labour-intensive systems of grain agriculture, including high-maintenance irrigation networks, to increase crop yields and shorten fallow times. These different strategies in the same environment were based on different kinds of resources in terms of land and labour, and on different needs. The less intensive approach of the family field tended to preserve the agricultural environment by allowing the land to recover its fertility during fallow periods, but the demands of the palace and temple elites may have caused one of the first man-made environmental disasters; intensive irrigation resulted in the salinization of the rich alluvium, destroying its productive potential.

The people who lived at Godin and the surrounding valleys didn't record their transactions and contracts, so it is much more difficult to reconstruct their system of land ownership and use, but highland agricultural systems are usually much less labour-intensive than the irrigation agriculture of the Mesopotamian plains. Godin team member Carol Kramer's study of a modern village near Godin (published in her book *Village Ethnoarchaeology*) revealed how complex these systems of land tenure could be even with less-intensive methods of farming. The men of "Aliabad" (a pseudonym used by Carol Kramer to protect the anonymity of her sources) provide most of the labour for their own family's fields, which tend to be dispersed across a fairly wide area of the valley. Most of the available land is divided into small plots, scattered across zones of soil quality and water access. A man may walk up to one hour to work in one of his many small fields, but the villagers say that this system works well because the best land is owned by different families. It is likely that this division of land actually originated many hundreds of years earlier. Traditionally, nobles owned vast estates of cultivable land in the highlands of Iran, which they would rent to political factions. These competing factions, sometimes within the same tribal family, would distribute the land equally among its members, who then farmed the land as sharecroppers. When land reform legislation was enacted in the 1960s, and the sharecroppers were allowed to buy the plots they farmed, the small dispersed plots of land became fixed in the land-ownership system. We have no idea how land was controlled or distributed at Godin in its many phases, but it is likely that the Godin villagers also exploited a range of fields surrounding the site.

The farmers of Aliabad in the Kangavar Valley rely mainly on the spring rains to water their fields, but simple irrigation ditches are also dug in the summer months to harness subterranean water brought to the surface by a neighbouring *qanat*. There is some debate about when *qanats* were introduced in Iran, but with the exception possibly of the local leader who built his palace at Godin in Period II, the farmers who lived at Godin would have had to rely mainly on rainfall to grow their crops. The farmers of Aliabad rotate the crops grown on any one field and leave fields fallow in alternate growing seasons. This increases the fertility of the land and decreases the need for irrigation. In all likelihood the farmers of Godin practiced a similar regime of crop rotation and fallowing.

The exact system of farming that was practiced at Godin in any given period is difficult to reconstruct from the available evidence, but we do have a fairly good picture of the crops that were grown in all the major periods at Godin. Cuyler Young and his team recovered two types of plant material during the excavation of Godin. The first were large chunks of charcoal that were collected primarily as potential sources of radiocarbon dating. These were found in a large variety of contexts including hearths and garbage heaps. In a few places in Periods VI and III, very large pieces of burnt roof beams, which had fallen when buildings burned and collapsed, were also recovered. Half of these samples were subsequently lost (see "Archaeological Dating at Godin," p. 36), but about one hundred large chunks of burnt wood remained in storage boxes at the ROM and were sent to Naomi Miller at the Museum Applied Science Center for Archaeology of the University of Pennsylvania Museum for analysis in conjunction with this publication.

Naomi Miller had previously analysed the only other source of evidence for the plants that were cultivated around Godin, some of which had been previously sorted by an unidentified person in the field. In spite of the great rush at the end of the 1973 season of excavations at Godin, the excavation supervisors who were working frantically to clear the remains of the Godin Period VI oval compound, realized that because of the relatively sudden abandonment and fire of a few of the VI buildings, there was a good chance that some charred plant seeds could be recovered from the deposits. Soil samples were collected for sieving back in Toronto and some flotation was undertaken in the field. In flotation, soil samples are placed into a drum of water, often with a hose running into the bottom to make a gentle movement in the water. Because charred remains are lighter than soil segments or stone, they will rise to the top of the tank to be scooped up. The seeds collected by flotation as well as the bags of unsieved soil samples were sent to Naomi Miller for analysis in the 1990s. The results of this analysis are summarized below ("Ancient Agricultural Landscape at Godin"), and further detail is provided in the discussion of individual periods.

Ancient Agricultural Landscape at Godin
Naomi F. Miller

The analysis of plant remains (charred seeds and wood) from Godin provides clues for reconstructing the ancient agricultural landscape. The farmers of Godin sowed and harvested at least four cereals and two pulses: two- and six-row barley, emmer (an ancient wheat known as *farro* in Italy), bread wheat or macaroni wheat, lentils, and chickpeas. Weeds long adapted to cultivation (*Vaccaria,* cow soapwort, *Cephalaria,* Syrian cephalaria, and *Lolium,* ryegrass) as well as other wild and weedy plants grew alongside the crops and provided fodder for the flocks.

Vineyards must have dotted the landscape closer to the settlement, for early on grapes were fermented for wine, as evidenced by residues in a fourth-millennium Period VI:1 ceramic jar. In Godin Periods III and II seeds of domesticated grape and vine wood provide even more direct proof of grape cultivation.

In the settlement itself, people roofed their mud-brick dwellings with poplar beams. They collected the wood of ash and hackberry and the dung of their animals for fuel. Like today, the Kangavar Valley experienced cold damp winters and hot dry summers. A surprising paucity of oak charcoal suggests that either the present-day woodland had not yet become established, or that the valley-bottom riverside forest supplied more than enough fuel for cooking, heating, and small-scale ceramic and metal production.

Animal Raising at Godin

Animal herding has been an essential part of Middle Eastern economies for at least 9,500 years. Since the eighth millennium BC, the people living in the highlands of Iran raised sheep, goats, cattle, and pigs. Sheep and goats were the most adaptable and widespread herd animals, providing milk, wool, meat, and sinews to their owners. Cattle were used for their milk and meat and served as important draught animals for ploughing fields. Pigs were exploited mainly as a valuable source of meat, but because they need to be fed with the same kinds of products as humans and cannot be easily herded, pig-raising tends to be most common in periods of abundance. Animals used primarily for transporting goods and people were domesticated at a slightly later date; donkeys became common in the fourth millennium BC, horses in the middle of the second, and camels in the first millennium BC.

Figure 3.10. Seal impression of sheep in front of a building, from a fourth-millennium BC temple at Tepe Gawra, Iraq

During the five seasons of excavation at Godin Tepe, more than 34,500 animal bones were recovered and brought back to the Royal Ontario Museum. Various collections of these were sent out for analysis to a number of researchers over the years, but with the exception of a 1979 PhD dissertation by Alan Gilbert, these analyses were never completed. In 2006 when this publication project was initiated, all the Godin animal bones, by now lying in disintegrating boxes in unused corners of various university labs, were tracked down, gathered together for the first time in many years, and sent to zooarchaeologist Pam Crabtree at New York University. Crabtree and her students spent a year identifying, counting, and measuring these faunal remains with some very interesting results. The inhabitants of each period of the site used slightly different proportions of animal species (Figure 3.11), as described in more detail in each of the following chapters, but throughout the occupation of the site the people of Godin raised mostly caprines (sheep and goats), a substantial number of cattle, some equids (donkeys, onagers, and horses), and a small number of pigs.

Zooarchaeologists can identify the species and often the sex of the animal bones recovered at an archaeological site by comparing them to modern collections, and they can then reconstruct the proportions of different animals that were exploited at a site. Certain features of the bones, including the eruption of molars and the fusion of limb bones, can also indicate the age of the animal when it was killed, providing an important clue about people's strategies of animal management. If animals are being raised primarily for milk and cheese, males tend to be killed at a young age, and females are culled only when they are no longer productive. If the emphasis is on meat production, both males and females will be butchered in their prime, and if the sheep and goats are most valuable for their wool, some members of both sexes are allowed to live long productive lives. Pam Crabtree dis-

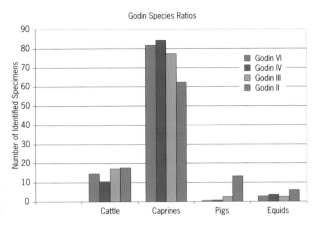

Figure 3.11. Counts of animal species at Godin Periods VI–II

covered that the pattern of sex and age ratios was different from period to period at Godin, indicating that although the people of Godin exploited the same range of species over the three millennia from Period VI to Period II, their reasons and methods for doing so were quite variable.

A key factor in the exploitation of sheep and goats is their natural habitat. They are temperate animals who do not like to be too cold or too hot and need large areas of pasture and easy access to water. One strategy is for village families to keep a small number of animals in their dwelling compounds. Nomadic pastoralists, on the other hand, use otherwise uncultivated land as pasture, and take their sheep over very long distances in winter and summer to accommodate the animals' needs. After the harvest, their animals often fertilize farmers' fields with their dung as they eat the remaining straw and stalks. Between village pastoralism and full nomadism is transhumance in which only a part of the population of settled people move with animals to pasture. These strategies actually are a continuum, each fitting particular natural and societal conditions, as will be discussed in relation to the villagers of Godin Period IV. In times of political or environmental upheaval, settled farmers may adopt pastoral nomadism, and strong, central governments often try to settle nomads.

The social and political organization of each strategy of animal herding varies in response to the challenges of pastoral goals and circumstances. Nomad camps, the ownership of pasture, and arrangements with settled farmers during migrations determine the overall organization of these pastoral nomad tribes and confederations. They tend to be egalitarian and independent of permanently settled people. The potential tactics of pastoralism vary depending on whether pastoralists are producing milk, cheese, meat, or wool only for themselves or also for exchange with settled populations for needed agricultural and manufactured goods.

Travel and Transport

The title of this book, *On the High Road*, refers to another critical component of the natural environment of the Zagros Mountains: the constraints and advantages created by the difficulty in traversing this rugged terrain. The plains of Mesopotamia can be crossed overland with ease in every direction or by using rivers and canals for transporting bulk goods. A typical Early Bronze Age barge on Mesopotamian waterways could carry up to 30 tonnes. No such capability existed in the highlands. Unlike lowland plains, mountains funnel transportation through a limited number of passes. Transport by barge is impossible and even wheeled wagons cannot negotiate much of this terrain. A man could carry a mere 15 kilograms (33 pounds) across 300 kilometres (200 miles) in 30–60 days. A donkey would increase that load to 50 kilograms (110 pounds) over the same distance in the same time period. Rivers, such as the Diyala, provide a guide for travellers, but in the mountains they do not permit the same kind of ease of water travel as do the waterways of the alluvium. Ancient and modern roads tend to follow the banks of the Zagros streams, but not all the rivers are equally useful as guides. For example, the Dez River flows in a fairly direct route as the crow flies from Godin to lowland Susa, but because of a series of tangs, most notably at the southern end of the Borujerd Valley, this route was probably rarely used. Rather, the ancient route from Kangavar goes the long way around via the Nehavand and Borujerd Valleys and over the easy pass to the Khorramabad Plain, emerging near the Bronze Age town of Maysur, then south in a route over three passes and down the left bank of the Karkeh River to the Susiana Plain.

The High Road (also called the Great Khorasan Road) is the section of what later came to be called the Silk Road that runs from Baghdad to Tehran. The natural topography of the Zagros Mountains meant that the High Road remained one of the main east-west routes through the Zagros throughout much of human history. From Baghdad the route follows the Diyala River to the foot of the Zagros at the Kabir Kuh. It turns southeast and ascends the mountains, and then runs through the plains of Hasanabad, Mahidasht, Kermanshah, Bisitun, Kangavar, and Asanabad. The road then crosses the Asadabad pass to Hamadan and on to Qazvin south of Tehran on the central plateau of Iran. From the Hellenistic era to modern times, the route ran through the northeast part of the Kangavar Valley past the towering Alvand range through the Asadabad pass, and onto the Iranian plateau. But during the period that Godin was occupied the road through the Kangavar Valley took the shorter if narrower and steeper route, through the pass cut by the Gamas Ab River, which flows past Godin, and from there to the Asadabad Valley and onto the plateau. Godin may in fact have been permanently abandoned towards the end of the first millennium BC because the traffic in people and goods had shifted some 4 kilometres to the north. A north-south extension of the High Road runs along the edge of the Iraqi piedmont branching in one direction toward Lake Van in Turkey and in the other toward the southern end of Lake Urmia. Other important routes to Godin run up the Lesser and Greater Zab rivers from modern Kirkuk and Erbil and from Fars in south central Iran.

The limited number of passes through the Zagros Mountains created cultural boundaries and constraints on trade, but the people of Godin were able to exploit this natural limitation of life in the mountains. The strategic location of Godin directly on the High Road through the Zagros, meant not only that the inhabitants of Godin could control the movement of people and goods through the mountains, but also that people living in the site participated in the diverse cultures that passed by its doors.

Raw Materials

Even in places with great agricultural potential, natural resources, such as metal ores, stone for tool-making, wood, and precious or semi-precious gemstones, can be scarce. Mountainous zones often have the resources that the lowlands lack. Such resources can be the basis of economic production and systems of exchange. Large, wealthy towns can exist in areas where such materials are found, or, as at Godin, along the routes used to transport these resources, even when the agricultural potential of the area is limited. Toward the end of the fourth millennium BC, one of the earliest exchange networks encompassing all of Greater Mesopotamia was based on such a disparity between the Mesopotamian heartland of cities, rich in soil, people, and complex economic and political organization, and its highland neighbours, rich in natural resources. Godin Period VI people were active participants in this extended trading network.

People had significant natural resources to exploit in the highlands of central Iran, including metal ores, minerals, and semi-precious stones. Of particular importance were copper, tin, and iron. Mines for copper and iron ores are scattered throughout the Zagros and Taurus mountains. In western Iran they are located mostly north and east of the central western Zagros at the edges of the Dasht-i-Kavir and near Lake Urmia. The area west of Urmia has a source for arsenical copper attested by archaeologists and mineralogists. After 3000 BC objects made of tin bronze first appear in significant numbers. The source of the tin used in making this bronze has long been debated. Many researchers believe it came from Afghanistan. Some texts of the late third and second millennia suggest that it reached southern Mesopotamia from the Indus Valley by way of the Gulf, and was transported to the Zagros via an overland route. Gold comes from eastern Anatolia, silver from

Figure 3.12. Carnelian shell and lapis found at Godin

scattered mines throughout the highlands. Chert for making stone tools is one of the widespread resources of the Zagros Mountains. Semi-precious stones including turquoise and lapis lazuli are found farther east, as is chlorite (soapstone) for making statuary and seals, and carnelian comes from the Transcaucasus. All these goods travel along the mountain routes through the Zagros. Because none of these mineral resources occurs naturally in the Tigris-Euphrates alluvial plains, the growing urban centres of Mesopotamia traded with the highlands for these valuable materials throughout the period that Godin was occupied. This trade in natural resources would play a significant role in structuring the societies of which Godin's residents were a part.

Further Reading

Note: Additional references are available in the Godin Web archive at https://tspace.library.utoronto.ca.

Adams, Robert. "Strategies of Maximization, Stability, and Resilience in Mesopotamian Society, Settlement, and Agriculture." *Proceedings of the American Philosophical Society* 122, no. 5 (1978): 329–335.

Aswad, Barbara. *Property Control and Social Strategies in Settlers in a Middle Eastern Plain*. Anthropological Papers 44. Ann Arbor: University of Michigan, Museum of Anthropology, 1971.

Barth, Frederik, *Nomads of South Persia*. Boston: Little, Brown and Company, 1961.

Bates, Daniel. *Nomads and Farmers: A Study of the Yörük of Southeastern Turkey*. Anthropological Papers 52. Ann Arbor: University of Michigan, Museum of Anthropology, 1973.

Brookes, Ian. *The Physical Geography, Geomorphology, and Late Quaternary History of the Mahi Dasht Project Area, Qara Su Basin, Central West Iran*. Toronto: Royal Ontario Museum, 1989.

Ehmann, Dieter. *Bahtiyaren, Persische Bergnomaden im Wandel der Zeit*. Wiesbaden: Dr. Ludwig Reichert, 1975.

Galaty, John, and Douglas Johnson, eds. *The World of Pastoralism: Herding Systems in Comparative Perspective*. New York: Guilford Press, 1990.

Harrison, J. V. "Kuhgalu: Southwestern Iran." *Geographical Journal* 88, no. 1 (1936): 20–36.

Jacobsen, Thorkild. *Salinity and Irrigation Agriculture in Antiquity*. Malibu: Undena Press, 1982.

Kramer, Carol. *Village Ethnoarchaeology*. New York: Academic Press, 1982.

Kroeber, Alfred. *Cultural and Natural Areas of Native North America*. Berkeley: University of California Press, 1939.

Lambton, Ann. *Landlord and Peasant in Persia*. Oxford: Oxford University Press, 1953.

Levine, Louis. *Geographical Studies in the Neo-Assyrian Zagros*. Toronto: Royal Ontario Museum, 1974.

Miller, Naomi. "The Near East." In *Progress in Old World Palaeoethnobotany*, edited by Willem van Zeist, Krystyna Wasylikowa, and Karl-Ernst Behre, 133–160. Rotterdam: A.A. Bakema, 1991.

———. Godin Tepe, Iran: Plant Remains from Period V, the late fourth millennium B.C. MASCA Ethnobotanical Report 6 (1990). http://masca.museum.upenn.edu/ethnobotanical_reports/godin_text.pdf

———. "Paleoethnobotanical Evidence for Deforestation in Ancient Iran: A Case Study of Urban Malyan." *Journal of Ethnobotany* 5, no. 1 (1985): 1–19.

———. "The Use of Dung as Fuel: An Ethnographic Example and an Archaeological Application." *Paléorient* 10, no. 2 (1984): 71–79.

Moorey, P. R. S. *Ancient Mesopotamian Materials and Industries*. Winona Lake: Eisenbrauns, 1999.

Oberlander, Theodore. *The Zagros Streams*. Syracuse: Syracuse University Press, 1965.

Peattie, Roderick. *Mountain Geography: A Critique and Field Study*. New York: Greenwood Press, 1936.

Pigott, Vincent. "The Question of the Presence of Iron in the Iron I Period in Western Iran." In *Mountains and Lowlands: Essays in the Archaeology of Greater Mesopotamia*, edited by Louis D. Levine and T. Cuyler Young, 209–235. Bibliotheca Mesopotamica 7. Malibu: Undena Publications, 1977.

Redding, Richard W. "The Role of Faunal Remains in the Explanation of the Development of Complex Societies in South-West Iran: Potential, Problems and the Future. *Paléorient* 11, no. 2 (1985): 121–124.

Rothman, Mitchell S. "Palace and Private Agricultural Decision-Making in the Early 2nd Millennium B.C. City-State of Larsa, Iraq." In *The Economic Anthropology of the State*, edited by Elizabeth Brumfiel, 149–168. Lanham, MD: University Press of America, 1994.

Spooner, Brian. *The Cultural Ecology of Pastoral Nomads*. Addison Wesley Module in Anthropology 45. Boston: Addison Wesley, 1973.

Vayda, Andrew. "An Ecological Approach in Cultural Anthropology." In *Explorations in Anthropology*, edited by Morton Fried, 249–253. New York: Thomas Crowell Company, 1973.

Wilkinson, Tony J. *Archaeological Landscapes of the Near East*. Tucson: University of Arizona Press, 2003.

Yener, Aslihan. *The Domestication of Metal: The Rise of Complex Metal Industries in Anatolia*. Leiden: Brill Academic Publishers, 2000.

Young, T. Cuyler. "The Kangavar Survey: Periods VI to IV." In *A View from the Highlands: Archaeological Studies in Honour of Charles Burney*, edited by Antonio Sagona, 645–660. Herent, Belgium: Peeters, 2004.

Zeder, Melinda. *Feeding Cities: Specialized Animal Economy in the Ancient Near East*. Washington, DC: Smithsonian Institution Press, 1991.

Zimansky, Paul. *Ecology and Empire: The Structure of the Urartian State*. Studies in Ancient Oriental Civilization, no. 41. Chicago: Oriental Institute, 1985.

4 | Contact and Development in Godin Period VI

Mitchell S. Rothman and Virginia R. Badler

The momentous social transformations that took place in the Mesopotamian alluvium during the Uruk period could not—and did not—occur in a vacuum . . . The emergence of civilization in southern Mesopotamia during the Uruk period can only be understood in the context of a wider system of interaction tying together the nascent state polities of the Mesopotamian alluvium and contemporary communities in the surrounding highland areas.

—Guillermo Algaze, 2001

Godin Periods VI and VII span the fourth millennium BC, the period when many features of the modern world emerged. All the hallmarks of complex society came into existence at that time, including leadership with the authority to make and enforce policies, taxes and tribute, social differentiation, bureaucracy, extensive economic specialization, writing, life in cities, and organized militias. Although many of the most dramatic changes of this early social evolution toward complexity occurred first on the lowlands of modern southern Iraq, all the societies involved from northern Mesopotamia, highland eastern Turkey, western Iran, and even the Transcaucasus of Georgia, Armenia, and Azerbaijan and North Caucasus steppes of Russia were affected by it. This was a multi-regional transformation.

Figure 4.1. The Godin VI oval compound

The difference between patterns of development in the highlands and those in lowlands, especially as they reflect different adaptations to the natural environment, are one of the themes of this book, but the path to these complex societies involves much more than the natural environment. Culture and society at any given time period are the result of both unique conditions and processes of change common to many evolving societies. This chapter will explore how the society of Godin Tepe Periods VI–VIII and the associated sites in the Kangavar Valley of highland central western Iran were the product both of a long history of development in the mountains and intercultural connections with lowland societies.

At the core of understanding Godin VI and its larger importance for Greater Mesopotamian prehistory are three fundamental areas of inquiry:

- When and how was the pattern of food and craft production typical of the highlands established? In what ways is it typically highland versus lowland?
- The earliest phases of this evolutionary trajectory are in a context of what anthropologists call simple societies, simple only in the sense that their organization tended toward

small, kinship-based groups with the most rudimentary types of leadership. What was the path that led to larger societal units, more highly developed leadership organizations, and more specialized economies?

• What were the connections of these highland societies with each other and with lowland Mesopotamian societies? What were the types of interactions among them? To what degree did these connections motivate local residents of the Kangavar Valley to retain or alter their behaviour and social structures?

All these questions are essential to try to answer because of what has emerged as a set of theories about why cities and leadership with authority developed for the first time midway through the fourth millennium BC when Godin Periods VI and VII were occupied. Those theories rest on the idea that the natural resources missing in the alluvial basins of the Tigris and Euphrates, but present in the surrounding highlands, created the need for a controlled, intra- and inter-regional trading system. Because the lowland societies had developed more sophisticated economic and political systems, they controlled the highland societies either as economic colonies or as trading partners. For the past four decades, these theories have been hotly debated and have spawned many archaeological projects. Godin Tepe VI is often cited as evidence for this model.

Most of the data we have relating to the study of the fourth millennium BC at Godin is from its last phase, Period VI:1 (originally called Period V). Godin levels VI:3 to pre-XI yielded samples of artifacts that are too small and too much out of architectural context for us to analyse their cultural meaning. Because Godin was such a deep site and it was clear that it would be difficult to reach these early levels, in 1971 and 1973 the Godin Project conducted excavations at Seh Gabi, a Neolithic to Chalcolithic site some 6 kilometres northeast of Godin in the Kangavar Valley. The data from Seh Gabi formed the basis for understanding these early periods in the area, although the site remains largely unpublished.

The chronology of the broader period covered by this chapter is summarized in Table 4.1. Traditionally archaeologists named this period and its sub-phases after Uruk-Warka, the first major excavated site in which it was identified. As our understanding of the period broadened however, scholars realized that the system of nomenclature no longer sufficed to characterize the cultural complexity of the period in the region as a whole. At a recent symposium of archaeologists and historians published in 2001 as *Uruk Mesopotamia and Its Neighbors*, a more neutral chronological framework (labelled Late Chalcolithic or LC 1–5) was developed that could better account for these cross-regional cultures. It is that framework that will be used here.

Table 4.1. Chronology of Greater Mesopotamia from the Neolithic to the end of the Chalcolithic Age

BC	Greater Mesopotamia Godin Tepe			Nippur Inanna	Uruk Eanna	Susa Acropole
3000	VI:1/V	LC 5	Late Uruk	XV–XVI	IVA IVB	17
3200					V	Late 18
3400	VI:2	LC 4	Middle Uruk	XVII	VI	Early 18
				XVIII	VII	
3600		LC 3		hiatus	VIII–IX	19–22
				XIX–XXI		
3800	VI:3 VII	LC 2	Early Uruk		X–XI	
4000	VIII				XII	hiatus
4200		LC 1	Terminal Ubaid		XIV–XV	23–27 Susa A
4400	IX	Middle Chalcolithic	Ubaid 4			
4600	Seh Gabi					
4800			Ubaid 3			
5000	X	Early Chalcolithic				
5200	XI	Halaf	Ubaid 2			
			Ubaid 1			
5500			Samarran			
6500–9000	NEOLITHIC					

Neolithic Precursors to Godin

To understand the nature and dynamics of Godin VI we must start thousands of years before the fourth millennium. Some key economic elements of the society of Godin Period VI including the first domestication of plants and animals, the beginning of settled life, and the appearance of economic specialization began to emerge during the so-called Neolithic Revolution. Although the Neolithic is often thought of as a uniform phenomenon, these three elements represent partially independent spheres of change. For example, settled village life preceded domestication at Hallan Çemi in the Taurus Mountains, Zawi Chemi Shanidar in the Zagros, and numerous sites in the Levant. Domestication of grains first occurred in the shadow of the mountains in the Levant, whereas some of the earliest animal domestication preceded plant domestication in the high piedmont and mountains. Pastoralists, who moved their flocks from highland pastures in the summer to lowland ones in the winter, also first appeared in the mountains. These early economic specialists provided animal products to villagers in exchange for craft goods and grains and often acted as transporters of goods. Theirs was a symbiotic relationship although at times rife with conflict.

In the Zagros, Early Neolithic villagers at sites such as Asiab, Sarab, Ganj Dareh, Guran, and Abdul Hosein evolved step by step over millennia from collectors to cultivators, village farmers, and pastoral nomads. Paleolithic peoples had a strategy of utilizing a broad spectrum of foods, because they were dependent on whatever nature provided. Residents at early Ganj Dareh continued this strategy. However, by its second phase excavators at Ganj Dareh found no wild grains; domesticated cereals provided the major component of the diet. Researchers also found evidence there of the first steps toward specialized nomadic pastoralism. While plant foods were similar throughout the Neolithic countryside, the specific sources of meat and animal products within the mountains varied according to locality; residents of some sites raised sheep and goats and domesticated cattle, while others exploited wild boar and deer. Pigs provided a small amount of meat in all these places.

Craft production in the Neolithic presages that of the Late Chalcolithic. Clay figurines of humans and animals were first made in considerable numbers during the Neolithic at sites such as Ganj Dareh and Sarab. Technologies for chipping stone into bifacial blades and flake tools from cores, grinding stone into querns and rubbing stones, forming clay into pottery with painted designs, and producing spindle whorls for making yarn appeared in the Early Neolithic.

Craft production is important because it reflects the technology of the period, but also because it indicates underlying social structures. Economic specialization is one of

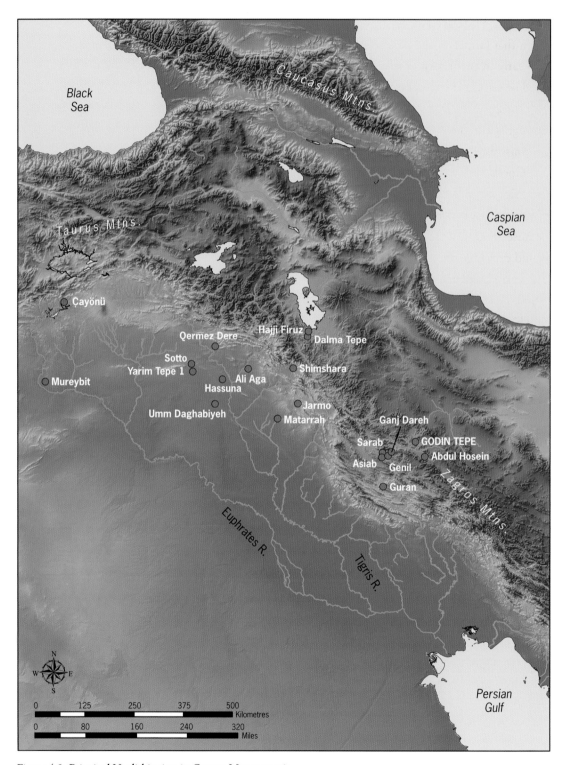

Figure 4.2. Principal Neolithic sites in Greater Mesopotamia

the defining characteristics of complex societies. On a simple level, specialization might mean that farmers make pots or sickle blades in their non-agricultural seasons, as was the case early in prehistory, or it can describe a system like ours in which we all produce one good or service and depend on the specialized production of others for almost everything we consume. The former is a basis for exchange that can strengthen or create social bonds through gifts; the latter is a complex system of interdependence that normally requires administrative organization and allows for administrative interference and control.

Goods were exchanged over a surprisingly large area since as early as the Upper Paleolithic period. Widespread finds of Red Sea dentalium shells demonstrates the scope of early exchange systems. This earliest exchange is often characterized as down-the-line trade, because those nearest the source of the valued item would take what they wanted, and would exchange the remainder to the nearest settlements. The process would start again in this second settlement and so forth down the line. The quantities would therefore decrease as one moved farther from the source area. A more formally organized system of exchange in which distance from the source was not the prime factor appeared later at the time of Godin VI:2.

The Neolithic villages were not so simple in their organization that they did not display some new social forms. Many of the earliest village sites, such as Ain Mallaha in the Levant, Qermez Dere in northern Iraq, and Novalı Çori and Hallan Çemi in the Taurus foothills, had distinctively larger structures, perhaps community buildings. Public ritual emplacements also became more commonplace. Private houses continued to be built in non-standard, ever-changing configurations. Such communal facilities and presumably the social organization necessary to coordinate them are the foundation for later more elaborated institutions evident at Godin and other sites.

Godin and the Central Western Zagros During the Early and Middle Chalcolithic

The earliest evidence for occupation at Godin comes from Periods XI through VII, spanning the Early and Middle Chalcolithic into the beginning of the Late Chalcolithic. Remains of these periods consist of pottery sherds, a few objects, and some animal bone excavated in a deep test trench, called Operation XYZ, as well as in the two soundings (Operations A and B) that Cuyler Young excavated in 1965. Operation XYZ was a small (2 metre by 4 metre) trench below the northern wall of the Period VI:1 oval compound that was dug in 1973 in order to try to uncover some of the earlier sequence at Godin. This trench was recorded in arbitrary 20-centimetre units instead of by archaeological strata, so it is difficult

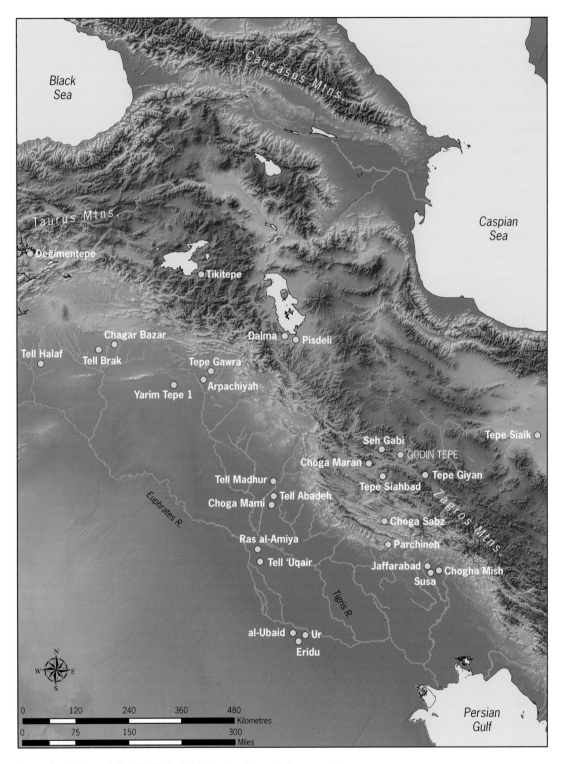

Figure 4.3. Early and Middle Chalcolithic sites in Greater Mesopotamia

to reconstruct a cultural sequence for these early levels. From the very fragmentary remains that were recovered it would appear that Godin Period VIII is in the transitional phase between the Middle Chalcolithic and the Late Chalcolithic (LC 1). Period VII, falling in the first part of the fourth millennium BC, belongs to the Late Chalcolithic (LC 2/Early Uruk) period. The neighbouring site of Seh Gabi, which was also excavated by the Godin Project, extends this sequence back into the Neolithic period.

The story told by the sites of these periods in the Zagros Mountains is of an ever-shifting distribution of communities and overall flux in the highlands throughout the Early and Middle Chalcolithic periods. One indication of that flux is found in the ecological niches that Early and Middle Chalcolithic groups chose. Early Chalcolithic sites clustered either on small streams or wadis (seasonally wet run-off streams) or were located at somewhat higher elevations that were not as dependent on readily available water. By contrast, in the Mesopotamian lowlands the first settlements could not have existed without immediate access to water for irrigation and transport routes.

This flux is represented by a series of painted pottery traditions including J ware (Godin pre-XI), "streaky," painted, and impressed Dalma ware (Godin XI/X), Black on Buff, Red on Buff, and Red, White and Black wares (Godin IX and VIII) that are associated with the Chalcolithic period within the central western Zagros (Figure 4.4). If we can interpret the distribution of these pottery design types as representing broadly interacting social groups, we can see that early highland groups were in one sense self-contained, but also that they had already begun to communicate and interact with lowland societies.

The people who made and used one of the earliest of these pottery traditions, J ware, lived on flood-plain streams. Their pottery was related to Halaf pottery of the piedmont of northern Mesopotamia. Dalma ware, on the other hand, contained many elements of the pottery traditions from the highlands north of Godin, especially the area of Lake Urmia. It did not extend into southern Luristan. While Ubaid pottery blanketed the piedmont and lowland plains of most of Greater Mesopotamia in the Middle Chalcolithic, the central western Zagros was largely isolated from these lowland pottery traditions until the end of the fifth millennium, although as Figure 4.4 illustrates, all these traditions share a common overall aesthetic as well as some specific design elements.

Pottery-style distributions indicate interactions, but the Middle Chalcolithic period in the central western Zagros represents other kinds of changes as well. Population size is a critical element for catalyzing change; the necessity of controlling and providing for the needs of larger populations often requires more complex organization. As agricultural technology was refined, the overall size of the population measured by the occupied area of sites in these mountain valleys grew in the Early Chalcolithic period.

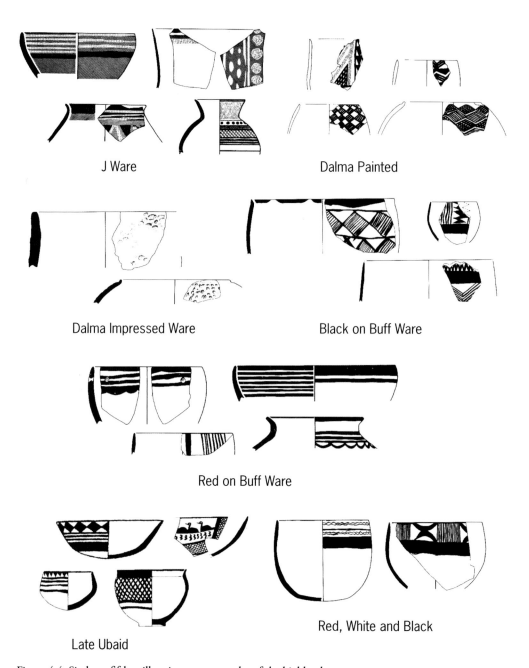

J Ware

Dalma Painted

Dalma Impressed Ware

Black on Buff Ware

Red on Buff Ware

Late Ubaid

Red, White and Black

Figure 4.4. Sixth- to fifth-millennium pottery styles of the highlands

Yet, by the end of the Middle into the beginning of the Late Chalcolithic period (Godin IX–VII) population numbers as represented by the occupied area of settlements had drastically declined throughout the Zagros from Iranian Azerbaijan to Fars. The Kangavar

Valley seems to have been the one exception to this trend. Some researchers argue that real population actually remained steady, but that a shift to a nomadic pastoral adaptation with its temporary encampments meant that fewer people left a trace in the archaeological record. There is a long history in the Middle East, continuing until very recent times, of people moving from village to pastoral nomad life in times of political or economic upheaval.

The increasing complexity of political organization, however, is demonstrated in a number of ways. An early way of controlling access to raw materials and goods was to seal them in storerooms or portable containers such as jars, baskets, and sacks. Access to these materials was limited by placing clay impressed with a carved seal signifying an individual or office over the string knot. The seal design carried information about who sealed the container and therefore also who had access to its contents (see The Seals of Godin Period VI, p. 113). Although seals and sealings pre-date Godin VIII, they became more frequently used in this period, and the uniformity of some designs suggests that they were more likely to be the symbols of institutional affiliation than of personal identity.

One reason for an increase in control mechanisms, and probably more controlling political organization, was an increase in the movement of goods. Greater Mesopotamia has an uneven distribution of resources. The alluvium lacks much beyond dirt, water, people, and animals. Any metals (gold, silver, copper), precious or semi-precious stones, wood for constructing larger buildings and boats, or chipping stone (including obsidian) must be imported from or through the surrounding highlands. During the time of Godin VIII, the LC 1, a real increase in the movement of these goods is evident across the region. For example, lapis lazuli, a semi-precious blue stone known to occur naturally only in the Badakshan area of northeastern Afghanistan, began to appear in LC 1 sites in significant amounts. The trade route used was the High Road north of the Dasht-e-Kavir. In the LC 1 the primary route continued down through the Jebel Maqlub near Lake Urmia onto piedmont near Tepe Gawra and connected with the Tigris corridor (see map on p. xvi). Later on in the LC 2–5 (Godin VII–VI:1), traffic shifted to a north-south route through the central western Zagros toward Susa. Obsidian and other chipping stone and finished blades as well as metal ores of hammered or cast copper travelled along the same route. In the northern piedmont, finely fired and decorated ceramics were traded over a surprisingly wide area, as determined by chemical characterization of pottery from Tepe Gawra, Shelgiyya, and Tell Brak. In other words, the route past Godin became a more and more important one for regional and even inter-regional exchange. Such an increased role is often an opportunity for would-be leaders to insert themselves into societies, forcing a real change in the basic relationships of different members of a society.

Often, during periods of such political change, religion comes into play. In order for people to accept the idea that they should give over power to leaders with the authority to make decisions for them, the gods often play a role in what anthropologists call the sanctification of political rule. For example, in fourth-millennium BC alluvial Mesopotamia the concept of the gods as providers, especially from afar, mirrors the images of kingship that emerged and the importance of exchange for exotic goods that elites promoted and used to signal their new social status.

One probable example of this is found in lowland southwest Iran at the site of Susa. There, residents built a truly massive high platform (called the *massif funeraire* by its excavators), composed of some 570,000 mud bricks covering one hectare (Figure 4.5).

The top of the structure was mostly removed by later rebuilding, but the shape of the one exposed side was recessed at the corners, suggesting that the platform was originally in a cruciform shape. On its apex were remains of a building with massive walls, large storage rooms, and a shrine decorated with ceramic models of caprid horns. A painted pot found at Godin phase VI:2 bore a painting of a horned animal that is very similar to the images found on some of the pottery from this period at Susa (Figure 4.6).

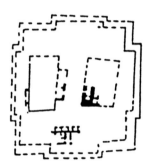

Figure 4.5. Susa *massif* showing the excavated face and drawing of possible plan

At the foot of the Susa *massif* was a cemetery with graves containing unusually finely made painted vases. These same special vases are found on survey in smaller numbers across contemporary sites of the Susiana Plains. One interpretation of this pattern is that a more hierarchically organized society had emerged, in part organized through the recruiting of labour to build and maintain the *massif* temple. The finely painted vases may have been tokens of rank used to reward the local leaders who participated in this new hierarchy. Meanwhile, in the northern piedmont, excavators at Tepe Gawra and Tell Brak recovered specialized buildings for storage of exotic goods.

Leaders cannot rely on sanctification alone. Among the services these new leaders had to perform were central storage of foodstuffs and other goods; the distribution of water for irrigation; and defence against pastoral nomads, other cities, and landless peoples.

One reason that the highlands and lowlands differed in their organization and in the

Figure 4.6. A pot of Godin VI with a painted checkerboard and horned animal

overall size of their political units has to do with the natural environment of agriculture; whereas an estimated 20,000 people lived in Uruk-Warka by 3500 BC, such numbers would not be found in the highlands for millennia. In the alluvium, population growth, clustered near the river banks for access to irrigation, also put pressures on these societies. Rainfall agriculture in the highlands did not require clustering. Population density in the highlands was lower and the size of political units was smaller, yet pressures that spurred greater social complexity still existed.

All the institutions of these LC 2–5 societies in the lowlands are associated with seals and sealings, indicating that a system of administered centralization had begun to evolve in earnest. Seals and sealings are also evident in the central western Zagros at this early stage of the Late Chalcolithic period. In general, however, we have much less knowledge of what was happening in the Zagros Mountains than in the lowlands. Only Tepe Giyan in Nehavand, Seh Gabi in Kangavar, and Baba Jan in the Pish-i Kuh have yielded relevant data other than pottery. The collection of seals and sealings from Giyan are especially important because of design parallels to Tepe Gawra, which lies some 500 kilometres to the north, as well as to the Bakun culture in southern Luristan to the southeast. These sites were stops on the intermontane exchange routes to the northern piedmont.

This pattern of links between distant sites suggests that extensive, integrated, controlled exchange networks in the Zagros had replaced simple down-the-line exchange.

The presence of thick-walled buildings at the village site of Seh Gabi, Mound A, near Godin indicates some social changes in Kangavar as well (Figure 4.7). Excavators uncovered eight rooms dating to Godin Period VII with cruciform hearths whose shape mirrors that of the temple on the Susa *massif*. The walls of these buildings were thick enough to support additional stories, although no foundations for staircases were recovered. Evidence for the production of pottery, sickle blades, stone beads, textiles, and clay figurines, as well as the remains of metal working, suggest a very lively craft-working tradition at this village. Finds of both seals and sealings indicate that this small village near Godin was part of a system evolving toward more complex organization, possibly with Godin as its centre.

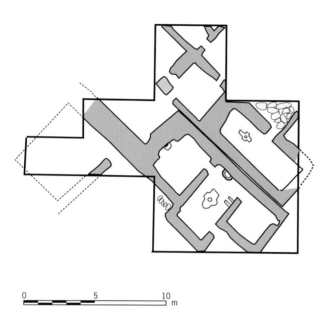

Figure 4.7. **Buildings of Seh Gabi, Mound A, Godin Period VII**

Such a societal system in Kangavar implies that geographical and societal centralization was developing. In more centralized systems the most important economic, social, and ritual activities are limited to a few sites. Cities or more appropriately urban systems represent a physical index of the degree of centralization of societies. Different functions from governance to farming to manufacturing to religion are distributed across sites in a pattern in which the most specialized functions, or ones that the leadership controls, tend to exist in city centres.

By the mid-fourth millennium BC, a very complex system of urban-centred social organization would be established throughout Mesopotamia. The development of these earliest state-based societies, traditionally associated with the Uruk culture, catalyzed change as far away as the northern Caucasus in Central Asia where very large settlements also appear for the first time. The immediate cause of these changes was in part the movement of goods and people in greater numbers and over a wider area than ever before. This new social complexity would be marked by qualitatively and quantitatively different kinds of economic, governmental, and religious interdependence. For some scholars the heart of the state is in its internal, hierarchical organization. For others it is the emergence of elites of power and privilege and the tools that these leaders used to work their will. All researchers acknowledge that specialized craft-making and high levels of exchange are part of the economic landscape of the state.

One of the hallmarks of the state in Mesopotamia was the development of a region-wide exchange network. Because the heartland of cities on the southern alluvium of Mesopotamia was so resource-poor, many of the raw materials needed to produce goods and to signal the new status of leaders were imported from areas to the north and east. Unlike earlier down-the-line exchange, these networks short-cut the gradual movement of exotic goods through space by sending agents into resource-rich areas to facilitate the movement of desired goods directly to their final destinations.

One of the major reasons why Godin VI is important to larger anthropological and Middle Eastern research is the theory that it was a colony of lowland alluvial city-states. Cuyler Young and Harvey Weiss initially made this argument for Godin VI:1. They saw the Godin compound within its oval wall as a colony of merchants from lowland Susa to its southwest. Co-author of this chapter, Virginia Badler, proposed that the oval compound was not a merchant colony, but a fort guarding the High Road. Yet a third researcher, Roger Matthews, proposed that it was a local administrative centre.

Those who favour the theory of economic colonization point to a distribution of distinctly southern Uruk cultural artifacts in the northern piedmont and highlands. This along with the political and economic sophistication of southern Uruk city-states is the evidence to support their theory. Those who see an alternative theory point to the indigenous development of societies in the so-called peripheral or colonized areas before the controlled international trading system, known as the Uruk expansion, had begun; trade in exotic goods was already prominent in the Middle Chalcolithic period. Even if the opponents of the colonization theories, modelled on the World Systems model of Immanuel Wallerstein, disagree with the nature of the periphery, including the central western Zagros, they agree that the trading system did exist.

The central question in the discussion of Godin VI material is how to define the nature of this site in terms of its relation to the lowland Uruk world. Was there an actual population of Uruk, lowland people living in the oval compound, as Young, Weiss, and Badler argued? Was there an indigenous highland population with its own developing leadership structures based on local needs, as Matthews suggested, or is there another, third possibility not yet considered?

Godin Tepe Period VI

Godin Period VI was reached only in the final month of the final season of excavation at Godin. With the funding coming to an end, speed was of the essence. As it became clear that the Uruk-related Period VI architecture was substantial and significant, and because a numeric tablet was found on the first floor to be exposed, the Period IV remains that still lay over much of the Period VI architecture were removed quickly and with less than optimal attention to detail and recording. As a result, the transition from Godin VI to IV is very poorly understood and there are many mixed lots and untraceable walls in these late Period VI and early Period IV deposits. Vertical elevations were recorded for the tops of walls and some floors of both levels, but the artifactual lots were not tied into this vertical grid, so that it is sometimes difficult to establish the stratigraphic relationship between the architectural phases and the artifacts that were found in them. The only really useful stratigraphic sequence for this period is the 1965 Operation B (originally recorded as C and G), but here again it is difficult to correlate the strata recorded in the stratigraphic section and the recording system used for the pottery collection. Strata 21, 18, and 13 in particular are so badly mixed that they are unusable.

In spite of the speed with which Period VI was excavated, the graduate students who were supervising the area convinced Cuyler Young that given the remarkable preservation of the architecture and floors it would be worthwhile to screen the dirt as it was removed so that the smaller artifacts and bones that might have otherwise been missed were recovered. They also undertook some flotation of the deposits to collect the charred seeds discussed in Chapter 3.

The Dating of Godin Period VI

In earlier publications Godin phase VI:1 was called Period V, and phases VI:1–3 had been much more finely subdivided. Young explained this rephasing in a 2004 article on the survey material:

> Unfortunately, because in the original test trenches dug in 1965 materials of lowland origin such as Late Uruk trays and beveled-rim bowls appeared to be stratified above materials of Period VI, the levels in which they were found were labeled Period V. In an effort to eliminate this confusion and make it clear that what was originally called Period V is chronologically just late Period VI . . . Period VI will henceforth be divided into three phases: VI:3, which represents the indigenous culture before any contact with the Uruk Period lowlands, VI:2, in which the

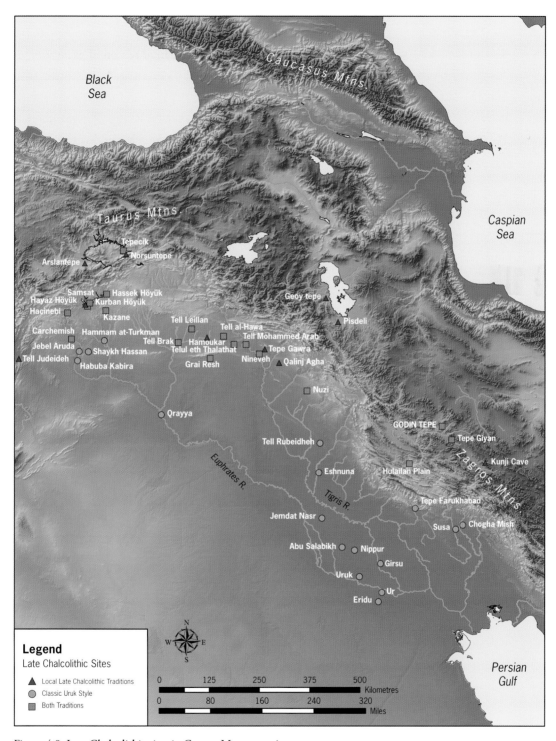

Figure 4.8. Late Chalcolithic sites in Greater Mesopotamia

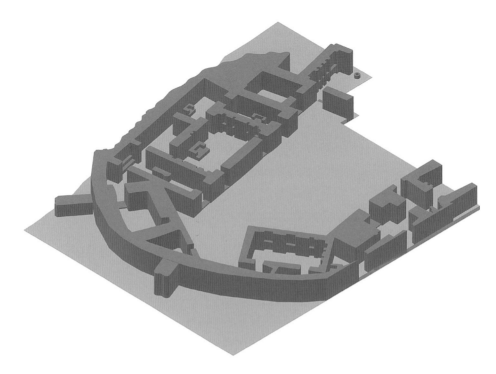

Figure 4.9. Raised plan of Godin VI:I oval compound

first hints of some contact with the lowlands appear; and Period VI:1, in which the Oval is built. Period VI:1 is divided into VI:1b and VI:1a based strictly on the architectural changes which occurred within the oval.

How can these phases be dated and how do they correlate with comparable sites in the Greater Mesopotamian world?

The dating of Godin VI is based on both relative chronology and radiocarbon dating. Our best understanding of the overall chronology appears in Table 4.1. Table 4.2 summarizes the absolute dates for Godin VI. Although absolute dates derived from radiocarbon analysis are in many ways the best source for chronology, they provide only a possible range of dates; these ranges can sometimes be narrowed by comparison with other sites. Chronological schemes that most archaeologists use are often the somewhat intuitive correlation of absolute and relative dates. The radiocarbon dates analysed by the Smithsonian lab (sample numbers beginning with SI) from Godin VI are fairly consistent and can be combined with Bayesian statistics (using the OxCal modelling program developed by Bronk Ramsey). With 95 percent probability these carbon samples came from plants that were last alive sometime between 3490 and 3050 BC. From the depth of deposit and other factors, it seems likely that the buildings of the Period VI:1 oval compound existed for less

Table 4.2. Radiocarbon dates for Godin VI

OxCal v4.1.3 Bronk Ramsey (2009); r:5 IntCal04 atmospheric curve (Reimer et al., 2004)

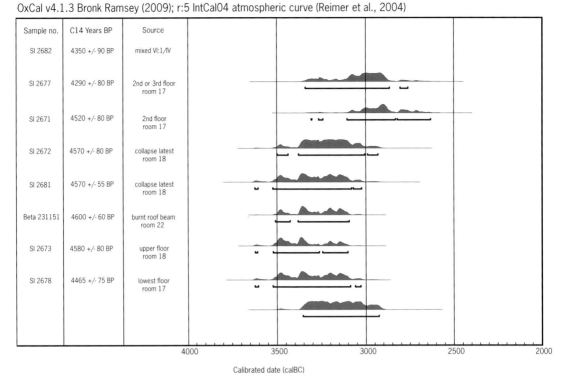

Sample no.	C14 Years BP	Source
SI 2682	4350 +/- 90 BP	mixed VI:1/IV
SI 2677	4290 +/- 80 BP	2nd or 3rd floor room 17
SI 2671	4520 +/- 80 BP	2nd floor room 17
SI 2672	4570 +/- 80 BP	collapse latest room 18
SI 2681	4570 +/- 55 BP	collapse latest room 18
Beta 231151	4600 +/- 60 BP	burnt roof beam room 22
SI 2673	4580 +/- 80 BP	upper floor room 18
SI 2678	4465 +/- 75 BP	lowest floor room 17

Calibrated date (calBC)

than 250 years; this time span probably fell sometime within that range of dates. Since the oval wall that defines the compound was clearly built after some of the buildings within it—the wall cuts some of the original buildings—the life of the oval wall is considerably shorter, probably less than 150 years. Two dates (SI 2674 and 2676) that were originally assigned to Period VI on the basis of our re-analysis of the stratigraphy belong rather to pitting from Period IV.

Unfortunately, no carbon samples were recovered from phases VI:2 and VI:3. These phases can be dated only by comparison with other sites. The relative chronology of Period VI and its overall relationship to other sites will be discussed below.

The Pottery of Godin Periods VI and VII (Figures 4.44–4.53)

Virginia Badler analysed the pottery from Godin Period VI. She used the 1965 Operation B to trace the changes in pottery style through the sub-phases of this period, although there were stratigraphic problems with the Operation B sounding.

We first need to define the ceramic assemblage that is to be compared. As at most archaeological sites, pottery was the most ubiquitous category of artifacts recovered from

Godin Tepe. There are more than 4,000 pottery sherds from Periods VI and VII stored in the Royal Ontario Museum, and about fifty vessels with full profiles. Other complete vessels remained in Tehran.

Making a vessel entails many important decisions by the potter. These manufacturing decisions are profoundly influenced by available clay and temper resources, the training of the potter, and the purposes for which, or persons for whom, he or she is making the pots. For the purposes of discussion, the Godin VI pottery will be divided first into functional shapes. The largest percentage is made up of small bowls—bowls with a rim diameter of 24 centimetres or less were classified as small, and those with a rim diameter of 25 centimetres or more were classified as large—serving bowls and beakers (58 percent of early Period VI sherds). The remainder of the assemblage is divided into vessels which would have had a group-use function: large bowls (group serving and food preparation; 17 percent in early Period VI), spouted vessels (serving of liquids; 2 percent in early Period VI), pots (food storage or cooking depending on burn marks; 10 percent in early Period VI), pithoi (for food storage; 1 percent in early Period VI), jars (for food storage; 11 percent in early Period VI), and lids (1 percent in early Period VI). There are similar percentages throughout Period VI. Table 4.3 presents the major types.

Table 4.3. Godin VI and VII pottery types

Type I Bowls Small <24 cm> large	Type II Jars	Type III Spouted Vessels	Type IV Beakers, Bottles, and Jugs	Type V Various
a. Beveled-rim	a. Four-lug	a. Uruk Droop	a. Beer jars	a. Eating Trays
b. Rolled rim	b. Rolled rim	b. Uruk Short funnel	b. Pedestal bases	b. Lids
c. Inturned rim	c. Collared or everted neck	c. Trough	c. Beakers	c. Strainers
d. Flaring plain rim	d. Fine	d. Straight tubular	d. Bottles	d. Cooking pot/ trays
e. Plain everted		e. Short wide/ cannon		e. Pithoi

Manufacture, Finish, and Decoration of Godin Periods VI and VII Pottery

All the pottery of Periods VI and VII was fired at a fairly low temperature with exposure to a considerable amount of air (oxidation), as opposed to being fired in a kiln, which is sealed, reducing the amount of oxygen (reduction). Its fabric colours ranged from pink to buff when not slipped (a slip is a thin layer of liquid clay applied before firing). When they are slipped the colours tend to be cream or red. Fine-painted pottery is most commonly decorated in brown or black paint on a cream ground. Two vessel forms, the rolled-rim small bowl and small jars, are almost always slipped, usually with a cream slip that sometimes burns pink in the firing.

Red lightly burnished pottery appears early in the Godin VII–VI sequence. That treatment, parallelled in the piedmont at Tepe Gawra, appears in the lowland later. Most researchers assume that lowland forms always move toward the highlands, but lowlanders do adopt highland forms. This is one of a number of examples.

Potters in Period VI and VII were also quite consistent in their use of tempering material. Throughout the entire period, the primary tempering agent is vegetal, most often chaff, or in the case of very fine chaff perhaps it is from dung, which mixed with straw in dried cakes was

Figure 4.10. Slipped, incised, and painted forms (see the core and slip colour on the incised four-lug jar)

Figure 4.11. Red-slipped vessels of Godin VII and VI:3

Figure 4.12. Early VI red-slipped jar

Figure 4.13. Inturned-rim bowls and a pedestal-base bowl

Figure 4.14. String-cut base typical of Uruk wheel-throwing technique

a common fuel for heating, cooking, and other pyrotechnic activities. There are certain exceptions, most notably medium sized jars and cooking pots. Cooking pots were made to withstand thermal shock, and to that end, small stones were added to the temper. However, very large pithoi were still tempered with a very coarse straw.

Most Godin pottery is hand formed. Forms are often quickly made and crudely trimmed by paring off the excess clay from the base as exemplified by the inturned rim-bowl shape. However, there is evidence for use of the potter's wheel, a technical advancement first utilized in the LC 3 period. The probable date when the wheel is first used at Godin is VI:2, the beginning of more intense contact with the Mesopotamian world. The pottery of VII and VI:3 is indistinguishable in many ways other than the percent of VII that were painted. The pottery of Period VII and phase VI:3 is the most finely made. The potters of phases VI:2 and VI:1 valued speed over quality, which is significant because mass production often accompanies overall increases in economic specialization and societal complexity.

Among those forms categorized by Badler as small bowls are the highly straw-tempered utility wares of the Uruk world, the beveled-rim bowls, which are important because of their connection to the lowlands. These were mass produced in the millions across Mesopotamia beginning in about 3600 BC. Some researchers think these vessels were mould-made, but it is more likely that someone took a wad of prepared clay holding it between the thumb and two fingers, quickly formed it, and finished it with a sweep of a thumb around the rim giving it its bevelled edge. These vessels can vary in height; the higher forms were called *blumentöpfen* (flower pots) by those who first found them. Badler's experi-

Figure 4.15. Wheel-cut base typical of Uruk technique

ments with various substances suggest that they were used to contain liquids, both because the rounded-rim bowls they replaced late in the Godin VI sequence were apparently used for drinking and because the formation of the bevel makes it fit a lower lip at a good angle for drinking. Evidence, including textual evidence, suggests that they were ration bowls, made by common workers rather than skilled potters, to feed the dependent or corvée work force of the central authorities.

Overall, the pottery of Periods VII and VI provides evidence for distinctive patterns of development and change. The changes that mark the transition between Periods VII and

Figure 4.16. Beveled-rim bowls

VI include decreases in the percentage of painted pottery, slipped and burnished pottery, and handmade pottery, including decreases in Period VII coarse-burnished wares. In late phase VI:2 flared plain-rim bowls and beveled-rim bowls emerged as new forms and quickly became the predominant bowl shape thereafter for Godin VI potters. New large forms appeared as well: ledge-rim bowls, bowls with an interior bevel, and vessels with straight and funnel spouts. Potters for the first time applied raised and incised decoration including rope decoration on everted-rim jars. In phase VI:2 potters also added disk and ring bases, medium and large beakers (with pinched lips in late VI:2), rolled-rim pithoi, pithoi with interior ribs and pinched knobs, exterior lugs, exterior decorative knobs, and serving trays and strainers.

The transition to phase VI:1 saw a return to painted jars and expanded use of the fast wheel as evidenced by unfinished string-cut bases and rilling (the undulating surfaces of wheel-thrown pots). The quantity of slipped pottery and pithoi decreased. Handmade beveled-rim bowls became the predominant small-bowl form, small rolled-rim bowls were more flared and the roll more tapered, and Uruk-type serving trays with either a rolled rim (with single thumb-print on rim, perhaps for pouring) or a straight rim became common. Ring bases increased in size. Only in the oval compound did excavators recover everted-rim jars with rope decoration and nose lugs, Uruk droop and trough spouts, cooking bowls ("woks"), Uruk-type bottles, and flared bowls with interior decoration.

Comparanda and Relative Chronology of Godin Period VI Pottery

The pottery of Period VI is significant because of our ability to date it by comparison to other sites. It is equally important because it tells us about cultural connections among ancient peoples.

The pre-Uruk contact or early Uruk contact material can be placed in time through relative chronology (Table 4.1). The nature of that contact in VI:2 is very limited in that it consists of the almost universal beveled-rim bowl, which we now know was already in wide circulation from 3600 to 3000 BC. String-cut bases and trays also appear then.

Godin VII and VI:3 into VI:2, the period when the site was very much part of the Zagros mountain culture area can be best dated by sites to its north and east in central Iran. The sites of Gabristan near Qazvin and Sialk near Kashan both have levels with ceramics comparable to Godin VII and early Godin VI. For Godin VII just before and at the beginning of the fourth millennium BC the comparison is with the earliest level at Gabristan and Sialk III, phases 4–5. Gabristan IV and Sialk III, phases 6–7, compares with Godin VI:3 into VI:2. A bowl type with three black painted finger marks from the rim can place Godin in the LC 2 with parallels to the piedmont of northeastern Iraq and southeastern Turkey.

Godin VI:2 on the basis of these comparisons falls in the LC 3 and LC 4 periods, and Godin VI:1 into LC 5 (Table 4.1). The pottery from this period also establishes very clear cultural links between the residents of Godin and the lowland Uruk world, particularly the part of the Tigris and Euphrates south of modern Baghdad (Nippur and Uruk), as well as the extension of the alluvium into southwestern Iran (Susa and Choga Mish). There are surprisingly few commonalities in pottery style with the Diyala Plain through which travellers from the south would have had to pass. Kunji Cave is clearly related to this VI:2 period.

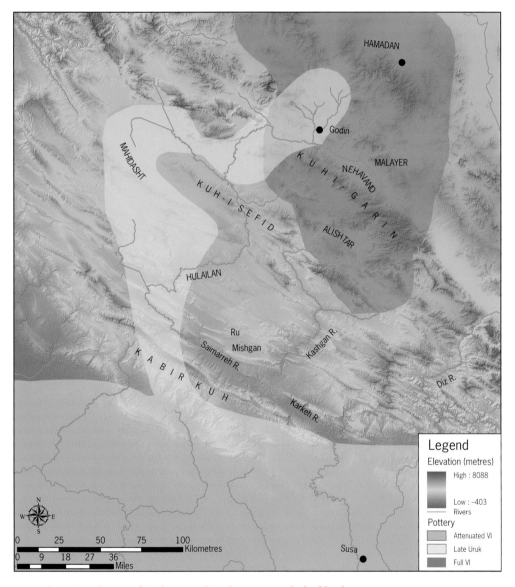

Figure 4.17. Distribution of Godin VI and Uruk pottery in the highlands

Godin VI:1 shares many parallels with the Uruk traditions of the lowlands at Nippur, Uruk, and Susa. It also shares styles with Baba Jan and other sites in the Pisht-i Kuh closer to the lowlands, presumably also copies of Uruk styles. An unusual connection with Arslantepe VIA of the LC 5 is the fenestrated stand, also present in the Diyala. In the last sub-phase of Godin VI, phase VI:1a, an additional cultural connection is made with pottery of the Transcaucasian cultures from the mountains of the south Caucasus in the modern countries of Armenia, Georgia, and Azerbaijan. This other cultural movement, which is the subject of Chapter 6, will also prove important for understanding the functioning of the site in its final VI:1 days. It establishes the date of Godin VI close to the end of the fourth millennium BC.

Certainly, the corresponding geographical distribution patterns of Uruk-like ware and local Godin VI pottery suggest a directed flow of influence or exchange, not a blanketing effect (Figure 4.17). The full Period VI ceramic assemblage is found in the central Zagros northeast of the Kuh-i Sefid and even more so northeast of the Kuh-i Garin, extending north to the Qazvin Plain near modern Tehran. This is the high mountain front adjoining the Dasht-i Kavir. The so-called attenuated VI, defined as having fewer VI elements, covered an area where only a partial set of the VI types are found to the south and west of the Kuh-i Sefid in the Mahidasht and Hulailan valleys. In the succeeding Godin IV period, surveyors did not find any of the Early Transcaucasian wares that dominated Godin in these valleys, suggesting that some kind of cultural barrier separated them. However, the clearest presence of the Uruk pottery occurred in the broadest agricultural plains of the Central Western Zagros, the Mahidasht and Kangavar. Contact snaked its way up the rivers along the High Road into the richest of the valleys. Parenthetically, it was in the Kuh-i Sefid and Kuh-i Garin, as well as the lowlands where population (mostly new villages) grew in the fourth millennium, while in the Mahidasht and Hulailan valleys population declined. Kunji Cave outside the VI or attenuated area is generally interpreted as a seasonal pastoral site southwest of the Kuh-i Garin on the route into the lowlands. Because it was one of only a few excavated sites other than Godin with this typical Godin Period VI pottery perhaps Kangavar or its environs was a home base for these pastoral nomad groups.

The Architecture and Function of the Godin Phase VI:1 Oval Compound

The latest and most important set of buildings in Godin VI are those within the oval wall. This compound consists of a group of structures around a central courtyard placed at what would have been the high point of the mound. The entire compound is surrounded by an oval enclosure wall, and covers an area of approximately 560 square metres. The structures within the wall can be divided into separate buildings composed of adjoining rooms. The

Figure 4.18. Plan of Godin VI:1b (earlier) oval compound

oval compound was abandoned and what remained was in fairly good context. Area 21 and room 22 in the northeast corner of the compound were burned.

A number of rooms including the northwest corner of the northern building (room 14) were cut away by the construction of the oval wall, suggesting that the oval wall was built after some of the buildings inside it. There are also three triangular rooms (rooms 5, 10, and 13) that accommodate the curve of the oval wall, which suggests that these at least were built after the wall. The overall impression is that the builders of the oval compound were taking advantage of the limited space available. The remodelling of the buildings of phase VI:1b in phase VI:1a (Figure 4.19) consisted of the addition of large rooms or enclosed areas (rooms 7–9) inside the courtyard. Based on the way this additional structure

Figure 4.19. Plan of Godin VI:1a (later) oval compound

appears to block one side of the entryway door, it may have been an unroofed enclosure, perhaps even for animals. Near the end of the occupation of the oval compound, the door-ways to rooms 2, 10, 12, and 13 were sealed.

These buildings share certain features. Four of the rectangular rooms have interior niches on their long walls (rooms 2, 6, 18, and 22), and one of these rooms (room 6) also has interior niches on its short walls. From ethnographic parallels, these niches were probably used as storage shelves. Of the thirteen completely excavated rooms in the VI:1b compound, only five have hearths on their initial floors. Three of the hearths (in rooms 17, 18, and 19) are heating fireplaces, while two of the hearths (in rooms 5 and 6) are constructed as cooking hearths, complete with griddles. In the modern Near Eastern village of Titriş Höyük, interior rooms

room 5

room 6

Baking Ovens

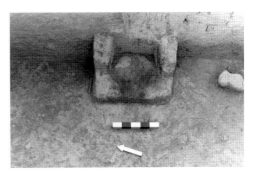

room 18

room 19

Heating Ovens

Figure 4.20. Varieties of hearths in the oval compound of Godin VI

can be divided into two basic groups based on use: living spaces with hearths where villagers cook, eat, and sleep, and storage rooms that are without hearths or windows.

One reason that Godin is important is its potential role in the Uruk expansion. Was it a colony or fortress built by lowland merchants? If so, were the occupants from outside the highlands or local leaders coordinating or regulating economic activity from inside the oval compound? These questions are best answered by reconstructing the function of the site's buildings through their architecture and contents. Comparison with the VI:1 and VI:2 phases of the Brick Kiln Cut outside the oval compound, although a small sample, will also aid our analysis.

What would one expect if Godin were occupied by lowland people? At Habuba Kabira and Jebel Aruda in

Figure 4.21. Wall niches and fallen burnt roof beams in room 22

Figure 4.22. Distribution of pottery types in the Godin VI:1b and VI:1a oval compound. (Numbers on pots indicate quantity of sherds found.)

northern Syria the occupants of newly founded colonies of Uruk people used the full range of Uruk pottery types. Their architecture followed the southern alluvial architectural plans. They also had a full range of seals and sealings. Habuba Kabira yielded numerical tablets like those at Godin. At Hacınebi, a site in southeastern Turkey in which a colony of lowland people lived side by side with a local Late Chalcolithic population, Uruk residents also had a full set of Uruk pottery types and sealings. Arslantepe on the Upper Euphrates, on the other hand, was a site that had developed significant administrative and economic centralization before the Uruk expansion, as we discussed above. Excavators there found locally made copies of Uruk types, although they are a minority of all pottery types, and many retained distinctly northern features. There was not a full corpus of Uruk types. Sealings had long been in use. Overall, the style of their seals is different from Uruk seals, although Uruk designs do appear in very small numbers in Arslantepe's last fourth-millen-

Figure 4.23. Distribution of objects in the Godin VI:1b and VI:1a oval compound. (Artifacts from primary and secondary contexts only are shown.) (Numbers beside artifacts indicate quantity of artifacts found.)

nium phase. The Italian excavation team also found a set of unsealed, round, thin tablets with punctured holes.

Whether occupied by local or foreign people, an administrative centre should have buildings whose primary function is not domestic. Such buildings often have large public areas for congregating, and rarely have artifacts typical of a residence. A fortress would contain weapons, stored supplies, and material for sustaining a siege. A merchant colony should have evidence for stored goods or raw materials exotic to the merchant's home base, but available locally, or for the manufacturing of products made from such materials.

At Godin, the southernmost set of buildings forms an entryway. Visitors or residents would have entered through room 4. If they brought material sealed or noted on tablets, they would have carried those materials through the gate and checked in with the guard who would deposit it for future audits on a shelving unit in room 3. Room 5 may have been

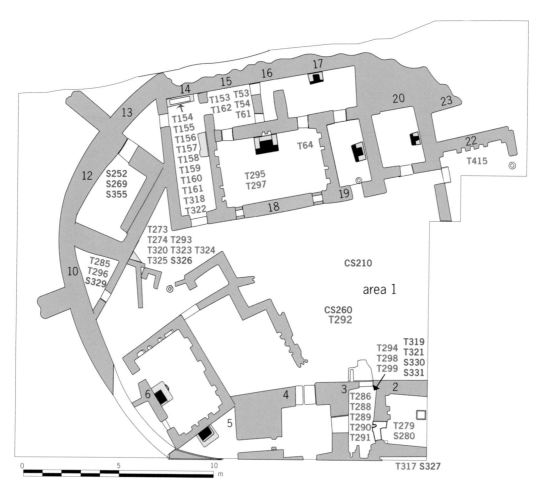

Figure 4.24. Distribution of tablets (T), cylinder seals (CS), and sealings (S) in the Godin VI:1b and VI:1a oval compound. Numbers are object numbers from the 1973 Godin field season.

Figure 4.25. Artifacts on floor on eastern side of room 18

where guards stayed and possibly cooked meals while on duty. The purpose of room 2 with its bin and remains of a wine jar and eating vessels is not clear. It was closed off near the end of the oval compound's occupation.

The building most likely to have had a special function is the northern building (rooms 14–19 and maybe 20). The main room, 18, cannot be approached from the courtyard. Its two openings to the courtyard are windows. A visitor would have entered through room 14 or 19 and then gone through room 15 or 17. A deep trough in the rear of room 14 contained many discarded tablets, and five tablets lay beside the trough in room 15. Charred lentils were recovered from near a bench. Room 15 has a small curtain wall. It creates area 16 which is less than 1 metre wide, too small to be a working space, but perhaps it was a newel wall for a staircase to a second floor over rooms 15 and 17. Against the eastern window of room 18 were a number of large pots, apparently smashed as walls fell in after abandonment (Figure 4.25). Around them were 1,759 small clay balls and some scattered grain. Additional sets of less than 100 clay balls each were recovered from the entryway, room 4, and from room 10. Unbaked clay balls have many uses, including as bobbins or loom weights in weaving, and as clay blanks for softening and then shaping into sealings or tablets. Their association with a metal spear and a macehead in room 22, however, implies a use as weapons.

The Function of the Clay Balls from the Godin VI Oval Compound
Virginia R. Badler

Almost 2,000 clay sling balls were found in the rooms within the Godin VI:1 oval wall. They were made of unbaked dense clay and were generally ovoid in shape with a rounder wider end and a pointed end, ranging in weight from 39 to 57.5 grams. Most were found near the east window of room 18 of the northern building.

Sling balls have been found in a wide variety of sites in Mesopotamia and Iran as early as the late fifth millennium BC. Standardization in the manufacture of sling balls was needed to provide a relatively uniform weight so that the combatant did not have to compensate for a different weight at every cast, and to provide a uniform, somewhat streamlined shape

Gd 73-416

0   10
                                                            cm

Figure 4.26. Clay balls (left) and macehead (right) from Godin VI oval compound

Figure 4.27. Sling balls on floor of room 18

in the interest of accuracy, velocity, and distance. Pure clay was used to provide density and perhaps because it would fall apart and could therefore not be returned by the enemy. The sling balls were sun-dried rather than baked to prevent cracking.

Significantly, one of the Sumerian words for sling ball, IM.DUGUD, literally means "heavy clay"—pure clay not lightened with straw or other tempering material. The other Sumerian word for sling ball, Á.SÀG, for which there is no literal translation, occurs in two passages where its use is clearly as a weapon of war:

In the mountain I will fight, I will renew (?) battles,
The arrow out of (my) quiver I will direct against it,
The sling stone I will … like a thick rope,
The long spear … I will hurl upon it,
The throw-stick, the weapon, I will direct upon him.
(Inanna and Ebih 40–44, Sjöberg 1967)

A letter from Tell Shemshara requests 500 slings for use by the army:

You know yourself that the grain stores are empty and that there is no grain for this army which is coming. Now, arrange a peace on good terms with Lullum and arrange for the transport (i.e., delivery?) of grain and flour so that your lord and the country may rejoice and (so that) he may establish your name forever. And let 500 slings be requisitioned for me! (*Chicago Assyrian Dictionary*, s. v. "aspu.")

Room 18, as well as rooms 17 and 19, contained large heating hearths, suggesting that this building served a different function than a normal house. However, potential signs of domestic activity did exist: some beads, bone tools, two stone spindle whorls for making yarn, a ground stone quern, two lithic cores (for making blades or used secondarily as a large grinder or hammer) and some blades and flakes. The pottery from room 18, aside from the storage jar containing the clay balls, consisted of sherds from a set of eating vessels. For this period the small bowl, beveled-rim bowl, and eating tray appear to constitute an eating set. Excavators recovered similar sets in rooms 14, 15, and 18, and the open area 1. Additional sherds are parts of serving and storage vessels. Although the hearths are forms that are not usually classified as cooking hearths, a number of sherds classified by Badler as cooking vessels based on their ware lay on the floor of the northern building.

A person could enter rooms 13 and 12 only from room 14 of the northern building. Room 12 had unusually thick walls, which Badler has previously interpreted in a 2002 article in the book *Artefacts of Complexity* as evidence of a safe storeroom. Its contents do indicate that it was a special-function room, lacking any potsherds in good context, but with

Figure 4.28. Beads from Godin VI oval compound

Figure 4.29. Ground stone objects from Godin VI oval compound

Figure 4.30. Spindle whorls from Godin VI oval compound. The one with two projections may alternatively be a model wagon wheel.

Figure 4.31. Flake cores from Godin VI oval compound

Figure 4.32. Flake tools from Godin VI oval compound

Figure 4.33. Blade tools from Godin VI oval compound

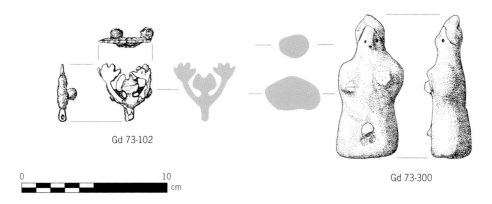

Figure 4.34. Figurines from Godin VI oval compound

a variety of tools: spindle whorls, beads, a bone awl and horn flaker, a grinding tool, a few clay balls, and a figurine of a woman (Figure 4.34). This would suggest a workroom rather than a storeroom. The presence of three sealings but no tablets reinforces this interpretation. As discussed above, sealings were placed on containers whose contents were controlled. When the containers arrived at their destination, authorized persons would break them open to access their contents. Tablets were normally used to record goods not easily stored in small containers, such as animals or large quantities of grain rather than raw materials.

Room 10 appears to have been used as a place to deposit trash in the final days of the compound's occupation. Its contents include a blank tablet, an unsealed tablet with three wedges, a sealing, lots and lots of pottery sherds, some clay balls, a core, and many lithic flakes. Also, most of the small collection of animal bones found within the oval compound were recovered from this room: 11 fragments from cattle, 32 from sheep or goats, and one from a red deer.

At the southwestern side of the oval compound, room 6 constitutes a seeming residence. Excavators found the only two cooking hearths in this area. Unfortunately, this area was excavated even more quickly than much of the rest of the compound and its finds are badly mixed. Serving bowls, a spindle whorl, a grinder, a quern, lithic tools, and one of the only sickles recovered from the oval compound also remained in reasonably good context in this area.

The remaining areas are either only partially excavated or poorly understood. The rooms in the eastern side of the oval compound were beyond the balks. Room 22 had charred grains and legumes on its floor, whether for household stores or part of a larger site-wide storeroom we cannot know. One possible material stored there was dung fuel, because barley, wheat, lentil, and weed remains are a typical diet for village sheep and goats. The number signs in most so-called Uruk IV tablets are traditionally those for grains (see "The

Godin Period VI Tablets" p. 116). A quern, a macehead, a few clay balls, a metal chisel, a sealed numeric tablet, and eating and serving vessels were recovered in rooms 22 and 23. Room 20, a thick-walled room separated from any other building, did yield one spectacular find (now in Tehran), a necklace of 208 black and 2 white stone beads. Its other remains, a heating hearth, sherds of a wine jar, grinding stones, and lithic blades, do not imply any particular set of activities.

The artifacts from the open courtyard are mostly lithic blades, flakes, and cores, and pottery of the same types as in the rooms, as well as tablets near the entrance to room 14. In 2002, Christopher Edens published a study of the lithics of Godin VI and IV. He concluded that there were two lithic industries. One was a flake industry (Figures 4.31 and 4.32). Flakes were roughly removed from pebbles of chert or flint. They were used as rough cutting implements or were more finely chipped into points, scrapers, or blades. The other industry used much more carefully prepared cores from which finer bifacial blades (Figure 4.33) were struck (see Chapter 5, Figure 5.30 for a photo of such a core). Although these techniques are widespread across the highlands from before the beginning of the fourth millennium BC, they were first identified in the Levant and are therefore called Canaanean blades. No Canaanean blade cores were identified from Godin VI. Edens therefore concludes that the bifacial blades were made elsewhere in the highlands and exchanged with the residents of Godin. Similar specialized blade-making workshops have been identified in southeastern Turkey from the fourth and third millennia at Değirmentepe and Titriş Höyük. On one point we disagree with Edens: he asserts that materials used to make blades were different from those used to make flake tools. An examination of the lithics stored at the ROM did not confirm this conclusion.

Figure 4.35. Cylinder seal Gd 73-260 from Godin VI oval compound

The only cylinder seal recovered from Godin VI (Gd 73-260) was also found in this courtyard area (Figures 4.35 and 4.42). Another cylinder seal (Gd 73-210, Figure 4.42) was found built into a brick of Godin Period IV:1b. It was probably accidentally included in the brick when the clay for its manufacture was dug from the earlier Period VI levels.

Taken as a whole, the compound within the oval wall would be unusual for a domestic neighbourhood. Few of the buildings appear to be houses, although people ate there. The presence of weapons certainly indicates conflict, although it is not clear whether the enemy were simply outside the oval wall or outside the site. Administered goods were entering and leaving the compound, as indicated by the tablets, seals, and sealings. Beads of shell, and black, grey, and white stone were common—their source is unknown—as were all the stages of flint-knapping, including a flaking tool. Metal objects occur in small numbers. As analysed by Lesley Frame, a fairly sophisticated metallurgical technology was in use at Godin VI:1 (see "Metallurgy of Godin Period VI," below). The presence of Early Transcaucasian pottery in VI:1a may be meaningful in this regard, as the Early Transcaucasian people were known for their skill in metalworking and wine-making. At the same time, evidence of metal smelting at Seh Gabi in the Middle Chalcolithic period indicates that metallurgy was an old craft in the Kangavar Valley.

Metallurgy of Godin Period VI
Lesley D. Frame

The earliest evidence for metallurgical activity at Godin Tepe appears in Period VI. Seh Gabi yielded earlier material; however, these remains have not yet been analysed. The metallurgical materials include a small fragment of a melting crucible, a furnace fragment with evidence of smelting, and many small copper oxide ore fragments. The crucible and furnace fragment each contain high-purity copper prills (globules of metal) with sulfide inclusions.

In addition to the processing debris, numerous metal artifacts were also recovered from this period. Only one of the twelve Period VI objects contained enough metal for analysis. Gd 73-312 is a cast unworked figurine fragment made of an arsenic and copper alloy. Arsenic was a common feature of early Middle Eastern metallurgy before tin was added to make true bronze.

It is clear that both smelting and melting practices were known to the Godin Tepe craftspeople during Period VI and later in Period IV.

Figure 4.36. Ceramics used in metallurgy or other pyrotechnic activity

Additional data on the metallurgy of Godin are available in the Godin Web archive at https://tspace.library.utoronto.ca.

Wine and Beer Residue Analysis on Godin Period VI Pottery
Virginia R. Badler

The chemical analysis of residues in Godin Tepe pottery established that the technique could be used to determine the existence of ancient wine and beer in prehistoric contexts. Tartaric residue suggesting a grape product that would have fermented into wine was found in a distinctive jar type (piriform, with impressed decoration in an inverted U shape on opposite sides of the vessel) from Deep Sounding room 18 and room 20 (latest VI:1a). The later vessel from room 20 has a bung hole a short distance from the base drilled after firing that was presumably to decant the beverage, as the colour of the dregs intensified below that point. Calcium oxalate residue suggesting the presence of beer was found imbedded in the interior slashes on the interior of a large two-handled jar found in the same room 18 as the early wine jar. The slashes on the jar interior are depicted on the early Sumerian sign for beer (KAŠ), which is clearly a jar marked by diagonal lines.

The earliest known wine residue was found in Transcaucasia (an early-sixth-millennium BC jar from Shulavenis-Gora), and it has been suggested that this region may be the homeland of viticulture. At Godin Tepe there is an intriguing link between wine-making and the appearance of the first Transcaucasian-type pottery. The earliest evidence for wine production at Godin Tepe correlates with an increase in the number of Transcaucasian-style sherds, including drinking cups. The wine-making artifacts themselves are suggestive: the funnel is similar to the Transcaucasian sherds in its method of manufacture (handmade and fired in a reduction atmosphere), and the heavy lid is a Transcaucasian pottery type that continues later in Godin Tepe IV.

Figure 4.37. Wine jar from Godin VI

The Godin VI oval compound contains some evidence to suggest that it may have been occupied by administrators of some sort: weapons suggest a military component; tools and raw materials indicate the presence of craft manufacture; and tablets, sealings, and jars may be involved in the collection and possibly storage of local agricultural and pastoral products.

The Godin Period VI:2 and VI:1 Architecture from the Brick Kiln Cut

Our only real glimpse of life outside the oval compound comes from the Brick Kiln Cut area south and down the slope from the Deep Sounding. The BKC VI:2 phase (Figure 4.38) predates the oval wall, and the VI:1 phase is probably contemporaneous with an early

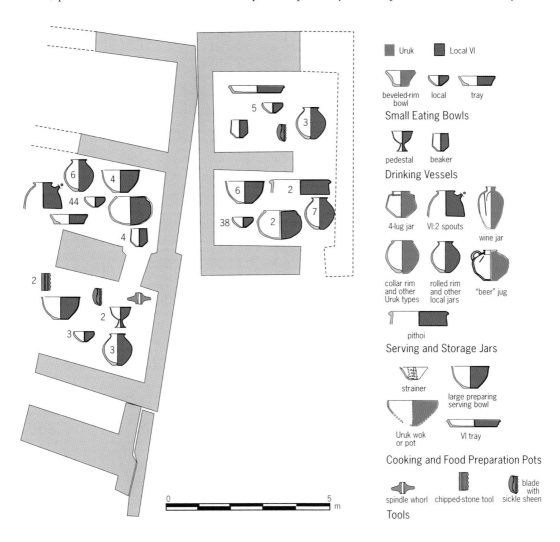

Figure 4.38. Plan of Godin VI:2 and distribution of artifacts in the Brick Kiln Cut

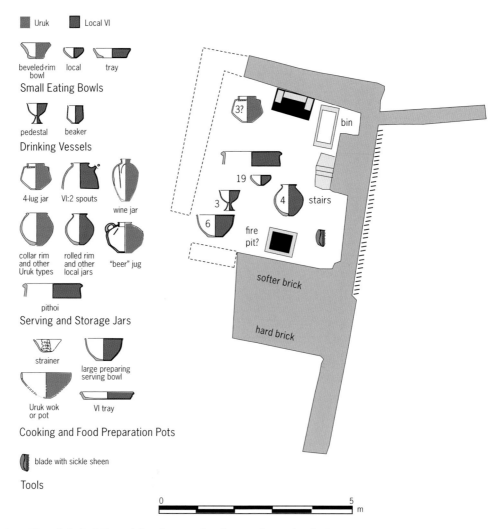

Figure 4.39. Plan of Godin VI:1 and distribution of artifacts in the Brick Kiln Cut

phase of the wall. The two BKC phase VI:2 buildings date to the earliest period of increased contact with the lowlands and are of a simple domestic type. Excavators found few tools, but among them were lithic blades with sickle sheen, and much pottery, again a serving set, this time without the beveled-rim bowl, as well as cooking, serving, and storage vessels. These suggest local farmers. None of the pottery was of the Uruk type. The BKC phase VI:1 building, which is contemporaneous with the VI:1 phase of the oval compound, has a hearth much like those found in the oval compound. Some Uruk-related pottery forms are also found in this level although they form a smaller percentage of the assemblage than in the oval compound. An interesting feature of this building is a staircase, indicating that there was either a second floor or that the roof was used to perform some activities.

Perhaps more important than the man-made artifacts in this area were the animal-bone remains. The vast majority of animal bones found from Godin VI came from the Brick Kiln Cut. As the analysis by Crabtree details (see "The Animal Bone from Godin Period VI," below), the emphasis appears to have been on raising animals primarily for their meat, and secondarily for their wool. This is a pattern of a fairly prosperous settlement that was probably more important in the economic system of the valley than a simple village.

The Animal Bone from Godin Period VI
Pam J. Crabtree

The faunal assemblage from Godin VI was dominated by the remains of sheep, goat, and cattle, along with smaller numbers of equids, pigs, and red and roe deer. About 25 percent of the sheep and goats were killed during the first year of life, and an additional 40 percent were killed between the ages of two and four years. The older adult sheep may have been kept for wool production. A small number of the cattle were killed during the first year and a half of life. Nearly half the cattle were killed just when they reached bodily maturity; those who survived to adulthood were probably used as breeding stock and for secondary activities such as ploughing. The goat age profile matches a herd-security model, but the sheep profile does not. I think that there may be some emphasis on wool production but not specialization.

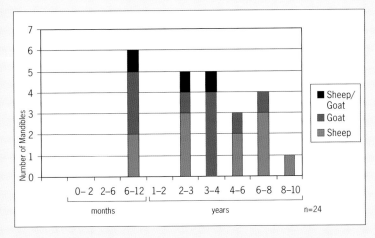

Figure 4.40. Mortality profiles for caprids (sheep/goat) from Godin VI

This is not a pastoralist strategy, which depends on milk, and secondarily on wool, rather than on meat. Pastoralists tend to kill their animals for meat only when they have stopped being useful for milk or wool. For a fairly prosperous village or perhaps small town, this animal-exploitation strategy, however, makes sense. The extraordinary amount of bone suggests that this part of the mound may have been used for provisioning its residents.

Additional data on the animal bone of Godin are available in the Godin Web archive at https://tspace.library.utoronto.ca.

The Kangavar Survey

The central role of Godin during Period VI can be inferred from the site's place in the system of settlement in the Kangavar Valley (Figure 4.41).

Godin was not an isolated settlement. It was part of its local polity and connected to larger networks of interaction with the broader Uruk and highland worlds. As we saw by mapping the spread of Uruk types (Figure 4.17), that connection followed the High Road. The settlement data from Period VI paint an interesting picture of what Godin's role might have been. The problem we face in assessing these settlement data is that only very general ceramic types were collected to date sites. We can distinguish Period VI from Period IV pottery, and we can tell if the presence of beveled-rim bowls places settlement sometime after 3600 and before 3050 BC. However, in that long span of time, mounds could have been occupied, abandoned, and re-occupied many times. Within those limits, what settle-

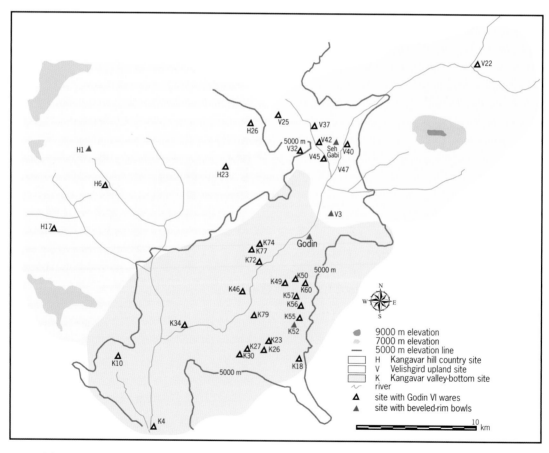

Figure 4.41. Kangavar survey with Godin VI sites

ment data appear to tell us is that Godin was the centre of the Kangavar Valley system in Period VI. The valley is divided among three quite distinct ecological niches: the floodplain, the Velishgird uplands, and the Kangavar hill country. From the time that VII and VI:3 pottery was used, the number and occupied area of mounds increased dramatically. Most of this increase was in the well-watered floodplain (6 percent of sites and 70 percent of total occupied area.) The sites in the floodplain cluster toward the southeast. In the Velishgird uplands they cluster near the main branch of the Gamas Ab River. As it is less effective for agriculture, the Kangavar hill country has fewer and more scattered sites. Godin surveyors collected Uruk pottery (beveled-rim bowls) from four sites. With the exception of the nearby site labelled V3, the sites with beveled-rim bowls tended to be in the middle of clusters of village sites. Seh Gabi in the uplands and K52 in the plain are equidistant from Godin, at approximately 4.5 kilometres distance. The one site with beveled-rim bowls in the Velishgird uplands is 20 kilometres away at the head of one tributary of the Gamas Ab.

Godin's central geographic position at the intersection of these two zones makes it a natural place for leaders to control the flow of goods. In particular, the increase in occupation of the best agricultural land raises the possibility that the function of Godin as a centre would involve collecting surplus grain either to feed dependants for their public works or as a hedge against bad agricultural years. This is also indicated by the tablets found at the site.

Godin then would find its best analogy with a site such as Arslantepe. That is to say, it was a society developing complexity over a long period from the Middle Chalcolithic onward. That development was further catalyzed by contact with lowland consumers and benefited from advances in the technology of administration. Leaders' most basic power derived from their access to local resources but was increased by the specialized production of beads, stone tools, and perhaps wine and beer.

Chemical Characterization of Godin Period VI Ceramics by Instrumental Neutron Activation Analysis
M. James Blackman

Neutron activation analysis takes a small sample of clay from pottery or other clay objects and puts it in a nuclear reactor, where neutrons blast the clay body into constituent elements. Those elements are then counted in parts per million. The sum of these counts gives a kind of chemical fingerprint. Because the geological formation of clays varies widely, the fingerprint of any area is quite specific.

The purpose of the analysis was to determine if the ceramics from Godin Period VI were locally made or imported. Eighteen ceramic samples from Godin VI were selected to represent a broad range of paste, form, and stylistic types. Three non-ceramic clay samples were also used, including a piece of what appears to be a tablet, and two clay balls also from Godin VI. Three ceramic samples of comparable age from Seh Gabi were also analysed, as were samples of Early Transcaucasian Culture pottery from Godin Period IV (see Chapter 5). The clay objects were included because they were likely to represent locally available Godin clays. The Godin VI ceramics were compared to an even larger sample of ceramics previously analysed from Godin Period III. To test for their origin, the results of this analysis were compared to previously analysed clays from Khuzistan (near the site of Susa) and from Nippur in the Euphrates Valley. Based on style, these were likely sources of Uruk immigrants and products. The ceramic samples from Khuzistan were taken from a number of sites and represent a general Khuzistan composition, not a specific site. To source the Godin VI ceramics for membership in comparator groups from various source areas, a cluster statistic of Mahalanobis distance was calculated using seventeen elements.

After testing, the following conclusions can be drawn:

1) None of the Godin VI samples analysed have a probability of greater than 0.9 percent of being drawn from the Khuzistan or Nippur comparator groups.

2) Half of the Godin VI ceramics, the Godin VI clay tablet, the two Godin VI clay balls, and two-thirds of the Seh Gabi ceramics are compatible with the same clay source as the previously studied Godin III ceramics and are most likely locally made. These nine samples include a VI:2 painted-pedestal bowl, a VI:1 incised four-lug jar, a VI:1 tall wine jar, a VI:1/2 beveled-rim bowl, a VI:2 short funnel-spout jar, a VI:2 trough spout, a VI:1 collared jar, a VI:1 red-slipped four-lug jar, and a VI:1 collared four-lug jar.

3) Half of the Godin VI ceramics and one of the Seh Gabi ceramics are compositionally incompatible with the Godin III ceramic clay source. Nine Godin VI ceramic samples and a single Seh Gabi ceramic were not closely associated with any of the three comparator groups, nor do they seem to form a separate compositional group. They include a VI:1 red-slipped four-lug jar, a VI:1 white-slipped painted jar, a VI:1 rolled-rim wine jar with impressed strip, a VI:1 red-slipped four-lug jar, a cooking pot, a VI:1 cream-slipped inturned bowl, a VI:1 striped polychrome jar, a VI:1 double-rimmed jar, and a VI:1 droop-spouted jar. These samples also do not form a single compositional group of their own. Whether they were made of several compositionally different clay sources or from the addition of differing types or amounts of temper in the Godin area cannot be determined with the current sample. Nor can the possibility be eliminated that they were imported from other manufacturing locales.

Additional data from this analysis are available in the Godin Web archive at https://tspace.library.utoronto.ca.

The Residents of the Godin Period VI Oval

It is critical to try to determine not only what the residents of the oval compound did, but who they were: local people as Matthews proposed, or foreigners as Badler and Young suggested. Comparison with contemporaneous sites of Uruk influence and Uruk personages gave us an indicator. The Uruk colonies had a full set of Uruk vessels; those with smaller percentages were not true colonies. The often cited counter-example is the Old Assyrian, second-millennium BC trading colony at Kaneš in central Turkey. Those merchants from Aššur were trading tin for various other materials. From the pottery, one would never have known that they were foreign, as they used almost exclusively local wares. Only the texts they left told us what was going on. At Godin, however, we do have foreign Uruk wares. The small percentage of Uruk pottery in the oval compound (30 percent of all the pottery in all contexts, very much less in primary and secondary contexts) does appear to be more similar to independent centres with Uruk contact than to lowland populations transplanted to north Syria. Missing were cooking pots, ovoid storage pots, small grit-tempered conical cups, many categories of bowls, and jars. Food and the way it is cooked can be an important marker of ethnicity. The absence of Uruk cooking pots suggests that locals were cooking food in a highland manner. The analysis of the chemical fingerprints of the Godin VI pottery indicates that much of this pottery was locally made, and none was imported from the southern sources of Nippur and Khuzistan.

The Seals of Godin Period VI
Holly Pittman

Among the important finds made inside buildings within the oval compound at Godin were numerical tablets and a few container sealings that were impressed with the imagery carved on cylinder seals. The administrative use of seal-impressed numerical tablets at Godin precisely mirrors the practice known from Susa in the Acropolis sounding, and from the site of Uruk.

The subjects engraved on the seals almost always involve animals. The most frequently occurring animals on the Godin seals are felines. They are shown walking (Gd 73-294, Figure 4.43c) or threatening bovids or wild goats (Gd 73-329, Figure 4.42). Felines are also shown alone. In one instance, impressed on the single tablet carrying an inscribed sign, lions are seated on their haunches facing some kind of standard (Gd 73-295, Figure

4.43c). This regal posture suggests some symbolic reference, perhaps to a distinct centre of administrative authority. Another distinct posture assumed by felines is rearing on their hind legs, looking back over their shoulder and with their tails crossed or entwined (Gd 73-153, Figure 4.43b). Images of humans are rare; the only representation is of a kneeling archer hunting a quadruped (Gd 73-320, Figure 4.43c).

Both functionally and iconographically all the seals impressed on the Godin tablets and container sealings are closely comparable to ones found either at Uruk or at Susa in levels that can be dated to level 17 of the Acropolis sounding (LC 5, see Table 4.1, p. 70). They are in fact so similar that they must have been made in the same workshop. For example, the image of a kneeling archer confronting a quadruped with its head turned back finds its close parallels on seals impressed on numerical tablets from Susa. A cylinder seal carrying the same imagery was found at Nineveh on the Tigris. The image of the feline seated on its haunches mentioned above is unknown at Susa but is closely parallelled in an example from the Eanna temple at Uruk. This theme is also attested at Nineveh impressed on a large sealing. Seals carrying images of large jars held in nets are found at almost all sites that have Uruk-related material, including Uruk, Susa, Tell Brak, Hacınebi, Habuba Kabira, and Godin (Gd 73-161, Figure 4.43b) (see my 2001 article in *Uruk Mesopotamia and Its Neighbors*).

Several seals from Godin carry a distinctive type of imagery that serve as early examples of what becomes the distinctive Proto-Elamite style of the following centuries. Although the Susa state and those of the southern Mesopotamian alluvium are very similar in iconography as well as political and economic structure during the fourth millennium BC, in the early centuries of the third millennium BC there is a regional realignment. The region to the east of the Tigris River realigns with Susa, the hilly flanks of the Zagros, and areas around the highland desert of Iran to form a cultural unit that has been called Proto-Elamite. The most characteristic example of the early Proto-Elamite style from Godin that illustrates the iconographic changes accompanying the cultural realignment is seen on an actual seal-stone found in a brick of Period IV at Godin, but which necessarily belongs to an earlier phase (Gd 73-260, Figure 4.42). The use of hatching on the shoulders of the bovid has been cited as one feature that links this seal to the highland tradition of the Proto-Elamites. But what has not been observed before is the presence of two distinct species of bulls shown side by side. This juxtaposition of a wild and a domesticated bull is a hallmark feature of the seals of the Proto-Elamite phase, and should probably be understood as a symbolic embodiment of a fundamental characteristic of the period during which there was a balanced integration of various centres of power. Another precursor of later highland imagery is the use of plants to suggest location in a particular landscape.

The exact message conveyed by the seals at Godin is still uncertain, but from later use we think that the seal referred to the administrator responsible for the transaction recorded on the tablet. The same type of reference to an administrator was probably also the function of seal-impressed container sealings.

Additional data on the tablets are available in the Godin Web archive at https://tspace.library.utoronto.ca.

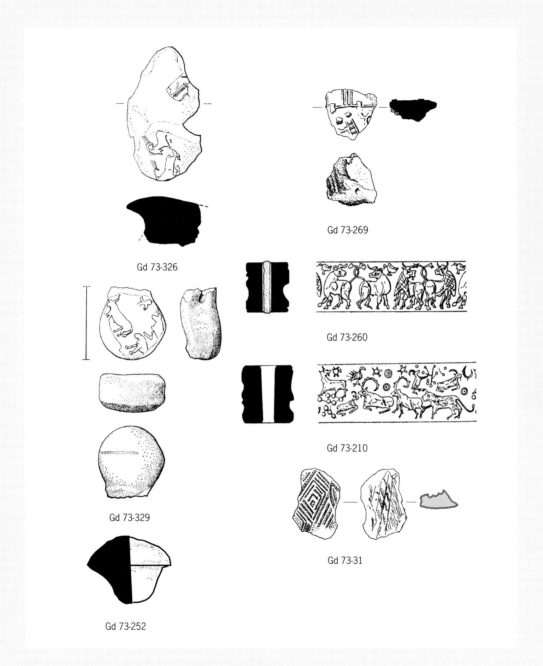

Figure 4.42. Seals and seal impressions from Godin VI

The Godin Period VI Tablets
William Hallo

The inscribed Godin tablets consist almost entirely of numbers. Numerical tablets from other sites need to be considered, but there is not as yet a conventional form of notation that bridges the geographical horizon of all the finds, which can be regionally distinct. Even when there are transregional similarities in the number signs, there may not be any easy way to compare them with the forms of numeral notation in historic periods.

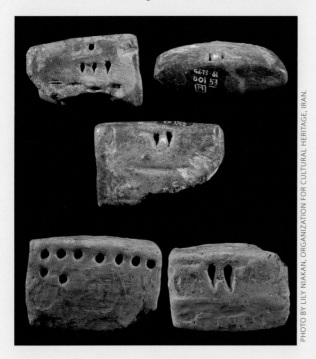

The Godin corpus of tablets is linked to archaic numerical tablets from elsewhere. In fact, the similarities are striking and the divergences minor, when one considers such factors as the date of the assemblage, the size and shape of the tablets, the appearance of the units from "1" up, the arrangement of the number signs on the tablets, the use of seal impressions, and of course the medium (clay) on which the seals and number tokens are impressed. Clearly, the Godin material is part and parcel of an inter-regional phenomenon that embraces, in modern terms, Iraq, northern Syria, and western Iran or, in ancient terms, what has come to be regarded as Greater Mesopotamia.

Figure 4.43a. A selection of Godin VI tablets

The token system that preceded the numerical tablets indicated not only the quantity but the nature of the commodities being counted. The slightly later archaic tablets from Uruk IV perpetuate these distinctions, albeit on a more sophisticated level, using different systems of counting for different commodities. Since the Godin system most nearly resembles that used for barley at Uruk, one may venture a guess that barley is also at issue here. The Godin VI:1 oval compound where the tablets were found indeed contained storage rooms and pottery, and there were legumes and grains stored in room 22.

Additional data on the tablets are available in the Godin Web archive at https://tspace.library.utoronto.ca.

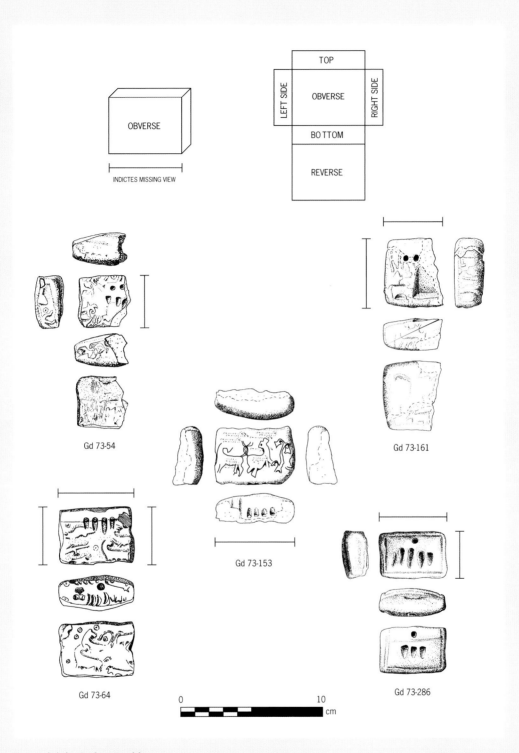

OBVERSE

INDICTES MISSING VIEW

TOP

LEFT SIDE

OBVERSE

RIGHT SIDE

BOTTOM

REVERSE

Gd 73-54

Gd 73-161

Gd 73-153

Gd 73-64

Gd 73-286

0   10
cm

Figure 4.43b. Godin VI tablets

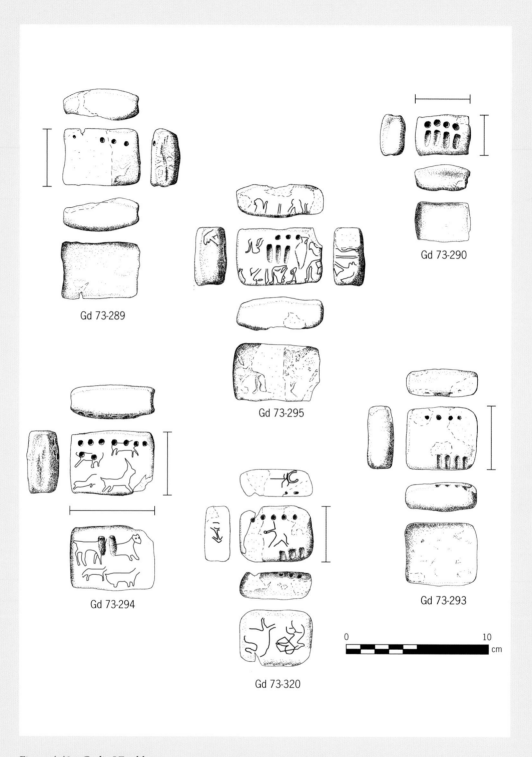

Gd 73-289

Gd 73-290

Gd 73-295

Gd 73-294

Gd 73-320

Gd 73-293

0   10
         cm

Figure 4.43c. Godin VI tablets

Concluding Remarks

Godin Tepe Period VI provides us with a fascinating picture of a mountain-culture area in the last prehistoric period of the Middle East. The residents of Godin Period VI shared cultural adaptations with other valleys in the area. These form a pattern typical of highland developments from the Neolithic period. The mountainous environment, with its limited access to the lowlands through few and difficult roads, had a tendency to isolate the Kangavar Valley during Periods VII–VI:3. This isolation, if only because of Godin's position on the High Road and its access to desirable raw materials, could not be sustained forever, and with each wave of people and influence, the structure of the society changed, while at the same time preserving elements of its earlier adaptations.

Who were the residents of the Godin oval compound and what were they doing at the site? The choice presented so far has been either foreigners or locals. This dichotomy may, however, hide a third alternative. The lowland Mesopotamians may have needed to guarantee a sufficient flow of goods. Instead of establishing their own trading posts in the desired resource zone, they may have collaborated with already existing local leaders to achieve the same result. They may have given the local elites some special tribute or technological advantage in exchange for a guarantee that desired goods would continue to flow. We believe that the much later Assyrian empire built this kind of relationship with local leaders at Godin in Period II. The position of the local leaders would be maintained by a strategy built on native traditions to fulfill their role as coordinators of defence, grain storage, and religious ritual. Yet, without the threat of military force that later empires could muster, these early relationships would be much more open-ended and equal. Thus, as happened at the end of the fourth millennium BC, they would be more easily disrupted by local changes, or by conflicts over power among the local leaders.

The structure of these societies may have followed a mountain pattern in which the leadership group tends to be a very thin layer of society, and the majority of the people follow older patterns more typical of simple chiefdoms or tribes. These leaders would have been the residents of the Godin VI oval compound, threatened as much by local people as by outsiders, and safest within the walls of the compound. They would have received goods from people in their local polity, but also some special products and even a very few examples of the finest foreign pottery from their lowland allies. It is possible that if the finest, rarest pottery were tested, it might prove to be from lowland sites. Their lowland benefactors might even have given local leaders seals in lowland style as a symbol of their authority or possibly to mark exports with their destination in the lowlands. In this model, the Godin oval compound is neither a colony nor a completely independent trading post.

Godin's leadership structure may have been less complex than that at Arslantepe because Arslantepe was not only the place where routes from central Anatolia, eastern Turkey, and Transcaucasia met at the Euphrates, but it is close to the Erganı copper mines and to sources of gold and silver lacking in the Zagros. This in part could explain the late development of the oval compound at Godin compared with the much earlier temple-palace compounds at Arslantepe. Godin Period VI came to an end at the beginning of the third millennium BC. Possibly, the coming of Transcaucasian people accelerated the decline of the leadership group. Possibly local people, still organized in a way more like the Early Transcaucasian societies than those of the heartland of cities, re-oriented their social structures to fit the newcomers, adopting the Transcaucasian markers of ethnicity.

Godin Periods VI–VII Pottery Typology and Tablets and Seals Catalogue

Table 4.4. Pottery comparanda to Godin Tepe VI

Phase	To southern Mesopotamia and Susiana	To central western Zagros and plateau	To other areas, especially Diyala and piedmont
VI:1	All Uruk = string-cut bases, Uruk trays, beveled-rim bowls, coarse conical cups, droop-spouted jars. Nippur LC5 (Late Uruk) flaring bowls with beveled-rims, straight-sided carinated bowls, bottle rims, neckless jars, and tall jars. Susa 17 = trough-spouted jars. LC 5 Nippur Inanna XIX, Warka Eanna IV, Susa Acropolis 17 = red-slipped, four-lug jars with "rope" appliqué.	Baba Jan = rolled-rim bowls, expanded-rim bowls, inturned-rim bowls with string-cut bases.	Arslantepe and Khafaje = fenestrated stands. Khafaje = beveled-rim bowls, cross-hatched triangle design on jars. Rubeidaeh vertical-sided Uruk bowls, four lug jars with impressed or incised decoration.
VI:2	Nippur Middle Uruk = beveled-rim bowls, plain flaring-rim bowls, funnel-spouted jars, tall jar, collar-necked jars, applied pellet decoration, expanded, rim bowls, inturned-rim bowls.	Kunji Cave KS 269 and Sagarab = rolled-rim bowls with higher profiles, large bowls with pinched rolled rims, large bowls with inturned beveled-rims, collar-neck jars, pedestal-based bowl, flaring plain rim bowls, pithoi with thumb-impressed strips, rolled-rim jars. Baba Jan = short-funnel jars. Sialk = IV.1 pedestal bases, short funnels.	Rubeideh cylindrical tumbler, flared-rim bowls, rolled-rim bowls, straight spouts, small rolled-rim bowl with cannon spout.
VI:3		Kunji = fine jars.	Many sites = bowls with three painted blobs

Note: Additional pottery figures are available in the Godin Web archive at https://tspace.library.utoronto.ca.

Type Ia. Beveled-Rim Bowls

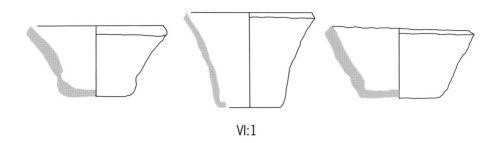

VI:1

Type Ib. Rolled-Rim Bowls

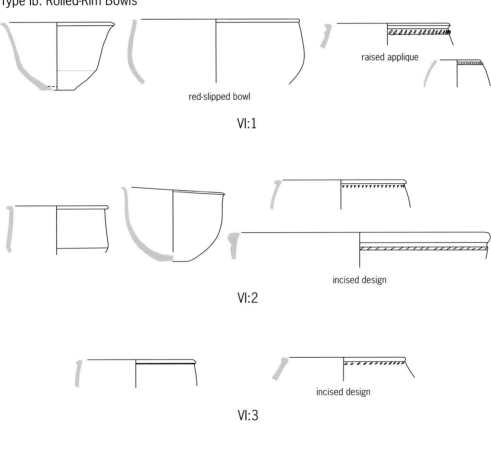

raised applique

red-slipped bowl

VI:1

incised design

VI:2

incised design

VI:3

0   10
cm

Figure 4.44. Godin VI–VII small bowls

Type Ic. Inturned-Rim Bowls

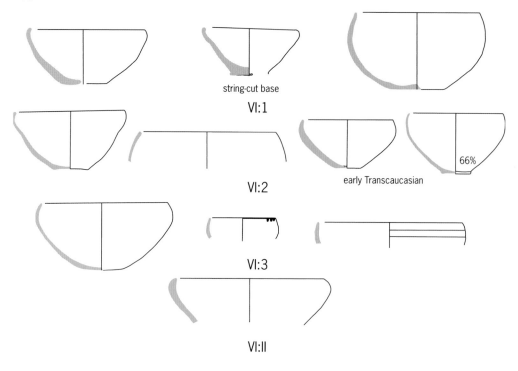

string-cut base

VI:1

VI:2

early Transcaucasian

66%

VI:3

VI:II

Type Id. Flaring Plain and Ledge-Rim Bowls

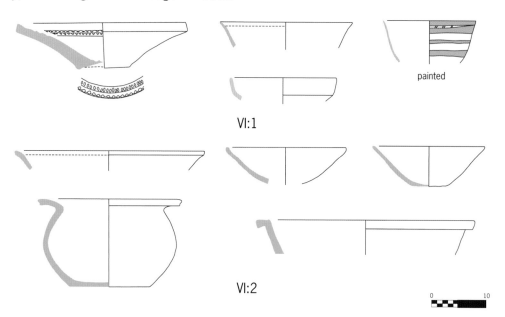

painted

VI:1

VI:2

0   10

Figure 4.45. Godin VI–VII small bowls

Type Ib. Large Bowls with Rolled Rims

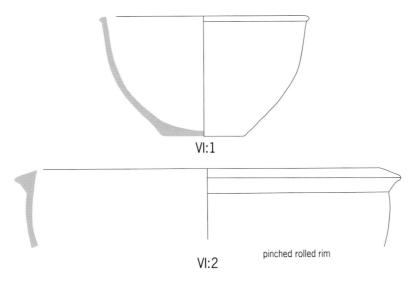

VI:1

VI:2

pinched rolled rim

Type Ic. Large Bowls with Inturned Rims

VI:2

Type Ie. Large Bowls with Plain Everted Rims

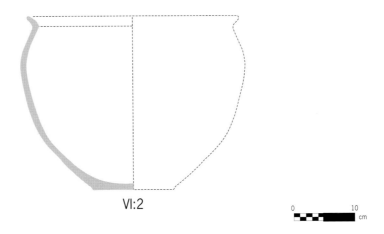

VI:2

Figure 4.46. Godin VI–VII large bowls

Type IIa. Four-Lug Jars

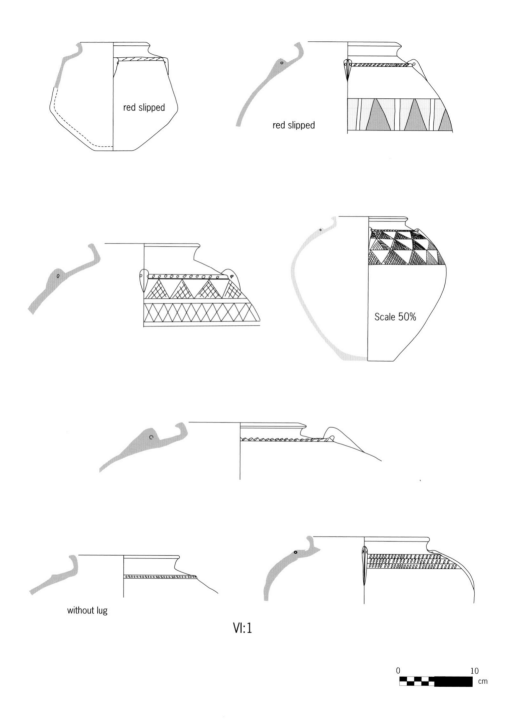

red slipped

red slipped

Scale 50%

without lug

VI:1

0   10
            cm

Figure 4.47. Godin VI–VII four-lugged jars

Type IIb. Rolled-Rim Jars

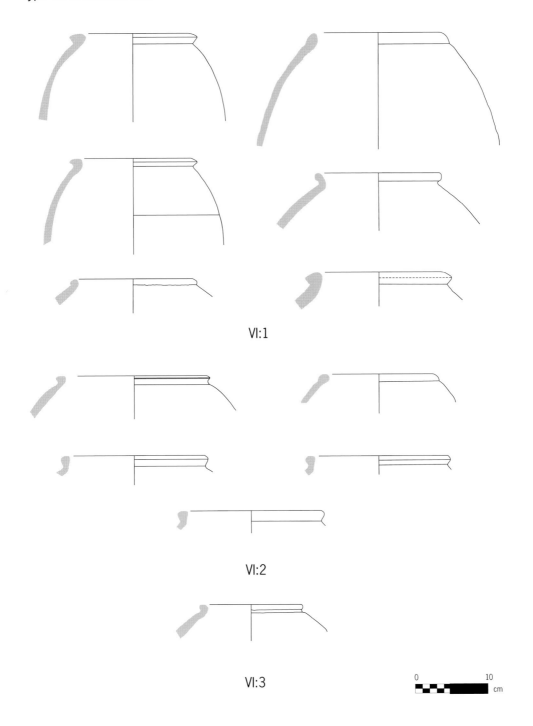

VI:1

VI:2

VI:3

Figure 4.48. Godin VI–VII rolled-rim jars

Type IIc. Collared-Neck Jars (Everted, Beveled Rims)

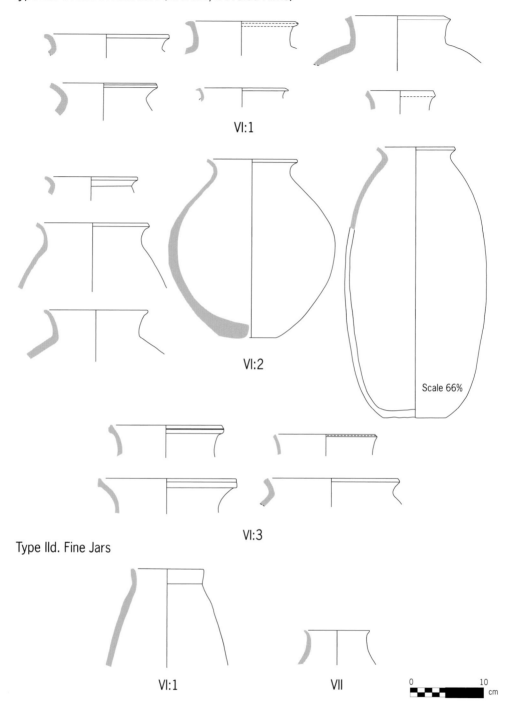

VI:1

VI:2

Scale 66%

VI:3

Type IId. Fine Jars

VI:1

VII

0   10 cm

Figure 4.49. Godin VI–VII collared-neck and fine jars

Type III. Spouted Vessels

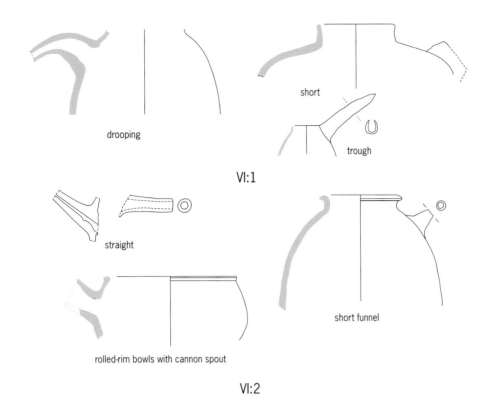

drooping

short

trough

VI:1

straight

rolled-rim bowls with cannon spout

short funnel

VI:2

Type IV. Handled Beer Jars

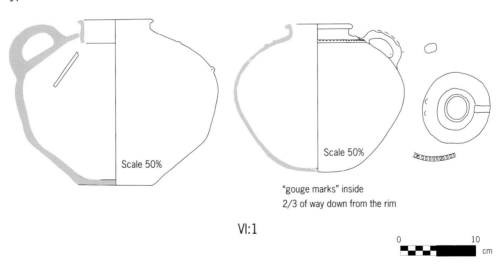

Scale 50%

Scale 50%

"gouge marks" inside
2/3 of way down from the rim

VI:1

0   10
[scale bar]   cm

Figure 4.50. Godin VI–VII spouted vessels and handled beer jars

Type IVb. Pedestal Bases

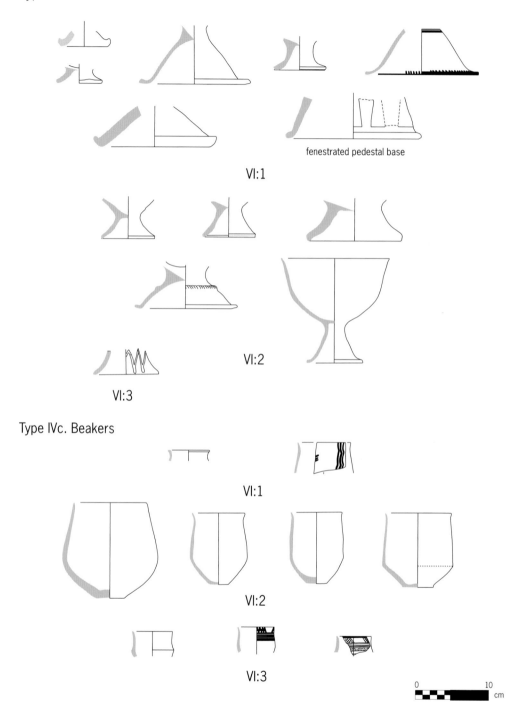

fenestrated pedestal base

VI:1

VI:2

VI:3

Type IVc. Beakers

VI:1

VI:2

VI:3

0   10
     cm

Figure 4.51. Godin VI–VII pedestal bases and beakers

Type IVd. Bottles

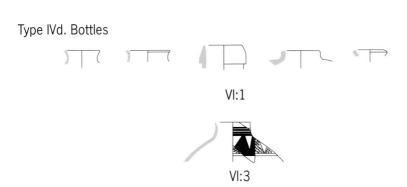

VI:1

VI:3

Type Va. Serving Trays

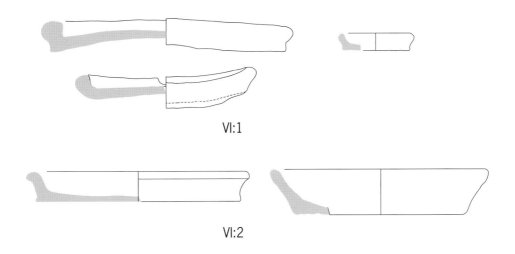

VI:1

VI:2

Type Vb. Lids

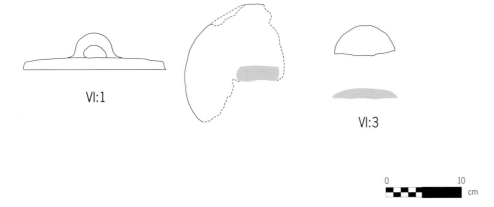

VI:1

VI:3

0   10
cm

Figure 4.52. Godin VI–VII bottles, serving trays, and lids

Type Vc. Strainers

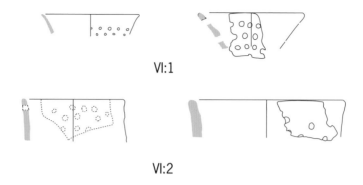

VI:1

VI:2

Type Vd. Cooking Pots and Trays

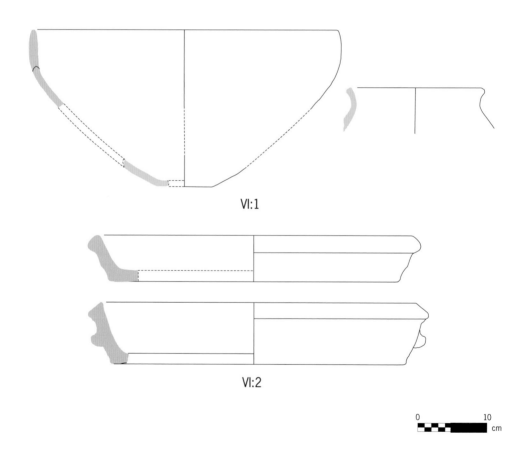

VI:1

VI:2

Figure 4.53. Godin VI–VII strainers, cooking pots, and trays

Type Ve. Pithoi

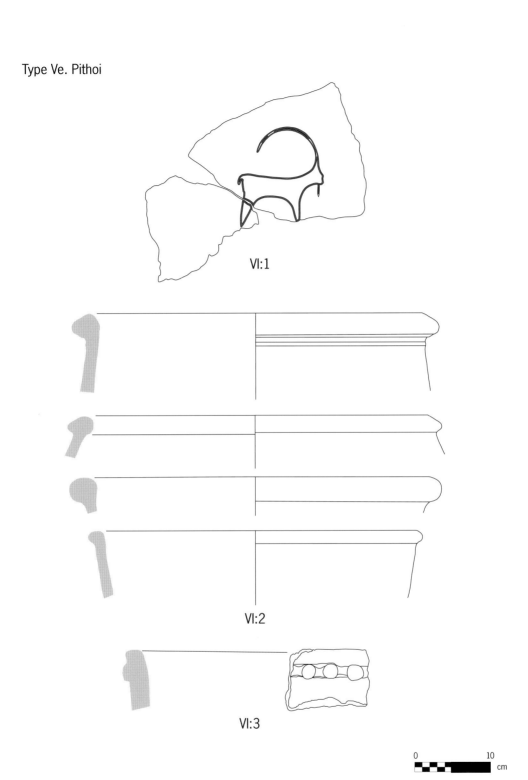

VI:1

VI:2

VI:3

0   10
cm

Figure 4.54. Godin VI–VII pithoi

Tablets and Seals Catalogue

Table 4.5. Tablets from Godin VI

Object number	Obverse	Reverse	Seal design	Illustrated*
Gd 73-53	fragmentary	blank	undetermined	Web archive
Gd 73-54	3 wedges, 2 dots	blank	horned animals	Fig. 4.43b
Gd 73-61	3 wedges, 2 dots	2 wedges	undetermined	Web archive
Gd 73-64	4 wedges	blank; bottom: 1 dot and 4 fingernails	equids?	Fig. 4.43b
Gd 73-153	blank	blank; bottom: 4 wedges	none	Web archive
Gd 73-154	2 wedges	blank	none	Web archive
Gd 73-155	fragment, 1 wedge	blank	undetermined	Web archive
Gd 73-156	fragment, 2 wedges	blank	none	Web archive
Gd 73-157	3 dots, 2 wedges	blank	none	Web archive
Gd 73-158	chipped, 6 wedges	blank	none	Web archive
Gd 73-159	3 dots	blank	none	Web archive
Gd 73-160	fragment, blank	blank	none	not illustrated
Gd 73-161	2 dots	none	quadrupeds	Fig. 4.43b
Gd 73-162	chipped, 2 dots, 3 wedges	2 wedges	none	Web archive
Gd 73-273	fragment blank	blank	none visible	not illustrated
Gd 73-274	chipped blank	indeterminate edge, 3 dots	none	Web archive
Gd 73-279	fragmentary, blank	blank	none	not illustrated
Gd 73-285	fragmentary, blank	blank	none	not illustrated
Gd 73-285	blank	blank	none	Web archive
Gd 73-286	5 wedges, 1 dot	3 wedges, 1 dot	none	Fig. 4.43b
Gd 73-287	fragment, 2 wedges	?	none	Web archive
Gd 73-288	3 wedges	1 wedge, 3 nail marks	quadruped	Web archive
Gd 73-289	4 dots	blank	quadruped	Fig. 4.43c
Gd 73-290	4 dots, 4 wedges	blank	none	Fig. 4.43c
Gd 73-291	5 wedges, 2 dots, 2 nail prints	3 wedges, 2 nail prints	none	Web archive
Gd 73-292	9 dots	3 wedges, 2 dots	none	Web archive
Gd 73-293	4 dots, 4 wedges	blank	none	Fig. 4.43c
Gd 73-294	9 dots	2 wedges	none	Web archive
Gd 73-295	3 dots, 3 wedges	none	KAS sign, lions	Fig. 4.43c
Gd 73-296	3 wedges	blank	none	Web archive

Table 4.5. Tablets from Godin VI (*continued*)

Object number	Obverse	Reverse	Seal design	Illustrated*
Gd 73-297	2 dots, 2 nail prints, 1 wedge	blank	none	Web archive
Gd 73-298	1 dot, 2 nail prints	blank	none	Web archive
Gd 73-299	2 wedges, 1 dot, 3 nail prints	blank, 1 edge 2 nail prints	none	Web archive
Gd 73-317	fragmentary, 2 dots	blank	none	Web archive
Gd 73-318	8 wedges, 4 dots	blank	none	Web archive
Gd 73-319	chipped, 2 nail prints	blank	quadrapeds	Web archive
Gd 73-320	5 dots, 3 wedges	blank	archer spearman	Web archive
Gd 73-321	chipped, 4 wedges	2 dots, 2 nail prints 1 wedge	none	Web archive
Gd 73-322	fragments	undetermined	none	not illustrated
Gd 73-323	fragmentary	none visible	horned animals	Web archive
Gd 73-324	fragmentary	none visible	none visible	Web archive
Gd 73-325	fragmentary	none visible	none visible	not illustrated
Gd 73-415	fragmentary, 2 dots	fragmentary	animals	Web archive

*Illustrations on Web archive at https://tspace.library.utoronto.ca/.

Table 4.6. Seals and sealings from Godin VI

Object number	Shape	Seal design	Illustrated*
Gd 73-31	Jar shoulder sealing	abstract shield	Fig. 4.42
Gd 73-210	Cylinder seal	wild horned animal threatened by lions	Fig. 4.42
Gd 73-252	Jar stopper	undetermined	Fig. 4.42
Gd 73-260	Cylinder seal	pairs of wild and domestic cattle	Fig. 4.42
Gd 73-269	Jar shoulder sealing	ladder shapes	Fig. 4.42
Gd 73-326	Jar shoulder sealing	horned quadrupeds	Fig. 4.42
Gd 73-329	Jar stopper	cattle threatened by lion	Fig. 4.42
Gd 73-331	Jar stopper	undetermined	not illustrated
Gd 73-65	Jar stopper	undetermined	not illustrated

*Illustrations on Web archive at https://tspace.library.utoronto.ca/.

Further Reading

Note: Additional references are available in the Godin Web archive at https://tspace.library.utoronto.ca.

Adams, Robert M. *The Heartland of Cities*. Chicago: University of Chicago Press, 1981.

Algaze, Guillermo. "The Prehistory of Imperialism." In *Uruk, Mesopotamia and its Neighbors*, edited by M. Rothman, 27–84. Santa Fe, NM: School of American Research Press, 2001.

———. *The Uruk World System*. Chicago: University of Chicago Press, 1993.

Badler, Virginia R. "A Chronology of Uruk Artefacts from Godin Tepe in Central Western Iran and Its Implications for the Interrelationships Between the Local and Foreign Cultures." In *Artefacts of Complexity*, edited by Nicholas Postgate, 79–110. Wiltshire, England: British School of Archaeology in Iraq, 2002.

———. "The Archaeological Evidence for Winemaking, Distribution and Consumption at Proto-Historic Godin Tepe, Iran." In *The Origins and Ancient History of Wine*, edited by P. E. McGovern, S. J. Fleming, and S. H. Katz, 45–56. Luxembourg: Gordon and Breach, 1995.

Balossi Restelli, Francesca. *Formation Processes of the First Developed Neolithic Societies in the Zagros and the Northern Mesopotamian Plain*. Studi di Preistoria Orientale, Volume 1. Rome: Visceglia, 2001.

Edens, Christopher. "Small Things Forgotten? Continuity Among Change at Godin Tepe." *Iranica Antiqua* 37 (2002): 31–46.

Flannery, Kent V. "The Cultural Evolution of Civilizations." *Annual Review of Ecology and Systematics* 3 (1972): 399–426.

Frangipane, Marcella. *Arslantepe Cretulae: An Early Centralised Administrative System Before Writing*. Rome: Universitá di Roma "La Sapienza," 2007.

———. "Local Components in the Development of Centralized Societies in Syro-Anatolian Regions." In *Between the Rivers and over the Mountains*, edited by M. Frangipane, H. Hauptmann, M. Liverani, P. Matthiae, and M. Mellink, 133–161. Rome: Universitá di Roma "La Sapienza," 1993.

Frangipane, Marcella, and Alba Palmieri. "A Protourban Centre of the Late Uruk Period." *Origini* 12, no. 2 (1983): 287–668.

Fried, Morton. *The Evolution of Political Society*. New York: Random House, 1967.

Hamlin (Kramer), Carol. "Seh Gabi." *Archaeology* 27 (1974): 274–277.

Henrickson, Elizabeth F. "Ceramic Evidence for Cultural Interaction Between Chalcolithic Mesopotamia and Western Iran." In *Technology and Style, Ceramics and Civilization,* Volume 2, edited by W. D. Kingery and Esther Lense, 87–132. Columbus, OH: American Ceramic Society, 1986.

Hole, Frank. "Archaeology of the Village Period." In *The Archaeology of Western Iran*, edited by Frank Hole, 29–78. Washington, DC: Smithsonian Institution Press, 1987.

———. "Symbols of Religion and Social Organization at Susa." In *Beyond the Hilly Flanks*, edited by T. C. Young, P. Smith, and P. Mortensen, 315–344. Chicago: Oriental Institute, 1983.

Levine, Louis, and T. Cuyler Young, Jr. "A Summary of the Ceramic Assemblages of the Central Western Zagros from the Middle Neolithic to the Late Third Millennium B.C." In *Préhistoire de la Mésopotamie*, edited by J. H. Huot, 15–53. Paris: Editions du CNRS, 1986.

Matthews, Roger. "Administrative Activity and Technology at Godin Tepe in the Later Fourth Millennium BC." In *Proceedings of the International Symposium on Iranian Archaeology: Western Region* (Kermanshah, 1–3 November 2006). Tehran: ICAR (Iranian Center for Archaeological Research), in press.

McGovern, P. E. *Ancient Wine: The Search for the Origins of Viniculture*. Princeton: Princeton University Press, 2003.

Nissen, Hans, Peter Damerow, and Robert Englund. *Archaic Bookkeeping: Early Writing and Techniques of*

Economic Administration in the Ancient Near East. Chicago: University of Chicago Press, 1993.

Pittman, Holly. "Mesopotamian Intraregional Relations Reflected through Glyptic Evidence in the Late Chalcolithic." In *Uruk Mesopotamia and its Neighbors: Cross-cultural Interaction in the Era of State Formation,* edited by Mitchell Rothman, 404–444. Santa Fe, NM: School of American Research Press, 2001.

Rothman, Mitchell S. "The Archaeology of Early Administrative Systems in Mesopotamia." In *Settlement and Society: Essays Dedicated to Robert McCormick Adams,* edited by Elizabeth Stone, 235–254. Los Angeles: Coetsen Institute of Archaeology UCLA, 2007.

———. *Tepe Gawra: The Evolution of a Small, Prehistoric Center in Northern Iraq.* Philadelphia: The University of Pennsylvania Museum Publications, 2002.

———. "Seal and Sealing Findspots, Design, Audience and Function." In *Archives Before Writing,* edited by P. Ferioli, E. Fiandra, G. Fisore, and M. Frangipane, 97–121. Rome: Universitá di Roma, 1994.

———, ed. *Uruk, Mesopotamia and its Neighbors: Cross-cultural Interaction in the Era of State Formation.* Santa Fe, NM: School of American Research Press, 2001.

Service, Elman. *Primitive Social Organization.* New York: Random House, 1962.

Sjöberg, Åke. "Contributions to the Sumerian Lexicon." *Journal of Cuneiform Studies* 21 (1967): 275.

Smith, Philip, and T. Cuyler Young. "The Evolution of of Early Agriculture and Culture in Greater Mesopotamia." In *Population Growth: Anthropological Implications,* edited by B. Spooner, 1–59. Cambridge, MA: MIT Press, 1972.

Stein, Gil. *Rethinking World-Systems: Diasporas, Colonies, and Interaction in Uruk Mesopotamia.* Tucson: University of Arizona Press, 1999.

———, ed. "The Uruk Expansion: Northern Perspectives from Hacinebi, Hassek Höyük, and Gawra." *Paléorient* 25, no. 1 (1999): 5–172.

Wallerstein, Immanuel. *The Modern World System I: Capitalist Agriculture and the Origins of the European World-Economy in the Sixteenth Century.* New York: Academic Press, 1974.

Weiss, Harvey, and T. Cuyler Young. "The Merchants of Susa and Plateau–Lowland Relations in the Late Fourth Millennium B.C." *Iran* 13 (1975): 1–18.

Wright, Henry. "Uruk States in Southwestern Iran." In *Archaic States,* edited by Gary Feinman and Joyce Marcus, 173–198. Santa Fe, NM: School of American Research, 1998.

———. "Toward an Explanation of the Origin of the State." In *Explanation of Prehistoric Change,* edited by J. Hill, 215–230. Albuquerque: University of New Mexico Press, 1977.

Young, T. Cuyler. "The Kangavar Survey, Periods VI to IV." In *A View from the Highlands: Archaeological Studies in Honour of Charles Burney,* edited by Antonio Sagona, 645–660. Herent, Belgium: Peeters, 2004.

Young, T. Cuyler, and Louis Levine. *Excavations of the Godin Project: Second Progress Report.* Toronto: Royal Ontario Museum, 1974.

Zeder, Melinda. *Feeding Cities: Specialized Animal Economy in the Ancient Near East.* Washington, DC: Smithsonian Institution Press, 1991.

GODIN 73
B1
FEATURE 143

5 | Migration and Resettlement: Godin Period IV

Mitchell S. Rothman

It is the great affinity, indeed almost homogeneity of the poetry, . . . shapes, surface treatment and decoration, which unifies the whole wide range of separated regions, from Transcaucasia, . . . Armenia and Azerbaidjan, through Eastern and Central Anatolia, to the whole length of the Levant, into one phenomenon. Diffusion of ceramic culture to such an extent requires the interpretation of an ethnic movement emanating from a region where that culture is at home, the Transcaucasian regions.

—Ruth Amiran, 1965

In the fourth and early-third millennia BC, societies in Mesopotamia were transforming into states and expanding their influence far beyond their heartland. In the mountainous regions north and east of the Tigris and Euphrates river valleys another fundamental cultural transition was occurring. Scholars refer to the consequences of this other transformation as Early Transcaucasian Culture. Godin Period IV represents one of the southernmost manifestations of this culture complex.

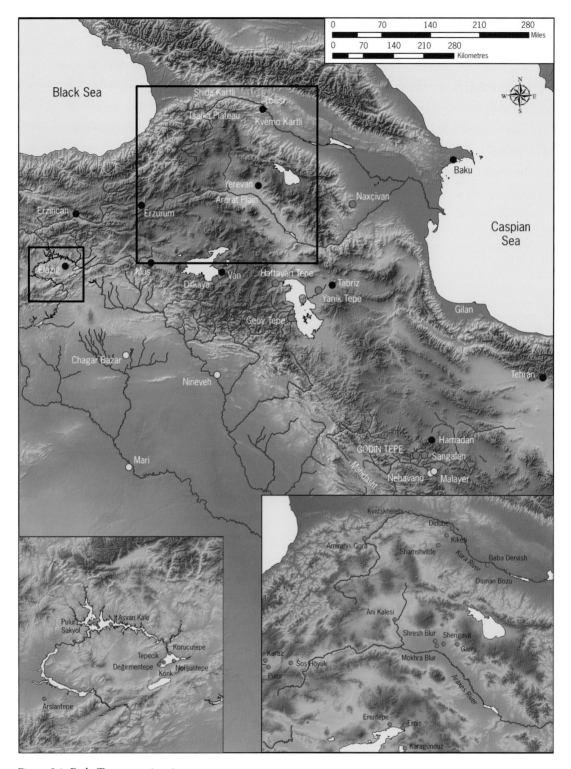

Figure 5.1. Early Transcaucasian sites

Early Transcaucasian Culture (ETC) originated in the modern countries of Georgia, Armenia, Azerbaijan, the adjoining lands of northeastern Turkey, and the Daghestan area of Russia, which forms a bridge along the Caspian shore from Central Asia through the North Caucasus Mountains into the Transcaucasus. The region borders Central Asia to its north and Turkey and Iran to its south and is defined by the basins of the Kura and Araxes rivers, east of the Black Sea, west of the Caspian Sea, and south of the northern high Caucasus mountain range (Figures 5.1 and 5.4).

The natural environment of the ETC is generally more open than the central western Zagros, and encompasses high mountains, broad river valleys, plateaus, and narrow valleys in the shadows of low mountain ranges. These mountain ranges merge into the Taurus Mountains of eastern Turkey north of Lake Van and into the Zagros Mountains of Iran north of Lake Urmia.

This is a physical and cultural landscape fundamentally different than that of the lowlands of Mesopotamia. As described in Chapter 4, people living on a resource-poor alluvial plain dependent on irrigation agriculture spawned the Mesopotamian revolution: cities, state-level organization, and the creation of regional and inter-regional exchange networks. In the Transcaucasus new cultural forms emerged from among pastoralists, farming communities, and short-lived towns beginning about 3500 BC as the Uruk expansion was continuing to develop in the lowlands.

Archaeologists identify the ETC mostly by its distinctive pottery: a small corpus of handmade, burnished forms, often black, or black on the exterior and red on the interior,

Figure 5.2. ETC pottery

but also red, grey, and dark buff in colour. Incised or raised plastic designs are another feature of this distinctive ware. These pottery styles are easy to identify, but the pottery alone does not define ETC. Later Middle Bronze Age cultures in the Transcaucasus used similar black, burnished pots, but their cultural patterns of adaptation, social structure, and belief really do not fit the ETC pattern.

The importance of ETC traditions lies in understanding the unique cultural trajectory shared by the mountain peoples of the ETC, and the way their cross-cultural contact at sites like Godin altered the course of both the larger ETC phenomenon and the local cultures that interacted with it.

As in Mesopotamia, the ETC involved a geographical expansion that occurred from approximately 3300 to 2500 BC, but the nature of this expansion is not like that of the Mesopotamians. The Uruk people of southern Mesopotamia had a great economic and cultural influence on the local societies they encountered outside their heartland, but not that many Uruk people actually moved into the local Late Chalcolithic sphere. The ETC expansion, on the other hand, was a migration of people. Populations of ETC peoples spread across the eastern Turkish highlands down into the northern Jordan Valley and also along the Zagros mountain front in western Iran. They arrived at Godin Tepe for the first time in Period VI:1a, but it was not until Period IV that they established an ETC settlement at the site.

The questions I explore in this chapter include: What was the nature of ETC traditions outside their homelands? Why and specifically from where did ETC peoples migrate? Because they did not migrate into under-populated environments, unlike the Uruk people,

Figure 5.3. Godin IV building 3

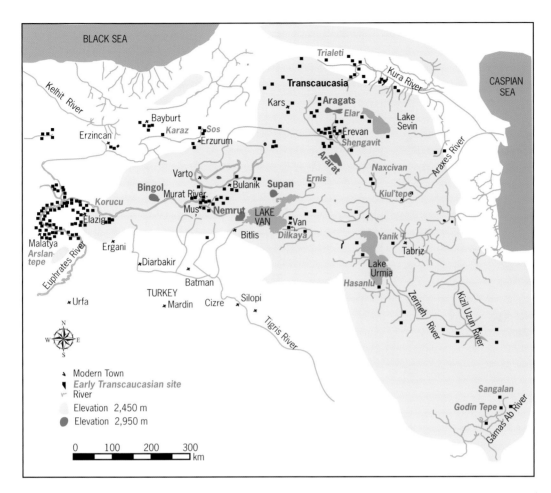

Figure 5.4. Distribution of Early Transcaucasian Culture

who migrated to northern Syria, how did they adapt to the natural and human environments they encountered as they moved, and how did they affect the native populations? These migrants encountered cultures with more advanced production techniques and very different organizational forms. Why did ETC peoples retain their own styles and presumably traditions for half a millennium or more? These more general questions will help clarify what was happening at Godin Tepe in the early third millennium and why the culture of Period IV took the forms it did.

The dating of the ETC is outlined in Table 5.1. The second column represents the broader dating system for Upper Mesopotamia. The next set of columns represents two alternative dating schemes for the South Caucasus, the classifications derived from the older three-age system (eras of copper and stone, bronze, and iron) on the left and periods based on local cultures to the right. The former aims to put the ETC into a global scheme, the

Table 5.1. Chronology of Early Transcaucasian Culture

BC	Godin Tepe	Upper Meso-potamia	South or Transcaucasus					North Caucasus
			Badalyn/Smith Aragats Armenia		Sagona Regional			
1500	Godin III	Middle Bronze	Middle Bronze 3	Karmir vank Karmir berd Sevin Uzerlik	Middle Bronze 2	Bedeni Martkopi	Trialeti	Maikop
2000		Early Bronze 4	Middle Bronze 2	Trialeti Vanadzor	Middle Bronze		Kurgan	
		Early Bronze 3	Middle Bronze 1	Early Kurgans	Early Bronze 3	Kura Araks III		
2500	Godin IV	Early Bronze 2	Early Bronze 2	Kura Araks II	Early Bronze 2			
		Early Bronze 1			Early Bronze 1	Kura Araks II		
3000								
	Godin VI	Late Chalolithic	Early Bronze 1	Kura Araks I	Late Chalolithic	Kura Araks I		
3500								

latter into one more specific to the mountainous regions. The last column relates the ETC to northern Caucasian culture history. The construction of a multi-regional chronological scheme has proven difficult. For example, one scholar will call 3100 BC Late Chalcolithic, while another calls it Early Bronze (EB) I and sometimes EB II. The chronological scheme that is the most consistent is the Kura Araks I–III periodization of Antonio Sagona, which I will use here. It is still much debated and far from set, but it does represent a fairly straight-forward temporal sequence that can be tied to cultural trends.

In Mesopotamia, cultures were homogenized by the openness and ease of travel in the lowland plains from the southern alluvium to the piedmont and hills of the north and east. Although there are commonalities that we use to define the ETC as a cultural entity, there are also many more local variants within each mountain area. The seeming uniformity of ETC pottery masks a great deal of internal variation, especially as migrants began to en-counter cultures foreign to them on their trek to new lands.

Pottery Style

Ceramic design traditions within Transcaucasia include Shida Kartli, Ťsalka, Armenian, and Kvemo Kartli styles (Figures 5.6–5.8). Their typical forms are shown in Figure 5.5. If pottery style represents shared traditions, maps of where each of these separate styles are found over

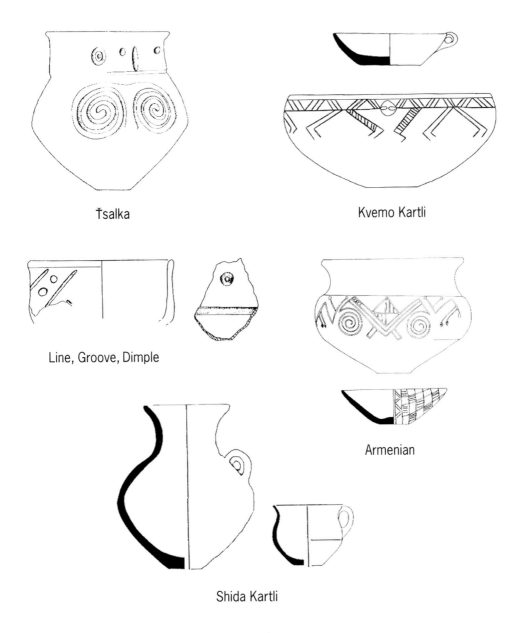

Figure 5.5. Examples of vessels from different ETC style zones

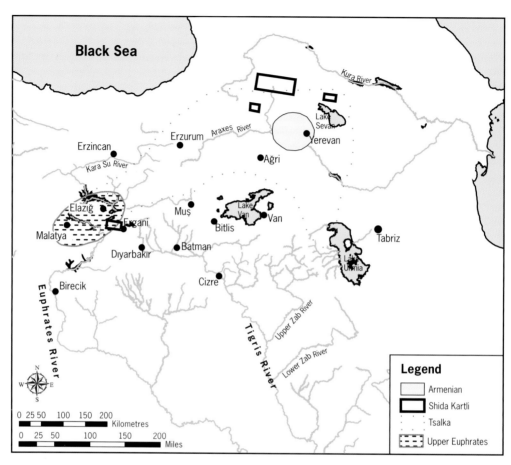

Figure 5.6. Distribution of Kura Araks II ETC style

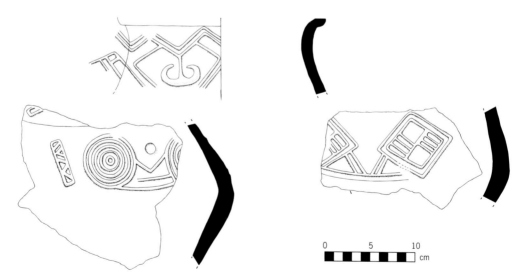

Figure 5.7. Tsalka-style pottery from Kazane in the Urfa Plain

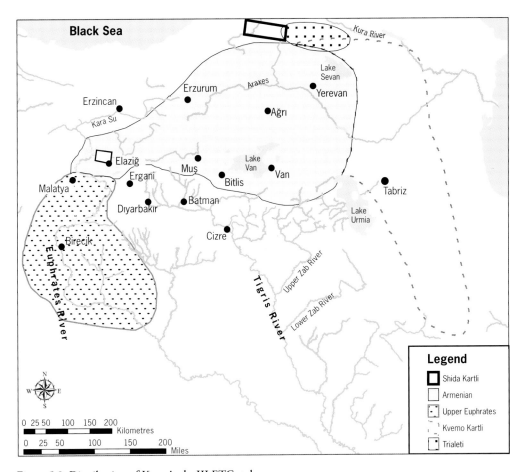

Figure 5.8. Distribution of Kura Araks III ETC style

time will indicate both their homeland and where people sharing these traditions went.

Figure 5.6 shows the Kura Araks II period distribution, beginning near the transition from the fourth to the third millennium BC. Ťsalka style was dominant wherever ETC appeared outside of Transcaucasia proper, although the earliest migrants in the Malatya area developed a second generation of styles fairly early on, called the Upper Euphrates style. A few examples also appear in Late Chalcolithic levels in the lowland piedmont (Figure 5.7).

By the Kura Araks III period (Figure 5.8), traditional Ťsalka styles became less popular even in the homeland. Styles associated with Armenia dominated to the west and Kvemo Kartli dominated to the east. Shida Kartli style remained concentrated in its former niche, and some of the intrusive Kurgan cultures, Trialeti, began to appear in the Transcaucasus. At the same time, in Kura Araks III period, we see the development of a new generation of pottery styles in the migration zones. For example, a Kura Araks III sub-set of the Armenian designs, the so-called dimple and groove, or line and groove, appeared in the Ararat

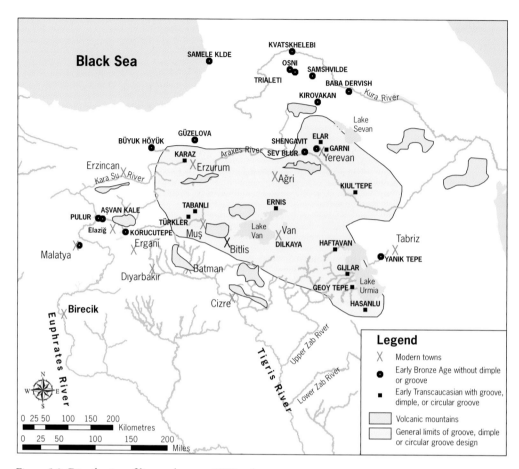

Figure 5.9. Distribution of line-and-groove ETC style

Plain of Armenia and throughout a very wide area from eastern Turkey into Iran, west of Lake Urmia (Figure 5.9). Its surface colour is often a lighter black or grey. This design is important, not because of its source, but because it is associated with the largest pastureland for sheep and goats in the highlands. The dimple and groove, or line and groove, represents a new generation of migrants, whose pottery style is an amalgam of Armenian styles and those of the local peoples with whom they then lived. In a study of this pottery from Muş west of Lake Van, published in 1997, Kozbe and I determined that the techniques of pottery-making there represented both the typical ETC methods and those of the earlier Late Chalcolithic population; they were merging with one another. The dimple and groove, or line and groove design appeared throughout the great Eastern Turkish zone of small farms and extensive pasturelands, but it never appeared in significant numbers in the more optimal agricultural zones to the west, east, or south.

The picture of ETC style zones that emerges is a bit of a confused puzzle of style areas. Even within the seemingly distinct zones of the Kura Araks III, styles zones crossed. For example, the sites of Haftavan and Yanik Tepe are both located on the northeast plains of Lake Urmia in Iran, yet the former shared design elements with Ernis at the northern tip of Lake Van in Turkey in the Armenian design zone, and the latter shared elements of Kvemo Kartli style. This mixing of styles suggests that rather than a single or a few large migrations, we are probably looking at many smaller movements outward and possibly even back over a long span of time. I have described this pattern as ripples in the stream. The streams consist of many smaller migrations along the same route. Even within a common stream of migration, however, ripples were created when small stones were thrown from other areas into the main stream.

The wares and designs of the Godin Period IV pottery corpus are fairly limited in terms of shape and design compared to the areas described above. They are related to Kvemo Kartli style, but are even more closely related to a second or third generation of local modifications of that style moving down the eastern side of Lake Urmia. Many of the best comparisons to Godin's pottery are not directly from the homeland but from later generations in the ETC migrations.

Andirons and Ritual

The ideological elements of culture are another important factor in the analysis of the ETC generally and of Godin Period IV in particular. Ideology is often the most difficult element of a culture for an archaeologist to recover, but for the ETC, the andiron, a mobile fireplace stand, may help. Andirons are placed in hearths in the centre of houses. These andirons come in a variety of shapes and are often decorated with human, animal, or abstract designs. Some of the shapes, for instance, those with horn-like projections, are most often found in the North Caucasus and northern Transcaucasian areas (inner Georgia). Horseshoe-shaped andirons are rare in the North Caucasus, but were the most common type in the areas of lower Georgia, Armenia, Azerbaijan, and throughout the remaining ETC territory. A circular form as well as sets of separate cylindrical stands also existed throughout the region from the Caucasus to the Taurus and Zagros mountain areas. The shapes of these andirons, as well as the particular designs carved on them, provide another indicator of the source areas for the ETC.

Godin Tepe yielded a number of andiron pieces, but most of them surprisingly were found in levels late in Godin Period III, well after the florescence of the ETC culture in Period IV. These late andirons were probably not the result of continuity of culture from Period IV, but represent instead contact with post-ETC populations of the Middle Bronze Age (see Chapter 6, Figure 6.23). The few andirons recovered from Godin IV are of the

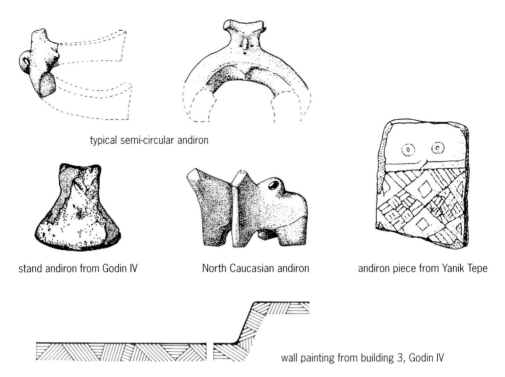

typical semi-circular andiron

stand andiron from Godin IV   North Caucasian andiron   andiron piece from Yanik Tepe

wall painting from building 3, Godin IV

Figure 5.10. ETC Andiron types

simplest cylindrical kind. There is, however, a stylistic connection between designs on an andiron piece from Yanik Tepe, a site on the eastern side of Lake Urmia, and a wall painting in the large building 3 of Godin Period IV (Figure 5.10).

The andirons may be even more important than pottery in understanding the nature of Early Transcaucasian Culture because of what they tell us about the organization of ETC life. Unlike Mesopotamian sites, most ETC settlements appeared to lack formal, centralized religious buildings. That does not mean that ETC peoples lacked religious ritual. Some researchers suggest instead that the ritual at the core of ETC belief was the hearth and its andiron. The religious focus of these cultures was domestic. Formal sanctuaries like churches, mosques, synagogues, and temples need community funding and usually larger organizations to train and maintain their clergy. The hearth is common to all residents without any need for formalized administration.

The exception to the domestic nature of religion in the ETC may come at the end of the period in the Transcaucasus after Godin IV. Mokhra Blur and Shegavit in Armenia had public, multi-site, ritual emplacements. At each of these sites excavators found large obelisks of basalt that must have been dragged 9 to 12 kilometres to their final resting place. At Mokhra Blur the obelisk was set on top of a tower some 6 metres high; it must have been visible to other sites in its vicinity. Each of these instances can be attributed to small local systems of sites rather than larger political units. They provide evidence for the recruiting and manipulating of labour to build and maintain these large monuments, which is a very important indicator that the social organization was more complex than the small size and lack of differentiation of houses at these sites imply.

Even among the more domestic manifestations of ritual in eastern Turkey, a number of variations have been reported. At the sites of Korucutepe and Norşuntepe sets of three andirons were positioned in special rooms. Plates were found on the andirons. At another ETC site, Pulur (Saykol), quite a few houses had hearth shrines with benches, andirons, and pottery (Figure 5.11). The building with rooms 88 and 83 was similar in plan to building 3 of Godin Period IV (Figure 5.16). Among the small wattle-and-daub houses of Sos Höyük in Erzurum, a religious ritual is also suggested. At the centre of round single-room structures residents intentionally buried horned animal figurines and the best quality bone and stone tools, including tanged obsidian arrowheads, in a clear pattern around the hearth and its andiron. The ETC use of vessels decorated with abstract animal and human designs and of different colour combinations may also reflect an ideological system symbolized in such rituals. The discovery of serving and eating vessels associated with the andiron shrine at Pulur may indicate that part of that ritual may have been a ritual meal or feast (Figure 5.12).

Feasting appears to be an ancient commu-

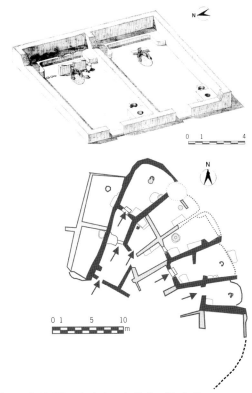

Figure 5.11. Hearth shrines in Pulur (Saykol)

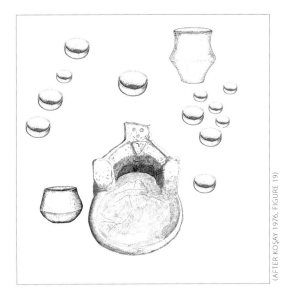

(AFTER KOŞAY 1976, FIGURE 19)

Figure 5.12. Remains of feasting in room 80 at Pulur (Saykol)

nal activity going back to the Neolithic. Feasting depended on the collection of surplus food and often involved a competition for who could put on the best feast. Chiefly lineages probably used feasts as a symbolic way to establish the legitimacy of their rank by tying the feast to the supernatural world through religious ritual. An example of feasting is represented by activities in building 3 of the Godin IV:1b and IV:1a phases.

Andirons often have handles, so that if a group moves as pastoral nomads or transhumants, they can take the hearth stands with them. The fact that these decorated mobile andirons increased in number in Transcaucasia toward the end of the fourth millennium BC, Kura Araks I, when the streams of migration began to increase, suggests that they were ideologically important. We do not have the "dictionary" to translate their precise meaning, but they are clearly connected to food production, fertility, and other economic activities.

In addition to structuring beliefs, religious ritual integrates members of a culture or ethnic group. Religion creates a moral community of divine belief that brings people together for more than just worship. The promotion of a cult is also one of the ways that people bring new members from other groups they encounter into their fold.

Architecture: Tradition and Function

The social meaning of architecture includes its functions, construction methods, and symbolism as reflected in the size, layout, and furnishings of buildings at a site. Smaller houses can be differentiated from specialized buildings like churches or factories. Even within the category of houses there can be critical differences in the way space is apportioned to distinct functions. In all societies from nomadic pastoralists to advanced states status is encoded in house type and floor plan.

For the ETC, four basic types of house shapes, construction, and layouts existed: single-room round houses of wattle and daub, often with adjoining storage units; square wattle-and-daub houses with a main room and a small entry room; round mud-brick houses with internal fittings; and square mud-brick houses, sometimes with multiple rooms. These buildings could be set side by side in a large semi-circle as at Pulur (Saykol) and at Godin in phase IV:1b, or they could be scattered about the village without a clear plan except that the doorways faced the same direction. Roofing was either mud over a frame of wooden beams, or thatch with a pitched or flat roof. A domed clay roof was at times built from the walls, as one can still see today along the Turkish-Syrian border or in Afghanistan where many of the other architectural forms mentioned here are also still being built.

All these buildings were quite small, measuring only 25–40 square metres. This is comparable to a larger nomad tent in the Middle East today. The organization of activi-

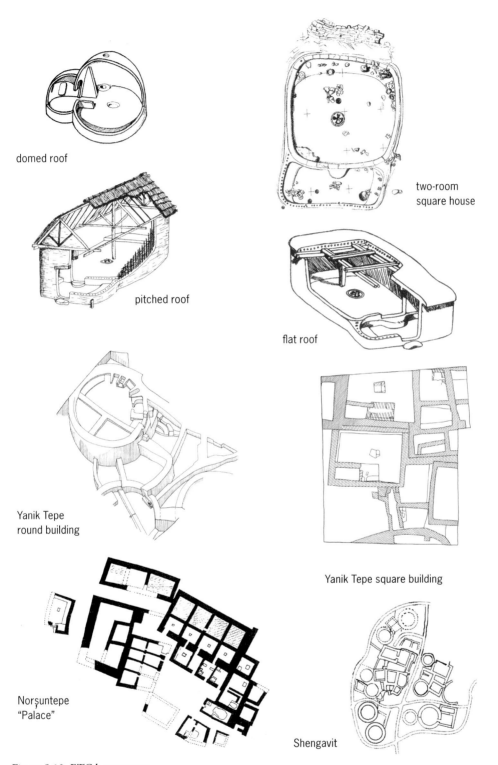

domed roof

pitched roof

two-room
square house

flat roof

Yanik Tepe
round building

Yanik Tepe square building

Norşuntepe
"Palace"

Shengavit

Figure 5.13. ETC house types

ties inside the houses probably mirrors that of nomad families as well. Domestic activities documented in ETC houses at the site of Dilkaya east of Lake Van displayed an expected range of functions: cooking, food serving, leather working, and weaving. These activities overlap in space. Grinding of grains, however, was done outside the house. Each house had hearths, often two, one in the corner of the room and one in its centre, as well as garbage pits, fire boxes (ash pits) near the hearths, silos, bins, and wall niches. Similarly, a typical nomad tent, like the modern village houses studied in the central western Zagros by Watson and Kramer, has a bench of mud or stone as storage for bedding and other goods that might get wet, external storage units, a small internal hearth for heat and small cooking tasks, and a large exterior oven for most cooking and baking.

At Norşuntepe, a square building, called the "palace" by its excavators, was much larger and more specialized. One hundred large storage pots found on a floor of this building indicate that the palace's role included storage. Its floor plan suggests that communal or public activities coordinated by socially ranked individuals happened there. Still, the Norşuntepe structures differ from the surrounding Mesopotamian-influenced sites in retaining ETC features such as benches and curved hearths. The implication is that either the ETC residents of this settlement adopted a model of organization closer to the complex Mesopotamian ones around them, or that the ETC tradition was producing a different form of ranked society, still following the Transcaucasian traditions as exemplified by the Armenian examples discussed above.

Economic Strategies

The people of the ETC practiced agriculture. Evidence for cultivation includes sickle blades, grinding stones (querns and rubbing stones), mortars and pestles, grain bins, and the remains of domesticated plant seeds. At Korucutepe and other sites in the Altınova Plain of Elâzig during the Kura Araks II period, barley (*Hordeum distichum*) and wheat (*Triticum aestivum* and *Tritium durum*) seeds have been found. There is some evidence to indicate that irrigation canals were sometimes dug, although in most of the ETC geographical area it would have been possible to grow crops with rainfall alone.

Animal husbandry was always an important element in the ETC economy. In Azerbaijan, cattle predominated in the Kura Araks I to early II periods, although sheep became more important in the Kura Araks III. A similar pattern of animal exploitation occurred at Arslantepe. At the town site of Korucutepe, during the Kura Araks III, 26 percent of identifiable animal bones were cattle, 66 percent were sheep and goats, and 8 percent were pigs. The smaller site of Sos Höyük near Erzurum yielded a similar pattern of animal exploitation.

The relative percentages of gender and age ratios of these species among animal-bone remains can indicate whether milk, implied by a higher proportion of females to males, meat, indicated by a higher proportion of younger males, or wool and hair, suggested by a high ratio of older to younger animals, were the main products obtained from these animals. For Sos Höyük in Erzurum and some northern Mesopotamian sites, sheep and goats were exploited for their meat. At Korucutepe in Elâzig, however, ethnozoologists determined that the gender and age ratios ratio were typical for obtaining wool from sheep and hair from goats. For cattle, herd-management curves suggest that significant numbers of females were kept, presumably for milk and cheese-making, and more males were kept than were necessary as breeders; some may have been killed for meat or hides but many of the larger males were probably kept for their ability to pull a plough. Available data suggest that ETC peoples used a subsistence strategy emphasizing flexibility to take advantage of whatever the local conditions were, as opposed to a focused one that would work only under a limited set of conditions. This is an ideal strategy for migrants.

The ratios discussed above may not represent the animal exploitation of the fully nomadic portions of the ETC populations. It is difficult to recover the remains of any nomadic people because their temporary campsites are difficult to find archaeologically. Modern pastoral nomad groups focus on activities for exchange with settled populations, like processing milk products or providing wool or hair, in order to obtain agricultural and craft goods that they do not make. They want to maintain their capital in animals by using secondary products instead of killing their animals for meat.

Understanding the Organization of ETC Groups in the Diaspora

How, then, do we conceptualize the role of ETC migrants in their new environments? Charles Burney, one of the early researchers on the ETC, categorizes them as ethnicities. Ethnicities are most commonly found in pluralistic or multi-cultural settings, especially where immigration is common.

Ethnicities can be defined either by what binds ethnic groups together (an essentialist definition) or by what distinguishes them from other ethnic groups (a boundary definition). The essentialist definition distinguishes ethnicities by their cultural content, including cultural values, systems of government and economics, environmental adaptations, and religion. Ethnic groups often share a common language, customs, food preferences, and cultural artifacts that reflect their commonalities symbolically. According to the boundary definition, some of the cultural essentials are emphasized to establish identity, maintain close alliances within the group, and compete with opposing ethnic groups.

Ethnicity, then, is constructed by identity, adaptation, and competition. It is marked by artifact, custom, attitude, behaviour, and organization. These ethnic identities are fluid, and their strength depends on many social, political, and economic factors. Archaeologists discover them by seeing how the ancients *used* symbols in establishing identity without assuming that we can really know what each of the symbols *meant* to the ancients.

Origin and Spread of ETC Traditions: Models of Migration

The earliest evidence for the artifactual hallmarks of Early Transcaucasian Culture is found in the mid-fourth millennium BC. However, the ETC did not arrive with new peoples or represent a totally new set of cultural arrangements, technologies, and perceptions. Rather, a continuum from the Neolithic through Proto–Kura-Araks culture is evident.

Perhaps the most critical change of this pre-ETC period was a change in the exploitation of the natural environment. Whereas earlier Neolithic peoples of the Transcaucasus lived on the agricultural soils of the Kura depression, populations thereafter used a wider range of ecological niches, including the pasturelands at higher elevations.

Demographers speak of a "push" and a "pull" in all migrations. There must be some reason to be pushed out of an earlier homeland, but there must also be something that pulls the mobile population in a particular direction. At the same time, the potentials and problems of living in a particular place will make it more likely that people will settle. Sometimes, migration is a strategy for improving one's lot in life. Primogeniture or other customs favouring one family member, kinship segment, ethnicity, or class over another, for example, may cause the less economically fortunate to migrate. On the other hand, a way for would-be leaders to be promoted is to lead their followers to new settlements. This was the model of the Vikings. Ideology may also factor into the equation. For example, the filling of America's western frontier was caused by more than population pressure or economic opportunity; it was the idea of Manifest Destiny that sent many settlers westward.

At times the informational pull to a specific location involves "leapfrogging": relatives or others who have migrated may draw migrants over large areas of available territory to a more distant locale. Diffusion of information and exotic goods along the stream may occur even in areas where the migrants do not settle.

A number of models have been proposed to explain the geographically wide distribution of Early Transcaucasian cultural elements over a period of more than 1,200 years. The earliest theory proposed a single mass migration of small farmers out of the ETC homeland in the Transcaucasus. Some scholars attribute this migration to a hunt for fields and pastures. It is also possible that some of the population was pushed by new mobile populations of the Kurgan culture. Some scholars reject the migration theory altogether, emphasizing rather the role of trade and emulation, in which ETC pottery passed along the same trade routes as metals, obsidian, precious and semi-precious stones, and perhaps viniculture (the cultivation of grapes) rather than accompanying large-scale migrations. The last theory appears to ignore too much evidence for the movement of populations, although trade certainly played a role in the spread of ETC artifacts.

In the areas outside the core zone where the ETC pottery types are found, migrants apparently mixed with local populations. ETC ware became the dominant style in some places, and in other places elements of ETC culture existed alongside local pottery-making and cultural/ethnic traditions.

In order to make sense of the patterns we see at Godin, what models can we derive from other areas of the ETC diaspora that have been more extensively researched?

The Muş Province west and northwest of Lake Van in highland eastern Turkey provides one example. Muş is situated in a snowy region with poor agricultural soils, but large areas of rich pasture for sheep and goats. It is endowed with sources of fine obsidian for tool-making, providing opportunities for trade.

This case is significant because it provides evidence for a demographic shift typical of migrations. During the Kura Araks II period ETC people migrated into the high north-eastern hills of Muş. In the subsequent Kura Araks III period, the number of sites increased dramatically, especially on the valley floor, which had been the home of earlier native populations. Not only did the immigrant population increase, but signs of assimilation are evident in the pottery-making techniques.

This trend in migrant settlement seems to indicate the existence of two ETC migrations. The first one, during the Kura Araks II, consisted mostly of pastoralists, while during the Kura Araks III it consisted mostly of transhumant farming communities mixing with the local population. The pull in this case was available pasture and farmlands.

A contrasting picture is presented by the Malatya plain. Malatya has a more optimal environment with rich agricultural and horticultural soils, and a more moderate highland climate. It was also at a transportation hub, as Godin was for the High Road through the Zagros Mountains. The residents of the site during the fourth millennium BC included leaders who used Arslantepe as their local centre to regulate a system of exchange and tribute. Leaders built a series of superimposed palace/temple complexes with ample storage and an auditing system for keeping track of receipts and disbursements of grain and other goods.

ETC pottery appeared in small numbers at Arslantepe in its Period VII during the first half of the fourth millennium BC, almost 500 years before any was present at Godin Tepe. As the fourth millennium progressed, the number and percentage of ETC pottery types increased. At the same time, the more mobile sheep and goats dominated the animal remains at the site, and cattle and pigs declined dramatically in number. Arslantepe's close proximity to the Ergani copper and other silver, copper, and lead mines was also an important factor in its regional role. The presence of minerals from Azerbaijan found as part of the smelting and alloying process at Arslantepe suggests that a group of ETC metallurgists lived at the site.

After the burning of the temple/palace complex at Arslantepe in about 3000 BC, people using largely ETC-styled pottery built wattle-and-daub houses on top of the remains of the last temple/palace complex. Seasonal occupation of small ETC sites on natural hilltops away from the Euphrates and central valley increased. A tomb was built at Arslantepe with sacrificed individuals and rich funerary goods, containing both ETC and local Plain Simple wares as well as metal weapons and containers made from unique alloys of silver and arsenical copper that are reminiscent of Maikop metallurgy from the North Caucasus.

Arslantepe therefore appears to represent a different pull from that of the immigrants to Muş. These immigrants were not looking for land. Rather they were pulled to Arslantepe because of its participation in local and then regional exchange networks, and because of opportunities for the talents of ETC metallurgists and others. Settlers or nomads seeking pasture or fields followed, but only after the decline of the Arslantepe palace/temple system.

Another variation is represented by the 'Amuq Valley west of Malatya between the Anatolian plateau to the north and the low plains of the Levant to the south, closer to sea level than either Malatya or Muş. Snows are limited in winter, and the valley's fertile soils are fed by many streams, rivers, and springs, providing rich agricultural and horticultural potential along with pastureland and mineral deposits in the surrounding foothills and mountains.

At the end of the Kura Araks I and beginning of Kura Araks II, the first ETC ceramics appeared in this area, followed by a dramatic increase during the Kura Araks III. This increase in ETC ceramics corresponds with a dramatic shift in settlement from relatively large sites found in the valley's centre during the earlier period to a proliferation of small sites (1–2 hectares) along its outskirts during the latter period. Furthermore, at large sites (e.g., Tell Tayinat) excavators found a mixture of local wheel-made pottery and handmade ETC wares. In contrast, the smaller sites (e.g., Tabarat al-Akrad) yielded almost exclusively ETC ceramics.

This situation is more like Muş than Malatya and again indicates multiple migrations and internal changes from the earliest occupations: first came mobile populations, maybe from Malatya or Elâzig, followed by farmers who established themselves on the outskirts of the indigenous settlement system, and no doubt provided some skills or animal products to local leaders. Sources of copper in the 'Amuq, however, were still part of the pull. During the Kura Araks III, the local and "foreign" cultures blended with each other. Variations in the fabrics of the ceramics suggest that all were made locally, perhaps in households, following local forms yet retaining some styles from Elâzığ. The 'Amuq's pull appears to be both metallurgical and subsistence.

Even farther south, the diffuse subsistence strategy of ETC populations is evident. Contrasting with the eastern Turkish areas, the Levant presents an environment completely different from the Transcaucasus. At 200 metres below sea level, with higher temperatures and lower precipitation, it is still marginal in some ways. However, sites are located on predominantly arable or irrigable land that, like the 'Amuq, have high agricultural and horticultural potential.

Although ETC ceramics (the local variant is called Khirbet Kerak ware) are found at forty-five sites over substantial parts of the southern Levant, they are most intensely concentrated along the north Jordan and its tributary river valleys. ETC wares make a sudden appearance in the southern Levant around 2700 BC close to the end of Godin IV at sites generally located in the lowlands on fertile soils with good access to water. Once again, larger sites such as Khirbet Kerak or Megiddo yielded a mixed assemblage of local pottery and ETC wares, while smaller sites (less than 2 hectares) such as Beth Shean or Tell Yaqush produced almost exclusively handmade and heavily burnished ETC ceramics.

Subsistence, rather than mineral resources, appears to have played the largest role here in pulling the second or third generations of ETC population south into the Jordan Valley. Although some pottery appears to be inspired by local traditions, a number of forms are originally found among the 'Amuq assemblage to its north. Some forms can even be traced back to eastern Turkey. ETC populations establish themselves in one place and then either because of growing numbers or the other factors discussed above, some sub-set of the population moves on into new territory, in this case clearly in search of land.

The ETC represents groups of people who were ethnically different from the cultures that occupied the lands into which they migrated. A flexible subsistence strategy based on animal husbandry and simple agriculture, often in less than optimal areas, is a shared characteristic of these groups, as are modes of pottery production and style, living arrangements, domestic ritual, and technical crafts, especially in metals and obsidian. In their movements they were likely pulled toward areas where some opportunity to use their expertise and resources in large trading networks existed, or where subsistence resources were readily available and competition with local populations was minimal. They quickly established symbiotic relationships with the locals, and more ETC peoples migrated to these places.

The pattern of ceramics linked with settlements is fairly consistent. First a trickle of potsherds appeared at sites, then the number of sites with almost exclusively ETC ceramics often in more marginal areas, increased, and finally, a mixture of ETC pottery types and local wares appeared at large sites, while small sites with only ETC wares continued as scattered enclaves.

Although the pattern is becoming clear, the details of the social dynamics behind these streams of migration remain to be explained.

Godin Tepe Period IV

Although Godin IV presents a rich collection of artifacts for study, a number of problems in the excavation and recording of these levels limit the conclusions one can reach. Most of Period IV was dug in 1973, the final season of excavation at Godin. At the beginning of this final season excavators had realized the potential importance of the Period VI (then called Period V) oval compound and a general rush was on to reach Period VI before the end of the project.

As a result, excavators were forced to hurry their work on the less imposing structures of Period IV. Gaps in the architecture of the earliest phase of IV (IV:2), especially in Operation A1, do not necessarily reflect the absence of architectural remains but may be the result of the hurried pace of excavation, which failed to allow the time to recover these eroded mud-brick or wattle-and-daub walls. The demands of drawing and recording the impressive buildings of the VI oval compound meant that the draftsperson of the project did not have time to draw all the walls of the small Period IV houses, and some elements of the plans published here had to be pieced together from scale sketches or crude hand drawings.

An overall problem at the site was a lack of consistent recording of elevations for the artifactual lots, and matching up building levels and deposits of artifacts is sometimes difficult. The problems of recording also affect the pottery analysis, because it is not always clear why certain potsherds were saved and shipped to Toronto and others discarded.

Dating Godin Period IV

The earliest appearance of ETC wares at Godin is in Period VI during the LC 5 period (see Chapter 4). This is before the beginning of significant migration in the Kura Araks II period. Within Godin Period IV, it is possible to detect a number of phases as structures were rebuilt and plans changed. The earliest Godin IV phase, IV:2 (Figure 5.14), represents a time when small buildings were anchored by postholes, and were therefore most likely wattle-and-daub houses. Builders of the next phase, IV:1b (Figures 5.15 and 5.16), retained nothing of the IV:2 plan and built mud-brick buildings, including the large build-

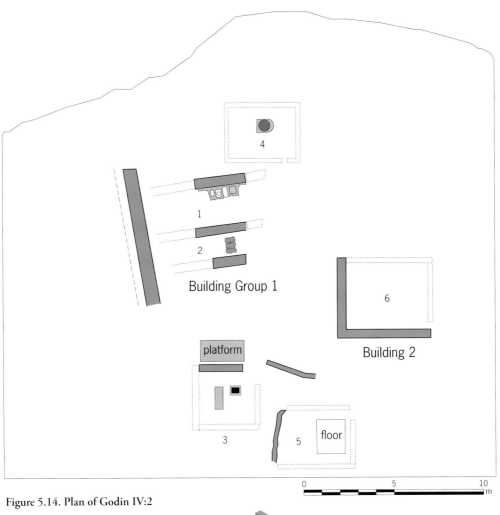

Figure 5.14. Plan of Godin IV:2

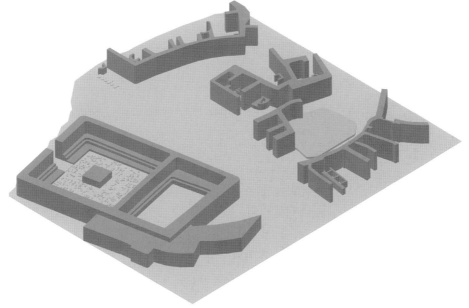

Figure 5.15. Raised plan of Godin IV:1b

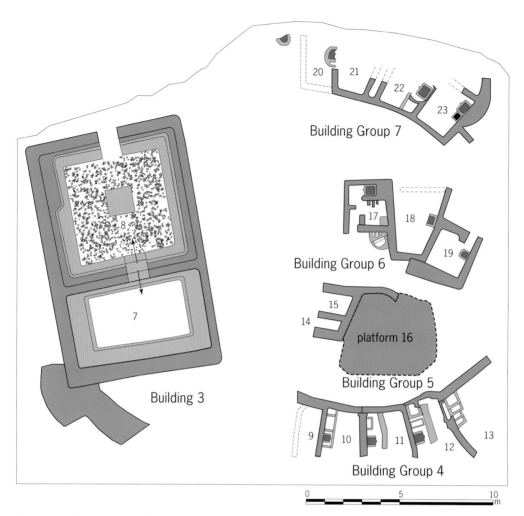

Figure 5.16. Plan of Godin IV:1b

ing 3 in the western side of the excavation area. The houses of phase IV:1b, in the eastern
half of the sounding, shared walls, especially curved north or south walls like the buildings at
Pulur (Saykol) in Elâzig. Phase IV:1a (Figures 5.17 and 5.18) retained building 3, but builders removed all the structures to the east of this building and laid out new square buildings
instead. Within phase IV:1a one building was significantly remodelled, and therefore the
phase is divided into IV:1a2 and IV:1a1 (Figure 5.18).

In terms of absolute dates, VI:1 ended not much later than 3050 BC (see Chapter 4, pp.
84–85). However, there may have been some time gap between the end of the occupation of the
oval compound and the occupation of Period IV. Excavators discovered a metre-deep deposit of
erosion between the latest Period VI deposits and the earliest Period IV levels in the Brick Kiln Cut

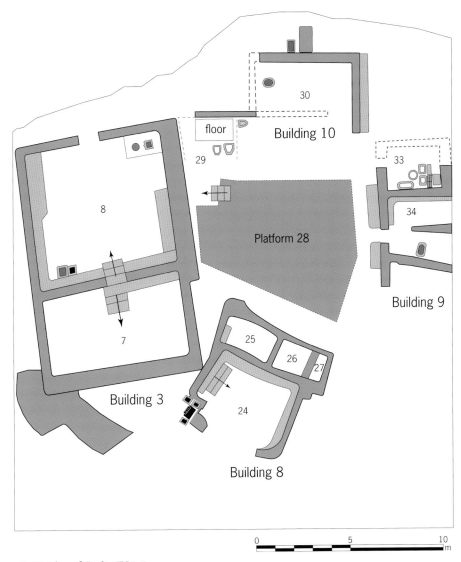

Figure 5.17. Plan of Godin IV:1a2

(Figure 5.19). The problem is that the slope of the mound was very steep. The excavated buildings of Godin IV were built on the pinnacle of the mound. At some point during its occupation, building 3 was buttressed to its south to prevent it from being undermined, because the mound sloped so sharply on that side of the mound. The Brick Kiln Cut (BKC) begins below the level of the buttress. Slope wash could therefore have accumulated quickly over a short period of time.

Precise dating of Godin IV from either radiocarbon or relative chronology is difficult. Newly run dates for Period IV and older dates from Period IV pitting into Period VI indicate that the Period IV occupation fell sometime between 2900 and 2600 BC (Table 5.2). Relative pottery chronology suggests that the occupation began during the earlier part of this range and that Godin IV:1a1 ended about 2700 BC.

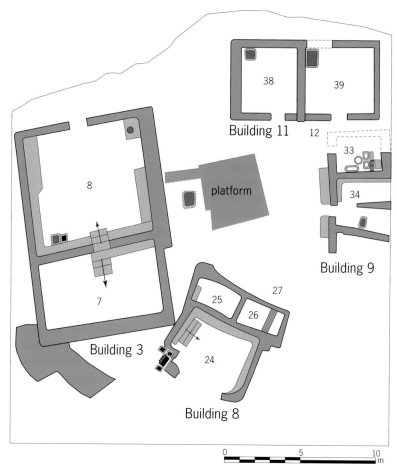

Figure 5.18. Plan of Godin IV:1a1

After the end of Godin IV the earliest secure dates for the succeeding Period, III, are in the twenty-sixth century BC, but they are not from the lowest strata and are not from very secure proveniences. There could be a hiatus between Godin IV and Godin III, but if so, there is no good way to determine its length. The builders of Godin III:6 cut the standing walls of building 3 when they dug their wall trenches for a very large building, and they seem to have filled in building 9 as a foundation for smaller structures. Presumably, they knew that the buildings were there.

Two factors mark the transition between Godin IV and III. In the earliest III phase, III:6, black burnished pottery continued to constitute 6 percent of the pottery assemblage. None of it has incised designs like Godin IV pottery, however. Closely packed complexes of square buildings typify Godin III:6, as opposed to the separate square buildings of Godin IV:1a. Godin III:6 appears to be contemporary in time with the square building phase of Yanik Tepe, best analog is Yanik Tepe west of the modern city of Tabriz and east of Lake

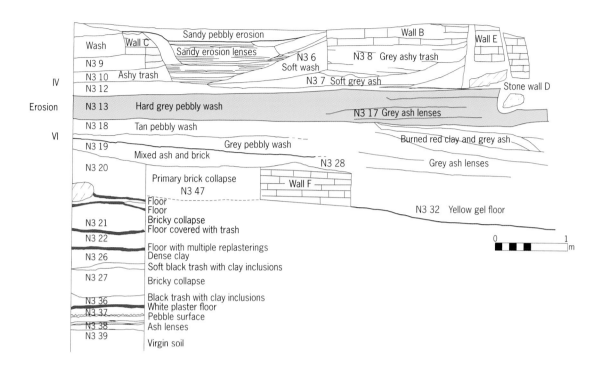

Figure 5.19. Stratigraphic section of the Brick Kiln Cut, east balk, north half; see Web archive for complete section.

but that too is not securely dated. It is noteworthy that phase IV:1a had the fewest potsherds with incised designs of Godin IV's three phases.

The broad chronological and geographical range, as well as the conservatism, of ETC pottery styles make relative dating of ETC sites difficult. Pottery was hand-made in houses rather than mass-produced in workshops, and fragile pottery with new styles was unlikely to be traded over difficult mountain roads. As Figure 5.21 illustrates, except for bowl-type IV and jar-type IV, the numbers of each type within each phase of Godin Period IV are too similar to differentiate. Even if we could have established a solid type set with significant variations among the phases of Period IV, there are no other well-excavated sites in western Iran from which absolute dates are available. The

Figure 5.20. Retaining wall for building 3

Table 5.2. Radiocarbon dates for Godin IV

OxCal v4.0.5 Bronk Ramsey (2007); r:5 IntCal04 atmospheric curve (Reimer et al., 2004)

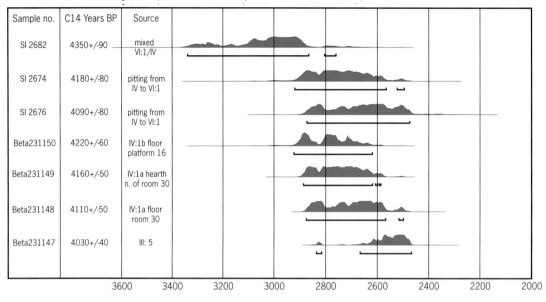

Calibrated date (calBC)

Figure 5.21. Counts of Godin IV pottery types by phase (from measured sample)

Urmia, but that site was dug quickly with a very limited number of supervisors and is not well dated. Fine-scaled chronology is not possible for the phases of Godin IV.

Godin IV was not a very long period compared to Periods VI and III. It almost certainly lasted less than 250 years. From the few pottery parallels we can draw to better-dated sites, Godin fits within the later Kura Araks II and the beginning of Kura Araks III periods. The transition to Godin Period III was fairly gradual.

Artifactual Remains of Godin Period IV

In order to reconstruct the activities people engaged in, archaeologists map artifact types onto the architectural and open spaces on the mound. Where sets of artifacts that may have been used to pursue a single activity, whether craft, ritual, social, or political, are found, they establish the presence of that activity in a particular building or open space.

Often these same clusters of activities can define other aspects of society such as social status, economic specialization, or organization. Taken together, these functional spaces can encode economic and social dynamics that extend beyond the limits of the settlement. Residents of any site depend on other sites for such resources as raw materials, prepared goods, mates, political or ideological alliances, pools of labour, and administrative organization. These activities create networks of interaction that can be local or extend to the limits of travel and communication.

Societies develop social organizations to facilitate the performance of these functions: to maintain order, to set policies, to define group goals, and to connect to other networks. Cities usually employ a state-level of organization with central control mechanisms, leaders with authority to make and enforce decisions, and hierarchies of power and privilege. Small, less independent systems or polities can be organized by chiefly lineages. Even smaller and still less interdependent societies can function by forging consensus when needed among kinship or communal groups.

If we envision a settlement as a set of functions within larger networks, we can then build a picture of both local functions and the organization lying behind them by plotting artifacts in the context of buildings and open spaces. We can also determine which, if any, of the models of migration discussed above apply to Godin IV.

Pottery

Approximately 3,000 pottery sherds and a few whole pots from Godin Period IV are stored at the Royal Ontario Museum. A small number of whole pots are housed in Tehran. For this analysis I inspected the ceramic sherds in Toronto, from which I constructed a typology (see Figures 5.56–5.61 at the end of this chapter). Of the 3,000 sherds, 627 were measured in detail. These included all those from the better (primary or secondary) proveniences and a few samples of each type wherever they were found. This analysis can paint a good general picture of the Godin IV pottery.

One usually thinks of ETC pottery as being black, but Godin IV pots were made in a range of colours. Of those, black is the most common exterior colour with 322, grey-brown 134, light brown 42, light red 42, dark buff 21, burnt sienna 20, grey 19, buff 15, and pale red 12. Virtually all the pots have a thin clay slip inside and out, and if the predominance of core colour is a true reflection, the fabric colour is generally grey-brown. The interior colour tends to match the exterior colour. Only 15 sherds of those recorded in detail have the characteristic black exterior and red interior, and a handful of the other exterior colours have a contrasting interior colour. The vast majority of black and burnt sienna exteriors are burnished, often highly. A few open bowl forms are also burnished on the interior.

The manufacture of Period IV pots indicates a fairly low level of technology. A technical analysis of its manufacture by Robert Henrickson in his 1989 article, "The Buff and the Grey," demonstrated that the pottery

is a technically inferior product. Beneath the carefully burnished surface adorned with striking white-filled excised geometric decoration is a poor quality fabric.

Figure 5.22. Colours of Godin IV pottery

Xeroradiographs of Godin sherds from two sites in two different areas (Godin Tepe in the Kangavar Valley and Sangalan in the Hamadan plain) reveal numerous internal voids, cracks, and flaws. The coarse grit inclusions tend to be at least 1 mm in diameter; many have maximum dimensions of at least several millimetres. This fabric is generally quite friable, crumbling readily. Such friability suggests a relatively low firing temperature.

Potters used an unusually high percentage of grog (ground up pottery) to temper the fabric of the pots. This grog tempering has many advantages in simplifying the production of pottery because the temper already contains the clay body. This theoretically simplifies the shaping process. The black/grey wares of Godin III lacked this grog tempering, a factor which Henrickson suggests may have been the result of major cultural, even ethnic, shifts in which pottery had begun to be made in more centralized workshops. During Godin IV, in addition to grog, coarse grit (quartz and basalt), sand, and occasionally straw were used in tempering. Analysts could find no evidence of the use of a fast or slow wheel. Most likely, pots were fired by digging a pit or building an above-the-ground stack of pots, surrounding them with straw or other fuel, and setting the pile on fire.

Figure 5.23. Grog inclusions in Godin IV pottery

This technology does raise an interesting question: how was the bichrome (black outside, red inside) pottery created, especially in such a low-technology environment? Ceramicists have offered a number of theories. One is that the clays were basically of a reddish colour. The interior, which remained

Figure 5.24. Godin IV vessel with bichrome firing colour

red, would be stuffed with straw and sealed. In the fire, the flash of flame would make the exterior black while the interior remained red. This theory does not, however, account for the fact that in many bichrome pots, the interior colour often spills over in an irregular way on the outside of the pot near the rim (Figure 5.24). A theory that seems to make more sense is that some kind of grease was applied to the exterior, which when burned at low temperature turned the greased surface black but retained some of the interior colour.

Godin Period IV Pottery Typology (Figures 5.56–5.61)

Typologically, all Godin IV pottery fits into eleven categories: conical bowls, rounded bowls, hole-mouth bowls, carinated bowls, cooking pots (with or without handles), storage jars, trays, S-shaped jars (short-neck or narrow-mouth), tall pointed-base jars, cups or mugs, and lids (a more detailed typology is available in the Godin Web archive at https:// tspace.library.utoronto.ca).

Bowls (Figures 5.56–5.57)

Bowls constitute 45 percent of the 627 measured sherds that could be identified to type; these numbers exclude body sherds that were apparently saved only for their design. The four basic types of bowls are characterized by different shapes of rims, profiles, and depths. The basic size characteristics are fairly uniform.

Type I bowls are all conical in shape. They tend to have feathered rims or rims with a slight inner ledge (for a lid?). Type I,2 bowls are deeper than Type I,1 and occasionally have a lug at the rim. Although they show little sign of burning or calcification—key character-

Figure 5.25. Godin IV bowl handles

istics of cooking pots—Types I,1a and I,2a bowls have drill holes near the rim, as do a few Type II round bowls. Presumably, they were hung, perhaps as warming trays, or to keep goods that were not in storage bins away from pests. The conical bowls are the most common bowl type; they constitute 38 percent of all measured bowls.

Round-sided and round-bottom bowls, Type II, are the second most common bowl form (33 percent of the bowl sample). They have characteristics similar to Type I bowls in terms of diameter at the rim and body thickness, although they tend to be shorter. Rim shapes similar to Type I show a common manufacturing technique, although an out-flaring rim and a handle exist.

The rarest bowl shape, Type III, is the hole-mouth bowl that almost fits in the category of jars. Carinated bowls are the second rarest (eight examples). Many have lugs with thickened rims. Some have flattened strap handles of a kind known as the Naxçivan handle, a very typical ETC form named after sites in the Naxçivan area of modern Azerbaijan just north of the Iranian border. These bowls have the largest rim diameters and on average the greatest height of any of the bowls.

Again, the thickness of the body is consistent with the other bowls, suggesting that the basic clay was made of a certain thickness for bowls (or thinner for jars), and then shaped over a mould form or in slabs to suit a particular purpose. There is little evidence of coiling. Decoration would then be added by incising designs on the surface of the bowl.

Cooking pots (Figures 5.57–5.58)

Cooking pots comprise 10 percent of the pottery sampled. Compared to bowls, they are taller, their walls and rims are thicker, while their rim diameter is about the same as bowls. They sometimes have handles or lugs and would have been placed on andirons or a tripod of stones. They often have stone in their temper to insulate them from the cooking fire.

Trays (Figure 5.59)

Trays are fairly crude, thick-walled functional items. They could have been cooking trays, although there were griddles in Godin IV houses. Alternatively, they could have been used in processing grains or other materials as similar trays were used for food processing in ethnographic examples. Their mere one percent of the sample may not reflect their real number, as many may have been used away from the site in or near fields.

Jars, storage jars, and cups (Figures 5.58–5.61)

Jars constitute 35 percent of the whole sample of measured pots, second only to bowls. All but Type IV conform to what ceramicists call S-shaped forms. Like bowls, the average body thickness (about 5 mm), rim thickness (close to 7 mm), and height (12 cm) fall within a fairly narrow range. What differentiates Types I, II, and III are the width of the mouth opening, the shape of the bottom, and the presence or absence of handles; Type I jars have the widest diameters at the rim, and Type III jars have pointed bases and often handles.

Figure 5.26. Typical Godin IV jar

Figure 5.27. Typical Godin IV beaker or cup

Figure 5.28. Top of handled Godin IV storage jar

Except for their size and the shape of their base, cups could easily fit Type III jars. They have the thinnest rims (average 5.2 mm) and body walls (average 3.97 mm) and are the shortest. Storage jars, to the contrary, have the thickest rims (1.4 cm), and bodies (1.2 cm) and are the tallest (44.6 cm). Some of the jar rims which lack enough of the body to determine their shape, Type V, could easily be storage jars.

Lids (Figure 5.61)

The final category of pottery is the lid. Lids are either simple convex circles of clay, or they have handles, either strap in the middle or Naxçivan type near the rim. Although the range of bowl and jar diameters at the rim is quite broad, those diameters appear best suited to cooking pots, ledge-rim bowls (Types I and IV), or storage jars.

Pottery Functions

The function of these pottery types can be determined by their characteristics, such as shape, rim diameter, and height. For example, most cooking pots are short and squat, thick walled, with a height of 6–41.5 cm, roughly a third as wide as they are tall. The vessels independently classified as cooking pots fit these criteria. An additional criterion is calcification.

All Middle Eastern clays are high in calcium carbonate and when wet or repeatedly heated this salt comes to the surface.

In a study of modern pottery use in an Iranian village published in 1983, Elizabeth Henrickson and Mary McDonald found that serving and eating vessels differed in size depending on whether they were meant for individuals or groups. Vessels for individual servings range from 6 to 8 cm in height and from 10 to 23 cm in maximum diameter, while pots for serving groups range from 4.4 to 23.4 cm in height and from 8.4 to 95 cm in maximum diameter. These figures suggest that jars of Types I, II, and IV may have been used as individual eating vessels, and bowls of Types I and IV and jars of Type III as serving dishes. This

may explain the generally small size of jars (including storage jars) compared to contemporaneous Mesopotamian examples. The height of Godin jars is barely more than most bowls. It is possible that the decorated small jars of Godin Period IV were used to serve food. In room 80 of Pulur (Saykol) Level X, a cooking pot and a set of small Type II bowls surround a hearth with a larger serving jar, again suggesting that small vessels were used for eating (Figure 5.12). Communal serving in the larger bowls, especially those with lids, is equally possible. From ethnographic analogy, bowls of Types I and IV fit the average family-size serving bowls.

Figure 5.29. Griddle hearths from Godin IV, showing the firing chamber and the griddle with drain

There is evidence for two major cooking techniques in Godin Period IV: cooking pots that were placed on andirons were used for stewed meals and grain porridge, and griddles were used for frying skewers of meat and vegetables. The draining lip at the front of these hearths appears designed to drain off fat or other liquids. In phase IV:1b, drains were built under the floor for whatever was flowing off the hearths.

Trays from Godin IV match the average cooking trays in the study mentioned above; however, there are so few of them at Godin that it seems unlikely that their primary function was cooking. A function involving roasting or otherwise processing grain appears more likely.

What I defined as cups fit the study norms as well. Compared to jars, they have a smaller diameter at the rim and thinner walls. The cups have handles, although some of the smaller Type I or II jars could be tumblers. The jar, bowl, and cup types specified as probable serving vessels are also the most likely to be decorated with incised designs.

Storage jars have larger rim diameters and heights than jars. Compared to many Mesopotamian storage jars, they are quite small. What the Mesopotamians kept in jars may well have been kept in bins at Godin.

In the real world most ceramics have multiple functions. What is used to serve food may easily be used at another time to mix food or other substances or to store small items. The characteristics of these vessels, coupled with which ones tended to be decorated, indicate that cups, many of the small jars, and a couple of types of larger bowls were used primarily for serving or eating food either by a group the size of a family or by individuals.

The Functions and Organization of Godin Period IV

The functions of Godin IV are presented through a series of artifact-distribution plans. Only artifacts in primary or secondary contexts were used. Information for most of these artifacts was obtained from lot sheet lists of discarded objects that did not provide a detailed description of individual objects. More detail was available on registry cards for those select objects that were registered and kept either in Tehran or at the ROM (for a complete list of registered objects see the T-Space Web archive, https://tspace.library.utoronto.ca).

Artifact Categories

A number of categories of artifacts appear on the distribution plans. For pottery, general functional categories (eating, serving, cooking, trays, and storage vessels) were used in the mapping. A few pottery-making tools such as burnishers were found, but there is no evidence for kilns.

Stone tools are divided into cores, waste flakes, flake and bifacial blades, and bifacial blades with use sheen that were probably used as sickles. As described in Chapter 4, there were two stone industries at Godin in Periods VI and IV represented by flakes tool and Canaanean blades. In a 2002 article, Edens argues that there is continuity from VI to IV in the technology. One distinct difference between the two technologies is that blade tools were made at Godin Period IV, as the find of a blade core demonstrates (Figure 5.30). There are clearly different sources for the flints and cherts used, although there is no evidence for a correlation between raw materials and flint-knapping techniques.

Metallurgy was an important craft in Godin IV. A pyrotechnic installation in the south-

Figure 5.30. Core for producing Canaanean blades

Figure 5.31. Godin IV blades. Different sources of flints are identified by their colours, relating to the minerals in their deposits.

western corner of building 8 of phase IV:1a seems to have been used for metallurgical activities. Smelting was already being practiced in the earlier Period VI at Godin and in Kangavar before Godin VI (see "Metallurgy of Godin Period VI" in Chapter 4, p. 105). As in Period VI, excavators recovered crucibles, some with slag attached. The sample of metal objects is small and few were preserved well enough for analysis.

Food production must have been a critical part of the activities conducted in Godin IV. The presence of sickle sheen on many of the stone blades and the location of many ETC sites in the rich valley bottom indicate that grain agriculture was a major part of the local economy and that the ETC residents at Godin were not predominantly pastoralists (Figure 5.34). Grinding stones used to process grain were found in some quantity at the site (Figure 5.35).

Pastoral products were also an important product of the Kangavar Valley. In Periods VI and IV sheep and goats (caprines) were the dominant species with cattle next in numbers (see "Animal Remains at Godin Period IV," p. 178). Pigs were rare, as were equids (probably donkeys and onagers).

Figure 5.32. A metal celt and wires from Godin IV

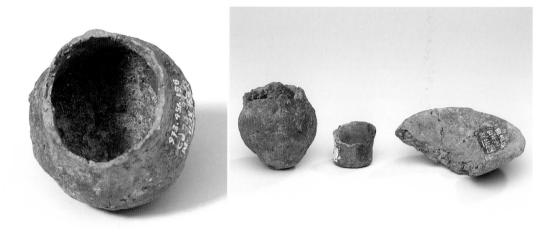

Figure 5.33. Godin IV crucibles used to smelt metal ore

Figure 5.34. Godin IV blades with sickle sheen

The strategy of exploiting domesticated animals in Godin IV was different from that of Godin VI. Whereas in Period VI animals appear to have been raised largely for meat, in Period IV they were being exploited for wool and hair, and killed only when they were older. If it is true that most of the animals were being raised outside of Godin, then there was either a transhumant element among Godin's residents or there were significant numbers of pastoral

Figure 5.35. Grinding stones used to process plant crops and minerals

nomad camps that the Kangavar Survey did not recover. The strategy of most pastoral no-mads is to preserve their capital in live animals by exploiting the renewable products (wool and milk) that their animals produce rather than meat.

Most of the recovered animal bones from Period IV were concentrated in and around building 3, and may be the remains of feasting on the older, non-productive animals of the herd.

The presence of wool and/or leather crafts can also be inferred by the tools used in conducting these activities. Three categories of artifact were probably involved: spindle whorls, bone awls, and burins. Spindle whorls are rounded weights through which a stick is passed. In the process of making the raw wool into yarn for weaving, the wool is attached to the stick and the spindle is spun with one hand

Figure 5.36. Bones tools from Godin IV

Animal Remains at Godin Period IV

Pam J. Crabtree

The sample of animal bone from Godin Period IV was relatively small. Caprines (sheep and goats) made up 85 percent of the total bone. Dental and epiphyseal patterns indicate that most of the caprines were killed when they were mature adults, including a number of quite elderly sheep and goats. The data are consistent with wool (or goat hair) production. In addition, there are almost no really young animals, which may be an indication that the caprines were being raised outside Godin. A number of two- to four-year-old animals appear to have been culled for meat, but many of the animals were mature and elderly. These animals either were culled from wool-producing flocks or were females that were no longer productive.

Additional data on the animal bone of Godin are available in the Godin Web archive at https://tspace.library.utoronto.ca.

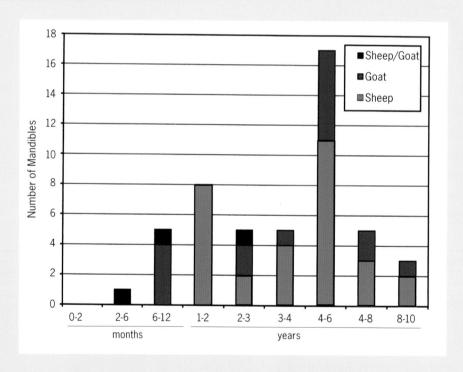

Figure 5.37. Bar chart of the ages when domestic sheep and goat were killed

Figure 5.38. Godin IV spindle whorls used for making yarn. Spindle whorl with protrusion may be a model wagon wheel.

as the wool is twisted with the other. Awls are used to pierce woven wool or hide for sewing, as are the sharper and stronger burins, which are blades that have been snapped at a forty-five-degree angle near one end. Awls and burins could be used for other tasks as well, but ethnographically, making clothing is among their most common uses.

Beads are few and are most significant because of the source of their materials. One bead of lapis lazuli was found in phase IV:1a. The only known source of lapis is Afghanistan. Unfortunately, the bead was found in removing walls, so it could be from an earlier period and could have been incorporated into a Period IV brick with the clay. Shell beads were also present in Period IV and are also unlikely to be local. This again implies inclusion in networks of exchange outside the local area.

Lastly, excavators recovered a number of animal figures. Figurines of sheep and cattle are ubiquitous across the region at the beginning of the third millennium BC (Early Bronze Age or Kura Araks II and III), both in the mountains and lowlands. Their

Figure 5.39. Beads of various materials recovered from Godin IV

Figure 5.40. Figurines from Godin IV

function is unclear; some scholars believe that they were toys, others identify them as religious icons. Their similarity and ubiquity would suggest that they are more than just toys and perhaps less than formal religious items. Another plausible explanation is their use in magic. Many such figurines appear broken in antiquity as some of the Godin figurines were. The sample at Godin is small, so a pattern of where these were found or how they were treated is hard to establish, but given their importance, some kind of spell for fertility would not be out of the question.

Artifact Distributions

Phase IV:2 was the earliest occupation of the Godin IV ETC peoples after initial contact in phase VI:1. As described above, this level is poorly documented. However, when the artifacts in the best contexts are assembled, they do give us a sense of what the occupants were doing. We know from field notes that structures were not formal mud-brick buildings. The few chineh (piled mud rather than individual bricks) walls appear to outline square as opposed to round buildings. Notes describe the presence of post holes, although excavators did not draw their pattern. These were in all likelihood wattle-and-daub constructions, much like those illustrated in Figure 5.13. In room 1, a series of adjacent bins and a hearth were found. This same combination would re-appear in subsequent phases.

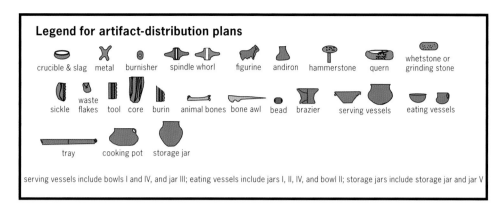

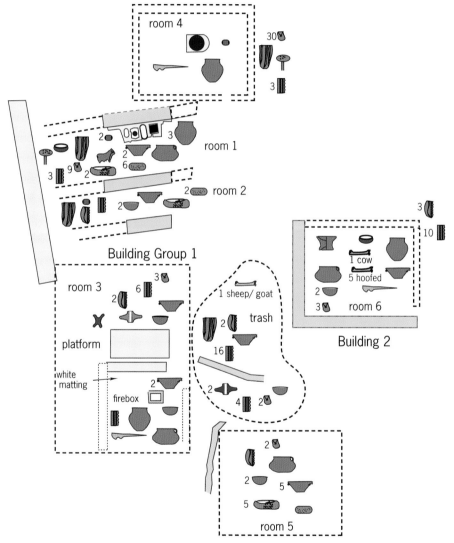

Figure 5.41. Distribution of artifacts in Godin IV:2. (Numbers beside artifacts indicate quantity of artifacts found.)

Put back into context, the artifacts appear to cluster into sets of similar functional types. Common to these clusters are grinding stones, cooking pots, and serving, eating, and storage vessels.

Craft activities are evident. Flint-knapping occurred in a number of places. Outside reconstructed room 4, waste flakes, a core, a hammerstone, and a few finished blades were deposited in a pit. Excavators recovered a similar set of core, waste, and bifacial flakes in rooms 1 and 3. Based on finds of crucibles, some with slag, in rooms 1 and 6, metallurgy was a common household activity. A brazier in room 6 suggests other pyrotechnic activities. A few spindle whorls indicate cloth-making.

Surprisingly little animal bone was recovered from phase IV:2. Bones include some cow, other ungulates, and a few sheep or goat. Sickles and storage bins are signs of agriculture.

Overall, phase IV:2 represents a settlement of Early Transcaucasian people. The Deep Sounding, a small Operation F at the lowest point of the mound in the south, and the Brick Kiln Cut all had ETC material. In fact, everywhere on the mound that excavators dug, they found ETC remains. What we have is therefore a small sample of a much larger settlement. Like the round-house phase at Yanik Tepe, the excavated buildings consisted of a set of undifferentiated households with very limited goods and very similar activities.

The residents of Godin IV:2 were clearly settled or at least transhumant people. Still, it is possible that these were not year-round occupations. They certainly grew grain crops,

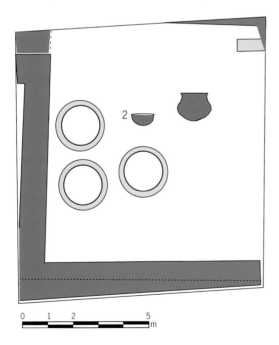

Figure 5.42. Plan and distribution of artifacts of Godin IV, Operation B, building 12. (Numbers beside artifacts indicate quantity of artifacts found.)

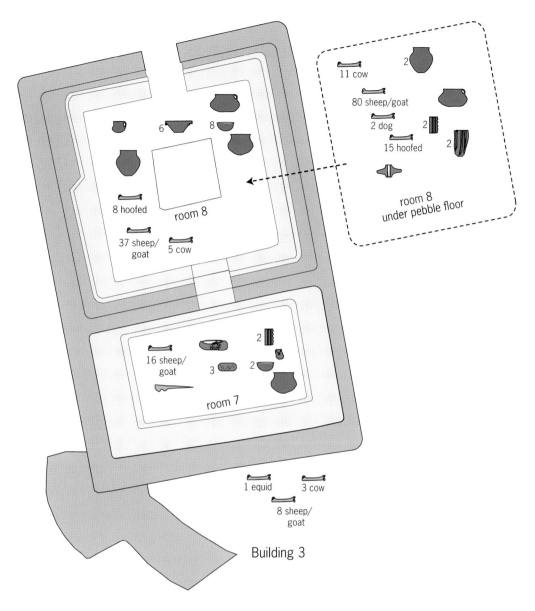

Figure 5.43. Distribution of artifacts in Godin IV:1b, building 3. (Numbers beside artifacts indicate quantity of artifacts found.)

raised domestic animals, and made tools of stone and metal. Their organization appears to have been simple and egalitarian, rather than ranked although, again, this conclusion is based on a small sample.

Godin phase IV:1b represents a significant change in the nature and role of the site. The core of this change is defined by the function of building 3 (Figures 5.3 and 5.43). Like the building with rooms 80, 83, and 88 of Level X at Pulur (Saykol) (Figure 5.11), this building is rectangular. It has an entrance on the short northern side and stairs to go from the first room (8) into the second room (7). Unlike the Pulur buildings, the more important activities appear to occur in the first room entered. That first room had black painted benches all the way around its interior. The northeastern wall had a painted design (Figure 5.10). In the centre was a low, raised platform, probably not an altar because field notes say nothing about burning, and the architect's notes imply that it was not much higher than 20 centimetres off of a pebbled floor. What is striking about the contents of the floor, as well as the area under the floor, is the quantity of animal bones, 158 in all. Most of these are sheep or goat bones (117), with 16 cow bones, 23 small-hoofed ungulate bones, and 2 dog bones. The floor area yielded one cooking pot, as well as serving, eating, and storage vessels. No other activities are indicated.

At more than 25 square metres, room 8 is by far the largest Godin IV enclosed space, in area comparable to the main room of Late Chalcolithic temples. Its size, decoration, structure, and contents indicate that the building served a public function, possibly as a place for ritual sacrifice or public feasting. After some minor remodelling, the contents of building 3 in phase IV:1a are almost the same, with 143 animal bones and cooking, serving, and eating vessels.

The adjoining room 7 has, in addition to more bones, tools one might use in food preparation: a quern, two cylindrical grinding stones and a grinding ball, a bone awl, and three flint cutting tools, as well as a couple of serving vessels and an eating bowl. Under the pebble floor were what appeared to be trash deposits, including a cooking pot, two serving vessels, a spindle whorl, two cores, two blades, and many animal bones. Oddly, excavators found no hearths or cooking ovens in the phase IV:1b version of building 3 although two hearths and a firebox were constructed in the front room during phase IV:1a.

The importance of this building is what it implies about the role of Godin Period IV. If phase IV:2 represents a set of egalitarian families, perhaps only seasonally occupying the mound, phase IV:1b is a permanent settlement, whose reach extends beyond the mound. Certainly, there were community or possibly valley-wide social rituals occurring on the mound. These would require a coordinating group. The fact, discussed above, that the animals may not have been raised by residents of Godin, suggests that Godin might have drawn mobile populations into the site for specialized activities.

The remaining buildings of Godin IV:1b appear to be small residences with sets of remains similar to building 1 of I phase V:2. In each small house there are cooking, serving and food-preparation tools, hearths, and storage bins, as well as sickles, spindle whorls, and some sheep or goat figurines.

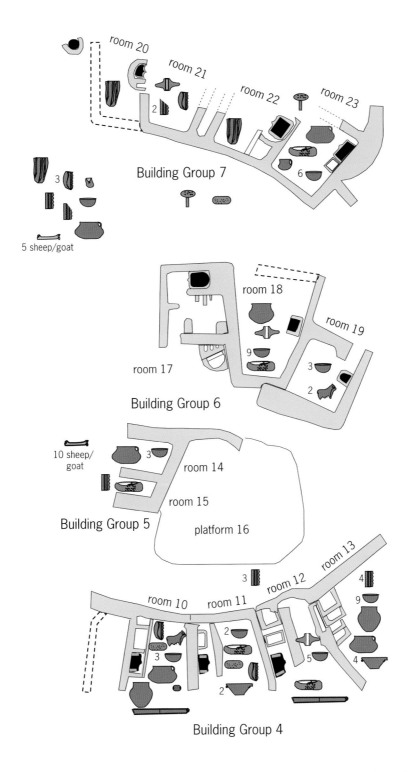

room 20
room 21
2
room 22
room 23
6
Building Group 7
3
5 sheep/goat

room 18
room 19
9
3
2
room 17
Building Group 6

10 sheep/goat
3
room 14
room 15
Building Group 5
platform 16
room 13
3
4
room 12
9
room 10
room 11
2
3
5
4
2
Building Group 4

Figure 5.44. Distribution of artifacts in Godin IV:1b, building groups 4–7. (Numbers beside artifacts indicate quantity of artifacts found.)

The lack of semi-circular andirons at Godin during phase IV:1b or 1a is surprising; the griddle hearths represent a very different solution to cooking. As is clear in Figure 5.29, the traditional horseshoe-shaped hearth was there, but a cover with a lip for drainage was added to the top. I am unaware of parallels to this type of cooking surface.

From what is really a relatively small area of a much larger mound, the picture of IV:1b that emerges is one in which most of the buildings and the activities occuring in them would be typical of any village. The residents very likely lived on the site year-round and were an established part of the local population. Building 3, however, indicates another level of organization.

Figure 5.45. Small buildings in Godin IV:1b

The last phase of Godin IV is IV:1a. Its major building (building 3) was the same as in IV:1b with what appear to be the same functions. A number of changes mark the building. The platform in the middle of room 8 must have been plastered over. Two hearths with associated fireboxes for ash were built in the northeast and southwest corners of the room. The bench along the east wall appears to have been built over and incorporated into the outside wall.

The building that was hardest to reconstruct and whose purpose is most unlike the other IV houses is building 8. The northern part was very haphazardly put together with a buttress of chineh on its northwestern edge and no apparent entrance. Room 26 contained items typical of a house, including an andiron stand. The southern part, room 24, does not seem connected to the northern rooms. It sits on the part of the mound that dips down dramatically. Two wide steps into room 24 may reflect the same mound topography. The contents of this room are also unusual. In the southwest, a fire installation consisting of three columns of clay filled with pebbles with shafts between each was constructed. The remains of three crucibles, two with pieces of crucible slag nearby, suggest that this was a metallurgical workshop. A hammerstone may also be part of the same manufacturing process, or may have been used on the lithic core also found there. Three benches adjoin what appears to be a craft-activity area. Making less sense are the large numbers of animal bone found in its general area. Given the wide area covered by the artifact lot in which they were found, I would suggest that they were discarded outside building 3, and therefore have little to do with the manufacturing going on in room 24.

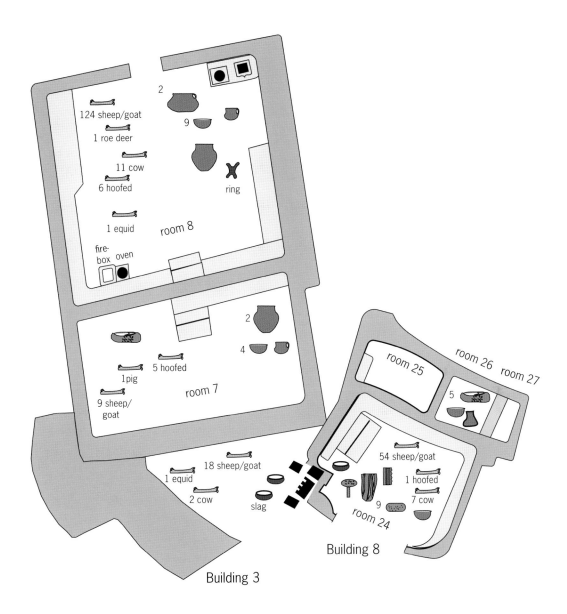

Figure 5.46. Distribution of artifacts in Godin IV:1a, buildings 3 and 8. (Numbers beside artifacts indicate quantity of artifacts found.)

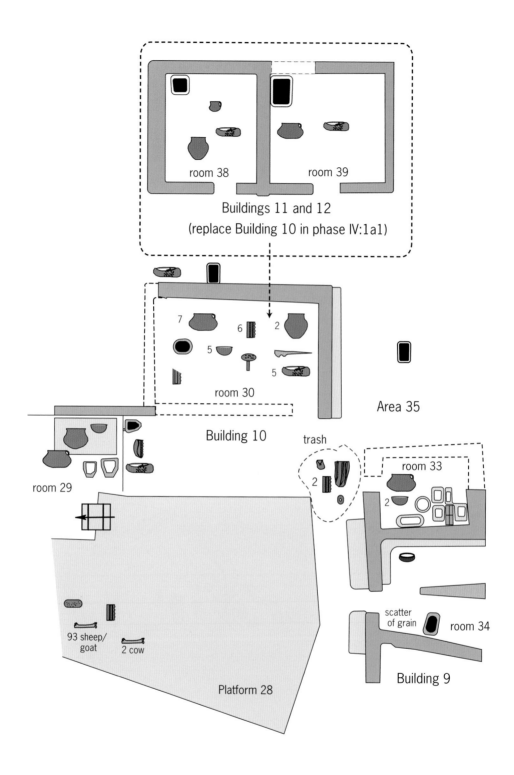

room 38

room 39

Buildings 11 and 12
(replace Building 10 in phase IV:1a1)

7

6 2

5

5

5

room 30

Building 10

Area 35

trash

2

room 33

2

room 29

room 34
scatter
of grain

93 sheep/
goat

2 cow

Platform 28

Building 9

Figure 5.47. Distribution of artifacts in Godin IV:1a1 and IV:1a2. (Numbers beside artifacts indicate quantity of artifacts found.)

Aside from the continuity of building 3, the rest of the architecture of Godin IV:1a was radically remodelled. The two sets of small buildings attached by a common curving wall in phase IV:1b were replaced. Building 9 with a fairly large single room was built with the bench outside the wall, a common feature in phase IV:1a. As in modern villages, the courtyard with a cooking hearth was perhaps a meeting area for a number of houses.

Adjoining building 9 was a white plastered brick platform. Its full extent is not clear. Along its western edge a set of stairs appears to lead into a room with a hearth, bins, and eating vessels. To its east, building 10 had two benches outside its western walls facing the platform. In general the platform has the characteristics of a public space, but we have no evidence to show how it was used.

Building 9, especially room 34, was mostly empty other than for an area of burned grain, in part because after the building fell out of use, the doors were blocked and it was filled in with bricks. Room 33, the northern room presumably of the same house, has the bins and the cooking and eating pots of a typical house; it was also bricked in. One section from the architect's drawing book of 1973 shows a wall of Period III built immediately on top of such a filled-in "platform."

Building 10 was replaced before the end of phase IV:1a. Its replacements, buildings 11 and 12, appear to be normal ETC houses.

Taken together, the remains of phase IV:1a appear similar to those of phase IV:1b in overall function. The group housing evident in the eastern buildings of IV:1b is missing and what looks like a formal workshop area with metallurgy is present. The platform, assuming it is not a foundation for Godin III buildings, suggests a distinct grouping as a coordinated set of buildings, with the public building 3 and the platform tying buildings 8, 9, and 10 into a cohesive unit. The position of this unit at the pinnacle of the mound suggests its possible role as a political and ritual centre.

Godin Period IV Pottery Designs

The most distinctive aspect of the pottery of Godin IV is its incised designs. Some analysts have suggested that these designs reflect woven designs on textiles that would not survive archaeologically; other researchers have proposed that the designs and generally the shapes reflect metal vessels. As discussed in Chapter 2, the relationship between cultural identity and artifact style is very complex, and archaeologists' attempts to use pottery design to differentiate identities within one cultural group have not always been successful. In some ethnographically known cultures, such as the Pueblo of the southwest United States, each small town has a pottery design tradition that is distinct from other towns. The designs of

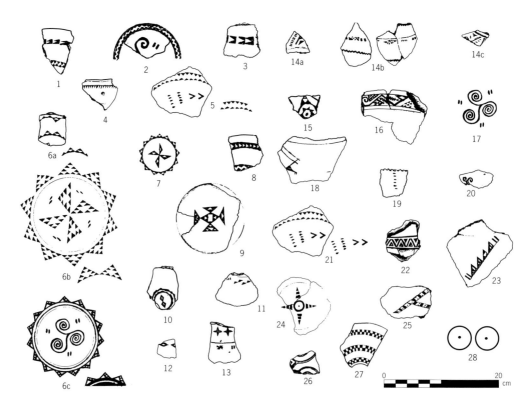

Figure 5.48. Incised designs on Godin IV pottery

Figure 5.49. Godin IV vessels with incised designs

Figure 5.50. Incised vessels   Figure 5.51. Incised base of Godin IV storage pot

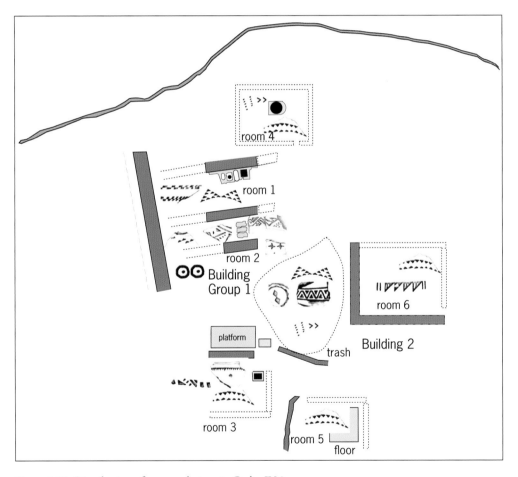

Figure 5.52. Distribution of pottery designs in Godin IV:2

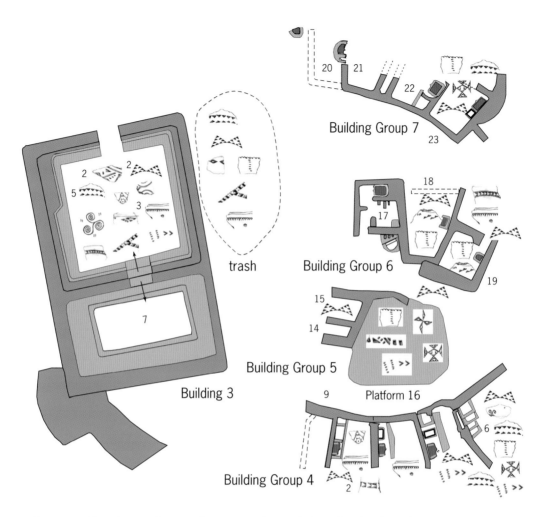

Figure 5.53. Distribution of pottery designs in Godin IV:1b. (Numbers beside artifacts indicate quantity of artifacts found.)

pottery from Godin IV, especially the ones more complicated than a squiggly line, may reflect such cultural identities.

Only sherds from primary and secondary contexts were used in this analysis. The distribution of pottery designs in phase IV:2 (Figure 5.52) shows commonalities, but mostly differences. The only design that occurs in most of the buildings of phase IV:2 is design 5. Otherwise the buildings appear to have different sets of designs, implying both individual household potters and some clear differentiation in the symbolic association of their occupants.

The distribution of designs in phase IV:1b is quite different from that of phase IV:2. Figure 5.53 shows a lot of commonality among all the separate buildings and open areas.

Building 3 contains a couple of designs not found in the other buildings, but they occur elsewhere in phase IV:2 or on a number of other vessels that are in unreliable contexts. This distribution seems to show that the residents of the mound had close cultural affinities. Whereas the residents of phase IV:2 appear to share few designs, the residents of phase IV:1b share a common set of identifiers. This makes a lot of sense if building 3 is an indication of a more complex society in which one chiefly group coordinated many of the activities of the residents of the site and the Kangavar Valley.

Pottery Parallels to Godin Period IV

One of the essential questions in the study of Godin Period IV is the origin of the site's residents. The best way to answer that question is to examine the origin of its shared pottery styles. Table 5.3 lists the comparisons of Godin IV pottery types as defined above with other ETC sites.

In addition to similarities in shape, design parallels can be used to determine the cultural affiliations of these people (Figure 5.48). Design 16 appeared on a bowl and a cup of phase VI:1, and then again on Type II rounded bowls in phase IV:2, but not thereafter (Figure 5.54). Its closest parallel is from the site of Baba Dervish in Azerbaijan along the Kura River in the Sharur Plain from the Naxçivan area of Azerbaijan. Another simple design appeared at Elar and Shengavit in Armenia, Pulur (Saykol) in Elâzig, and at Yanik Tepe. Some of these designs are highlighted by the inclusion of a white paste, possibly lime. Such lime inclusions are evidenced only at Yanik, Godin, and the Gilan site of Diarjan. Most of the parallels to Godin pottery designs are from Yanik Tepe. The round eyes, Godin design 28, is parallelled by Yanik type 13, Godin 12 by Yanik 18, Godin 25 by Yanik 43, Godin 15 by Yanik 51, Godin 18 possibly by Yanik 79, Godin 5 by Yanik 99, Godin 21 by Yanik 84, and Godin 22 by Yanik 123. The few published sherds from Diarjan in Gilan share Godin designs 1, 2, and 8.

Most of the comparisons therefore relate Godin IV to Yanik Tepe east of Lake Urmia and areas to its east in Iran. Where direct connections with Transcaucasia existed, they are mostly to the Ararat Valley in Armenia or southern Azerbaijan north of Iranian Azerbaijan. Type IV bowls show a possible relationship to Georgia, but only 4 Type IV bowls were found in our sample compared to 92 Type I bowls and 80 Type II bowls. Somewhat surprisingly, a significant number of comparanda relate Godin to sites along the Murat River, a tributary of the Upper Euphrates River, in Muş and Elâzig.

Table 5.3. Parallels to Godin IV ceramic types

Godin Type	Parallels to other sites
Bowls I,1	a–c = Yanik Tepe, Iran; Tepecik, Norsuntepe, and Avcili in Elâzig, Turkey; (with a handle) Shengavit, Armenia. d = Degirmentepe and Norguntepe in Elâzig, Pulur (Saykol), and various sites in Muş, Turkey.
Bowls I,2	Same as I,1.
Bowls II	a = Korucutepe in Elâzig, Turkey. b = Yanik Tepe, Iran. c = Pulur (Saykol), Degirmentepe, and various sites in Elâzig, Malatya, and Muş, Turkey. e = Yanik Tepe, Iran. f = Van, Turkey; Garni, Armenia.
Bowls III	Too generalized to compare to other sites.
Bowls IV	a & d = Elar and Metsamor, Armenia; Samshvilde and Kiketi, Georgia. b (lug, not bowl shape) = Korucutepe, Turkey. d = Yanik Tepe, Iran.
Cooking pots	Unclear from descriptions in other sources which are cooking pots.
Storage jars	Yanik Tepe, Iran; Karaz in Erzurum, Turkey; Asvan Kale, Könk, and Degirmentepe in Elâzig, Turkey.
Jars I	e = Degirmentepe, Korucutepe, Norsuntepe, Tepecik in Elâzig, Turkey. g = Baba Dervish, Azerbaijan.
Jars II	a = Shengavit, Armenia. g = Anı Kalesi in Kars, Karaz in Erzurum, Turkey; Geoy Tepe, Iran.
Jars III	a = Yanik Tepe, Karaz and Cinis Höyük in Erzurum, Turkey. b = Yanik Tepe, Iran. c = Ernis, Iremir, Van, Turkey. e = Kvaskhelebi, Georgia. g = Yanik Tepe, Iran.
Jars IV	b = Yanik Tepe, Iran. e = Iremir, Van, Turkey.
Jars V	Rims only.
Cups	d (shape not size) = Amiranis, Gora, Georgia.
Lids	Yanik Tepe, Iran. Various sites, Georgia. Various sites in Erzurum and Elâzig, Turkey.

Presumably, these comparanda imply that ETC people followed one of a number of routes into the central western Zagros. The most important one was along the eastern side of Lake Urmia and down through the Zagros mountain front (see Chapter 3). This would have been part of the same pathway that brought lapis lazuli from Afghanistan over the central desert of Iran, the Dasht-i Kavir, past sites in Gilan mentioned above with Godin IV pottery. Another route must be from eastern Turkey, connecting with the north-south route.

Conclusions

What then is the larger picture that the remains of Godin IV paint?

ETC people came to the central western Zagros in the Kura Araks II period long after they first migrated to Malatya (the site of Arslantepe) and a bit later than the first migrants arrived in Muş, Yanik Tepe, and the other Lake Urmia area sites. The residents of Godin were in effect a second or third generation, coming not directly from the homeland, but from the diaspora of ETC migrants.

Figure 5.54. Incised vessels from Godin VI:1 and Godin IV:2 with variations of design 16

Godin was the farthest south and east that ETC populations moved. They came along the High Road from Hamadan—Cuyler Young once described Sangalan Tepe in Hamadan as one of the biggest mounds he ever saw—and stopped at Godin.

The pull toward this most southerly expansion of ETC culture in the Iranian Zagros is best explained by the expanding exchange networks, as was the case for Arslantepe. There is some evidence in Godin IV:1a of a sizeable, specialized metallurgical workshop, but excavators found no specialized craft area before IV:1a, at least in the small sample of the mound that they explored. In the absence of such craft-making, controlling one part of the trading network by controlling the High Road would seem the likely focus of immigrants. At the same time, the availability of good pasture and agricultural land must have been part of what drew them to Kangavar. Stephen Batiuk's proposal, in our joint 2007 article, that this represented a founder effect, in which new leaders would set out into new territory to establish their own colony, seems plausible for this case. I envision a few hundred clan members setting off on such a trek as the likely scenario for these migrants.

At the same time, there are elements of this Zagros migration that appear quite different

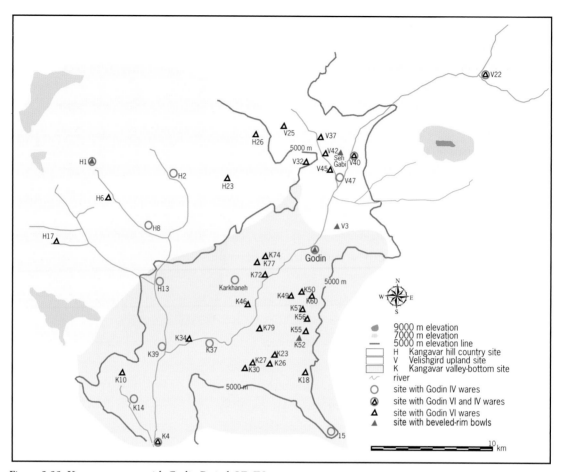

Figure 5.55. Kangavar survey with Godin Periods VI–IV sites

from that in eastern Turkey. The pattern there was incorporation into already existing local centres, and the occupation of outlying areas, so that a smaller percentage of the centre's pottery would reflect those of ETC ethnicity, whereas the majority of residents were still locals. Small outlying settlements yielded purely ETC pottery and other evidence of their ethnic style. In Kangavar, the central site appears to be entirely ETC. The other sites are also entirely ETC. They are scattered among the valley bottom and uplands at regular intervals. Most of the occupied hectares are represented by just two sites, Godin and Karkhaneh (18 out of 30.61 hectares). This is not the eastern Turkish pattern. Nor is it a lowland pattern where central sites are surrounded by many small village and town satellites.

As I described their basic subsistence above, ETC peoples had elements of settled village life, pastoral nomadism, and transhumance. The suggestion in earlier articles, including my own, was that pastoral nomads were a major part of the migrating population. We should, perhaps, visualize another social arrangement that combines all these elements; this would have involved smaller clans of a few hundred people who migrated as conditions impelled. Medieval and later historical Europe saw a number of these kinds of groups. They, too, were known for retaining their ethnic identities.

What happened to the local population when these migrants arrived? The total population of Period IV as represented in occupied mounds is almost identical to that of Period VI (30.24 versus 30.61 hectares for IV), but less than half the 73.45 hectare total in Period III (although since Period III lasted more than four times longer than Period IV, we would expect to find many more settlements associated with Godin III pottery types). Only three Period IV sites other than Godin were built on top of Period VI sites; each of those was at the north, south, and east entryway to the valley, as if guarding its gates. Although there is no direct evidence, a case can be made that a number of the former Period VI residents remained in their villages, cut off from all but the ETC world. They may therefore have retained their local potting traditions. This does not mean that there was an invasion, as some have proposed. The absence of weapons, walls, or other signs of defence suggests a peaceful and symbiotic relationship. Perhaps some of the remaining natives even adopted ETC potting traditions.

As at Norşuntepe, a degree of centralization and probably of rank is evident in building 3 of Godin phases IV:1a and IV:1b with its many discarded animal bones. Feasting may have been a mechanism to unite the valley under ETC coordination. The trajectory of change exemplified by Godin in the Zagros raises interesting questions about the nature of its society.

Certainly as the dawning of Period III approached, Kangavar was readily incorporated into the new cultural and political system of the Proto-Elamites, maintaining much of what must have been a common adaptation that continued from Period VI.

Godin shared some of the cultural change typical of the ETC migration, but the site displayed some rather different elements as well. New surveys and new excavations in this region should be able to explain this phenomenon better.

Godin Period IV Pottery Typology

Conical Bowls

Type I, 1

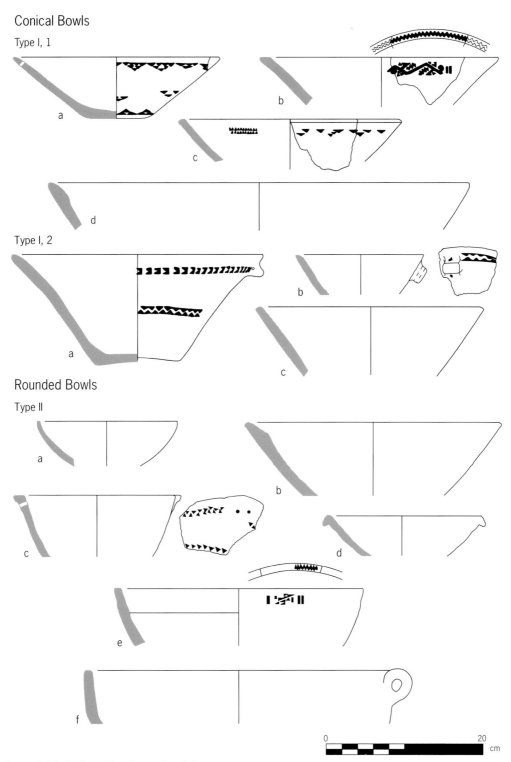

Type I, 2

Rounded Bowls

Type II

Figure 5.56. Godin IV bowl types I and II

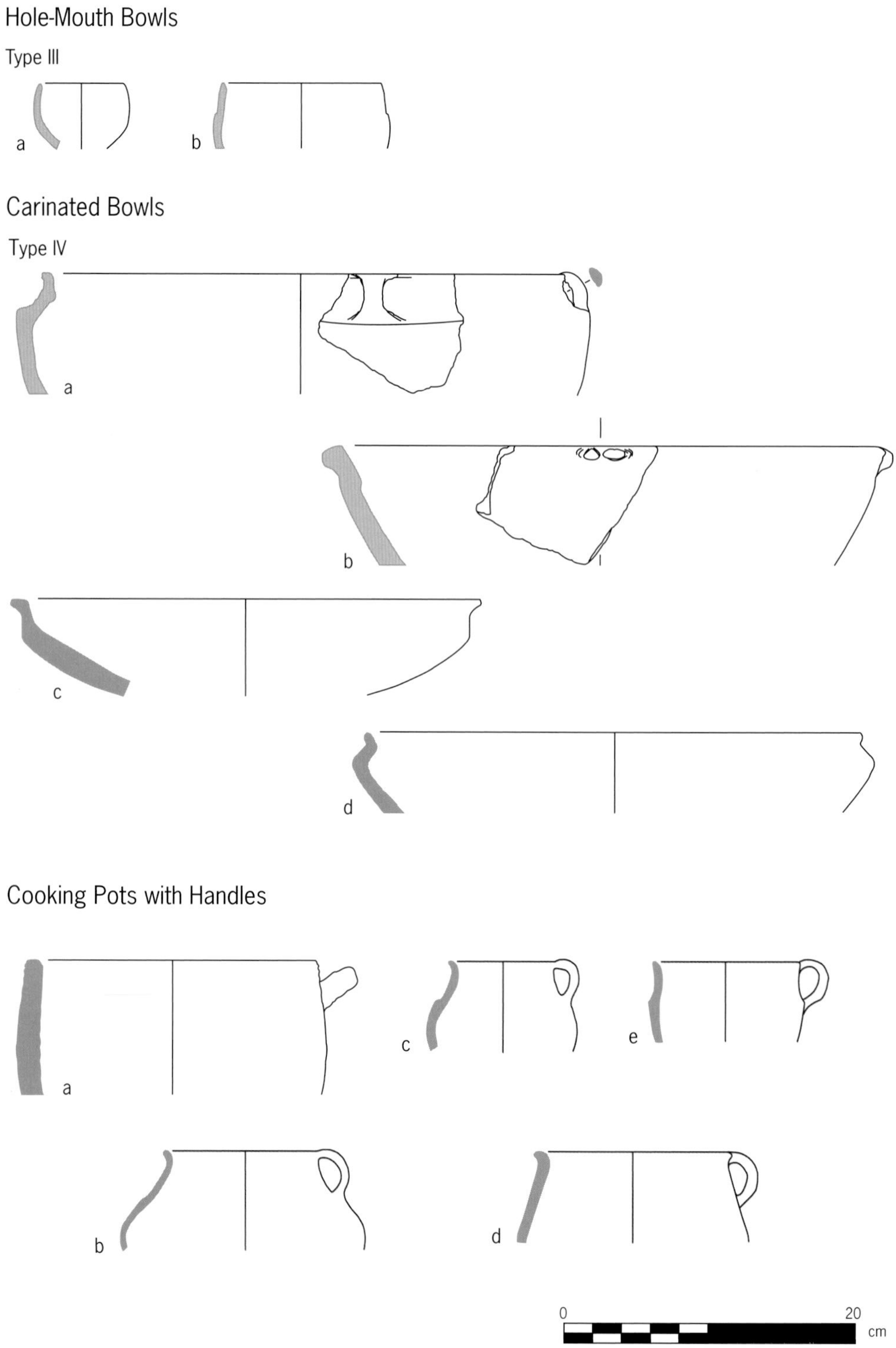
Hole-Mouth Bowls
Type III
a
b
Carinated Bowls
Type IV
a
b
c
d
Cooking Pots with Handles
a
c
e
b
d
0
20
cm

Figure 5.57. Godin IV bowl Types III and IV, and cooking-pot types with handles

Cooking Pots without Handles

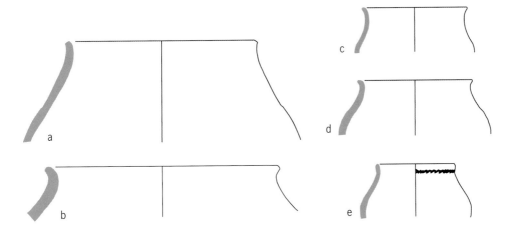

Storage Jars

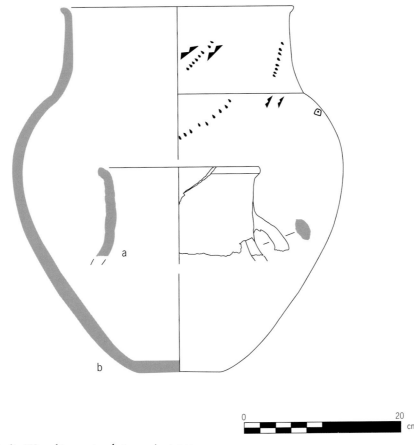

0   20
cm

Figure 5.58. Godin IV cooking-pot and storage-jar types

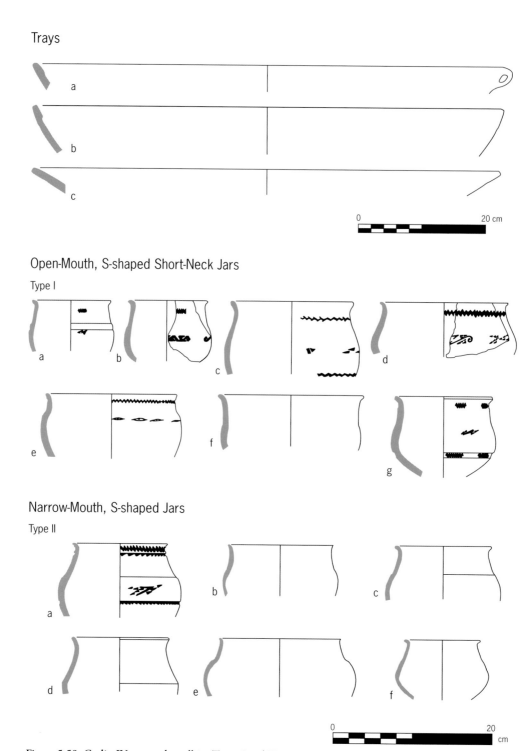

Trays

Open-Mouth, S-shaped Short-Neck Jars
Type I

Narrow-Mouth, S-shaped Jars
Type II

Figure 5.59. Godin IV tray and small jar Types I and II

Taller, Pointed-Base Jars

Type III

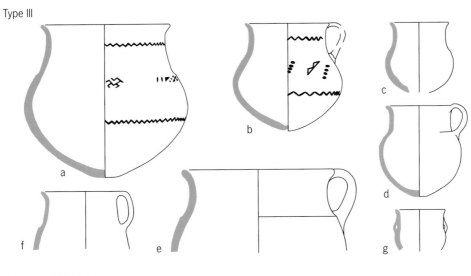

Straight-Sided Jars

Type IV

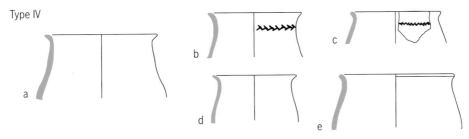

Miscellaneous Jar Rims, Shape Unknown

Type V

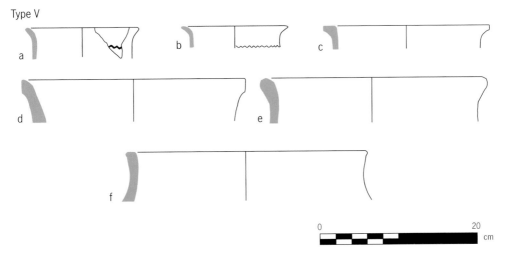

Figure 5.60. Godin IV jar Types III–V

Storage Jars

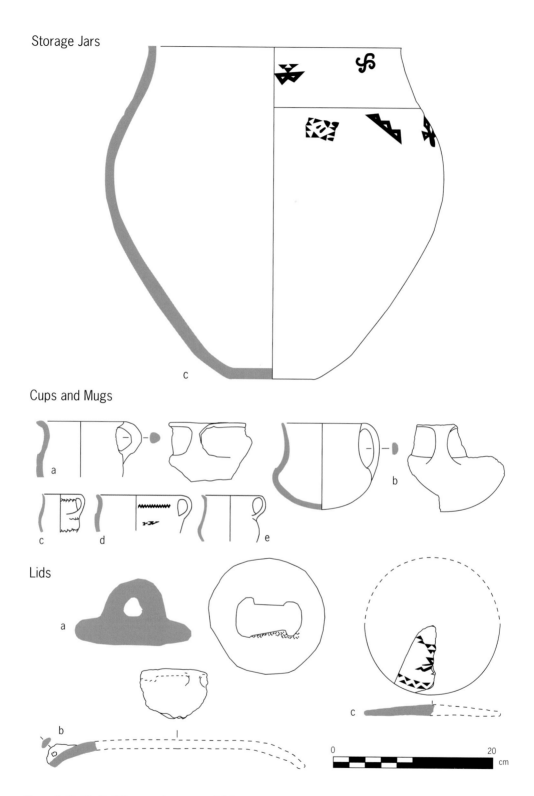

Cups and Mugs

Lids

Figure 5.61. Godin IV storage jar, cup, and lid types

Further Reading

Note: Additional references are available in the Godin Web archive at https://tspace.library.utoronto.ca.

Abay, Eşref. "The Expansion of Early Transcaucasian Culture: Cultural Interaction or Migration?" *Altrientalische Forschungen* 32, no. 1 (2005): 115–131.

Amiran, R., "Yanik Tepe, Shengavit, and the Khirbet Kerak Ware." *Anatolian Studies* 15 (1965): 165–167.

Anthony, David. "Prehistoric Migration as a Social Process." In *Migrations and Invasions in Archaeological Explanation,* edited by J. Chapman and H. Hamerow, 21–32. Oxford: British Archaeological Reports S664, 1997.

———"The Bath Refilled: Migration in Archaeology Again." *American Anthropologist* 94, no. 1 (1992): 174–176.

———"Migration in Archaeology: The Baby and the Bathwater." *American Anthropologist* 92, no. 4 (1990): 895–914.

Areshian, Gregory. "Early Bronze Age Settlements in the Ararat Plain and its Vicinity." *Archäologisches Mitteilungen aus Iran und Turan* 37 (2006): 71–88.

Batiuk, Stephen, and Mitchell Rothman. "Unraveling Migration, Trade, and Assimilation." *Expedition* 49, no. 1 (2007): 7–17.

Burney, Charles. "Hurrians and Proto-Europeans: The Ethnic Context of Early Trans-Caucasian Culture." In *Anatolia and the Ancient Near East: Studies in Honor of Tahsin Özgüç,* edited by K. Emre, B. Hrouda, M. Mellink, and N. Özgüç, 45–51. Ankara: Türk Tarih Kurumu Basımevi, 1989.

———. "Circular Buildings Found at Yanik Tepe, North-West Iran." *Antiquity* 35 (1961): 237–240.

Burney, Charles, and David Lang. *The Peoples of the Hills: Ancient Ararat and Caucasus.* London: Weidenfeld and Nicolson, 1971.

Cribb, Roger. *Nomads in Archaeology.* Cambridge: Cambridge University Press, 1991.

DiNocera, Gian Maria. "Mobility and Stability: Preliminary Observations on Early Bronze Age Settlement Organization in the Malatya Plain." *Archäologische Mitteilungen aus Iran und Turan* 37 (2006): 63–70.

Earle, Timothy. *Chiefdoms: Power, Economy, and Ideology.* Cambridge: Cambridge University Press, 1991.

Edens, Christopher. "Small Things Forgotten? Continuity Amidst Change at Godin Tepe. *Iranica Antiqua* 37 (2002): 31–46.

Fahimi, Hamid. "Kura-Araxes Type Pottery from Gilan and the Eastern Extension of the Early Transcaucasian Culture." *Archäologisches Mitteilungen aus Iran und Turan* 37 (2006): 123–132.

Frangipane, Marcella, and Alba Palmieri. "Cultural Developments at Arslantepe at the Beginning of the Third Millennium: The Settlements of Period VIB." *Origini* 12 (1983): 523–574.

Frangipane, Marcella, and Giovanni Siracusano. "Changes in Subsistence in East Anatolia during the 4th and 3rd Millennia BC." In *Man and the Animal World,* edited by P. Anreiter, L. Bartosiewicz, E. Jerem, and W. Meid, 237–246. Budapest: Archaeolingua,1998.

Henrickson, Robert. "The Buff and the Grey: Ceramic Assemblages and Cultural Process in the Third Millennium BC Central Zagros, Iran." In *Cross-Craft and Cross-Cultural Interactions in Ceramics,* volume 4, edited by M. McGovern, M. Notis, and W. Kingery, 81–146. Westerville, OH: American Ceramic Society, 1989.

Howell-Meurs, Sarah. "Exploitation of Upland and Lowland Environments: Early Bronze and Iron Age Sites From Eastern Turkey." *World Archaeological Bulletin* 10. http://www.worldarchaeologicalcongress.org/site/bulletin/wab10/Howell.php.

Kiguradze, Tamaz, and Antonio Sagona. "On the Origins of the Kura-Araxes Cultural Complex." In *Archaeology in the Borderlands: Investigations in Caucasia and Beyond*, edited by Adam Smith and Karen Rubinson, 38–94. Los Angeles: the Cotsen Institute of Archaeology, UCLA, 2003.

Kohl, Philip. *The Making of Bronze Age Eurasia.* Cambridge World Archaeology Series. Cambridge: Cambridge University, 2007.

Koşay, Hamit. *Keban Project Pulur Excavations 1968–70.* Keban Project, Series III, 1. Ankara: Middle East Technical University, 1976.

Kozbe, Gülriz. "Activity Areas and Social Organization within Early Trans-caucasian Houses at Karagündüz Höyük, Van." In *A View from the Highlands: Archaeological Studies in Honour of Charles Burney*, edited by Antonio Sagona, 35–53. Herent, Belgium: Peeters, 2004.

Kramer, Carol. *Village Ethnoarchaeology: Rural Iran in Archaeological Perspective*. New York: Academic Press, 1982.

Kushnareva, K. Kh. *The South Caucasus in Prehistory*. Philadelphia: University Museum Publications, 1997.

Mason, Robert, and Lisa Cooper. "Grog, Petrography, and Early Transcaucasians at Godin Tepe." *Iran* 37 (1999): 25–31.

Morphy, H. "On Representing Ancestral Beings." In *Animals into Art*, edited by H. Morphy, 144–160. London: Unwin Hyman, 1989.

Palumbi, Giulio, "Red-Black Pottery: Eastern Anatolian and Transcaucasian Relationships around the Mid-Fourth Millennium BC." *Ancient Near Eastern Studies* 40 (2003): 80–134.

Renfrew, Jane. "Food and Feasting in Antiquity." Review of *Food, Cuisine and Society in Prehistoric Greece*, by Paul Halstead and John C. Barrett, eds.; *The Mycenaean Feast*, by James C. Wright, ed.; and *Food in the Ancient World*, by John M. Wilkins and Shaun Hill. *Antiquity* 80, no. 310 (2006): 1000–1003.

Rothman, Mitchell, and Gülriz Kozbe. "Muş in the Early Bronze Age." *Anatolian Studies* 47 (1997): 105–126.

Rothman, Mitchell. "Ripples in the Stream: Transcaucasia-Anatolian Interaction in the Murat/Euphrates Basin at the Beginning of the Third Millennium B.C." in *Archaeology in the Borderlands: Investigations in Caucasia and Beyond*, edited by Adam Smith and Karen Rubinson, 95–110. Los Angeles: Cotsen Institute of Archaeology, UCLA, 2003.

———. "Style and Adaptation along the Turkish-Iranian Borderland." In *Yeki Bud Yeki Nabud: Essays in Honor of William Sumner*, edited by Naomi Miller and Kaymer Abdi, 207–216. Los Angeles: Cotsen Institute of Archaeology, UCLA, 2003.

———. Environmental and Cultural Factors in the Development of Settlement in a Marginal, Highland Zone. In *The Archaeology of Jordan and Beyond: Essays in Honor of James A. Sauer*, edited by L. E. Stager, J. A. Greene, and M. D. Coogan, 429–443. Winona Lake, Indiana: Eisenbrauns, 2000.

Rouse, Irving. *Migrations in Prehistory*. New Haven: Yale University Press, 1986.

Sagona, Antonio. "Social Boundaries and Ritual Landscapes in Late Prestoric Trans-Caucasus and Highland Anatolia." In *A View from the Highlands: Archaeological Studies in Honour of Charles Burney*, edited by Antonio Sagona, 475–538. Herent, Belgium: Peeters, 2004.

———. "Social Identity and Religious Ritual in the Kura-Araxes Cultural Complex: Some Observations from Sos Höyük." *Mediterranean Archaeology* 11 (1998): 13–25.

———. "Settlement and Society in Late Prehistoric Trans-Caucasus." In *Between the Rivers and Over the Mountains*, edited by M. Frangipane, Harald Hauptmann, Mario Liverani, P. Matthiae, and Machteld Mellinck, 453–476. Rome: Universitá di Roma "La Sapienza," 1993.

———. *The Caucasian Region in the Early Bronze Age*. Oxford: BAR, 1984.

Smogorzewska, Anna. "Andirons and Their Role in Early Transcaucasian Culture." *Anatolica* 30 (2004): 151–177.

Summers, Geoffrey. "Yanik Tepe and the Early Transcaucasian Culture: Problems and Perspectives." In *A View from the Highlands: Archaeological Studies in Honour of Charles Burney*, edited by Antonio Sagona, 617–643. Herent, Belgium: Peeters, 2004.

Watson, Patty Jo. *Archaeological Ethnography in Western Iran*. Viking Fund Publications in Anthropology 57. Tucson: University of Arizona Press, 1979.

Whiting, John, and Barbara Ayres. "Inferences from the Shape of Dwellings." In *Settlement Archaeology*, edited by K. C. Change, 117–133. Palo Alto, CA: National Press Books, 1968.

Young, Cuyler. The Kangavar Survey: Periods VI to IV. In *A View from the Highlands: Archaeological Essays in Honour of Charles Burney*, edited by Antonio Sagona, 645–660. Herent, Belgium: Peeters, 2004.

Young, T. Cuyler, Jr. *Excavations at Godin Tepe: First Progress Report*. Royal Ontario Museum Occasional Paper 17. Toronto: Royal Ontario Museum, 1969.

6 | The Godin Period III Town

Robert C. Henrickson

The Šimaškian knows neither his god nor those elected priestesses. His soldiers are numerous like grass; his seed is widespread. He who lives in tents, who does not know of the places of the gods: like a wild beast which mounts, he knows nothing of flour and the offering of prayers. The evil namtar demon and the distressing asag demon do not approach him. Who [does not utter] a divine oath is committing sacrilege, yet his troops are in good health.

—Sîn-iddinam, King of Mesopotamia, describing the inhabitants of the Zagros Mountains

Godin Tepe was perhaps the largest settlement (15–20 hectares) in the highlands of central western Iran from the mid-third through mid-second millennium BC; the stratified sequence of architecture and associated artifacts is unmatched in the region. Analysis of the Period III occupation at this site, and in the surrounding Kangavar Valley, yields insights into socio-economic and political developments on both the settlement and regional levels. Regional surveys supplement the results from excavations.

My discussion will move outward from the site and its excavation to the regional context. The architectural history of the settlement provides a framework for the local economy. Tracing the development of the Godin III ceramic tradition and examining the structure of the potter's craft, provide the basis for looking at regional trends and the relationship of the Godin III cultural area to the larger world.

Godin Period III Architecture

Excavation of Period III remains at Godin Tepe was concentrated in the Deep Sounding, a 500–700 square metre exposure in the area of the ancient and modern summit of the mound. Six major phases of Period III occupation, designated phase III:6 (the earliest) to phase III:1 (the latest), were distinguished in the 7–9 metre depth of deposit. Each had a distinctive character, but a tendency toward ever denser occupation is evident through the first several phases. The following are some very general time ranges for these phases.

phase III:1	post–1400 BC
phase Post–III:2	1600–1400 BC
phase III:2	1900–1600 BC
phase III:3	1900 BC
phase III:4	2100–1900 BC
phase III:5	2400–2200 BC
phase III:6	2600–2400 BC

The persistent, basic physical organization of the settlement, as defined by road paths and building orientations, suggests a marked continuity of occupation at the site as a whole. The general trends in the changing character of the settlement at Godin Tepe are parallelled in regional survey data, which put this central settlement into context within the Kangavar Valley.

The excavated sequence in the Deep Sounding does not represent continuous occupation. Instead, each phase comprises one or more distinct, superimposed architectural configurations consisting mostly of domestic structures. Intervals of localized abandonment marked by erosion surfaces and stratigraphic discontinuities separate the phases. In the patchwork of replacement and change, as many as twelve superimposed architectural levels and sub-levels were distinguished in the eastern portion of the excavation. Allowing 30–50 years as the average use-life of mud-brick domestic structures, as is typical for such buildings in the region today, the excavated sequence represents perhaps 360–600 cumulative years of occupation. Since the Godin III period lasted roughly 1,200 years, the excavated portion of the settlement at Godin Tepe—that in the Deep Sounding—lay unoccupied for at least half of that period. In effect, the excavation reveals a series of discrete episodes in the life of the settlement.

Several lines of inference, however, suggest that occupation may have been essentially continuous at Godin Tepe as a whole. Repeated piecemeal abandonments, and later re-occupations, of areas within traditional Near Eastern settlements are typical. Furthermore, the area of the Deep Sounding was the summit of a large mound even in antiquity. Today, when traditional villages are built on mounds, settlement tends to concentrate on the perimeter and lower slopes, while the summit is often left unoccupied. Aerial photos of Karkhaneh, the second largest mound in the Kangavar Valley, illustrate this process over thirty years. In the 1930s, a dense band of household compounds extended across the top of the mound. By the 1960s, however, this band lay abandoned; occupation had shifted onto the slopes on either side of the band, spread to the surrounding plain, and become somewhat less dense. Thus, although the summit of a mound may be a poor place to seek a continuous sequence of occupation, it is probably a reasonable place to search for phases or periods of particular size or growth within a settlement.

At Godin, the summit area in the Deep Sounding was at various times an important component of the Godin III settlement, on its periphery, or abandoned while occupation may have continued elsewhere on the site. Only a few of the architectural plans from the many sub-phases of III can be presented here although all plans are available in the Godin web archive (https://tspace.library.utoronto.ca). The earliest Godin III occupation probably lay outside the Deep Sounding, on the perimeter or lower slopes of the mound left by earlier periods of occupation. Phase III:6 was long-lived, with considerable diversity of architecture. In phase III:5 at least part of the settlement lay on the north slope of the mound and barely extended into the area of the Deep Sounding, onto the very summit of the mound. Most is now lost to erosion by the river there. Later, in phase III:4, the area was a prosperous neighbourhood within the settlement. The following phase III:3 occupation seems to have lain on the southern slope of the mound, outside the area of the Deep Sounding. In phase III:2 the area was again part of a neighbourhood with sizeable houses. The settlement as a whole may have reached its largest size at this time. The remains of phase III:1 are badly disturbed by weathering due to prolonged abandonment and construction activity during the later Period II occupation.

Despite the lack of continuity of occupation within the area of the Deep Sounding itself, the persistence of the basic organization of the settlement from phase to phase indicates long-term continuity of occupation at the site as a whole, which must be anchored by continuing occupation in adjacent areas. The longest-lasting feature was "Avenue Road," a modest roadway which ran through the southeastern corner of the Deep Sounding during at least three distinct phases of occupation (phases III:6–4), spanning more than 500 years. A final echo may even appear in the early phase III:2 occupation. On a more localized level, the persistence of building orientations, property lines between households, and wall lines from phase to phase provides further support for continuity. This is most marked between phases III:5 and III:4, where building orientations and even major wall lines are repeated north of Avenue Road. Finally, the southern edge of the settlement served as a cemetery through much of the Godin III period (burials were found from phases III:6, 4, 2). These considerations, taken together, support the proposed general continuity of occupation at the site.

Villages fulfill many functions: shelter, workplace, and social and cultural setting. Probable functions of individual rooms and areas may be inferred from built-in features, such as hearths and bins, characteristic types of pottery vessels, other artifacts, location and access relative to other rooms, and other attributes. Ethnographic and ethnoarchaeological fieldwork on traditional architecture suggests further distinctive features of various types of rooms. Living rooms have well-plastered walls and floors; further decoration, such as whitewash, is typical. Kitchens have hearths, some storage facilities (permanent or movable), and equipment for cooking. Storerooms usually have roughly finished walls and floors, and provision for bulk storage. Due to the limited area of excavation (at least relative to house

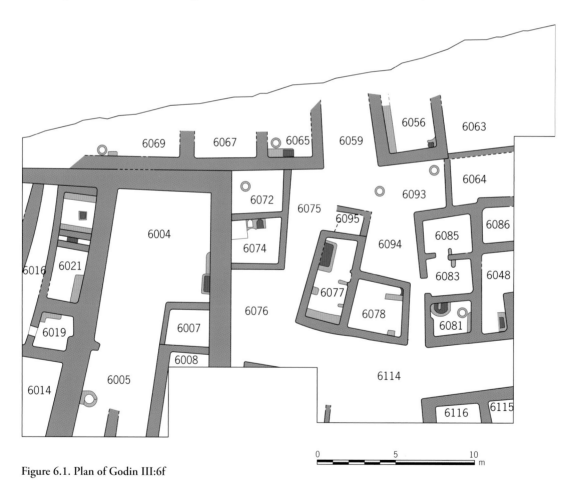

Figure 6.1. Plan of Godin III:6f

size), and the typically irregular outline of Near Eastern village houses, however, only parts of many households may be excavated; preservation can affect interpretation as well. The full range of possible room types may not be recovered or identifiable in each phase.

Each phase of the Godin Period III occupation had a distinctive nature. The changing scale, character, and associated features and artifacts in the buildings recovered in the various occupational phases of the Deep Sounding illuminate the character of an area within the settlement. Architectural changes in this relatively limited area of the site suggest socio-economic developments similar to those reflected by regional settlement patterns. Let us now turn to the architectural and stratigraphic sequence in more detail, since this provides the foundation for reconstructing social and cultural developments. Only a limited selection of plans can be illustrated, presenting some of the most complete and coherent configurations.

Phase III:6 makes up by far the deepest deposit of any phase in the Deep Sounding on the summit of the mound (Figure 6.1). Whereas during the other phases of Godin III

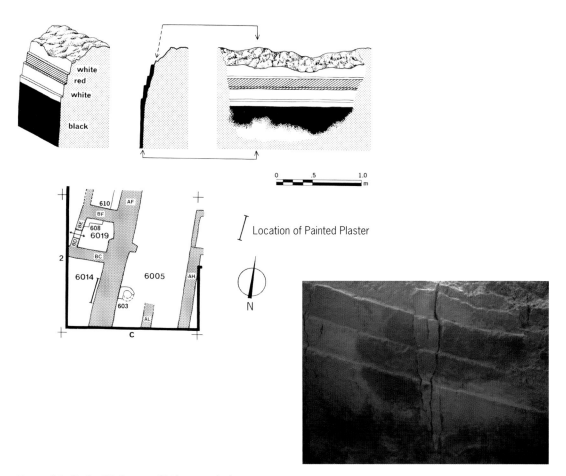

Figure 6.2. Godin III:6, room 6014, painted plaster

townspeople sometimes temporarily abandoned the summit in favour of the lower slopes, during Godin III:6, occupation of the excavation area was more or less continious. The early structures stand in stark contrast to one another. In the eastern portion of the Deep Sounding, a small household compound consisting of several blocks of two to three small rooms gradually coalesced; eventually a light courtyard wall enclosed the unit. It would not be out of place in a traditional modest, low-density village today. Yet less than 10 metres away to the west, the other half of the Deep Sounding is occupied by the Western Complex. Although an area of almost 300 square metres was cleared, the plan suggests that much additional area remained unexcavated. The major walls, set into foundation trenches more than a metre deep, were more than 1.5 metres thick, heavier than any other Godin III structure of any phase. In the southwest corner, a large block of fallen mud-brick wall was finely plastered and painted. Features in the row of rooms at the west, such as ledges and hearths, suggest use of that area for habitation rather than storage. The eastern half was simply open space. Although its plan, sheer size, and position on the summit and upper western slope of the mound suggest considerable importance, the role of this major complex remains uncertain. Artifacts were interchangeable with those from the modest households to the east; no metal or finely finished objects were found. The complex may have been involved with trade.

A second massive structure was built to the north (North Building), but it is almost completely lost to later erosion of the mound face by the river. Open space along the east face of the Western Complex gradually filled with the opportunistic construction of a house in the corner formed by the two major buildings.

As the phase III:6 occupation continued, the eastern household compound was renovated and rebuilt. More notably, however, the Western Complex was gradually abandoned. Modest domestic structures were built over part of its former area, incorporating parts of the massive walls as foundations and lower courses. This old neighbourhood clearly lost importance as the focus of occupation moved elsewhere on the mound. As the settlement aged, the architecture in the area of the Deep Sounding became more modest and socio-economically homogeneous. Phase III:6 ended in gradual abandonment of the area following a decline in the size and quality of architecture there.

During Godin III:6, the relatively diffuse settlement at Godin Tepe lay in the centre of numerous small settlements scattered throughout the valley and surrounding hill country. Given the length of the phase and the small size (less than 2 hectares) of all but the central two settlements (Godin and Karkhaneh), not all of these outlying settlements are likely to have been contemporaneous. Thus, small settlements scattered on the valley floor and in the hill country characterized the initial phase of the Godin III occupation in the Kangavar Valley.

Most of the area of the Deep Sounding lay abandoned long enough in late phase III:6 for the architecture to decay until probably no wall remained standing. The local high point of the mound lay in the northern half of the Deep Sounding, with a slope downward to the south. The persistent village lane in the southeast lay at a considerably lower elevation than the summit.

The phase III:5 occupation adapted to these contours and used only the relatively flat summit of the mound at the north. Phase III:5 structures continued to the north, on the part of the mound now lost to erosion by the river, judging from the incomplete rooms. The sloping southern half of the Deep Sounding probably lay vacant. The southern ends of southern rooms are lost to the later phase III:4 construction activities, but if the rooms had extended much further southward, there would have been problems with the downward slope. Three basic structural units may be distinguished based on doorways and solid walls. These divisions continue into the following phase (III:4). The phase III:5 occupation was relatively brief, judging from the limited architectural change, and ended in an abrupt destruction. At least half a metre of bricky collapse filled the rooms and courtyards, covering dozens of pottery vessels smashed on the floors. Abundant charcoal, apparently not from fire associated with the destruction, was found on the floors of two rooms. Three partial human skeletons lay on the floor of one. More human bone was found on the floor in a room to the west, and yet another skeleton probably also belongs to this destruction. The bodies and the bricky collapse covering *in situ* pottery suggest an earthquake—a not uncommon event in this region.

During Godin III:5, the overall settlement pattern shifted toward the pattern that sharpened over the next 700 years. The balance between hill-country and valley-floor settlement shifted decisively toward the valley floor, as occupation in the hill country began to decline. This trend continued in later phases.

Most of the phase III:4 construction seems to have been relatively contemporaneous, judging from the predominance of party walls rather than paired parallel exterior walls, as well as the relatively integrated plan and the widespread use of stone (Figures 6.3–6.5). Phase III:4 is notable for its immediate high density of occupation. Dense existing occupation on lower slopes must have constrained building here on the summit of the mound. Thus we see infilling on the scale of a neighbourhood rather than a single structure, quite unlike the more gradual and less dense process seen earlier in phase III:6. Space seems to have been at a premium. Construction dealt with slope by cutting and terracing with retaining walls. The rooms of each structure step upward to the north, employing a series of stone steps in several areas (Figure 6.6).

Although none of the architectural units or individual rooms are large, the intensive

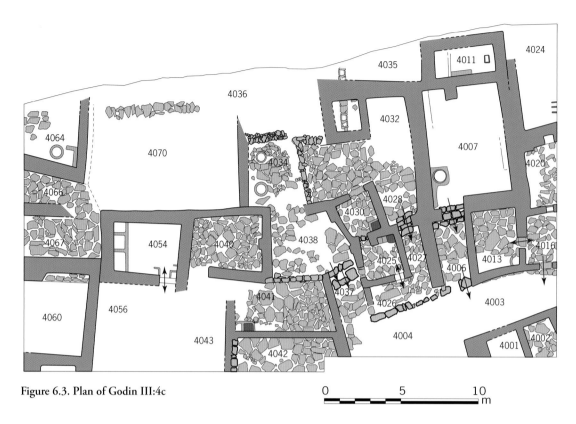

Figure 6.3. Plan of Godin III:4c

0 5 10
m

use of space, large quantities of stone, quality of construction, and thickness of walls all suggest greater investment of time and resources than seen before. The unparallelled, widespread use of stone for paving floors, steps, and retaining walls is most notable. Architectural units, as defined by interconnections among rooms, remain essentially unchanged through the occupation, although numerous internal alterations and repairs are evident. As it did in phase III:5, occupation here ended abruptly in sudden destruction, probably due to an earthquake. One body lay crushed by fallen mud-brick on the floor of room 4040, and most houses had vessels on the floor.

Phase III:3 was a restricted phenomenon, consisting primarily of architectural fragments within 5 metres of the southern edge of excavation. A number of pits in the northern half of the Deep Sounding cut into phase III:4 architecture and collapse. The phase III:3 deposition in the Deep Sounding raised the southern sloping portion so that the entire area became essentially flat. It is unclear whether this was the result of deliberate filling or a product of occupation almost entirely outside the area of excavation. The nature of the phase III:3 deposit—extremely hard with numerous brickbats throughout—is consistent with either possibility. Little if any pottery can be reliably attributed to the actual occupation of this phase.

Figure 6.4. Plan of Godin III:4a

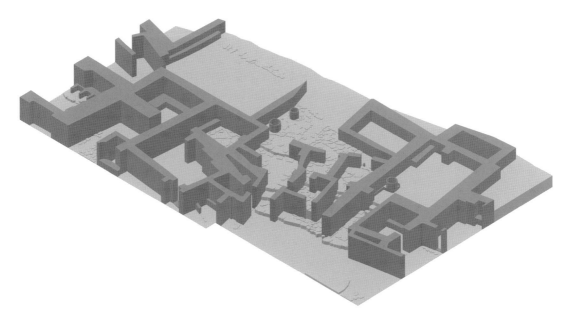

Figure 6.5. Raised plan of Godin III:4a

Figure 6.6. Godin III:4a, stairs to room 4038 (above) and hearths in room 4062 (below)

Phase III:2 architectural units tend to be larger and contain new features; some rooms are larger than any seen before (Figure 6.7). But as occupation progresses some infilling occurs and houses become less elaborate. Only two large structures yield coherent plans; both are unlike structures seen before. At the east is a house with an elaborate entrance that has shallow benches or ledges on each side (room 2016). It opens onto what had been the path of Avenue Road, which had gone on almost forever. Off this entryway is a relatively large room (2014) with a unique central feature—a hearth surrounded by a low mud-plaster bench (Figure 6.9). Local workmen immediately interpreted this as a "kursi." In traditional villages, during cold winter months, a low square wooden framework is placed over a hearth or brazier and covered with a blanket; family members gather around with their legs under the blanket to enjoy the warmth. From this room there is access to two further rooms, the innermost a more typical living room with a cooking hearth. While the western portion of this house remained relatively static, its eastern end underwent a complete rebuilding on a more modest plan, replacing the room with the "kursi." It is uncertain whether the rooms to the north are part of this structure because of the absence of doorways, but wall thicknesses, masonry bonding, and the likelihood of storerooms being integral in such a household suggest a connection. Yet another unique feature of this structure is the kitchen (2001) with a raised hearth and ceramic tray, and a flue in the wall. At least ten andiron fragments, the largest group from any Godin III structure, were found in this house.

To the west, room 2050 is perhaps the largest, single roofed room found in Godin III. Given its size, two posts to support an east-west roof beam are likely; one possible column

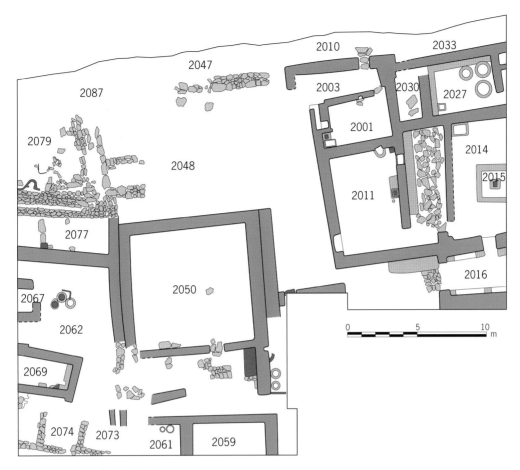

Figure 6.7. Plan of Godin III:2c

base was recorded. Low mud-plastered benches along two sides of the room are the only features. Although there is a raised hearth area just outside the doorway, there is no provision for heating in the main room. It would seem to have served best as a gathering area. Eventually a small two- or three-room structure was built between these two main structures.

The architectural character of phase III:2 is notably different from previous phases—larger units and, at least initially, less dense construction. In the first progress report on the excavation, Cuyler Young suggested that this phase had been destroyed by an earthquake, since the southern wall of room 2011 was shifted bodily as it fell as a block. But the widespread destruction, collapse, and material smashed on floors seen in phases III:5 and III:4 is lacking, and a slower abandonment seems more likely by comparison. Prolonged weathering and the construction of the Godin Period II citadel denuded the western architectural remains, leaving them difficult to interpret.

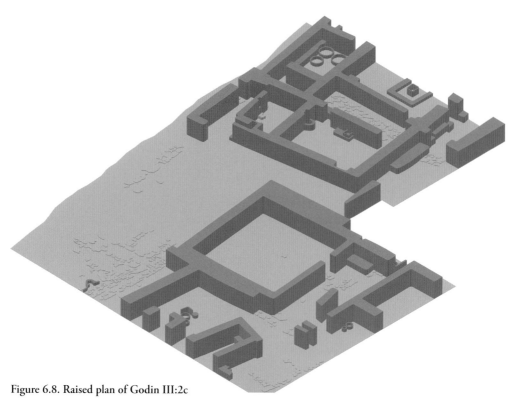

Figure 6.8. Raised plan of Godin III:2c

Figure 6.9. Godin III:2c, "kursi" in room 2014 (left) and raised hearth in room 2001 (right)

The trend toward settlement concentrating on the valley floor culminated in Godin III:2, when the hill country had almost no identifiable settlements. As population reached a long-term high, occupation concentrated on the valley floor in a three-tiered hierarchy of agricultural settlements. Around the large central settlement of Godin Tepe was probably a network of irrigation canals serving the nearby villages, similar to the situation in that area today. The hill country probably continued to be used for pasture. This settlement seems to have collapsed well before the end of Godin III.

The subsequent phase lacks any architectural remains and is (infelicitously) designated Post–III:2 since it was recognized as a separate phase only after the numbering of architectural phases had long been set. There is no architecture. It is, however, of crucial importance that two graves were securely stratified between the architecture of phases III:2 and III:1. Grave goods included a distinctive ceramic repertoire. The distinctive painted wares are not part of the assemblages found in either phase III:2 or phase III:1. This pottery both helps date the grave assemblage and emphasizes its lack of association with permanent architecture. Previously the assemblage had been known only from graves at other sites across much of Luristan ("Giyan II"); other graves from this phase are found across the summit under Period II citadel floors and down the slopes of Godin Tepe. I will return to the implications of these graves in the discussion of regional developments.

After an interval of abandonment (Post–III:2) during which at least part of the area of the Deep Sounding and lower slopes served as an occasional burial ground, occupation resumed. The surviving architecture of phase III:1 is essentially the remains of a single house. The cut made to create the flat surface for the largest columned hall of Period II removed much of the latest Period III deposit in the western two-thirds of the Deep Sounding. The phase III:1 house was modest in size but carefully built, with extensive use of stone, although little survives above the foundation. The plan is unlike those found in earlier levels. The pottery from the house is derived from what had been seen in phase III:2, but painted wares had almost completely disappeared. The Godin III tradition and occupation ended.

Settlement Economy in Godin Period III

The architecture and artifacts recovered from Godin III strata document a wide range of daily or recurrent activities within the settlement or associated with it. Still other activities may be inferred from by-products or end-products. In some cases, tools that must have been used have not have survived. Much of what may have been lost can be inferred from indirect evidence and ethnoarchaeological studies of traditional Zagros village societies and technologies.

I will discuss the variety of activities in terms of several overlapping topics: 1) basic subsistence; 2) the built environment (houses and other structures within the settlement);

Figure 6.10. Godin III ground stone tools

3) individual households; 4) possible toys; 5) specialist crafts; 6) trade; and 7) ritual. Pottery will be treated at greater length after this overview.

The mixed farming economy of agriculture and pastoralism, which still underpins Zagros village subsistence, had long been established by Godin Period III. Fields in the plain surrounding the settlement supplied cereal grains (wheat and barley) and pulses (lentils and chickpeas) (see "Ancient Agricultural Landscape at Godin," p. 59). Barley could also have been used for brewing beer, and evidence for cultivation of grapes suggests wine-making; both are known at Godin in Period VI:1. With the possible exception of flint sickle-blades, no agricultural tools (e.g., ploughs, threshing sleds, or winnowing tools) were recovered, but most would have been wooden and would not have been preserved. Sickles had flint blades, of which a limited number have been recovered; a few have retouched edges and sickle sheen. Four cores suggest local production, although none is in reliable context. Threshing would have been done at the edge of the settlement. Almost all houses have storage space, some with permanent bins; large pottery storage vessels are ubiquitous. Grinding stones, probably used primarily for grinding grain, are one of the most commonly found artifacts after pottery. Godin III:6 settlement in the Kangavar Valley as a whole consisted primarily of relatively small villages scattered across the plain and up into the hills, with Godin and perhaps Karkhaneh larger than the rest. As time passed, settlement tended to concentrate on the valley floor; Godin became a large town. In his 1975 article on the

Kangavar survey, Cyler Young interpreted the distribution of later Godin III settlements on the plain as evidence for the development of irrigation networks; examination of the survey collections and records suggests that this would most likely have occurred in Godin III:2, perhaps extending back to Godin III:4.

The slopes of the valley and the areas around fields and watercourses provided pasturage for flocks of sheep and goats. These animals would primarily have been sources of dairy products and fibre for textile production, rather than meat. The basic diet remained the same for millennia. Equids, and perhaps bovids, might have drawn ploughs and provided transport. There is little evidence for hunting weapons, although a number of clay pellets, presumably used with slings on small prey, were recovered. Lance or spear heads may have been used for hunting larger animals, as well as warfare. We do have the bones from the prey, including deer, various birds, and other animals. Some of the bones bear marks left by butchering, others the results of gnawing by dogs. Presumably those villagers had to chase away hungry dogs as one does in Near Eastern villages today.

Figure 6.11. Godin III sling pellets

The basic construction materials were mud-brick for walls and wood (poplar) for roof beams. Villagers would have made mud-brick on the edge of the settlement, probably near the river, where dirt, chaff, and water would be mixed, formed into bricks, and left to dry in the sun. Most mud-bricks incorporate sherds, from the use of material from earlier decayed structures. For example, walls of several rooms in the eastern house in phase III:2 yielded large numbers of Godin VI:1 sherds (including beveled-rim bowls), showing that the mud-bricks had been made from fourth-millennium BC deposits on the mound itself. Poplar may have been either harvested from wild stands, or perhaps grown specifically for roof beams, as is traditional in the region. Matting, rushes, or brush would have been placed over the beams to support the mud/clay roofing. Walls and roofs were finished with mud-plaster. Packed mud (pisé) was used for some walls and built features, such as bins or benches. Most of the basic materials would therefore likely have come from near the settlement. The only major exception would have been stone, generally used sparingly for wall foundations, door sockets, steps, and occasional paved floors. It would have to come from the hills surrounding the valley several kilometres away. Thus, extensive use of stone in construction may suggest relatively greater wealth. The nature of the architecture at Godin suggests household-based construction, rather than a need for true specialists.

Individual households carried out a wide variety of production activities. Houses usually included at least one room used for storage. These backrooms might have large built-in bins, such as free-standing cylindrical bins (e.g., room 2027 in phase III:2, Figure 6.7) or rectilinear bins along walls (e.g., room 4054 in phase III:4, Figure 6.3). Large pottery vessels, found in all households, would provide additional protected storage. Containers made of perishable materials (e.g., basketry, cloth, leather, or wood) are not preserved archaeologically but were probably the most common form of storage. Items stored would include not only grain, but dairy products (cheese, butter, or dried yogurt), and perhaps beer or wine, in addition to household or agricultural equipment. This storage capacity in households suggests basic self-sufficiency.

Figure 6.12. Godin III bone tools

Hearths mark the main living area in the household, providing for food preparation and heat in the cold winters. Additional evidence for food preparation includes cooking pots and grinding stones for making flour.

Ethnographic studies, such as those by Carol Kramer and Patty-Jo Watson, document other household activities for which direct evidence is often limited or absent from the archaeological record. Inventories of traditional village households show most household tools were probably perishable (e.g., wood, rush, bone). Those made of more durable materials might be recycled rather than discarded. Textile production, using both wool and goat hair, was certainly a major household activity but is represented by very modest artifactual evidence. After the wool or hair was removed from the animal, it had to be cleaned and prepared for spinning into thread or yarn. The spindle used in twisting wool into thread is an important tool. The weight, or whorl, on the spindle was often made of baked clay in other periods, but none has been found in Godin III deposits. Since spinning is essential, the whorl apparently was made from some perishable material, such as wood; traditional whorls in the region are entirely

Figure 6.13. Godin III animal figurines

wooden. The thread or yarn then was woven into cloth on looms made of wood. Traditional looms are simple, usually wooden, and thus leave little direct evidence. All that an archaeologist would find from such a loom are small holes left by pegs or posts in the courtyard surface.

Holes in house floors (such as in rooms 2064 and 2078 in phase III:2) may mark the locations of vertical looms. On such looms, loomweights for tension on the warp are usually unbaked clay "doughnuts" 10–15 centimetres in diameter. They would not be particularly durable and only one such possible weight is recorded (Figure 6.14). Pierced disks (4–6 centimetres in diameter) chipped into shape from sherds may have served as weights for smaller or lighter-warp weaving projects. While these might also be spindle whorls, they show no use wear and are

Figure 6.14. Godin III wheels and a loomweight (right)

both large (generally more than 5 centimetres in diameter) and heavy for such a purpose. Pottery occasionally preserves possible impressions from cloth or basketry. Bronze needles indicate sewing. Bone may have been used as tools "as is" (such as scapulas for paddles or scoops, and

Figure 6.15. Godin III bronze objects and moulds

lower jaws of sheep or goats for scrapers) or worked into needles, pins, or combs (Figure 6.12). Likewise, wood, reeds, and other perishable materials may have been used for various items.

Other artifacts shed light on less serious aspects of life. Small animal figurines made of lightly baked clay, usually in poor condition, were probably children's toys (Figure 6.13). Most appear to be sheep, goats, and perhaps cows and dogs, the common animals around the village. Incised lines on one figurine might represent fleece. Some figurines have holes pierced through their necks, perhaps for stringing. A number of "wheels" (disks with enlarged hubs) may also be parts of toys (Figure 6.14). At least one of the larger animal figurines has a horizontal hole through the feet which could be used for an axle; these seem to be pull toys. The wear on the hubs of the "wheels" is consistent with such a use. Rough disks chipped from sherds are common and may be game pieces; usually there is no use wear, which might suggest use as a scraper or smoother.

The Godin III economy included several crafts involving specialist production. Pottery is the premier example, and will be discussed at greater length separately. Some relatively crude pottery may have been hand-made within individual households during the later phases of Godin III (phases III:2–1). From Godin III:6 through Godin III:4, perhaps even through Godin III:2, part-time, specialist potters made a great majority of the assemblage.

Godin III has also yielded evidence for metallurgical activity, particularly two moulds (Figure 6.15) (one from room 4030 in Godin III:4) and abundant by-products, such as slag (see "Metallurgical Activity during Godin Period III," p. 228). Which bronze items (such as the pins, needles, vessels, and tools, shown in Figure 6.16) are locally made is uncertain. The "firing holes" found in diminishing numbers from Godin III:6–4 may play some role, given their evidence for repeated episodes of

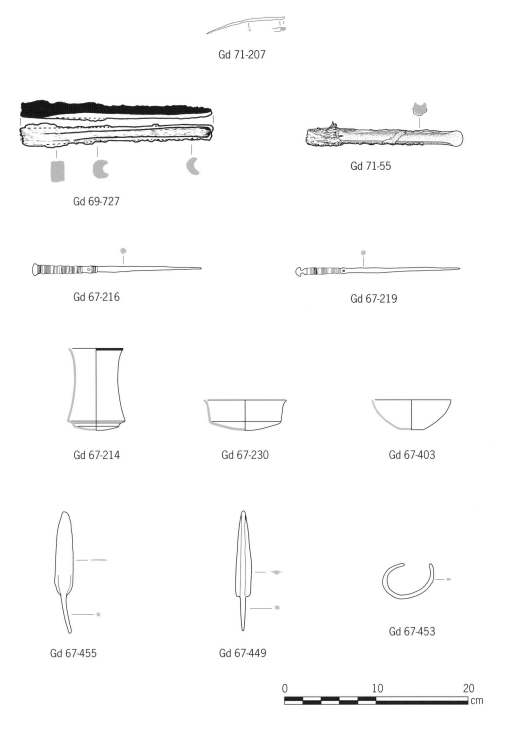

Gd 71-207

Gd 69-727

Gd 71-55

Gd 67-216

Gd 67-219

Gd 67-214

Gd 67-230

Gd 67-403

Gd 67-455

Gd 67-449

Gd 67-453

0   10   20
cm

Figure 6.16. Godin III bronze objects

intense heat. Carpentry tools (saw, gouges, awls, chisels), particularly the group of several such tools from a grave in Operation O, provide evidence for a specialist woodworker.

Various materials and artifacts document contact or trade with other regions. Copper and tin (or arsenical and tin bronze), and silver, came from well beyond the Kangavar Valley. Pottery likewise documents interregional contacts. Phase III:6 yielded several sherds related to Susa. Phase III:4 pottery shows contact with other central western valleys and lowland Mesopotamia (grey ware), and phase III:2 ceramics reflect contact with Mesopotamia and northeastern Iran. The source for the grinding stones is uncertain. Trade in such perishable goods as fine textiles, agricultural products, fine wood, and animals, was probably extensive, although we cannot document it archaeologically.

Metallurgical Activity during Godin Period III
Lesley D. Frame

Compared to the earlier periods, there was less evidence of metal processing from Period III contexts. These remains included only one fragment from a melting crucible (Godin III:4) and a tuyere fragment (Godin III:2, Figure 6.17).

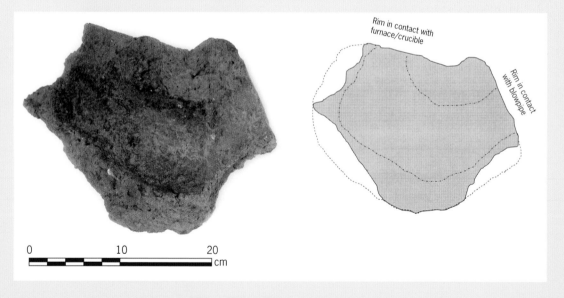

Figure 6.17. Godin III:2 tuyere fragment

The only other tuyeres found at this date are from Kiul Tepe and Yanik Tepe in Azerbaijan, making this artifact particularly exciting. Unlike the straight tuyeres from farther north, the

Figure 6.18. Two decorative pins from Godin III, Tomb 1, burial B (top: Gd 67-215, bottom: Gd 67-219)

Godin tuyere fragment is a right-angle tuyere. Because the outside surface is not heated and contains no droplets of metal, slag, or matte, this fragment is probably from the bottom side of the tuyere. The presence of multiple metal prills (globules of metal) on its interior surface indicates that the tuyere was close to the level of molten slag or metal rather than above the fuel source during use. It could have been used with a crucible or a furnace. In addition to the tuyere and crucible fragments, there were two moulds from Period III (Figure 6.15). The lack of crucible or furnace fragments from this period makes it difficult to determine the exact setup employed, but the use of a tuyere and the presence of moulds suggest a more permanent or larger-scale operation than the limited evidence indicates.

The numerous metal artifacts from Godin Period III reflect the styles, manufacturing techniques, and abilities of multiple craftsmen across the Iranian plateau. Support for this conclusion is two-part. First, similar examples of these metal artifacts appear at many sites along the major trade routes of the plateau.

Second, items whose functions do not necessarily dictate a particular method of manufacture—specifically pins and bracelets—have a much higher degree of variability in their microstructures and composition. Two pins from the same burial are particularly interesting since Gd 67-215 contains twice as much tin as Gd 67-219 (Figure 6.18). Because higher tin content yields a paler shade of yellow, this difference in composition may reflect a desire to have a pair of pins of slightly different colour. Variability in microstructure is present even among items that have very similar styles, suggesting the presence of multiple producers. Given the evidence for small-scale production at Godin Tepe and the high volume of goods that would have come through the site for trade, it is safe to assume that the majority of these metal artifacts were produced elsewhere. This is significant because it indicates the preservation of regional or workshop traditions in metallurgy regardless of the ultimate style of the object.

In addition, the well-stratified (and numerous) metal finds from Godin provide an opportunity to observe overall trends in the manufacturing abilities of the workshops across the plateau. The most obvious of these trends is the shift from copper-arsenic alloys to the first appearance of tin bronze in Period III:6. However, tin bronze is restricted to burial contexts until Period III:4. The appearance of tin bronze in non-burial contexts during the later part of Period III corresponds well with the appearance of tin at other Iranian plateau sites during the late third and early second millennium BC. Manufacturing styles are extremely conservative for utilitarian objects (chisels are produced in the same manner regardless of composition or date). On the other hand, the general trend in pins is a shift from highly variable microstructure during Period III (including examples of as-cast, heavily worked, heavily annealed, or fine-grained microstructures) to only worked and annealed microstructures of similar grain-size in Period II.

Additional data on the metallurgy of Godin are available in the Godin Web archive at https://tspace.library.utoronto.ca.

Moving finally to a much more speculative level, there are some hints of ritual. In Godin III:4 there are three possible foundation deposits associated with house construction, involving placing portions of sheep or goat carcasses and pottery beneath the stone foundations of walls. At the east, four such deposits lay under or near the wall between rooms 4020 and 4060 (Figure 6.3). Each was accompanied by small (diameter 4 to 6 centimetres, height 3 to 4 centimetres) crudely formed unfired bowls. To the west, at the eroded face of the mound and partially beneath the stone foundation of the northern wall of room 4070, some well-made pottery and an abundance of tiny "thumbprint dishes" accompanied three partial animal carcasses. A single diameter 4 to 6 centimetres, animal skeleton lay beneath the foundation stones of the wall between rooms 4025 and 4030. In two cases where walls were preserved, the rooms had niches in the north wall, but were not otherwise notably unusual.

An incomplete human figurine from phase III:2 (Figures 6.19 and 6.20) may be more than just a toy. The long-skirted figurine seems to be preserved to either the chest or the armpits, with an animal head protruding from its chest. There is nothing similar from Godin III, and its elaboration is noteworthy, especially in that phase. Unfortunately, its fragments came from mixed strata in an outdoor area. In the earlier phases, several fragments of theriomorphic (animal-shaped) vessels, some with painted decoration, have no obvious utilitarian purpose. These figurines were hollow, with a hole in the back and another from the nose into the interior, apparently for the flow of liquid.

Other objects and behaviours may have non-utilitarian dimensions. Andirons were a standard item of household equipment exclusively in phase III:2. Their variability and simplicity, or even crudity, suggest individual production. Although usually schematic or iconic in their simple form, several have human features (Figures 6.21 and 6.22). These might have significance beyond simple hearth equipment (see discussion of andirons and ritual in Chapter 5, p. 149). Red-slipped fenestrated stands in phase III:4 are distinctive (Figure 6.38c); the consistent absence of burn marks in the shallow dish on the top indicate they were not braziers.

The distinctive and limited choice of animals incorporated in painted decora-

Figure 6.19. Godin III:2 clay human figurine

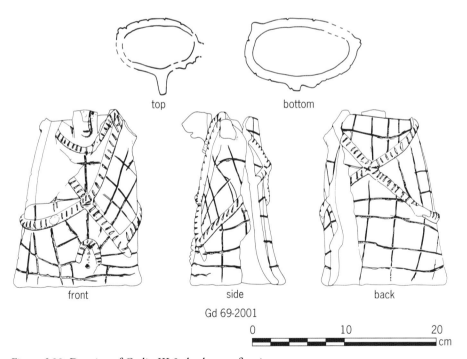

top   bottom

front   side   back

Gd 69-2001

0   10   20
cm

Figure 6.20. Drawing of Godin III:2 clay human figurine

tion may be significant. Animal motifs are essentially limited to Godin III:5–4. By far the most common animal has always looked to me like a duck or similar waterfowl. A distant second and third in frequency are "eagles" with wings spread wide, and goats (Figure 6.24). These frequencies are utterly at odds with the faunal remains; compare this to the animals portrayed by the small clay figurines (sheep/goats, and perhaps a few bovids).

Finally, burials provide evidence for social stratification and possible ritual. The consistent provision of grave goods reflects, at a minimum, respect for the dead; there is no firm basis for ideological inferences. The variation in the amount and value of grave goods must represent differences in wealth. Godin III burials, both at Godin and contemporary sites, are extramural, probably in discrete cemeteries. All burials at Godin before Post–III:2 were found south of the main mound; this again suggests occupational continuity. All Post–III:2 burials were found on the upper slopes of the mound. Despite high

Figure 6.21. Godin III:2 andiron with human features

Figure 6.22. Godin III:2 andirons

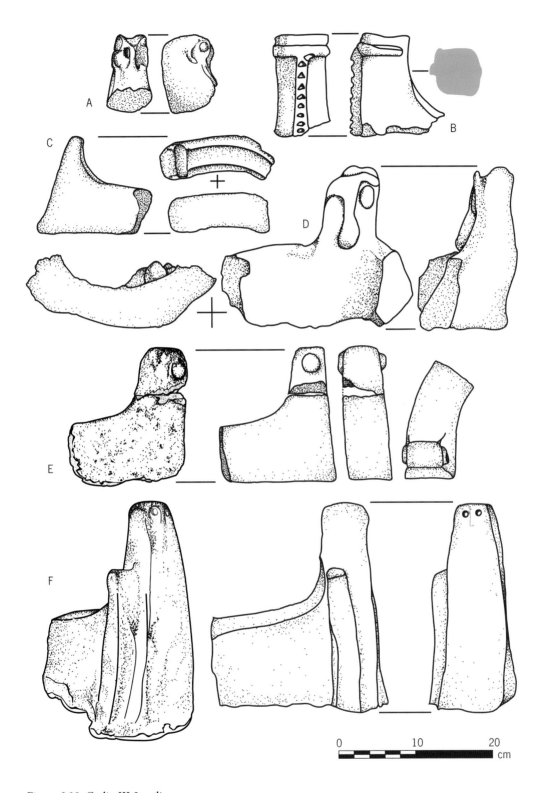

Figure 6.23. Godin III:2 andirons

Figure 6.24. Godin III:5 painted pottery with animal motifs

infant mortality in antiquity, however, not a single infant or small child burial was found either within houses or in the cemetery. The limited skeletal data available suggest that all Godin III burials may have been at least adolescents.

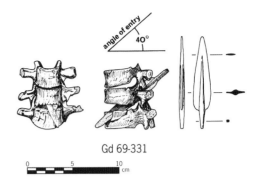

Gd 69-331

Figure 6.25. Vertebrae with spearpoint from Godin Post-III:2 burial

The contrast in grave goods between the two known Godin III:6 graves certainly suggests social stratification. The types of pottery vessels included—most related to food service and consumption—hint at ritual. One grave had only two grey-black vessels (bowl and tankard ["eat and drink"]). The other, apparently disturbed, nonetheless had seven grey-black bowls, two tankards, two cylindrical beakers, several buff-painted pots, and seven bronze items. Although only one, partially excavated grave in Operation EEE dates to Godin III:4, its eight painted buff-ware and fifteen red-slipped vessels clearly suggest wealth; contemporary graves at Tepe Giyan also display a range of wealth.

The single excavated grave in Godin III:2 is the richest of all. The stone-walled and stone-roofed chamber contained two bodies, each with grave goods, another separate group in the centre, and more outside on the roof. The grave goods included numerous pieces of bronze jewellery and vessels, local plain and painted buff pottery, and relatively fine, grey pottery which is probably not local. Close to the tomb chamber was a horse burial, which may have been associated with the tomb.

Finally, the twelve Post–III:2 burials on the upper slopes of Godin Tepe yield a range of grave goods. Some have only a single painted goblet, others have more, as well as coarse, plain-buff vessels. The richest yielded nine pieces of bronze jewellery, a bowl, five javelin heads, and six vessels. One other burial, lacking grave goods, had a spearpoint embedded in two vertebrae (Figure 6.25); the cause of death is not in doubt.

The Period III settlement at Godin Tepe ranged in size from village to town, depending on the phase. The mixed agricultural-pastoral economy supported a population that had clear differences in degrees of wealth, and included some craft specialists.

Let us now turn to the best-known and most common craft: pottery. I will first discuss the potter's craft at the midpoint of the Godin III sequence (III:5–4), then turn to the long-term development of the tradition. This will then lead to a broader interpretation of Godin III in its historic context.

The Godin III Potter's Craft (Godin III:5–4)

The sudden destructions, probably due to earthquakes, which ended phases III:5 and III:4 provide an opportunity to discuss the organization of pottery production during Godin III. At least a half-metre deposit of collapsed mud-brick walls and mud-plaster roofs preserved household assemblages *in situ* on floors, including more than a hundred complete or restorable pottery vessels in each level. The pottery preserved on each floor should represent a relatively short period of time prior to each destruction. Although some may have been made earlier than others, all vessels found on the sealed floors were in use at the end. Possible disparities in vessel ages are, moreover, unlikely to be notable, with the possible exception of the largest storage jars. The limited architectural changes in phase III:5 suggest a relatively brief occupation, on the order of years rather than decades. With proper maintenance and repair mud-brick village houses last up to fifty years, but numerous modifications are likely during that time. Even in the more prolonged phase III:4 occupation, the floor assemblages should still represent the period just prior to destruction for several reasons. Godin III pottery is unlikely to have had long use-lives. All of it, including the painted-buff ware, is rather utilitarian in form and finish and appears to have limited inherent value. The painted pottery was relatively abundant, and the assemblage lacks a notably fine ware.

At each phase the painted decoration on floor assemblages shows homogeneity, within which stylistic subgroups may be defined. Compare, for example, the two

Figure 6.26. Godin III:4 vessels with painted duck motifs

Figure 6.27. Godin III:4 red-slipped pottery

Figure 6.28. Godin III:5 painted pottery

pairs of painted ducks from phase III:4 (Figure 6.26), or the variable treatment of animals on III:5 pots (Figure 6.24). Basic vessel shapes are few and show limited variability; their simplicity suggests generalized uses. Only the very large storage jars, which would rarely be moved, are likely to have had long use-lives.

Burial goods, on the other hand, tend to show much greater stylistic homogeneity. Throughout the Godin III period, pottery placed in graves seems to have been unused, rather than drawn from the living household's goods. The grave pottery was apparently assembled at the time of burial, and generally shows marked stylistic homogeneity. The premier example is the III:4 tomb in Operation EEE south of the mound. Most of the major shapes of the assemblage are found among the eight painted buff-ware and fifteen red-slipped vessels: carinated vessels, beakers, and simple bowls. The overall typological and stylistic homogeneity is notable. The large and medium painted vessels have similar proportions. They are relatively open and have vertical walls with a sharp-thickened carination. In registers other than the main, the rendering and the choice of motifs and composites are similar, making allowance for the varying vessel sizes. All are slab-built, with smoothed or self-slipped surfaces, and painted rather carelessly as the vessel was rotated on a turntable. These general stylistic characteristics carry over to two of the small vessels, although these were thrown on a potter's wheel. Almost all of these vessels share a basic approach to vessel decoration and are quite distinct from the other three small painted vessels, as well as the pottery in the households. The red-slipped, plain-ware vessels, especially those with handles, are notably homogeneous in size and shape. None of the vessels shows any evidence of wear, suggesting that new vessels were put into the grave. The morphological and stylistic homogeneity suggests that most came from a single source.

Most of the pottery recovered *in situ* from the floors of phases III:5 and III:4 was made and used during a brief period of time. This diminishes concern about variability due simply to the passage of time. Furthermore, all the material comes from contiguous households within a single 500-to-700-square-metre area of a 5-to-10 hectare settlement. These reductions of possible sources of variability, combined with the detailed provenance data, enhance the value of those two corpora of

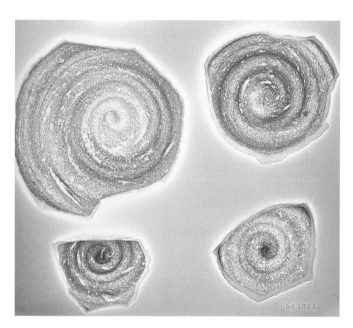

Figure 6.29. Xeroradiographs of Godin III:5–4 bases

pottery for analyses of the technology and organization of production.

The painted buff-ware has medium to fine sandy temper (maximum diameter less than 0.2 millimetres). It is well fired, at a temperature of 800–1000°C, in an oxidizing atmosphere; no grey core remains. The fracture is smooth and sharp. A number of primary and secondary forming and finishing techniques were used. Pigment for the painted decoration contained iron-bearing minerals (including hematite or goethite) mixed with quartz and clay.

In the entire assemblage, only one basic shape in buff-ware consistently received more than cursory decoration during Godin III:5–4: carinated vessels, with restricted mouths, in a wide range of sizes and proportions (Figures 6.37 and 6.38). A relatively soft carination marked the transition from a rounded lower body to an inward sloped shoulder; the everted rim had a simply finished lip. Painted decoration extends from the rim to just below the carination.

Shape and size affect potters' choices of forming methods. Shape is essentially a constant with Godin III:5–4 painted-buff ware since only one basic vessel shape has significant painted decoration or abundance. Size therefore is the primary morphological variable. Four size groups can be defined, based on dimensions (rim, neck, and carination diameters) and primary forming method used. Each size of vessel has a characteristic production sequence. The available clays and the apparent limitations of forming technology, particularly the potter's wheel, constrained choices of forming methods. While only the production sequences for painted-buff, carinated pots are discussed here, the relationship between size (maximum diameter is the most easily used measure) and primary forming method holds for all other buff-ware shapes.

Small vessels (maximum diameter less than 15 centimetres) were thrown on a potter's wheel (fast wheel); the centrifugal force from the

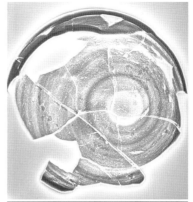

Figure 6.30. Xeroradiograph and photo of small Godin III:5 thrown vessel

Figure 6.31. Xeroradiograph of Godin III:5 medium-size jar shoulder, showing wheel finishing of shoulder

rotation of the wheel aids raising and shaping the vessel walls. Throughout the history of the Godin III assemblage, the potter's wheel was used exclusively for making small buff-ware vessels. The interior often retains a raised ridge, spiralling outward and upward from the centre (wheelmark); X-rays show that within the ceramic itself, temper and voids also show consistent diagonal orientation resulting from the forces exerted during forming (Figure 6.30).

Medium vessel (maximum diameter about 15 to 30 centimetres) construction involved hand-building techniques, such as coiling, for initial (primary) forming. Extensive secondary forming, perhaps including beating or drawing, and heavy interior scraping hinder identification of forming methods, even with use of xeroradiography. The base portion may have been built from slabs or coils in a mould, with the walls of the lower body coiled (Figure 6.29). Layered or stepped breaks document the use of at least several pieces of clay. The lower body, between the base and carination, is usually not restorable, since its walls are thin and undecorated. The varying thickness of the lower body profile, the obvious hollowing out of the interior profile below the carination, and scars document severe interior scraping which usually begins 2 to 4 centimetres below the carination. Sometimes half or more of the initial wall thickness was removed. This indicates that the lower body was originally considerably thicker to provide greater strength during primary forming. Surfaces within the frequent breaks at the carination suggest a join between the lower body

Figure 6.32. Xeroradiograph and photo of large Godin III:4 storage jar, showing coil construction

and the shoulder, indicating two-part construction. Circumferential imprints from cords and other bindings indicate concern with countering stress from subsequent forming of the upper body. Xeroradiographs of medium vessels often show diagonal orientation of inclusions and voids in the rim, neck, and uppermost shoulder, suggesting forming on a rotary device, while this patterning is absent in the lower body (Figure 6.31). Ethnoarchaeological accounts show that vessels may be hand-built on a turntable and the neck and rim shaped and finished by brief rotation at high speed, in effect giving the appearance of throwing this part of the vessel, in terms of residual traces.

Large vessels (maximum diameter around 30 to 60 centimetres) were built much like the medium ones, with coiling followed by aggressive interior scraping, which removed a third or more of the original wall thickness. Major horizontal breaks tend to be periodically spaced along the height of the profile, with a tendency toward smaller increments near and above the carination. In the lower body, such breaks occur at approximately 10-centimetre intervals, compared to 5 to 6 centimetres in the shoulder and neck. Such breaks mark the individual construction episodes. Given the height of coils found in xeroradiographs, construction increments comprised roughly four coils in the lower body and perhaps two in the shoulder/neck. Binding scars remain on the lower body of some large vessels.

Oversize vessels (maximum diameter more than about 60 centimetres) were formed using unmodified coiled construction. Potters smoothed the corrugated surfaces of the successive coils by slightly flattening both faces (giving the coils a squarer cross-section) and smearing the clay to fill the depressions. The minimal distortion of coil cross-sections indicates that little secondary forming was done (xeroradiographs clearly show the joins between coils inside the vessel wall, see Figure 6.33). The interior is only lightly scraped. As with the large vessels, wall construction proceeded in increments of 10 to 12 centimetres with the addition of perhaps four coils. Ethnographic accounts of very large jar production report similar construction increments, as do archaeological analyses (e.g., Early-Middle Phrygian [950–550 BC] and Hellenistic [200 BC] pithoi at Gordion). As distance from the base increases, the intervals between breaks decreases

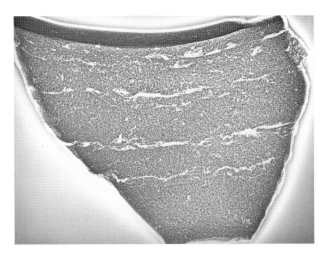

Figure 6.33. Xeroradiograph of Godin III:4 red-slipped jar, showing coil construction

to 5 to 6 centimetres, suggesting the addition of only two coils. Such smaller increments in the upper part of the vessel counter the ever increasing stresses on the partially formed and semi-hardened vessel. These would be particularly acute during the building of the incurved shoulder and shaping of the neck and rim. This method of construction, which included reworking the bottom portion of the vessel at the end of the forming sequence, was used in Godin III:6–5 for making oversize, ovoid storage jars with cable decoration. When this type of vessel disappeared after Godin III:5, the production sequence was adopted in Godin III:4 for making oversize carinated jars, a type not previously made.

Within the floor deposit assemblage from each phase, several groups of vessels whose proportions and absolute dimensions correspond closely can be distinguished.

Standardization of measurement in producing a given form is in terms of the potter's body rather than a uniform system; measurements are usually taken from the hand. Such measurements become unconsciously incorporated onto the potter's mental template. Consequently, if two potters with slightly different hand sizes are producing "identical" forms, the dimensions as determined by an absolute measuring system will vary proportionately to the relative size of their hands.

Clusters of closely similar pots may be the products of individual potters. Interacting potters can generally identify the work of individuals within the group from observation of idiosyncratic details. Morphology and metrology suggest, therefore, that the work of individual potters may be identifiable.

The structure of the Godin III painted style is dependent on the carinated vessel form (Figures 6.38a–c). Horizontal bands or registers of decoration are stacked from just below the carination to the neck. The focal, or main, register, where the largest and most elaborate motifs appear, rests on the carination. Stylistic groupings, defined in part by the type of motifs used in the main register, depend on vessel morphology. The length of the shoulder determines the relative openness of a vessel and the space available on the shoulder for the main-register decoration. Some motifs occur only on one size of vessel, others on two or more. Motifs on larger vessels tend to be either bolder or more elaborate. The motif repertoire varies within a hierarchy of vessel size, valley system, and time. When the proportions and dimensions of vessels are particularly close, the choice and rendering of motifs in the main register is usually equally close, lending further support for the identification of individuals.

The methods of production (particularly the use of the potter's wheel) and the standardization of vessel types, decorative styles, motif repertoires, and vessel morphology all suggest specialist production of painted buff-ware. The organization of production—how full-time the potters were, how workshops functioned internally, how broad each potter's or workshop's range of vessels was—remains unclear. That the potters were relatively few in number is the crucial inference. Neither forming methods nor painted style, beyond the basic structure of decoration, links all sizes of painted buff-ware vessels. Although the same overall structure of decoration is used on all vessel sizes, and some major motifs used in the main register occur on more than one size of vessel, these provide only tenuous links among various vessel sizes for workshop identification.

Given the varied forming methods used, did workshops concentrate on one or more of the sizes? In other words, did each workshop specialize in use of one or more forming methods, or did each use the full range? Throwing on the potter's wheel involves motor habits distinct from those used with turntables or hand-building techniques. Likewise, building oversize vessels requires considerable skill and involves an entirely different forming sequence from other sizes, so such vessels tend to be made by potters who specialize in these forms. Use of ceramic ring scrapers does, however, provide some evidence for interrelationships among production of vessels of differing sizes. These rings (8–10 centimetres in diameter) were thrown on a potter's wheel but were used exclusively for scraping the interior (and exterior?) of medium and large vessels built by hand.

Surface and fabric colours after firing suggest diversity of clays and/or preparation. Both Godin III painted-buff, common, and red-slipped wares were fired at similar temperatures (800–1000°C) in oxidizing atmospheres, yet yielded distinctly different fabric and surface colours (light browns and tans compared to reds). Neutron activation analysis has shown that the red-slipped ware pastes have a consistently higher iron and lower calcium content.

It is not clear whether potters prepared clay differently for use with the various forming methods for Godin III buff common ware. No marked difference between paste of various vessel size groups of Godin III:5–4 painted buff-ware is evident, either to the naked eye or under magnification. Indeed, some of the vessels with the finest pastes, in terms of size of inclusions, are either large or oversize! The aplastic inclusions in the paste of oversize vessels are not appreciably different in size from those in small vessels. Apparently, Godin III potters used levigation and/or grinding of the raw clay to reduce and control particle size.

Limited exploratory petrographic, thin-section analysis of primarily Godin III:5 pottery has noted that Godin III:5–4 painted buff-ware and contemporaneous red-slipped-ware pastes are distinct from one another, but each is quite homogeneous in itself. This is in marked contrast to the relative heterogeneity of paste observed within single Chalcolithic wares from the Kangavar Valley.

There is a suggestive, but not wholly consistent, relationship between paste and stylistic groupings. Tight stylistic and morphological groupings of vessels do not always have equally similar pastes. For example, samples were taken from three of eight medium vessels in a stylistically and metrically tight group with the solid diamond motif in the main register; one had markedly higher amounts of carbonate and shell inclusions than the other two. On the other hand, two stylistically and morphologically very similar vessels with the inverted V or "stingray" motif were alike in their presence/absence and amounts of various minerals. These two vessels share their general "petrographic fingerprint" with six other vessels of disparate proportions and motifs. Petrographic thin-sectioning thus permits some evaluation of stylistic groupings. Paste similarities corresponding to stylistic, morphological, or primary forming-method groups are gratifying. Paste similarities that crosscut such groups may suggest the range of a workshop's products. The petrographic evidence offers modest support for the hypothesis that a few potters or workshops used a variety of forming methods to make a range of vessel sizes.

Neutron activation analysis provides another approach to paste characterization—determining if various pots are made from similar or differing clays. In one study published by Vitali and others in 1987, four sets of samples (ninety-two in all) from buff-painted and red-slipped vessels found in Godin III:5 and III:4 floor deposits were run. For both the painted buff-ware and red-slipped wares, there was good but not perfect separation of Godin III:5 from Godin III:4 samples. Within each phase, the paste of each ware was relatively homogeneous yet distinct from the other. Thus, at a single site, over a span of no more than 200 to 300 years, potters working in a coherent and conservative ceramic tradition used distinguishable clays for different wares. More important, different phases of a single ware within a single assemblage, where clay preparation and forming methods remained essentially unchanged, could be identified. With both Godin III painted buff-ware and red-slipped wares, Godin III:5 and III:4 could be distinguished, although not absolutely.

A second neutron activation analysis, published by the author and James Blackman in 1992, concentrated on painted buff-ware from phases III:5–4. These analyses shed some further light on the relationship between paste on the one hand, and production sequence or scale on the other. The number of samples (fifty-four) was insufficient, however, to test possible relationships between paste and stylistic groups definitively.

In order to test the homogeneity of paste within large and oversize, hand-built, painted buff-ware vessels, samples were taken at intervals of 10 to 20 centimetres along the profile of two Godin III:4 storage jars. Taken with attention to the major horizontal breaks, almost every sample derives from a separate construction increment or episode. The paste from each of these two Godin III:4 jars was remarkably homogeneous within each vessel, particularly for such large, hand-built jars.

The homogeneity of the paste suggests that the clay was prepared using either levigation or grinding, or both, and that large volumes were prepared at one time. The marked homogeneity of paste throughout each vessel is the crucial observation. Ethnographic accounts of potters' making similar vessels suggest that large amounts of clay were prepared at one time. Production of large and oversize vessels involves brief episodes of building separated by extended periods of waiting for the vessel to harden enough to allow further work, and requires considerable skill. In order to make more efficient use of their time, potters therefore make a number of vessels at one time, moving continuously from one to the next in a cycle. For example, at Thrapsano in Crete, pithos makers construct ten to twelve pithoi at once. Large quantities of prepared clay must be ready at hand so that work can continue.

These ethnographic examples illustrate a rational and efficient approach to large vessel production, making the best use of time. The similar approach and production sequence suggests that the Godin III potters would have worked in a similar fashion, making at least several large or oversize vessels at one time. Fragments of a number of other such vessels were recovered from phases III:5 and III:4 at Godin Tepe. The clay requirements, the careful preparation of the raw clay evident in its homogeneity, and the high competence in forming and finishing seen in the products themselves, all indicate that production of Godin III:5–4 buff ware was a skilled craft.

When the entire pottery production cycle is considered, a large amount of time, effort, and skill is implicit. The clay first had to be dug and transported to the working area, wherever either may have been (no clay bed, workshop, or kiln has yet been identified in the Kangavar Valley). The relative fineness and homogeneity of the clay and aplastic inclusions (temper) suggest that the clay was either levigated or ground, or both. The relative standardization of production sequences for each vessel size, as well as painted decoration and vessel morphology, all suggest that Godin III potters were both skilled and few.

The marked homogeneity of the paste alone in these two vessels provides support for organized production by a limited number of skilled potters. These provide a vivid contrast to the Godin III:5–4 large, red-slipped, wide-mouth, storage vessels that are less well constructed, using a coarser paste, simple smoothed finish, and lower-temperature firing. The red-slipped-ware pottery is likely made by potters distinct from those making the buff ware. The painted-buff large and oversize vessels represent an entirely different level of expertise and approach to pottery production.

The number of samples run was not large enough to permit division of the Godin III:4 or III:5 vessels into statistically meaningful subgroups, but general clustering tendencies may be considered. Godin III:4 and III:5 pottery tend to fall into separate clusters. A group of phase III:5 vessels includes the full gamut of vessel sizes and forming techniques: small (wheel-made) to large (coiled). Right in the heart of it, moreover, is an oversize ovoid pithos, with cable decoration. A second small cluster consists of phase III:4 medium and small vessels. Again, wheel-thrown and hand-built vessels occur together in some of the closest groupings.

The data suggest that vessels of all sizes are interconnected by paste. Indeed, buff-ware vessels of all types (pithoi and two types of carinated vessels) are intermixed. Just as previous analyses of decorative style, morphology, and production sequences had concluded, paste characterization also suggests that production of various sizes of vessels was integrated, with a few potters or workshops supplying the society as a whole with pottery.

Paste characterization through neutron activation and petrographic thin-sectioning tends to support the hypothesis that relatively few potters, made Godin III painted buff-ware during each phase of Godin III. Most important, the marked homogeneity of the paste throughout the large vessels suggests careful preparation of large quantities of clay. The resulting products show high competence in forming and finishing. Ethnographic parallels indicate that skilled potters produce a number of such vessels at a time rather than singly. The case for limited numbers of potters or workshops is greatly strengthened. Paste groupings appear to crosscut forming methods. Similarity of paste among pots made using different methods of primary vessel forming, suggests that individual potters or cooperating groups of potters grouped in workshops, produced the full range of vessel sizes.

Table 6.1. Distribution of Godin III ceramic wares by phase

GODIN TEPE PERIOD III

CERAMIC SEQUENCE
WARE BY LEVEL
PRIMARY AND SECONDARY LOTS ONLY

LEVEL	BUFF-PAINTED	BUFF COMMON PLAIN	BUFF COARSE PLAIN	GREY-BLACK AND GREY	RED-	RED-SLIPPED-PAINTED	SAMPLE SIZE
III:1	4%	10%	79%	2%	5%	<1%	325
POST III:2	50	8	40		2		48
III:2	2	6	87	1	1	<1	586
III:3	4	7	70	4	14	<1	228
III:4	8	22	40	1	27		1671
III:5	18	25	38	3	14		1787
III:6	24	44	24	6	1		5291
TOTAL SHERDS PER WARE	1792	3268	3617	406	853	8	9936

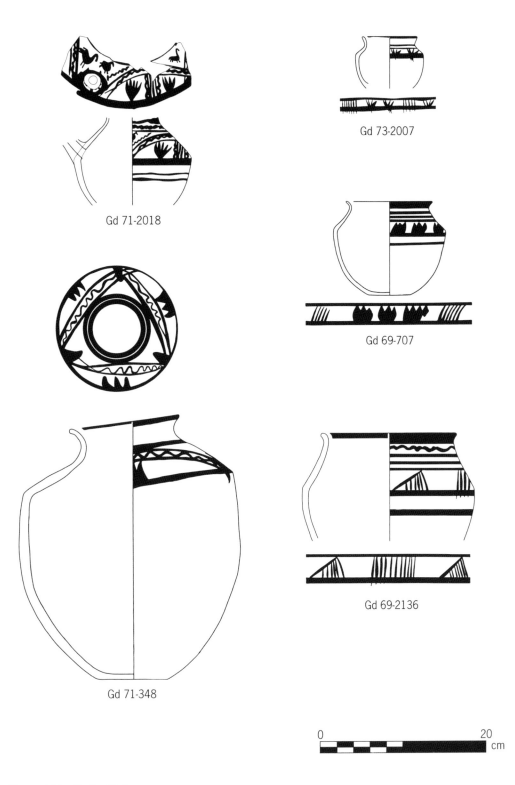

Gd 71-2018

Gd 73-2007

Gd 69-707

Gd 71-348

Gd 69-2136

0   20
          cm

Figure 6.34a. Godin III:6 pottery

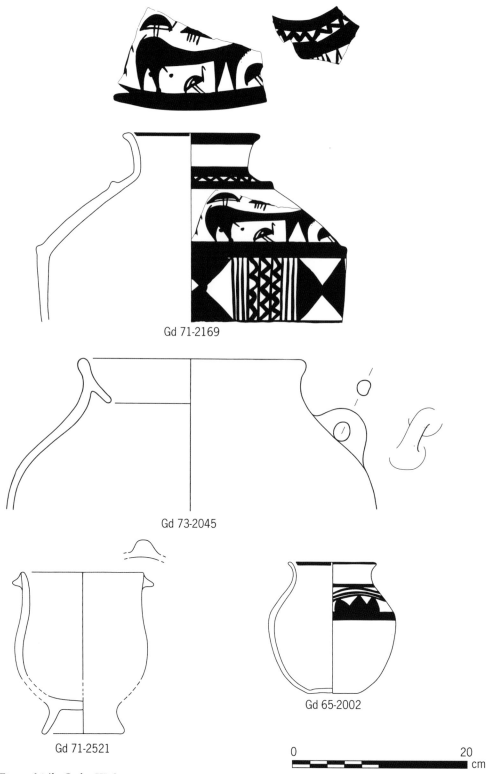

Gd 71-2169

Gd 73-2045

Gd 71-2521

Gd 65-2002

0   20
                     cm

Figure 6.34b. Godin III:6 pottery

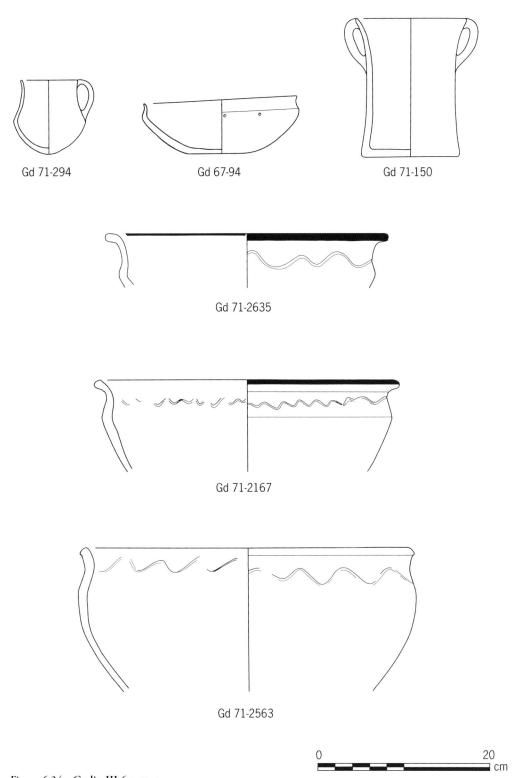

Gd 71-294

Gd 67-94

Gd 71-150

Gd 71-2635

Gd 71-2167

Gd 71-2563

0   20
cm

Figure 6.34c. Godin III:6 pottery

The Overall Godin III Ceramic Sequence

Although the ceramic tradition is referred to as Godin III, its origins clearly lie elsewhere. The date of the beginning of Godin III in one area need not, and indeed often will not, correspond to that in another. Indeed, there is no evidence that the initial development of the assemblage took place in Kangavar or the immediate region. Godin III:6 pottery is clearly related to the well-documented Susa Dc-d/Susa IVA ceramic tradition in southwestern Iran in lowland Susiana. As will be discussed later, its appearance in Kangavar, and the other eastern highland valleys east of the Kuh-I Sefid, may mark a Susiana polity moving northward to tap into the trade along the High Road. Classic Susa IV or Godin III:6 pottery is rare in the western valleys. The ultimate origins of the tradition probably lay in the piedmont polychrome traditions of the early third millennium, so dates in the western and southern valleys of Luristan would tend to be somewhat earlier than further east, such as Kangavar.

Figure 6.35. Godin III:6 grey-black pottery

The hallmarks of the Godin III:6 and later assemblage are buff-ware carinated pots and jars, and related rounded profiles, in a wide range of size and proportions (Figures 6.34a–c). Painted decoration, found only on the buff ware, is concentrated above the carination or shoulder. Other characteristic buff-ware vessels include: very large, ovoid, storage jars with applied cable decoration and piecrust bases.; bowls with enlarged or modelled rims, often painted, some with wavy lines incised below the rim, and carinated or rounded profiles; and various types of beakers. Buff ware constitutes almost the entire assemblage. Almost

70 percent of sherds come from medium-grit, tempered vessels, with an additional 24 percent from coarser vessels. The remaining 6 percent consists of handmade burnished, grey-black ware, perhaps derived from a similar Godin IV ware, was used for shallow carinated bowls, tankards, large concave-sided cylindrical vessels, and shallow dishes.

Painted decoration is simple and bold; only carinated vessels and beakers have more than simple painted bands. Decoration is arranged in registers on the upper body. An upper band (below the neck) and a lower band (below the

Figure 6.36. Godin III:6 grey-black pottery

carination or shoulder) consist of combinations of straight and wavy lines. These outline the main or focal register on the lower shoulder. Here geometric or abstract motifs (naturalistic is rare) tend to be discrete rather than continuous; often two such motifs may alternate three or four times around the circumference of the vessel. The "triple arc" is a common distinctive class of motifs (Figure 6.34a, Gd 71-348); three successive arcs in the main register, when seen from above, form a triangle, which frames the neck. This motif provides the primary link to the outermost western valleys of the Pusht-i Kuh, where the ceramic tradition is somewhat different. There is limited evidence for Godin III:6 or similar wares in the western highland valleys, with the major exception of Rumishgan, which is one of the outer southern valleys.

Grey-black ware may represent an element of continuity from Godin IV to Godin III:6 (Figures 6.35 and 6.36). This ware is found only in valleys where there was previously a Godin IV occupation. Almost every Godin III:6 site also has a Godin IV occupation. Grey-black ware has no analog in other regions, nor in the Susa IV assemblage. Its methods of production and fundamental attributes (reduction firing, burnished surfaces, wholly handbuilding) are alien to the buff-painted technological tradition, but similar to those of Godin IV. In their 1999 article Robert Mason and Lisa Cooper pointed out that Godin IV pottery typically uses grog temper while Godin III grey-black is grit-tempered, but the latter is characteristic of the Godin III buff tradition and might be expected as part of assimilation.

The central date for Godin phase III:6—mid-third millennium BC—is well established by the copious parallels to the Susa sequence. Additional parallels to a small number of

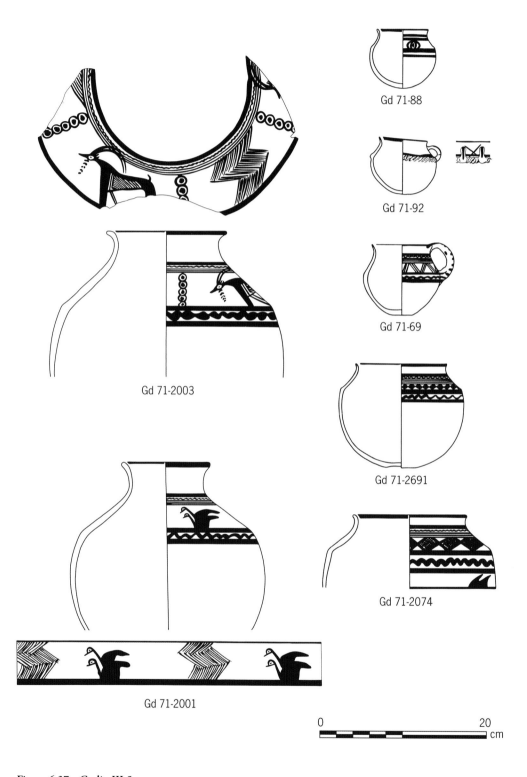

Gd 71-88

Gd 71-92

Gd 71-69

Gd 71-2003

Gd 71-2691

Gd 71-2074

Gd 71-2001

0   20
                     cm

Figure 6.37a. Godin III:5 pottery

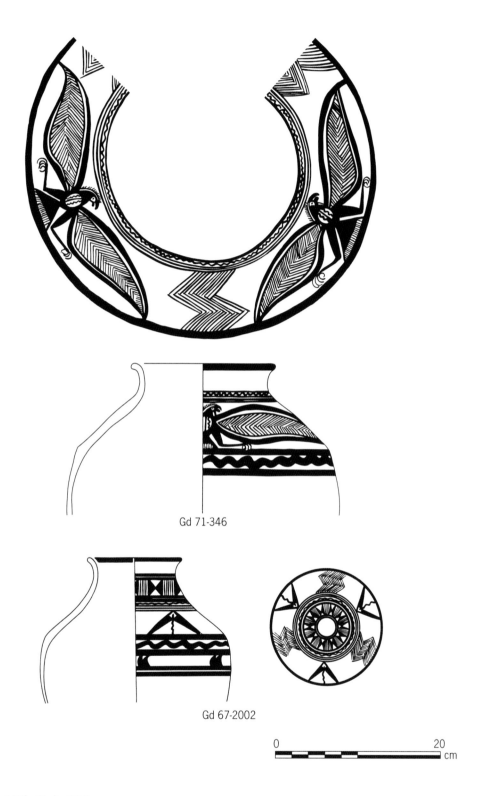

Gd 71-346

Gd 67-2002

0   20
                     cm

Figure 6.37b. Godin III:5 pottery

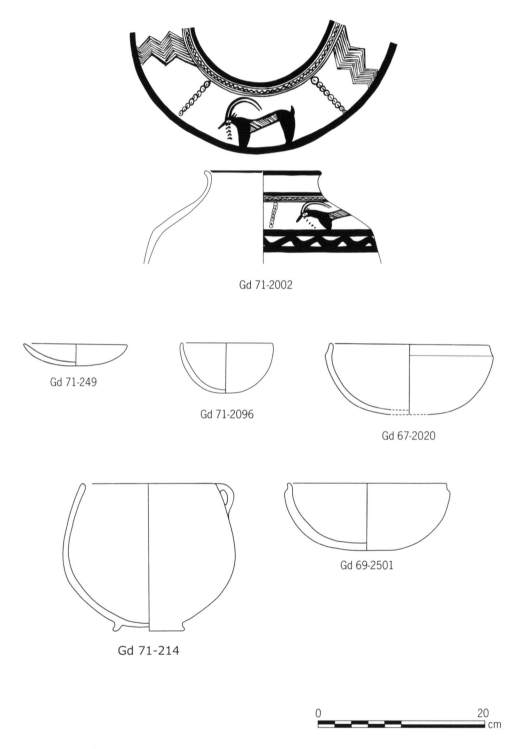

Gd 71-2002

Gd 71-249

Gd 71-2096

Gd 67-2020

Gd 71-214

Gd 69-2501

0   20
                      cm

Figure 6.37c. Godin III:5 pottery

sherds found at Early Dynastic III al-Hiba/Lagash in southern Iraq (Sumer) provide further evidence. In the Mahidasht, at Chogha Maran, the mid-third millennium assemblage consists of a red-slipped plain ware. Associated with this, however, were almost 200 sealings with Mesopotamian Early Dynastic II–III parallels and a limited number of Godin III:6 sherds.

In Godin phase III:5, carinated vessels continue as the characteristic, painted buff-ware vessel form, although the carination is often softer than before (Figures 6.37a–c). Some large jars have cable decoration and a painted X and small hole between two vertical handles; oversize cable-decorated storage jars continue. Roughly 45 percent of sherds are medium-buff ware; an additional 40 percent are coarser, undecorated buff. Grey-black carinated bowls, tankards, and simple dishes are less common than in Godin III:6 (3 percent). A handmade, well-finished and well-fired, sometimes burnished, red-slipped ware appears (14 percent), probably beginning to supplant the earlier grey-black. Common vessel forms include simple round bowls with grooved or rounded rims, hole-mouth jars, and neckless globular pots with raised bases, all in a wide range of sizes.

The register organization of the painted decoration continues in phase III:5, becoming perhaps less variable. The grammar, or rules, for painted decoration are quite clear and simple. The upper and lower registers now use composites of straight and wavy lines, except on the smallest vessels. A further register is sometimes added beneath the lower register, especially when the main register uses continuous motifs (e.g., successive solid or cross-hatched diamonds); it consists solely of groups of "flames" resting on two lines. Common discrete motifs in the main register are naturalistic (eagles, ducks, goats), geometric (nested diamonds, zigzags), and abstract (inverted Vs or "stingrays"). Usually zigzags alternate three times with another discrete motif, most commonly inverted Vs, ducks, eagles, and goats. The introduction of continuous motifs (usually strings of diamonds in this phase) marks a turning point, since such decoration increases in later phases, resulting in a progressive diminution and de-emphasis of the main register. Smaller vessels may have isolated bull's-eyes in the main register. The use of the wheel is also more notable in decorating some of the pottery of this phase—some painters would rotate the pot on a turntable to draw the horizontal lines, rather than using the more usual freehand approach, especially on pots with continuous motifs.

Godin III:5 pottery is widespread, though primarily in the northern valleys. The only concentration in southern valleys is in Rumishgan. Connections with the lowlands are very limited. The few Godin III:5 vessels found there, particularly at Susa, are imports, unrelated to the current, lowland-Susiana ceramic assemblage, which had become much more Mesopotamian. The few imports found in the lowlands, primarily at Susa, suggest a roughly Akkadian date (c. 2400–2100 BC).

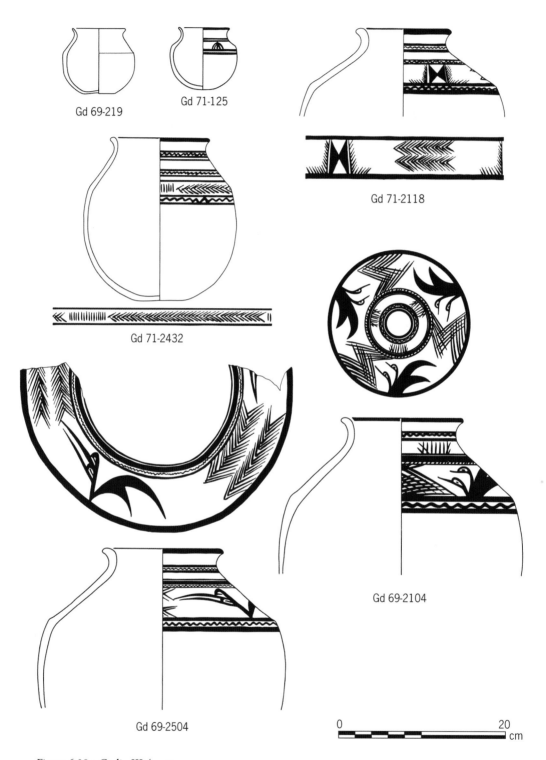

Gd 69-219

Gd 71-125

Gd 71-2118

Gd 71-2432

Gd 69-2104

Gd 69-2504

0   20
                     cm

Figure 6.38a. Godin III:4 pottery

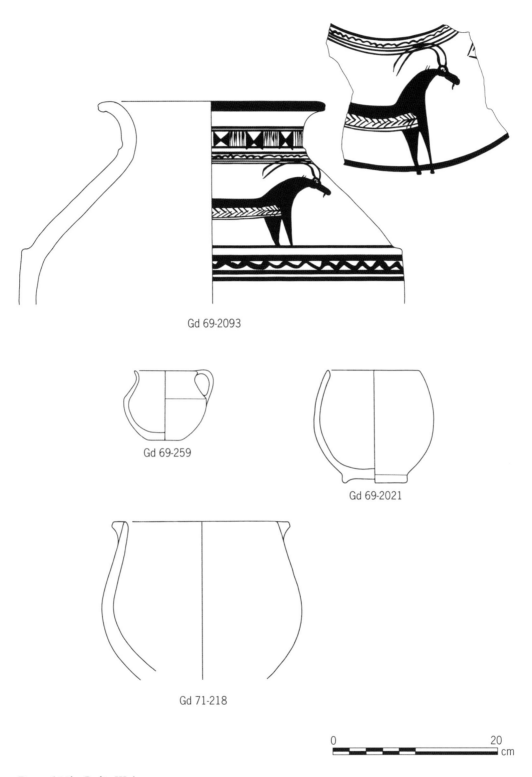

Gd 69-2093

Gd 69-259

Gd 69-2021

Gd 71-218

0   20
                cm

Figure 6.38b. Godin III:4 pottery

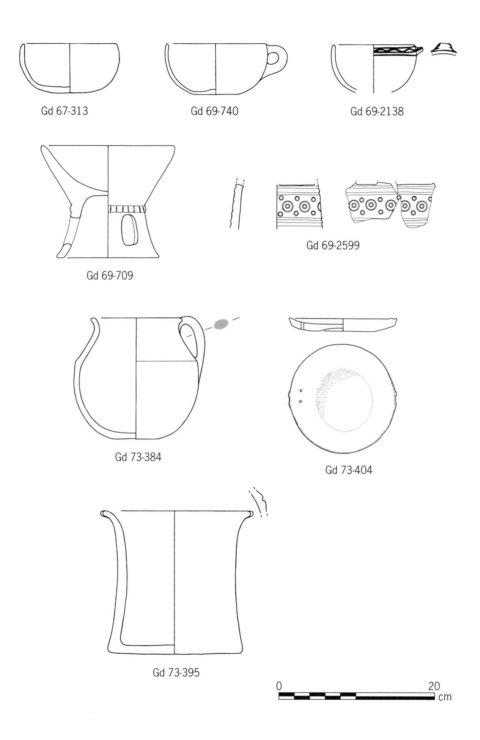

Gd 67-313

Gd 69-740

Gd 69-2138

Gd 69-709

Gd 69-2599

Gd 73-384

Gd 73-404

Gd 73-395

0   20
                     cm

Figure 6.38c. Godin III:4 pottery

In Godin phase III:4, painted, restricted-mouth vessels remain the principal diagnostic of the assemblage, but the former carination tends to become more of an angular shoulder, often with ridges added on larger vessels (Figures 6.38a–c). Both the softening of the carination and the addition of the ridge provide an antecedent to the later Godin III:2 vessels. The frequency of common painted buff ware continues to decrease, to 30 percent, while the coarser plain-buff ware increases to 40 percent. This coarsening of the assemblage begins a trend that continues to the end of the tradition. Red-slipped ware comprises almost 30 percent of the assemblage, being used for most utilitarian vessels (particularly simple rounded bowls, saucers, or lids, and a wide variety of carinated pots and storage jars). Some of the red-slipped vessel forms continue those typical of the earlier grey-black, which has disappeared (concave-sided cylindrical, carinated, or grooved-rim bowls, tankards). A finer grey ware appears, apparently as an import since it comprises less than 1 percent of the sherds and tends to have shapes unusual for the assemblage.

The painted decoration develops from that of the preceding phase, and is characterized by greater elaboration (typically more and finer brushstrokes), frequent use of decoration on the neck (in a neck register above the still-recognizable upper register), and a greater preference for linear geometric and continuous motifs. The neck and upper register often consist of bandlets made up of groups of straight and wavy lines combined with other fillers. In the main register, ducks continue to be a favourite motif but tend to be longer and leaner. Other animals are rare, including the "oiseau peigne" which is common in contemporary graves at Tepe Giyan in the nearby Nehavand Valley. Zigzags become long and limp, but more often are replaced by arrays of fine hatching. The increased use of continuous motifs in the main register and multiple bandlets above emphasizes the horizontal aspect of the decoration, so that the main register loses its prominence. The overall effect is multiple bands, which prefigures the style of Godin III:2. Inter-valley variation becomes more pronounced, so that Kangavar and the neighbouring Nehavand Valley to the south (Giyan IVA) have clearly distinguishable local styles. The use of abundant fine brushstrokes links the two, as do a limited number of vessels, which seem to have been exchanged between valleys.

The overall distribution is much as before, but regionalism is much more pronounced and makes precise mapping difficult. Each major valley system has a distinctive regional variant of the overall Godin III:4 style. Even adjacent valleys with decent access to one another, such as Kangavar and Nehavand, have readily identifiable, local substyles. Godin III:4 has to be dated primarily in terms of the better-dated previous and succeeding phases (c. 2100–1900 BC).

Godin phase III:3 consists of a very poorly preserved architectural stratum, with little reliably associated material.

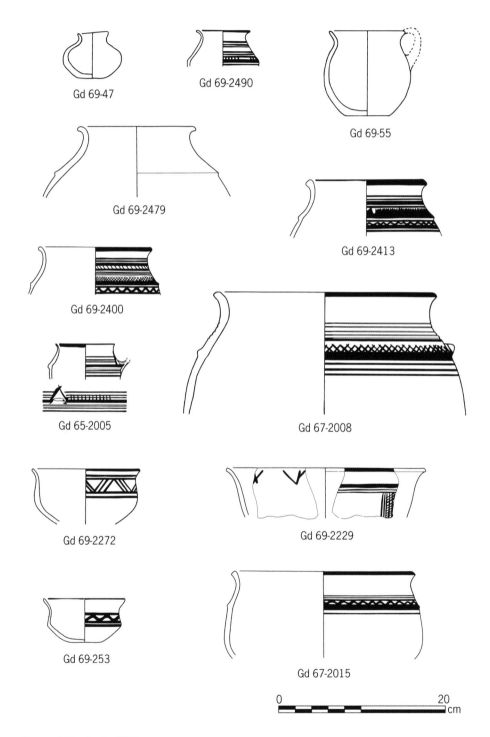

Gd 69-47

Gd 69-2490

Gd 69-55

Gd 69-2479

Gd 69-2413

Gd 69-2400

Gd 65-2005

Gd 67-2008

Gd 69-2272

Gd 69-2229

Gd 69-253

Gd 67-2015

0   20
                        cm

Figure 6.39a. Godin III:2 pottery

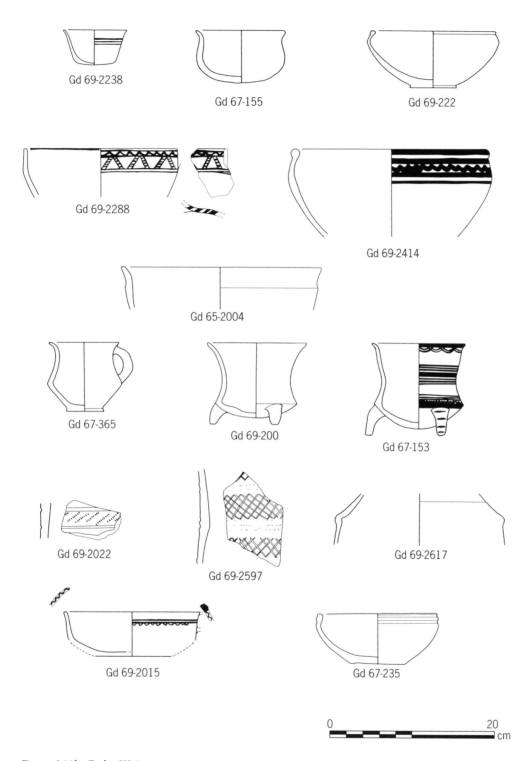

Gd 69-2238

Gd 67-155

Gd 69-222

Gd 69-2288

Gd 69-2414

Gd 65-2004

Gd 67-365

Gd 69-200

Gd 67-153

Gd 69-2022

Gd 69-2597

Gd 69-2617

Gd 69-2015

Gd 67-235

0   20 cm

Figure 6.39b. Godin III:2 pottery

Godin phase III:2 marks a major shift in the Godin III ceramic tradition, with the ceramic assemblage becoming much coarser overall (Figures 6.39a–b). The situation is rather paradoxical. The quality of the painted buff ware reaches a technical peak, with well-formed and well-finished vessels carefully painted. Rather bag-shaped vessels with shoulder ridges replace the earlier carinated profiles, with the decoration collapsing into a large band surrounding the shoulder ridge. The upper, main, and lower registers merge into a single broad belt of various linear bands, within which the main is relatively narrow and contains simple or repetitive motifs, such as grids or hatching. The other major painted vessel form is the tripod, with either tall concave, or shallow hemispherical bodies, and simple geometric decoration. Far more of the decoration is painted while rotating the vessel on a turntable than in any prior phase. Yet this painted pottery represents a much smaller proportion of the overall assemblage, as painted common buff ware shrinks to less than 10 percent of the assemblage. The majority of the assemblage is now undecorated, handmade, coarse buff (90 percent). Shapes are irregular, with curvilinear rather than carinated profiles and simple, often bevelled, rims. Skilled potters are producing the painted buff-ware, but the utilitarian, plain, coarse wares are likely produced by less skilled potters on a much smaller scale, though probably not within individual households. Several interrelated, well-made, grey wares comprise a minor element (1 percent), which may represent mostly imports since their shapes and finish are seldom related to the rest of the assemblage. Most such vessels are bowls and restricted forms, but istakans, tripods, and ridged jars are also present; some have pattern burnish. Red-slipped ware essentially disappears.

Regionalism is much less pronounced than in the previous Godin III:4 phase, but still evident. Bichrome or polychrome decoration is rare and tends to be found on medium or larger jars; it seems to be somewhat more common in valleys to the west of Kangavar. Ceramic parallels to the lowlands remain limited. The origins of the grey wares remain uncertain, although there are limited parallels to both contemporary Elamite grey wares and perhaps those of northeastern Iran.

Godin phase III:2 marks the maximal distribution of the tradition, both within individual valleys and in the central western highlands as a whole. More and larger sites are known in almost all valleys. This may be partially, but far from entirely, a result of patterns of occupation; many Godin III:2 sites have earlier (Godin III:6–4) phases of occupation, but few are occupied later, so the Godin III:2 occupations are more easily identified during survey.

A small number of painted sherds in phase III:2 at Godin Tepe are clearly not part of the Godin III tradition (Figures 6.39a–b, Gd 69-2272, Gd 69-2229, Gd 69-2288, Gd 69-2015) especially in the style and nature of their painted decoration, and their burnished surfaces. Limited parallels with sites such as Haftavan VI suggest contact with northwestern Iran, echoing the northeastern parallels for the andirons, which are found exclusively in

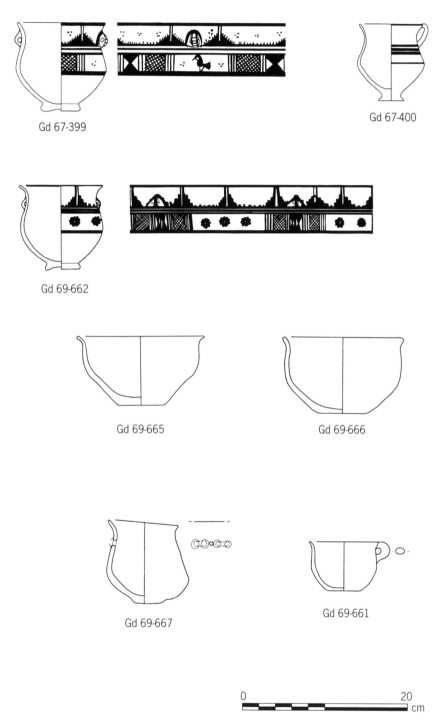

Gd 67-399

Gd 67-400

Gd 69-662

Gd 69-665

Gd 69-666

Gd 69-667

Gd 69-661

0   20
                                  cm

Figure 6.40. Godin Post–III:2 pottery

Figure 6.41. Godin Post–III:2 goblets

phase III:2 strata at Godin Tepe.

Radiocarbon and artifact parallels indicate a date of c. 1900–1600 BC. At this point, the development of the Godin Period III tradition becomes problematic. Although the ceramic assemblage of Post–III:2 is well defined, its relationship to Godin III:2 is ill defined. General parallels between the simple shapes of the plain wares suggest continuity,

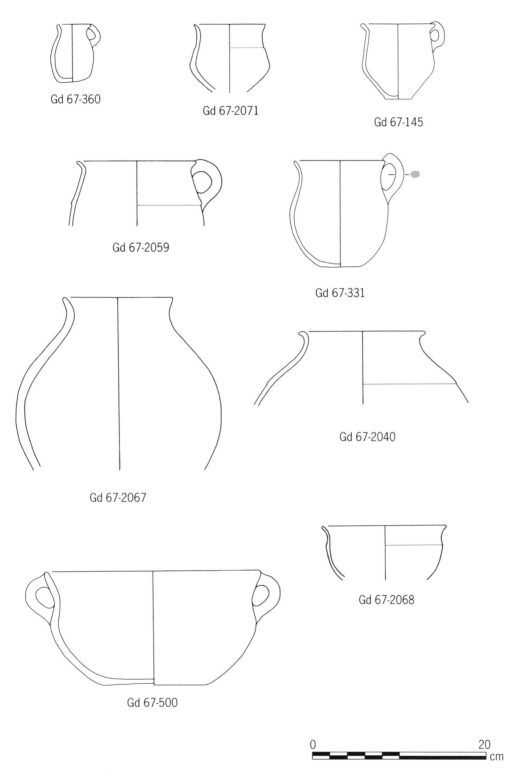

Gd 67-360

Gd 67-2071

Gd 67-145

Gd 67-2059

Gd 67-331

Gd 67-2067

Gd 67-2040

Gd 67-2068

Gd 67-500

0   20
                       cm

Figure 6.42. Godin III:1 pottery

and stratigraphy demonstrates that this phase is indeed Post–III:2 (i.e., it postdates phase III:2). The material culture of Post–III:2 is defined solely on the basis of grave goods at all sites where it is found. Two such graves are stratified between phases III:2 and III:1 in the Deep Sounding, and others are found scattered across the upper slopes of the mound at Godin Tepe. Although Post–III:2 material is found across central western Iran in almost all areas where earlier phases of Godin III are found, this pottery derives solely from graves. No associated settlements have been identified at any excavated site.

The documented typological range of the assemblage is narrow; some basic functional types are rare or absent. Cooking pots, large jars and pots, and lids are rarely found in these grave goods. Disproportionately large numbers of small vessels appear, particularly those suitable for drinking (Figures 6.40 and 6.41). Two types of footed goblets are typical: 1) "Bird and Sun," with a curvilinear profile, two horizontally pierced lugs, and finely painted decoration; and 2) "Banded," with concave cylindrical body with a low carination or belly, a single small handle at the rim, and simple painted line decoration. Footed bowls with painted bands are the other diagnostic form. None of these types is found in Godin III:2 contexts, indicating that Post–III:2 is a distinct and slightly later phenomenon. Other pottery in the grave groups is simple, rather coarse, handmade, and usually irregular in profile. The frequent presence of bronze artifacts, most often weapons (especially spear or javelin points), suggests a certain amount of wealth and inter-regional trade. The stratification of Post–III:2 and artifact parallels indicate a date in the mid-second millennium.

The limited phase III:1 architecture and the general lack of material in good contexts hamper definition of the Godin III:1 ceramic assemblage. Most consist of undecorated, irregular, and coarse, yet relatively well fired vessels. Restricted vessels have simple, curvilinear profiles; ridged jars resemble those of phase III:2. Smaller bowls tend to be carinated, larger ones curvilinear (Figure 6.42). Two small, carinated, wheel-made cups are the only painted vessels from good context, and, as such, are anomalous in both forming method and decoration. The Godin III painted style clearly has disappeared, and only some of the basics of what is known from phase III:2 continue among the unpainted buff wares. The scale of the potter's craft has shrunk to perhaps the household level. The date is problematic, though radiocarbon dating suggests somewhere in the third quarter of the second millennium. The architecture of phase III:1 seals two Post–III:2 graves, providing a terminus post quem. Regional distributions, even within Kangavar, cannot be defined, given the simplicity of the assemblage and its resemblance to the coarse, unpainted wares of Godin III:2. Godin Period III had come to an end.

With this background, let us now look at Godin III as a regional phenomenon, and put it in its larger historical context.

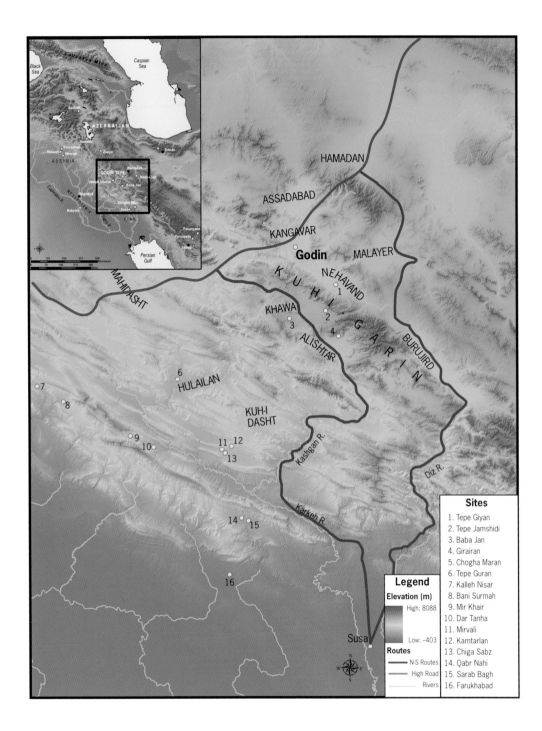

Figure 6.43. Sites occupied during Godin Period III

Regional and Historical Perspective

Central western Iran—modern Luristan and southern Kurdistan—is a pivotal region in the Zagros Mountains. This highland region looms over the lowlands: To the west lie Sumer and Babylonia, to the south, Susiana. The latter portion of southwestern Iran was the lowland component of Elam, a perpetual rival of Mesopotamian powers. Major trade routes run through the region. Jockeying for control of, or access to, resources has shaped the relations between highlands and lowlands for millennia. The socioeconomic and political interactions between highlands and lowlands had important, and often unforeseen, consequences for both; the impact of each on the other tends to be underestimated. The Iran-Iraq war has, in effect, recurred over more than 5,000 years.

Since the highlands have yielded almost no contemporary native written material for the second and third millennia BC, reliance on lowland Mesopotamian sources for writing history has yielded a one-sided account. The highlands are portrayed primarily as the objects of military campaigns or power diplomacy, the sources of plunder and tribute, or simply the home of uncivilized marauders who sometimes descend into the Mesopotamian lowlands to wreak havoc. This picture deserves redress. By default, archaeological data must be the primary basis for an understanding of the cultural history of the non-literate highland areas.

The topography of the central western Zagros highlands structures all interaction. Three major ridges of the Zagros define the basic geographical zones. First, at the west, the Kabir Kuh separates the Mesopotamian lowlands and the piedmont zone (Pusht-i Kuh) along the outer face of the Zagros from the highland valleys of western Luristan. Second, between the Kabir Kuh and the Kuh-i Sefid, the rugged topography yields isolated, narrow, poorly watered valleys, which have limited economic potential (Pish-i Kuh). Third, still farther east between the Kuh-i Sefid and the Alvand alignment, the higher valleys tend to be wider, with large undulating plains that are easier to irrigate. These valleys, and the Mahidasht to the west, have the greatest agricultural potential. To the east of the Alvand alignment lies the Iranian plateau.

This topography defines a limited number of routes among the intermontane valleys and restricts access to and from surrounding regions (Figure 6.43). Although moving parallel to the line of the ridges (northwest-southeast) is less difficult than moving across them, few natural north-south routes connect lowland Susiana with the highlands. These routes enter the highlands along river valleys and then move northwestward, parallel to the mountain ridges. In the western zone, the narrow, steep-sided valleys and gorges make travel even parallel to the ridges difficult. In the eastern zone, north-south travel is easier along either side of the Kuh-i Garin ridge. The better route runs northward along the Diz River from the Susiana lowlands to the Burujird Valley and onward through the Nehavand and Kangavar valleys. This had the added benefit, from the Elamite or highland perspective, of being the most distant from Meospotamia and thus more secure; the series of Islamic caravanserais along the route demonstrate the long-term importance of the routes. East-west travel is even more constrained. Few routes, most involving difficult passes, link the north-south routes. The High Road (or Great Khorasan Road or Silk Road), however, is the best east-west route from the Iranian plateau to the Mesopotamian lowlands; it is also marked by a series of Islamic caravanserais. From the Iranian plateau and the Hamadan plain, it winds westward through the Kangavar Valley past Godin Tepe, then through the Sahneh, Mahidasht, and Shahabad valleys, finally descending into the middle reaches of the Diyala River behind the Jebel Hamrin. From there, access to central Babylonia is relatively easy.

Traditional tribal and ethnic areas in the region are related to the topographic divisions. Today the northern valleys along the High Road are predominantly Kurdish, and mark the southern edge of Kurdistan. All valleys south and west to the piedmont are Luri. Within Luristan itself, three major tribal areas are defined by pastoral migration routes. These correspond repeatedly to distributions of ceramic assemblages in the archaeological record from at least the fifth millennium BC onward.

The traditional economy of Luristan has been a mixture of farming and herding since at least the fourth millennium BC. The small, narrow valleys of the western zone are unable to support either large, sedentary, human agricultural populations or local animal populations. In order to maintain their health and productivity, flocks must be moved between seasonal pastures in an annual migratory round. In the summer, the flocks are pastured in the upland, eastern valleys. In the winter, they are moved to the lower, outer Zagros valleys toward the piedmont. This strategy supports larger animal, and consequently human, populations. Although the eastern valleys have greater agricultural potential, herding is still a vital part of the economy. Such an economy is very sensitive to both the vagaries of the weather and, in the context of complex societies, human intervention.

Historical geography involves linking ancient toponyms and peoples with the physical landscape, recreating the ancient cultural landscape. Mesopotamian sources contain references to highland peoples, political, social, and ethnic regions, and topographic features. Since in many cases the writer probably had a hazy understanding, if any, of what was referred to, reconstruction of the historical geography remains ambiguous. Thus it is difficult to establish reliable identifications even in the outermost highland regions, and the problem only becomes worse with increasing distance in the absence of fixed points. In his book on the archaeology of Elam, Dan Potts provides an overview of the current interpretations of the historical geography of the region.

Table 6.2. Chronology of Godin III and related sites

BC	Godin Tepe	Tepe Giyan	Baba Jan	Mahi-dasht	Rumish-gan	Pusht-i Kuh	Susa Ville Royale	Meso-potamia
1400	III:1	graves 64, 65, 71, 72, 73, 77, 79, 82	Trench C grave 3			Late Bronze	Ville Royale I	Kassite
1500	Post-III:2 Graves							
	gap				Kamtarlan II (graves)			
1600								
1700	III:2	graves 83-101 105-107 108, 110 112, 115	Level 4 Op. F graves 1-4			Middle Bronze		Old Babylonian
1800					Chigha Sabz (graves)		Strata 3-6	
1900	III:3							Isin-Larsa
	gap							
2000		graves 111, 113, 114 116-119		Godin III				
	III:4							Ur III
2100							Strata 5-6	
	gap				Kamtarlan II (sherds)			Post Akkadian
2200			Level 5 Painted Chamber graves 1-2			Early Bronze II		
2300	III:5	grave 102			Dumavizeh	Kamtarlan I (sherds)	Strata 7-8	Akkadian
2400								
2500	III:6					Early Bronze I	Strata 9-12	Early Dynastic IIIb
2600					Mirvali		Strata 13-15	Early Dynastic IIIa
				Maran Red Slip				
2700	IV							Early Dynastic II

Figure 6.44. Susa D/IV style goat from Godin III:6

Figure 6.45. Godin III:6 pottery

In the early third millennium BC, central western Iran was a mosaic of diverse societies now defined primarily by pottery assemblages. In the northeastern valleys of the central Zagros, including Kangavar at Godin Period IV, the Early Transcaucasian Culture reached its southernmost substantial expansion from northwestern Iran. Its hallmark was well-burnished, handmade black pottery with white-filled incised decoration. Contemporary with its arrival, materials such as lapis lazuli ceased to arrive in the lowlands around 3000 BC, suggesting the cutting of Mesopotamia's long-distance connections with the East. Farther west, in the Mahidasht, simple, but well-made, red-slipped pottery was used. Developments in the central valleys of Luristan remain unclear. In the southern valleys and piedmont, an assemblage characterized by polychrome-painted pottery, related to the Scarlet Ware of Early Dynastic I Mesopotamia predominated a monochrome-painted tradition soon developed. To the west, in the middle reaches of the Diyala, east of the Jebel Hamrin, the small fortified settlements suggest that the region was a frontier, with great concern about the Zagros highlands just to the east.

As the later Early Dynastic period began in lowland Mesopotamia, archaeological patterns in the highlands changed markedly. A tradition of monochrome-painted pottery expanded from the Susiana lowlands and piedmont of southwestern Iran into the highlands. In particular, this assemblage extended northward in the eastern highland zone, reaching the High Road in the Kangavar Valley and beginning the Godin III period (Godin III:6) there. In Kangavar this yielded a complex sociocultural situation, as a period of co-existence and acculturation with the Early Transcaucasian Culture (Godin IV) seems to have ensued. Almost all sites with Early Transcaucasian Culture occupations also have evidence of early Godin III:6 settlement, suggesting a peaceful and gradual transition. In addition, some continuity of domestic pottery types may be traced, not only in eating, drinking, and serving bowls, but also for cooking pots and a distinctive form of storage jar. This contrasts markedly with other abrupt changes of (archaeological) cultures in the region, when many or most existing settlements were abandoned and new ones founded, and pottery assemblages changed radically.

Both the location and nature of the earliest Godin III architecture at Godin Tepe suggest the motivation for both the movement into Kangavar and a period of cultural co-existence. The first phase III:6 structure built at Godin Tepe was a very large complex, of which only part was excavated. Its scale remained unequalled in the region for perhaps the next two millennia. Foundation trenches more than a metre deep were cut into the top of the mound, and mud-brick walls almost 2 metres thick built into them. One wall had moulded and painted plaster decoration. Adjacent to this building, another, somewhat less massive building, was built later; unfortunately almost all has been lost to the erosion of the mound face. A few sherds, clearly more closely related to lowland Susa than the local assemblage, were found (Figure 6.44).

It is only after these massive structures were completed that modest, recognizably village-style houses and compounds began to fill in the remainder of the area excavated at the top of the mound; in one case being tucked into a corner formed by the two large buildings. This began a very long, continuous occupation at Godin Tepe; the street in the southeast corner of the area of excavation (nicknamed "Avenue Road" by the excavators) maintained its path for the next 500 to 600 years. Settlement in the Kangavar Valley included two major sites (towns) along the source of the High Road, and numerous small sites (villages) both on the valley floor and in the surrounding hill country.

The Kangavar Valley, and Malayer to the east, seem to define the northeastern limit of the Godin III tradition for centuries. It is noteworthy that while the monochrome pottery seems to have first moved quickly northward and eastward as far as Kangavar and Malayer, movement into the western highland valleys probably occurred only several centuries later.

What can account for this highly directional expansion? The economics of trade, based on the network of routes through the region, is a likely explanation. The Kangavar Valley straddles the High Road. The Malayer plain provides access to the Iranian plateau and north-south routes running along the eastern face of the Zagros. In Malayer, the earliest Godin III occupation at the largest site yielded pottery closely related to lowland Susa and was preceded by a large Godin IV Transcaucasian occupation. Control of this region, with the good eastern route leading southward to Susiana, was all that was needed; sheer distance and the intervening mountainous terrain secured it from Mesopotamian interference. In addition, these valleys provided the best subsistence base.

Therefore I would suggest that the pattern (and limits) of the initial expansion, and the nature and location of the initial Godin III occupations in these northern valleys, demonstrate a primary interest in securing and protecting access to the major trade routes through the central Zagros. The push into the Kangavar and Malayer valleys secured access to the High Road and gained access to the north-south routes along the western edge of the Iranian plateau. This served to divert trade southward through the eastern valleys to Elamite Susiana. The continued presence of a red-slipped pottery assemblage in the Mahidasht, and the virtual absence of Godin III:6 pottery there, suggests that movement westward along the High Road remained impeded. The sealings associated with this assemblage at Chogha Maran seem to reflect contact with the Early Dynastic II–III sites in the Diyala. The Early Dynastic city-states of lowland Mesopotamia thus had incomplete access to the highlands, the plateau and their products. Truncated access was available up the High Road to the Mahidasht but then blocked farther east, or through the Elamite lowlands. This is the era of

Figure 6.46. Godin III:5 painted pottery

the Royal Cemetery of Ur, whose rich royal burials included an abundance of imported materials. The distribution of the relatively few pieces of Iranian-style, monochrome-painted pottery (Godin III:6 or Susa IV style) found in lowland Mesopotamia support this pattern of trade connections. Most are found in the south, especially at Lagash but also at Ur and Telloh. Chogha Maran is the one major exception. In contrast, the very extensive excavations in the lower and middle Diyala sites have yielded little evidence for direct interaction with the highlands during this period.

The rise of the Akkadian state in lowland Mesopotamia (c. 2300 BC) had dramatic repercussions on the development of the highlands, setting the pattern of interaction for the next several centuries. Sargon and his successors conquered and unified the lowlands, incorporating even Susa and Susiana into their kingdom. This had two major effects: 1) severing the economic (and political) links between Susiana and the highlands; and 2) subjecting the highlands themselves to sustained political and military pressure. Year names and inscriptions record diplomatic efforts and campaigns directed at the highlands, although their scale and successes were probably exaggerated and the highland historical geography remains very problematic. Within a century, however, the Akkadian state collapsed, giving way to the ill-defined and poorly understood Gutian interlude in Mesopotamia. The Gutians are not identifiable archaeologically in the lowlands. Although they are generally regarded as coming from the mountains, no archaeological evidence links the Guti with the highlands.

The emergence of Ur and the establishment of the Ur III dynasty late in the third millennium renewed and intensified the confrontation with the highlands. The Ur III state controlled the Mesopotamian lowlands in a closely knit provincial system. On the eastern frontier, beyond a line of vassal polities, lay numerous semi-autonomous highland polities. The historical geography of this and later centuries remains a vexed question, with many basic problems yet to be resolved. Suffice to say that beyond direct military contact with the Ur III state in the highlands lay numerous small, autonomous polities, each perhaps consisting of several intermontane valleys. While the rulers of these polities are referred to in contemporary lowland documents as kings, they are probably better characterized as chiefs, given the probable size of their territories inferred from archaeological evidence. Ur III year-names and other sources demonstrate that the Zagros highlands were a major external concern. Indeed, the northeastern frontier in the Diyala region is the only area in which repeated Ur III military activity is documented, beginning as early as 2059 BC. In a critical thirteen-year period (2044–2032 BC), the Ur III state conducted repeated military campaigns into this region, penetrating an ill-defined distance into the highlands. Messenger texts document provisions for a constant flow of messengers and envoys travelling into the highlands to vassal and autonomous polities.

The depth of the Akkadian and Ur III penetration into the highlands is difficult to establish, given our uncertain understanding of the historical geography. Neo-Assyrian campaigns into the Zagros in the first millennium BC may, however, offer some guidelines despite scholarly disagreements over scale. Their deepest penetration was apparently along the High Road, reaching the Assadabad Valley (just north of Kangavar), as shown by the stele erected there by Sargon II. The Neo-Assyrians did not, however, incorporate anything east of the Mahidasht into their provincial administrative system. The valleys east of the Kuh-i Sefid would probably have been subject to diplomatic and, usually, indirect military pressure. Likewise, the Assyrians seem to have left Luristan proper, south of the High Road, alone; it was too difficult to campaign in and too poor to repay the effort. The Ur III state probably took the same courses, probably with less depth.

During the Akkadian period, the Godin III:5 assemblage seems to have spread further within the highlands, probably moving west of the Kuh-i Sefid into the Mahidasht at this time along the High Road and Luristan proper further south. The southern valleys had already been occupied. The ceramic tradition seems notably homogeneous in style across its distribution, perhaps at a maximum for its history.

At the end of the third millennium BC, however, distinctive regional stylistic variants of the Godin III assemblage appeared within clusters of valleys. Godin III:4 has been identified primarily in the more northern and eastern valleys, those more removed from direct military contact with the Ur III state. Coupled with this retrenchment of distribution is an apparent decline in both number of sites and total occupied area. In the northeast valleys, east of the Kuh-i Garin range, the elaborately painted decoration is highly stylized and quite different from all other regions, even those just to the west. Settlement in the western highland valleys remained relatively smaller in scale and sparser. At Godin Tepe itself, the

Figure 6.47. Godin III:4 pottery

town of phase III:4 seems to have been fairly prosperous, with large amounts of stone used in construction. The excavated area was densely built-up. "Avenue Road" still followed the same track as centuries before. Godin was now the single town in the Kangavar Valley, while the proportion of settlements on the valley floor increased relative to those in the surrounding hill country.

Archaeological evidence, such as small site sizes and limited numbers, suggest a relatively simple society, although the varied numbers and elaboration of grave goods at Godin Tepe and Tepe Giyan in Nehavand clearly provide evidence for at least some social stratification. Regional stylistic differences and results of neutron activation analyses indicate that specialist potters served market areas consisting of clusters of several adjacent valleys.

The apparent retrenchment, to the northern valleys, may have resulted from the prolonged Akkadian and Ur III military and political pressure on the outer highland valleys. Although Luristan itself would have been difficult to campaign in, the pastoral component of the regional economy may have provided leverage to exert some influence or control. In the annual migratory round, the herds spent the winter in the pastures of southwestern Luristan, in or near the piedmont. This area was quite accessible from the lowlands, exposing the tribal herds to threat; loss of herds would be a crippling blow to the subsistence economy. For example, when Reza Shah forced pastoralists in the region to give up the annual migrations in 1925–1939, their herds suffered critical losses and the population of the region suffered severe hardships. Lowland powers' ability to threaten the southwestern winter pastures would be sufficient and effective economic blackmail to exert control over the population of Luristan. Because the Ur III state controlled the outer fringes of the Zagros piedmont, such a strategy could easily have been applied. The repeated campaigns on the northeastern frontier of the lowlands argue for long-term concern and instability there. The underlying impetus may have been the protection of trade routes and access to resources via the High Road.

Why did regional differences develop at this time? Ethnographic studies suggest that one response of interrelated social groups, when pressed toward sociopolitical unification, is to emphasize individual group identities through material culture and other means. The regional variants in the Godin III:4 tradition may reflect such a process of self-differentiation. Even the neighbouring Kangavar and Nehavand valleys have rather different styles of painted decoration on pottery. The elaborate regional style in the northeastern valleys may reflect the areas of one or more of the small autonomous highland polities, near but not subject to Ur III control.

The sustained Ur III pressure, in particular, provided a catalyst for rapid political change in the highlands. Spurred by opposition to Ur, highland polities would have banded

Figure 6.48. Godin III:2 grey ware

together to resist. Intermarriage among leading families is a common method of sealing alliances. The network of kinship relations would have laid the foundation for emergence of a "dynastic figure" or family linking the various polities. Initial highland successes would have strengthened the movement toward collaboration, which quickly subsumed the Šimaški lands, the SU lands, and Anshan within the highlands., The numerous highland polities in central western and southern Iran coalesced politically under the dynasty of Šimaški within a span of thirty years (2033–2003 BC). The confederation then seized Susa and lowland southwest Iran, and went on to crush the Ur III state.

The number and size of sites throughout both lowland and highland Elam increased markedly during the first half of the second millennium BC. All the data suggest increased settlement and wealth in the highlands. The relative homogeneity of material culture indicates increased regional integration, with a limited amount of local variation continuing. In the central Zagros highlands, settlement patterns changed dramatically in the Godin III:2 period. Sites became far more numerous throughout the region, suggesting that more peaceful conditions prevailed and the population prospered. Although sites in the western valleys remained small, central sites in the eastern valleys reached their largest sizes, such as Godin Tepe in Kangavar. Political confederation yielded Elamite control of all routes and trade through the central Zagros highlands.

The Kangavar Valley, as a node of routes, reached an unprecedented height of prosperity and population, based on intensive agricultural exploitation of the valley floor and probably trade as well. Godin Tepe, in the middle of the valley overlooking the High Road, was a prosperous settlement with well-built and large houses. The total area of settlements in the valley was almost double that of any previous period, and indeed was not again equalled until the Parthian period 1,500 years later. The increased proportion of settlements located on the valley floor rather than in the surrounding hill country suggests intensified agriculture, and their apparent linear arrangements may reflect ancient canal courses, suggesting increased reliance on irrigation.

Although Godin III:2 pottery exhibits strong overall stylistic homogeneity, regional substyles or variants are still identifiable. The eastern valleys had complex trichrome, dark painted on red slip, and incised wares. The valleys farther west along the High Road had a simple, linear, bichrome-painted decoration. These regional distributions resemble both those of variants in the previous phases and pre-modern ethnographic tribal areas. Ceramic parallels to the Susiana lowlands are few and relatively weak.

After the fall of the Ur III state, numerous petty city-states in lowland Mesopotamia bickered with one another for two centuries, with some rising to brief prominence and then falling back in the Isin-Larsa period. Finally, as several lowland city-states emerged as regional powers, Elam also again became a major international power under the Sukkalmah from 1800 to 1750 BC, playing important military and economic roles in the lowlands, particularly in central and northern Mesopotamia. It is the central Zagros highland component of Elam that may make this focus of activity understandable. After a series of defeats, culminating in the rise of the Old Babylonian state under Hammurabi, Elam withdrew from further western adventures and ceased to influence Mesopotamia.

Mesopotamian contact with the central Zagros highlands, perhaps via Eshnunna on the lower Diyala, is just visible archaeologically. Sherds of Isin-Larsa grey ware (Figure 6.39b, Gd 69-2022) have been found primarily in valleys along the High Road, particularly the Mahidasht and Kangavar. Old Babylonian, Mesopotamian-style cylinder seals and pottery, rather than highland-related material, are found in the Zagros piedmont southeast of the middle Diyala River.

In the period 1850–1750 BC, a triangular relationship based on trade developed among Larsa, Eshnunna, and Elamite Susa. The prominence of Eshnunna, and its era as a regional power, may derive from both its geographical position and its interrelationship with the central Zagros highlands, which were most likely part of the Elamite confederation; again the historical geography is a problem too complex to explore here. The (Elamite) highlands and Eshnunna were complementary both geographically and economically. Eshnunna lay on the eastern edge of central Mesopotamia and was the crossroads region for other major lowland routes leading north, south, and west. By the late nineteenth century BC the city-state of Eshnunna included the lower Diyala region and extended upstream into the Jebel Hamrin basin of the middle Diyala. It thus controlled the lowland end of the High Road, as well as routes running northwest-southeast along the outer face of the Zagros. Eshnunna was one of the few lowland polities most readily accessible to Elam, either along the outer face of the Zagros, within the piedmont, or along the High Road to the middle reaches of the Diyala. Seen from a highland Elamite perspective, Eshnunna was the gateway into the economic crossroads of the Mesopotamian lowlands. Evidence for economic activity involving the two is slim, but quite suggestive. During this period Mari letters cite Eshnunna and Susa as sources for tin. Letters and documents from other sources, such as cities of central Mesopotamia, also cite the general area of the Eshnunna state as a source of tin.

Although the Sukkalmah lasted until c. 1600, its power had gradually faded. In the highlands, the Godin III tradition gradually disappeared through the mid-second millennium, although identifiable remnants persisted in the eastern valleys until the later second millennium BC The simplified pottery assemblage suggests that the local economy shrank in scale and complexity; pastoralism seems to have grown in importance.

The Post–III:2 assemblage and its distribution seem to mark a dramatic change toward a far simpler economy in the mid-second millennium. As noted in the pottery discussion, the assemblage is known only from graves. This is not to say that there were not permanent settlements at the time, only that they have not yet been reliably identified. The Post–III:2 distribution includes the regions of both summer and winter pastures. The absence of identifiable permanent settlements suggests a fundamentally pastoral economy.

The Godin III:1 occupation demonstrates that such settlements did exist somewhat later, but the material culture would make them difficult to identify in survey. The long history of the Godin Period III tradition had come to an end. Godin Tepe itself would see only intermittent activity for the rest of the second millennium.

Further Reading:

Note: Additional references are available in the Godin Web archive at https://tspace.library.utoronto.ca.

Amiet, P. *L'Age des echanges inter-iraniens, 3500-1700 avant J.C.* Paris : Ministère de la culture, 1986.

Carter, E. "Elamite Exports." *Contribution à l'histoire de l'Iran: Mélanges offerts à Jean Perrot,* edited by F. Vallat, 89–100. Paris: Editions Recherches sur les Civilisations, 1990.

———."The Piedmont and Pusht-i Kuh in the Early Third Millennium B.C." In *Préhistoire de la Mésopotamie: La Mésopotamie préhistorique et l'exploration récente du Djebel Hamrin,* edited by J.-L. Huot, 73–84. Paris: Centre National de Recherche Scientifique, 1987.

———. "Excavations in the Ville Royale at Susa: The Third Millennium B.C. Occupation." *Cahiers de la Délégation Archéologique Française en Iran* 11 (1980): 11–134.

Carter, E., and M. W. Stolper. *Elam: Surveys of Political History and Archaeology.* Berkeley: University of California, 1984.

Contenau, G., and R. Ghirshman. *Fouilles du Tepe Giyan.* Paris: Geuthner, 1935.

Dyson, R. H.,Jr. "The Archaeological Evidence of the Second Millennium B.C. on the Persian Plateau." *Cambridge Ancient History* 2(1): 686–715. London: Cambridge University, 1973.

Edwards, M. *Excavations in Azerbaijan (Northwestern Iran) 1: Haftavan, Period VI*. Oxford: British Archaeological Reports, 1983.

Gasche, H. *La Poterie élamite du deuxième millénaire a.c.* Paris: Geuthner, 1973.

Goff, C. "Excavations at Baba Jan: The Bronze Age Occupation." *Iran* 14 (1976): 19–40.

———. "Luristan before the Iron Age." *Iran* 9 (1971): 131–152.

Haerinck, E. *Bani Surmah: An early Bronze Age graveyard in Pusht-i Kuh, Luristan.* Leuven: Peeters, 2006.

———. "The Chronology of Luristan, Pusht-i Kuh in the Early Bronze Age I (ca. 3000 to ca. 2600 B.C.)." In *Préhistoire de la Mésopotamie: La Mésopotamie préhistorique et l'exploration récente du Djebel Hamrin,* edited by J.-L. Huot, 55–72. Paris: Centre National de Recherche Scientifique, 1987.

Henrickson, R. C. "A Comparison of Production of Large Storage Vessels in Two Ancient Ceramic Traditions." In *Materials Issues in Art and Archaeology IV*, edited by P. B. Vandiver, J. Druzik, J. L. Galvan, I. A. Freestone, and G. S. Wheeler, 553–572. Pittsburgh: Materials Research Society, 1995.

———. "Analysis of Use Wear on Ceramic Potter's Tools." In *Materials Issues in Art and Archaeology III*, edited by P. B. Vandiver, J. R. Druzik, G. S. Wheeler, and I. C. Freestone, 475–493. Pittsburgh: Materials Research Society, 1992.

———. "Wheelmade or Wheel-Finished? Interpretation of 'Wheelmarks' on Pottery." In *Materials Issues in Art and Archaeology II*, edited by P. B. Vandiver, J. R. Druzik, and G. Wheeler, 523–541. Pittsburgh: Materials Research Society, 1991.

———. "The Buff and the Grey: Ceramic Assemblages and Cultural Process in the Third Millennium B.C. Central Zagros, Iran." In *Cross-Craft and Cross-Cultural Interaction in Ceramics,* edited by M. R. Notis and P. E. McGovern, 81–146. Ceramics and Civilization IV. Westerville, OH: American Ceramic Society, 1989.

———. "The Godin III Revised Chronology for Central Western Iran, ca. 2600–1400 B.C." *Iranica Antiqua* 22 (1987): 33–115.

———. "A Regional Perspective on Godin III Cultural Development in Central Western Iran." *Iran* 24 (1986): 1–55.

———. "Craft Specialization and Pottery Production in Bronze Age Central Western Iran." In *Technology and Style,* edited by W. D. Kingery, 53–85. Ceramics and Civilization II. Columbus: American Ceramic Society, 1986.

———. "Šimaški and Central Western Iran: The Archaeological Evidence." *Zeitschrift für Assyriologie* 74 (1984): 98–122.

———. *Godin Tepe, Godin III, and Central Western Iran, ca. 2600–1400 B.C.* Doctoral dissertation, Department of Near Eastern Studies, University of Toronto, 1984.

———. "Giyan II and I Reconsidered." *Mesopotamia [Torino]* 18–19 (1983–1984): 195–220.

Henrickson, R. C., and, M. J. Blackman. "Scale and Paste: Investigating the Production of Godin III Buff Painted Ware." *Chemical Characterization of Ceramic Pastes in Archaeology*, edited by H. Neff, 125–144. Madison, WI: Prehistory Press, 1992.

Horne, L., *Village Spaces: Settlement and Society in Northeastern Iran*. Washington, DC: Smithsonian Institution, 1994.

Kramer, C. *Village Ethnoarchaeology: Rural Iran in Archaeological Perspective*. New York: Academic Press, 1982.

Mason, R. B., and L. Cooper. "Grog, Petrology, and Early Transcaucasians at Godin Tepe." *Iran* 27 (1999): 25–31.

Miroschedji, P. de. "Susa and the Highlands: Major Trends in the History of Elamite Civilization," *Yeki Bud, Yeki Nebud: Essays on the Archaeology of Iran in Honor of William M. Sumner*, edited by N. F. Miller and K. Abdi, 17–38. Los Angeles: Costen Institute of Archaeology, 2000.

Mortensen, I. D. *The Nomads of Luristan: History, Material Culture, and Pastoralism in Western Iran*. Carlsberg Foundation's Nomad Research Project. London: Thames and Hudson, 1993.

Potts, D. *The Archaeology of Elam*. Cambridge: Cambridge University Press, 1999.

Schmidt, E. F., M. N. Van Loon, and H. H. Curvers. *The Holmes Luristan Expeditions*. Chicago: Oriental Institute, 1989.

Stein, A. *Old Routes of Western Iran*. London: Macmillan, 1940.

Thrane, H. *Excavations at Tepe Guran in Luristan*. Moesgaard: Jutland Archaeological Society, 2001.

Watson, P. J. *Archaeological Ethnography in Western Iran*. Viking Fund Publications in Anthropology 57. Tucson: University of Arizona Press, 1979.

Young, T. C., Jr. "An Archaeological Survey of the Kangavar Valley." In *Proceedings of the Third Annual Symposium on Archaeological Research in Iran*, 23–30. Tehran: Iranian Center for Archaeological Research, 1975.

———. *Excavations at Godin Tepe: First Progress Report*. Toronto: Royal Ontario Museum, 1969.

———. "Survey in Western Iran." *Journal of Near Eastern Studies* 25 (1966): 228–239.

Young, T. C., and L. D. Levine. *Excavations of the Godin Project: Second Progress Report*. Toronto: Royal Ontario Museum, 1974.

7 | The Median Citadel of Godin Period II

Hilary Gopnik

*After the Assyrians had ruled Upper Asia for five hundred and twenty years, the Medes
were the first to begin to revolt from them; and, I think, they fought with the Assyrians
about their freedom and proved good men, and they thrust away from themselves their
slavery and were free.*

—Herodotus, Histories I.95

Most of what we know about the Medes comes either from the fifth-century stories of Greek
historian Herodotus or from the records of their enemies, the Assyrians. The Godin Tepe
Period II citadel stands as one of the only physical records of these "good men," the Medes.

In the early ninth century BC, Ashurnasirpal II (882–859 BC), king of Assyria, attentive prince, worshipper of the great gods, ferocious dragon, conqueror of cities and the
entire highlands, king of lords, encircler of the obstinate, crowned with splendour, fearless
in battle, lofty and merciless hero, he who stirs up strife, king of all princes, lord of lords,
chief herdsman, king of kings, attentive purification priest, destructive weapon of the great
gods and avenger (to quote only a portion of his epithet list), commanded his artists to
create a new decorative scheme for the throneroom of his palace at the city of Nimrud in
northern Iraq. Instead of the ritual scenes of fertility and piety that had adorned previous
palaces, Ashurnasirpal chose to receive his guests surrounded by images of violent warfare
and conquest. The litany of beheadings, impalings, looting, and mass-deportations that
lined the palace rooms of Ashurnasirpal and his successors, in the form of hundreds of
painted stone reliefs, was intended to intimidate the enemies of the state, but in our terms
it provides important evidence of the peoples that the Assyrians were trying to subdue,
including the Medes of Godin in the Zagros Mountains.

The first millennium BC was the age of empire in the Near East. Large centralized states had flourished in the region for two millennia, but they had tended to stay within their natural borders, extending their power outwards only for brief interludes. The state of Assyria, under protection of the great god Ashur, had been a powerful presence in northern Mesopotamia since about 2000 BC, when the governors of the capital at Aššur had established a thriving trading colony as far north as the city of Kaneš in central Turkey. Assyria's fortunes had ebbed and flowed since that time, but by about 900 BC a new line of powerful kings established a renewed military-based state. Assyria, with its political capital now moved from Aššur to Nimrud in northern Iraq, began to reach outwards for power, at first tentatively conducting raids and demanding tribute as its predecessors had done, but later taking direct political control of neighbouring states.

The Assyrians became the model of how to create an empire and how not to endear yourself to your subjects. The violent images of warfare that lined the most intimate rooms of their palaces and the graphic narrative accounts of battle that formed their royal annals paint a picture of a ruthless and brutal adversary. For particularly recalcitrant subjects, the Assyrians employed the tactic of mass deportations, shipping the entire population of towns from one end of the empire in ancient Israel to the other in the Zagros Mountains, thousands of kilometres away. The hardships of these enforced trails of tears can still be seen on the painted stone reliefs of the perpetrators; in one fragment now in the British Museum a deportee bends to offer water to an emaciated baby as they follow loaded pack mules to their new home. In other panels still more gruesome fates await the enemies of the state; we see men impaled on stakes, flayed alive with their skins stretched out for display in front of an enemy stronghold, or with their heads hanging from trees like ripe fruit. In spite of this seemingly well-orchestrated and purposeful culture of violence, the Medes of the Zagros Mountains appear to have fared somewhat better at the hands of the Assyrians than did other surrounding states.

The exact location and extent of the country of the Medes is not entirely clear, but the Assyrians write about Medes living all along the High Road through the Zagros, from Kermanshah to Hamadan. Godin Tepe lies in the heart of this area. The Medes had probably settled in this area sometime around the end of the second millennium BC, when large-scale migrations of people took place all over the Near East. Archaeology can't tell us anything about language groups, so it is impossible to know exactly when or how they arrived, but we do know from historical sources that people speaking Indo-European languages, including ancient Persian, had settled in Iran by the first millennium. The Medes were one of these newly arrived peoples.

The Medes first appear in the historical record in 835 BC as recorded in the Black

Figure 7.1. The capture of the Median fortress of Tikrakka by the Assyrians, from a carved relief at the palace of Sargon at Khorsabad. An Assyrian stele that was erected in an earlier campaign can be seen in front of the fortress.

Obelisk of the Assyrian king Shalmaneser III (858–824 BC), which recounts a campaign along the High Road from the Diyala through the passes of the Zagros Mountains, along which lay Godin Tepe (probably still abandoned following the desertion of the Bronze Age settlement). Some twenty years later, Shalmaneser's successor, Šamši-Adad V (823–811 BC), would write in his annals:

> I marched to the country of the Medes. They took fright in the face of the angry weapons of Aššur and of my strong warfare, which have no rival, and abandoned their cities. They ascended a rugged mountain, and I pursued them. I massacred 2,300 soldiers of Hanaširuka the Mede. I took 140 of his rider [horses] from him and carried away his property and possessions in numbers beyond counting. I razed, destroyed and plundered Sagbita, the royal city together with 1,200 of his towns. (Grayson, AO 103.1 iii 27–36)

The Neo-Assyrian kings had a notorious penchant for exaggeration, and the figures used here should be taken with a large grain of salt, but this passage establishes two important points: the Medes escape the Assyrian troops by fleeing into the mountains, and horses are the loot of choice for the Assyrians to carry away with them from the country of the Medes.

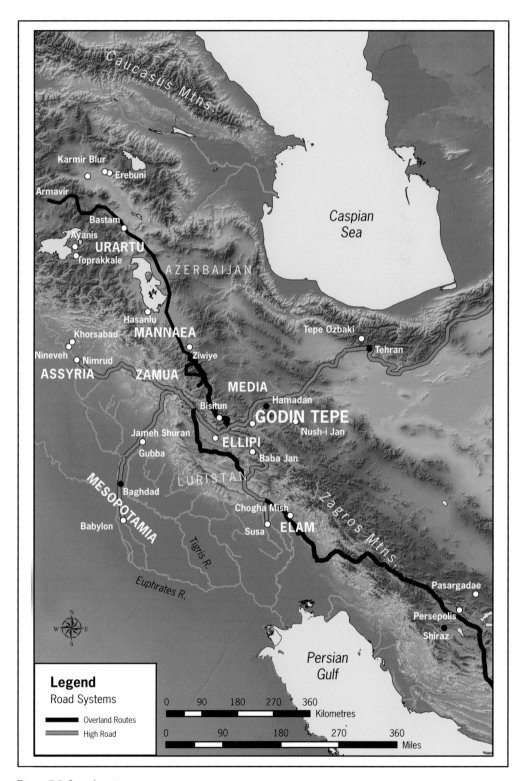

Figure 7.2. Iron Age sites

Horses were an integral and essential component of the indomitable Neo-Assyrian army. They were used as mounts for archers and nimble draught animals for chariots. But from what we can gather from the abundant texts, the Assyrians did not breed horses in large numbers within the heartland of Assyria itself. Although domestic horses had probably been exploited in Iran for some 2,000 years by that time, they were treated as herd animals, rather than individually bred and raised in enclosed corrals. The horses of the Medes were let loose to roam through the valleys of the Zagros Mountains, grazing on the grasses of the valley floors, and were captured and trained only as they reached maturity. The horse herds were probably culled and controlled, but horse husbandry nonetheless required an expanse of land that simply wasn't available in Assyria where agricultural land was at a premium. The Assyrians grew to depend on the horses provided by trade, tribute, and booty from the Zagros principalities, particularly once the rising power of Urartu cut off their supply from northwest Anatolia.

The state of Urartu was the thorn in the side of the Assyrian kings. Urartu was based to the north of Assyria, centred in the Lake Van area, but stretching from eastern Turkey to Azerbaijan. The cores of the two empires were never in dispute, but as each pushed its boundaries they had continual skirmishes over control of the surrounding territories. The Medes in the Zagros were one of the groups in the uncomfortable position of lying adjacent to both empires, and their history was subject to this shifting balance of power. When Urartu encroached on the Zagros area by forming alliances with the northern Zagros states of Parsua and Mannea, who provided horses and riders to the Urartian army in exchange for military protection, the Assyrian king Tiglath-Pileser III (744–727 BC)

Figure 7.3. Medes bringing horses to the Assyrian king Sargon II in a relief from Sargon's palace at Khorsabad

responded with a well-orchestrated show of force designed to intimidate the pro-Urartian rulers and to shore up the pro-Assyrian powers in the region. Tiglath-Pileser eventually annexed Parsua (not to be confused with the later Persian territory that lay much further south) and turned it into an Assyrian province controlled by an Assyrian governor. Sargon II (721–705 BC) expanded this province and created two more, but left a string of Median settlements lying to the east with their local rulers in place and nothing more than oaths of vassalage and threats of intimidation to ensure their cooperation. One of these rulers chose to perch his palace-citadel on the very top of the mound of Godin, by then a 20-metre-high hill of ruins commanding a strategic view of the Kangavar Valley below.

The citadel at Godin was an impressively large edifice. In its prime, it enclosed a space of almost 5,000 square metres, including a large columned hall, dining rooms, kitchens, storage magazines, and probably second-storey bedrooms. Its 3-metre-thick exterior walls were designed to keep intruders out, should they have managed to get past the shower of arrows that would have descended on them from the arrowslots looming over the cliff face. Although it was designed to intimidate and impress from the exterior, the main activity that seems to have gone on inside the building was not preparing for warfare, but eating and drinking on a large scale. The carefully made arrowslots were allowed to fill up with debris through time, so that shooting out of them would have been impossible. Although spearpoints and arrowheads were found in the earlier domestic occupations at Godin, here in the citadel where they should be expected in large numbers, only two bronze arrow-heads were recovered. Instead, the inhabitants left behind a few large garbage heaps filled with broken drinking bowls, serving platters, bones of butchered sheep and goats, and even the remains of dessert in the form of grape seeds.

Back in Assyria, Sargon had abandoned the old capital at Nimrud and built a brand-new, Brasilia-like city, which he called Dur-Šarrukin (roughly translatable as Sargonville), but which is generally now known by its modern site name, Khorsabad. On the walls of the pristine palace of his new capital, Sargon ordered his sculptors to inscribe the official version of his annals and to create carved stone reliefs illustrating his military conquests. In those inscriptions and reliefs, Sargon recounted his campaigns to expand the empire, including several forays to the mountainous east against the "madaaya dannu," or mighty Medes.

Khorsabad was excavated in the late nineteenth century by two French diplomats, Paul Emile Botta and Victor Place, who drew and then removed the carved stone slabs for shipment back to the Louvre in Paris. Unfortunately the leaky sailing ship and rafts that Place had hired to move the shipment down the Tigris River were attacked by brigands, probably in search of contraband bales of silk that had been smuggled onto the ship in order to avoid customs duties. The pirates quickly seized the ships' timbers, an even more

Figure 7.4. Bowl sherds from Godin II citadel garbage

valuable resource than silk in the treeless marshes of southern Mesopotamia, and the ships and rafts, unable to bear the weight of their historic load, promptly sank to the bottom of the river where some of the carved reliefs lie to this day. On those lost slabs, scribes had recorded the events of Sargon's sixth military campaign which brought him eastward to the distant mountains of the Medes:

> The people of Ḫarḫar drove out Kibaba, their mayor, and sent word to Talta of Ellipi (that they wished) to be his vassals. That city I captured and I carried off its spoil. People of the lands my hand had conquered I settled therein. I set my official over them as governor. The upper canal of Bit-Ramatua, the lands of Urikatu, Sikris, Shaparda, Uriakku, six districts, I captured and added them thereto. The weapon of Aššur, my lord, I appointed as their deity. Kār-Šarrukīn, I called its name. From 28 mayors (bēl āli) of the land of the mighty Medes I received tribute, and I set up my image in Kār-Šarrukīn. (ARAB 2, I.11)

Sargon resettled deportees from other conquered areas, renamed the city after himself, and to make sure that the populace didn't forget his power, he commissioned the construction of local monuments recording his deeds.

In the fall of 1965, Cuyler Young and Louis Levine were conducting the first season of excavations at the mound of Godin. They knew there was an Iron Age occupation at the site, and they had begun to uncover the fortified citadel that lay on the summit of the mound. One of the local workers had been telling them all season about an old carved stone that had been found in his village the previous year and urging them to come out to see it, but such stories are common in the Near East and usually turn out to be valueless. In any case, Cuyler and Lou were too busy with their own excavations at Godin to traipse off to other villages. As it happened, on a grey weekend in late October as the field season was beginning to wind down, their wives, Pam and Dory, had come to visit them and the two men decided that they would use the workman's "stone" as an excuse for a drive through the mountains. The four piled into the Land Rover with the worker as guide, and since it

Figure 7.5. Carved image of Sargon II on the Najafehabad stele

so happened that both Pam and Dory were in an advanced state of pregnancy, Cuyler took the wheel vowing to drive carefully in spite of the heavy autumn rain that had started to fall. A mile or so before they reached the village of Najafehabad, some 15 kilometres northeast of Godin, and in spite of Cuyler's vaunted ability to negotiate the treacherous mountain roads, the Land Rover skidded and landed in a ditch at the side of the road. Grumbling and convinced that this was all a wild-goose chase in any event, the two couples climbed out of the vehicle and made their way on foot through the mud to the village where they would be able to find men to help pull their Land Rover free. As Lou tells the story, he and Dory (who was a couple of months further along in her pregnancy than Pam) were lagging behind Cuyler, Pam, and the guide, when suddenly he heard Cuyler's normally deep, sonorous voice utter a shrill cry of excitement. "Don't get excited, Lou," he all but squealed, "but this is the real thing."

The villagers of Najafehabad had built their homes into the side of a mound of ruins and had tunnelled into the mound itself to make safe, protected stables for their sheep and goats during the winter. In the course of building one such room, a farmer had hit a 2-tonne block of stone with some kind of human figure carved on one side and on the other the wedge-shaped signs that make up the ancient cuneiform script used in Mesopotamia for 3,000 years. The farmer had dragged the stone out to the front of his house as an object of curiosity and placed it with the more attractive figure side up in the public street of the village. Cuyler and Lou immediately recognized the figure as an Assyrian king and the script as the distinctive signs of the Neo-Assyrian dialect of Akkadian, although these particular lines were clearly the production of a sub-par provincial scribe. Here almost certainly was the "image of the king" that Sargon had boasted of on the walls of his palace in Assyria as having been erected in the land of the mighty Medes.

The Najafehabad stele is remarkable for its find-spot in the heart of Media, as well as for the gaps it filled in our knowledge of the interactions between the Assyrians and the Medes. Intended for a local audience, the stele expanded on the summary of the sixth campaign that appeared in the official, homeland version of the annals. It names names and gets specific about the allegiance or treachery of each city ruler (*bēl āli*). Most importantly, the consequences of crossing an Assyrian monarch are laid out in detail. Time had worn away sections of the inscription, but the import of the message of intimidation remains clear.

> At that time, the people of the city of
> Harhār who are submissive to Aššur (and) perform
> corvée duty [. . .] They drove off [Kibab]a, their city ruler,
> and withheld the horses (which were) to be given
> yearly as their tribute. They strengthened their city
> wall and *repeatedly requ[ested (military) aid . . . befo*re]
> the day had progressed [x *double-hours*] I had brought
> about their defeat; I inflicted a major defeat on them. I
> impaled their fighting men on stakes
>
> . . .
>
> Moving on from the city of Harhār, I crossed a
> river with cold water (and) came to the city of Zakruti.
>
> . . .
>
> The land of Igali, the land of Sikris, (and) the
> land of Bīt-Uargi, distant regions whose *name*(s) the
> kings who preceded me *had never heard*, [. . .] My [awe-

in]spiring splendour overwhelmed them and they
abandoned their cities. They gathered their people
(and) their property and [. . .] the land of *Abra . . . or their
support* [. . .] I put to the sword and took the remainder of
them as booty, (namely) people, horses, mules, oxen,
sheep, (and) donkeys. . . . to/for [. . .] I tore down,
demolished, (and) set on fire.

. . .

I crossed the Pattaus River (and) came to
the land of Ukuta. The people of *th*[*at*] region . . . [. . .
who/which] I set on fire like a torch, I fed my troops
their grain crop in large quantities. My warriors in
order to plunder . . . [. . .] they took as booty.

. . .

Moving on from the land of Ukuta, I crossed
over Mount Arusaka, a mighty mountain, *with great
difficulty* (and) came to the land of Anzaknê . . . [. . .] . . . *I
made flare up like a star*. The Uriiakian Karakka *saw*
the smoke of the conflagration of the cities of the land
of Anzaknê . . . [. . .].

. . .

Uardatti of the city of Sibaraia who had neither stretched out his hand to
(any of) the previous kings (of Assyria) (nor) *inquired
about* their health . . . [. . .] district of the land of Aialaia . . .
of the camp which *covered the sky* for a distance of one
double-hour('s journey), the river . . . large horses
trained to the yoke . . . [. . . *At the command of the god* . . .],
who makes (me) triumph, and of the god *Nergal, my
protection*, the tireless one, fit for battle, [*he* (Uardatti*)
came to me*], to the land of Irnisa, in order to save his
land (and) allow (his) *people* to live in peace . . . [. . .] he
grasped my f[eet] and submitted himself to the yoke to
Aššur, my lord

. . .

At that time, I had a stela made and [*I
engraved upon it*] image(s) of the great gods, my lords,

who make me triumph . . . [. . .]. I inscribed upon it [(. . .)]
the victorious deeds of Aššur, my conquests which I
made over the four quarters (of the world), (*and*)
everything *I had done* in the city of *Kišēsim*. [*I erected*
(*it*)] in the city of *Kišēsim*, which (my) hands had
cap[tured], for . . . [. . .].
In the future, may a future prince — (one)
whom Aššur, king of all the Igīgū gods, shall summon
and name to be ruler of Assyria — read this stela and
ano[int (it)] with o[il! (. . .)] May he offer a sacrifice!
May he praise the kind deeds of Aššur and have future
generations taught to revere him (Aššur)!

(This translation of the stele was prepared by Grant Frame and Andreas Fuchs, who very generously gave me permission to quote portions of it here. It will be published in the Royal Inscriptions of Mesopotamia volume on the inscriptions of Sargon II.)

As argued in 2003 articles by Karen Radner and Giovanni Lanfranchi, the picture that emerges of the Medes from both the Khorsabad annals and the Najafehabad stele is markedly different from that drawn by the earlier report of Šamši-Adad V. In the earlier text the scribe writes of a "royal city" and refers to Hanaširuka the Mede as if he directly controlled a multitude of cities. In another text his scribes refer to the "šarru" or "king" of the Median town of Gizilbunda. By the reign of Sargon, the Median elites are almost exclusively called *bēl āli* (literally city-leader; the Akkadian plural for the term is *bēl ālani*, but it is seldom written out that way and to avoid confusion I use the singular form as a collective here). In fact the title *bēl āli* is reserved solely for the rulers of the Zagros after this time, and the term is never used for any of the other leaders of vassal states. We assume that this change in terminology was not the result of a change in the political system of the Medes, but that as the Assyrians took more direct control of the Median polities they became both savvier about how Median society was set up, and more adamant about distinguishing their own expanding territorial state from these "barbarian" neighbours. If we could understand what form of leadership is encompassed by the term *bēl āli,* and why the term becomes uniquely attached to the rulers of the Zagros in the mid-eighth century BC, we would be a long way towards understanding how Median society and culture were constituted. But since all of our information about the Medes comes from sources written by their opponents—either Assyrian or Greek—it is very difficult to know how much these descriptions tell us about the Medes and how much about their enemies' view of them.

For many years Herodotus's account of the Medes' evolution from a state of lawless villagers to one ruled by a judge-tyrant, and finally a far-flung empire, was accepted as, if not the complete truth, at least a partial version of what had happened:

All of those on the mainland were now free men; but they came to be ruled by monarchs again, as I will now relate. There was among the Medes a clever man called Deioces: he was the son of Phraortes. Deioces was infatuated with sovereignty, and so he set about gaining it. Already a notable man in his own town (one of the many towns into which Media was divided), he began to profess and practice justice more constantly and zealously than ever, and he did this even though there was much lawlessness throughout the land of Media, and though he knew that injustice is always the enemy of justice. Then the Medes of the same town, seeing his behaviour, chose him to be their judge, and he (for he coveted sovereign power) was honest and just. By acting so, he won no small praise from his fellow townsmen, to such an extent that when the men of the other towns learned that Deioces alone gave fair judgments (having before suffered from unjust decisions), they came often and gladly to plead before Deioces; and at last they would submit to no arbitration but his.

The number of those who came grew ever greater, for they heard that each case turned out in accord with the truth. Then Deioces, seeing that everything now depended on him, would not sit in his former seat of judgment, and said he would give no more decisions; for it was of no advantage to him (he said) to leave his own business and spend all day judging the cases of his neighbours. This caused robbery and lawlessness to increase greatly in the towns; and, gathering together, the Medes conferred about their present affairs, and said (here, as I suppose, the main speakers were Deioces' friends), "Since we cannot go on living in the present way in the land, come, let us set up a king over us; in this way the land will be well governed, and we ourselves shall attend to our business and not be routed by lawlessness." With such words they persuaded themselves to be ruled by a king. The question was at once propounded: Whom should they make king? Then every man was loud in putting Deioces forward and praising Deioces, until they agreed that he should be their king. (Herodotus I.96–98, trans. A. D. Godley)

Modern historians have questioned the historical veracity of this and many other of Herodotus' stories, which were written as much to convey a specifically Greek political ideology as to try to accurately reconstruct past events. But the passage does seem to confirm the Assyrian view of the Medes as organized in smaller political units than the nation-states of some of their other rivals. Assyriologists who first deciphered and translated Sargon's cuneiform inscriptions translated the term "*bēl āli*" as "mayor," in their worldview the name for a leader of a city. But "mayor" seems to imply the existence of a higher authority, and the texts simply never mention someone ruling above the *bēl āli*. In the mid-twentieth century, *bēl āli* began to be translated as "city chief," probably with direct reference to what anthropologists called "chiefdoms" (kin-based societies with inherited leadership). In the old anthropological model, "chiefs" (as opposed to the "headmen" of tribal societies or the "kings" of true monarchies) amass wealth and power, but retain that power only by their capacity to redistribute this wealth in periodic feasts. Anthropologists envisioned an evolutionary sequence of societal development in which tribes became chiefdoms, which in turn evolved into states (or what was often called "civilization"). This intermediate semi-king seemed to correspond in part to the *bēl āli* of the Assyrian texts, and the evolutionary sequence to Herodotus's story of the crowning of Deioces. In the early twenty-first century, when historians and archaeologists came under the influence of post-structuralist anthropology, which saw culture as a dense, multi-layered set of messages and counter-messages, the term *bēl āli* (translated as "city lord") was interpreted as a Neo-Assyrian construct that reflected as much about their view of Media as a marginal territory as it did any political reality on the ground. Modern scholars were no more immune from the bias of their intellectual culture than Herodotus had been in the fifth century BC.

Whether mayor, lord, or chief, it was almost certainly a Median *bēl āli* who held court at the citadel at Godin. Chances are that his father had preceded him in the position and the many additions to the original building may well have been ordered by his son. In Sargon's annals a certain Karakku, the *bēl āli* of the Median town of Uriakku, swore loyalty to Sargon in 714 BC. In a letter written some years later, the Assyrian governor of the province assured Sargon: "Concerning what the king my lord wrote to me: 'arrest and imprison the son of Karakku of Uriakku, and appoint Rametî in his stead!' I had the son of Karakku arrested and imprisoned, as the King my lord wrote, and we sent Rametî in his stead"(SAA XV, 85). Apparently Karakku's son had succeeded him as *bēl āli* but had then committed some offence against the king, probably by failing to pay sufficient tribute. So the position of *bēl āli* was dynastic, even though the Assyrian king could choose to depose rulers who displeased him. A tantalizing broken line follows this passage: "The Uriakkeans did not agree to be under him but said: 'The son of Irtukkanu . . . [broken line]" Were the Uriakkeans objecting to the appointment of Rametî, or was the governor justifying his actions by claiming that the Uriakkeans also wanted rid of the son of Karakku? Unfortunately we will never know what the Median villagers said about the son of Irtukkanu, but their opinion about their leader was apparently important enough for the governor to take it into account. In the event, Rametî was appointed although he too seems to have toyed a little with the Assyrian powers that be. A few months later, the governor writes, seemingly in Rametî's defence: "the son of Irtukkanu (Rametî), city lord (*bēl āli*) of Uriakku—after the magnates (Assyrian officials) had moved on from his presence, he visited me, brought the rest of the tribute, and will take it to the magnates"(SAA XV, 101). It would seem that even Rametî needed a little coaxing before agreeing to deliver up the whole of the tribute to the Assyrian officials. A postscript to this whole episode occurred the following year when the governor wrote to the king that, in his temporary absence on a trip to the capital and through no fault of the governor's, the deposed *bēl āli* had escaped from prison and had fled to his relatives in a nearby town. Obviously the power of the Karakku family had not been entirely quashed.

The primary wealth of the Godin *bēl āli* came from his control of the vast herds of sheep, goats, and horses, which fed on the rich pastureland of the Kangavar Valley in the winter, and the Zagros mountainsides in the summer. In the Assyrian kings' annals, whenever a Median area is conquered, the tribute demanded always comes in the form of livestock, particularly horses, instead of the gold, silver, and craft goods collected from other subdued nations. At Godin, the kitchen garbage piled in the back corner of the magazines contained enough sheep and goat bones to have supplied a number of hearty feasts; there must have been plenty of livestock left over even after the Assyrian king had been appeased with tribute. Lamb stew was thickened with barley and supplemented by bread baked in the elaborate ovens found in the citadel kitchen from the wheat grown in the valley fields. An exchange between Sargon and his governor at Kār-Šarrukīn implies that the wheat too was subject to Assyrian tribute payments, or at least that the king was vitally concerned about the state of the crops: "As to the harvest about which the king my lord wrote to me: 'Why have you not written to me how it is?'—the harvest has sprouted, but it is badly ravaged, and it is raining and snowing continually"(SAA XV, 100). The crops of the fertile Kangavar Valley may have been another important source of wealth for the Godin *bēl āli*, who presumably knew better than the Assyrian governor how to deal with the unpredictable mountain climate.

If nimble riding horses were the primary tribute demanded from the Godin Medes by the Assyrians, the site's location at one of the major passes along the High Road must also have played its part in the power of this local potentate. The Assyrian kings don't often specify their reasons for an "interest" in a particular region. Their ideology, like that of most imperial powers, simply asserted their god-given (in this case specifically Ashur-given) superiority over all other nations, and therefore their implied right, or even duty, to conquer and rule. Still, we know that the High Road must have been the main route for goods coming from the east, most particularly the bright blue lapis lazuli, which can be found only in the remote mountains of northern Afghanistan. Lapis was one of the most highly prized stones throughout the history of the Near East. It adorned the most precious pieces of jewellery and furniture of Mesopotamian kings, and the lapis trade may well have been a primary impetus for the establishment of contacts with the East as early as the sixth millennium BC when Godin was founded. The stone was so highly valued that imitation lapis, like cubic zirconium, became an industry in itself. The Assyrian kings used the real thing for inlay on their furniture as well as for architectural decoration

Figure 7.6. Carnelian, shell, and lapis lazuli beads from Godin III

on their palaces, boasting of adding friezes of basalt and lapis to line the cornices of their palace walls. The black and blue patterns haven't survived, but must have been a stunning addition to the palace façade. They also must have required very large quantities of lapis to be effective, and we know that in at least one case in the reign of Esarhaddon (680–669 BC) this lapis was provided by the Medes, who themselves probably obtained the precious stones from their eastern neighbours. "The Medes, whose country lies far off, who in the time of the kings, my fathers, had never invaded Assyrian territory, nor trodden its soil, the fear of the terrible might of Ashur, my lord, overwhelmed them and mighty steeds, lapis lazuli, the choicest products of their country, they brought to Nineveh, my royal city, and kissed my feet"(ARAB 2, 540).

With the exception of one carnelian bead and one ivory bead, which must have been accidentally discarded in a trash heap, no trace of any trade goods have survived in the citadel of Godin, but this is hardly surprising. If the large storerooms were used for any such precious items, they would have been thoroughly cleaned out before the site was abandoned. It is very unusual to recover any valuable objects at an archaeological site unless it was destroyed very quickly and without warning, as the earthquake destroyed some levels of Godin Period III. Most precious goods recovered archaeologically are found in burials.

If there was a cemetery near Godin during Period II—and it is possible that the Medes had already adopted the Ahura-Mazdean practice of exposure instead of burial—it hasn't been located. In the earlier Period III, one inhabitant was buried with a gorgeous string of translucent, red carnelian beads and a single, bright blue, oblong, lapis lazuli bead, so we do know that lapis was being brought to the site in the second millennium BC (Figure 7.6).

The Assyrians certainly thought of the Zagros area as a whole as useful for their trading networks. When Sargon renamed Median settlements, after incorporating them into the new Assyrian provinces, he used the prefix "kār" (as in Kār Šarrukīn), meaning port or trading post in Akkadian, instead of "dur," meaning fortress, as he did in other areas. Sargon must have wanted to emphasize the economic importance of these cities as trading hubs rather than defensive outposts of the Assyrian army. What's really striking about this is that Sargon and his successors seem to have made an effort to incorporate the Medes into the Assyrian Empire by appealing to their pocketbooks instead of using the terror tactics for which they were so famous. When the Assyrians "came down like the wolf on the fold," as Byron put it, on the towns of ancient Israel, they instituted a policy of divide and conquer that decimated the political and social systems of the conquered territories. Mass deportations, assassinations of local leaders, and the wholesale replacement of regional governments with Assyrian officials, were designed to ensure that the conquered people could not regroup and rebel. The Medes, on the other hand, were not only allowed to keep their local leaders in many cases, but the Assyrian governors who were appointed to govern the area seemed just as anxious to please the *bēl āli* as vice versa. When a new governor was appointed in Kār Šarrukīn, his first set of orders from the palace was to placate and reassure the Median *bēl āli*: "Concerning the city-lords [*bēl āli*] about whom the king my lord wrote to me (saying) 'Speak kindly with them! Your friend and enemy should not be treated differently' . . . The son of Asrukanu has come to visit. I dressed him in purple and put silver bracelets on his wrists" (SAA XV, 91).

The purple robes and silver bracelets were more than just gifts of friendship. They were potent symbols of peaceful relations and were brought out whenever treaties were sworn. From the reign of Sargon's grandson, Esarhaddon (680–669 BC), the oaths of fealty that would have been sworn in such a ceremony are actually preserved in a set of clay tablets that were found apparently deliberately smashed to bits in a temple throneroom at the Assyrian city of Nimrud. In a 1993 article Mario Liverani suggested that these *adê* (loyalty oath) tablets record not only the Median *bēl āli* Ramateia's promise to serve faithfully the Assyrian king and his heir as an ally, but possibly to serve as part of the personal bodyguard unit that protected the heir apparent, Ashurbanipal, from assassination. In a clause that is reminiscent of a modern legal disclaimer, Ramateia also swears to report any rumour he hears about threats to the crown prince "either from the mouth of his [Ashurbanipal's] brothers, or from the mouth of his uncles, his cousins, his family, members of his father's line; or from the mouth of magnates and governors, or from the mouth of the bearded and the eunuchs, or from the mouth of the scholars or from the mouth of any human being at all" (SAA II, 6:75–82). Esarhaddon's own father, Sennacherib, had been killed in his palace by Esarhaddon's brothers only a few years earlier, so the threat was very real, and the role of bodyguard must have been taken fairly seriously. Esarhaddon's enlistment of Medes in this capacity must be an indication that the "mighty Medes" had found a place of trust for themselves at the heart of the Assyrian court.

If the Assyrians treated the Medes more leniently than other conquered peoples, as it appears that they did from the preserved letters, treaties, and annals, then the reason for this leniency has essentially been lost to us. It may be that it wasn't leniency at work so much as impotence. As Šamši-Adad V discovered very early in the Assyrians' encounter with the Medes, these mountain dwellers could and did "abandon their cities and ascend a rugged mountain." It was one thing deporting the captives from a besieged city in the plain; it may have been something more of a challenge to round up dispersed Median villagers hiding in the snowy mountains that they knew so much better than their conquerors, especially given the Medes' skill on horseback. The large scale deportations that occurred in the western part of the empire also required a lot of bureaucratic intervention, specifically in terms of census lists and recording. Whenever scores of deportees are shown on the carved reliefs, they are almost always accompanied by Assyrian scribes painstakingly writing on wax and papyrus the numbers and names of the captives and their families. In a letter to the king, one weary official writes: "I went as far as Šabirešu to meet the people and oxen that were brought to me from Guzana: I checked them, received them, and provided them with shelter. Some of them were missing. Kimâ, a wineskin-raft man, three persons; Sandapî, a vegetable gardener, three persons; Hulî, a farmer, five persons; Kuzâ, a belt-maker, four persons—in all 15 persons missing from my writing-board! I sent the Bodyguard from Šabirešu back to Guzana for them, telling him: 'Go and get the rest of the people, and come and bring them to me!'"(SAA I, 128). This kind of detailed record keeping must have depended in large part on the existence of local census taking; we know from the Bible (2 Samuel 24) that there was a long and bitter history of head counting in these western provinces. In Media it is doubtful that the *bēl āli* kept census lists, and the complex lineages and family relationships that probably defined the make-up of Median village life were undoubtedly quite opaque to the Assyrian officials who were nominally supposed to govern them.

The Medes were more valuable as horse trainers and trading partners than they would have been as captive deportees, as long as they didn't directly threaten Assyrian interests by allying themselves with the Urartians. Conditions in the Zagros Mountains were difficult and foreign to the plain-dwelling Assyrians. The governor of Kār-Šarrukin had reason enough to complain to the palace back in Assyria about the king's ignorance of conditions in the mountains: "Concerning what the king my lord wrote to me: 'Be at Calah [the capital] on the 1st of Nisan [the first month of the calendar year]'—We are clearing the roads, but it is snowing and snow is filling them up. There is very much snow . . . The year before last when there was as much snow, he gave me two chariots, and the men and horses who were with me died in the snow. I shall be in the king my lord's presence on the 6th or 7th of Nisan"(SAA XV, 83). Direct administrative control of such harsh territory was probably simply not worth the trouble when the Median *bēl āli* were willing enough to cut deals with the Assyrians at the expense of their rivals. In the same passage in the annals in which Esarhaddon recounts the gifts of lapis lazuli by the three Median *bēl āli,* he goes on to explain why the Medes have come to him bearing gifts: "Because of the other chieftains [*bēl āli*] who had raised their hands against them, they implored my majesty, asking me to be their ally. My officers, provincial governors, who were stationed on the borders of their land, I dispatched with them and they trampled down the inhabitants of those cities, bringing them into submission at their feet"(ARAB 2, 540). In fact one of these *bēl āli* later went on to swear an *adê* oath, agreeing to serve the Crown Prince Ashurbanipal. Fifty years later, this oath was to be smashed to bits both literally and figuratively when a coalition of Medes and Babylonians invaded the Assyrian capital, ending the Assyrian's 300-year rule of terror. The invading Medes, possibly aided and abetted by a Median corps of the king's personal bodyguard, brought out the tablets containing their oaths of allegiance to the Assyrian king from the temple storeroom and crushed them under foot.

The Godin Period II Citadel

In 1965 Cuyler Young and David Stronach climbed into a Land Rover and set out on an exploratory survey through the mountains of western Iran in search of sites to excavate. Both young scholars knew that their choice would define their scholarly and, to a large extent, personal identity for a long time to come. Cuyler and David shared a highly developed, even devilish, sense of humour, a spirit of adventure, and a love of good food and old scotch; they were perfect companions for such an adventure. They also shared a passion for the early history of Iran, most particularly for the history of the Medes and Persians, the two nations known from Greek and Assyrian sources to have founded the single great military rival to Ancient Greece, the Persian Empire. As they set out on their search they knew that, although there were many criteria that they would look for in choosing a site to excavate, the one find that would please both of them most of all would be material evidence of the Medes. The Medes were tantalizingly present in historical sources from Assyria and Greece, but up until that time completely absent in the archaeological record. The ruins of the huge Persian palace/capital of Persepolis had stood mute testimony to the artistic achievements of the Persians for millennia, and the great Assyrian cities of Nimrud and Nineveh had been uncovered since the mid-nineteenth century, but no physical remains that could be definitively ascribed to the Medes had yet been discovered. Historians knew that the Assyrians wrote of them as unpredictable, distant mountain dwellers, and knew that to be called a Mede was considered an insult to the Greeks, but nobody was sure what being a Mede might have meant from the perspective of the Medes themselves. A Median excavation would not only clarify many technical issues about pottery sequences and dating, it would put a material face to the "group of good men" that Herodotus had written about 2,500 years earlier.

Cuyler and David's search for Median sites to excavate couldn't have been more fruitful. The excavations at Tepe Nush-i Jan and Godin Tepe would provide the only good, first-hand information about the Medes since they disappeared from history after the invasion of Persia by Alexander the Great in 331 BC. As it turned out, and although there was no reason to predict it from the surface material, each site provided a different angle from which to view Median culture: Nush-i Jan revealed an almost perfectly preserved fire temple of the pre-Zoroaster, Ahura-Mazdean religion of the Medes, and Godin Tepe was home to a fortified citadel of the Kangavar Valley *bēl āli*.

Before the excavation of Godin, our only image of what a Median city might have looked like came from the carved reliefs of the palaces of the Medes' Assyrian overlords. The courtiers and generals who gathered in the palace suites to celebrate their military victories must have enjoyed reliving their exotic experiences in foreign lands. The Assyrian artists went to some degree of trouble to include details of landscape or architecture that were characteristic of the countries depicted, and field sketches of campaigns in foreign territory were almost certainly produced for reproduction in stone back at the capital. The account of the Assyrian victories may have seemed somehow more convincing when you could see the "reality" of the different landscapes.

As the excavation of Godin progressed, it became more and more clear that the citadel actually looked quite a lot like the Assyrian depictions of Median fortresses, but that it also included details that were completely unexpected.

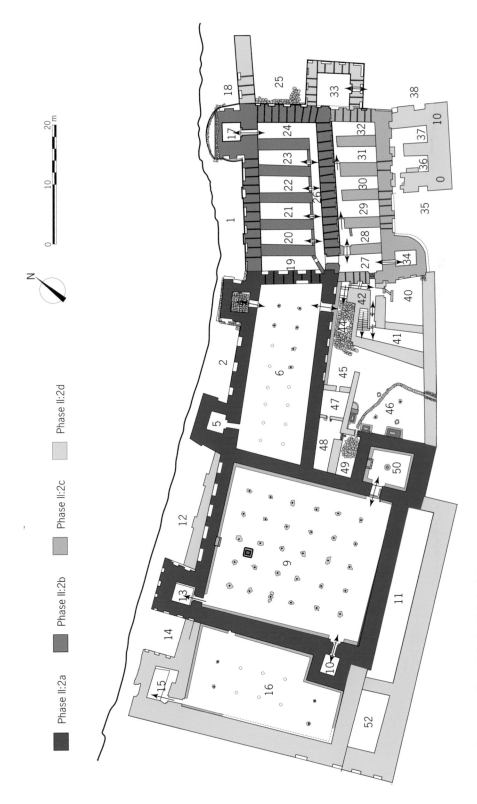

Phase II:2a

Phase II:2b

Phase II:2c

Phase II:2d

Figure 7.7. Plan of Godin II:2 citadel

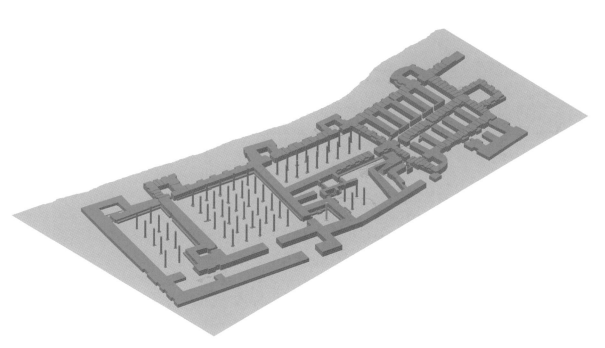

Figure 7.8. Raised plan of Godin II:2 citadel

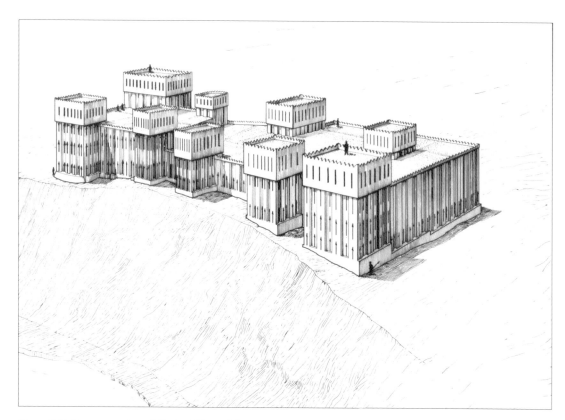

Figure 7.9. Reconstruction of Godin II:2 citadel

The Citadel Architecture (Phase II:2)

The Godin citadel was an impressively large building, measuring some 120 metres by 50 metres (just about exactly the size of a soccer pitch and a little larger than an American football field). It was clearly constructed in four main stages but it is impossible to tell how much time elapsed between the addition of each unit (Figure 7.7). The units may have been made in quick succession or the whole building may be the result of several generations of *bēl āli*, each striving to add his own mark to the family mansion. As each addition was made, features that were originally characteristic of exterior walls, including arrowslots and recesses between buttresses, were adapted to interior uses, being filled in with bricks or pottery sherds, or turned into bins. We can trace the sequence of construction simply by following these exterior walls and their conversion to interior spaces. With each new wing, the new walls were generally bonded into each other (by laying the mud-bricks alternately to form an interlocking corner) but not bonded to the old walls, so we can also determine which walls were built at the same time (Figure 7.16). In addition to these obvious extensions, several of the main citadel walls were actually damaged at some point, perhaps by an earthquake or perhaps from the settling that resulted from the builders' rather lax attitude towards foundations. Towers 13, 4, and 17 were almost certainly rebuilt, perhaps more than once, and the whole exterior wall facing the cliff edge was frequently repaired and shored up (Figure 7.21). After the citadel was abandoned and the wooden columns were removed, the roof collapsed, and some pastoralists or farmers built their houses in the ruins of the once grand building. This secondary phase of occupation, originally called the squatter phase, is here labelled phase II:1.

The first unit to be built was the large columned hall (room 9), the *raison d'être* of the Godin citadel. Room 9 is the largest and clearly the most important room in the building. The thirty wooden columns, aligned in five rows of six columns each, that held up the roof must have punctuated the space of the room, like the trees in a plantation. They were most probably plastered in red or white lime plaster, and perhaps even painted, although we have no evidence for any such refinements since the columns themselves were removed when the building was abandoned. Along the walls of the room ran a narrow bench that showed evidence of multiple layers of alternating white and red lime plaster. Towards the centre of the bench along the back wall, aligned with the space between the second and third rows of columns, was a carefully constructed "seat of honour" (Figure 7.11). This seat projected into the room slightly and was a little higher than the bench that ran beside it. A footrest was set into the floor directly in front of the seat, and the wall behind it was recessed by a few centimetres, as if to further set off the figure who sat there. About 5 metres in front of this feature, but not quite centered on it, was a raised brick hearth, three courses of brick

Figure 7.10. Seat of honour and hearth in the Godin II:2 columned hall

high (Figure 7.10). It was covered on all sides with thick mud plaster. The top of the hearth had been replastered several times after ash accumulated on its surface.

The west wall of this hall was rebuilt over the course of the citadel's occupation, and a column base was found partially buried beneath it. It seems that the whole columned hall may have been renovated, and perhaps narrowed, when room 16 was added to its western side. The entrance to this room was unfortunately badly eroded, and it was impossible to trace anything beyond the foundations of a narrow anteroom running in front of it (room 11). The placement of the door itself has been entirely lost. Our suggestion as to its possible location in the raised plan of the building is based on an analogy with the anterooms at Hasanlu and is purely conjectural (Figure 7.8).

This large hall was probably originally surrounded by four towers, although the southeast tower (room 50) was larger than the rest, and its central columned room clearly served a different purpose from that of the small guard rooms of the other towers (rooms 5, 13, and 10). Benches ran around all the walls of this room, and another "seat of honour," similar to the one in the main room but with slightly raised sides, was centred on its northern wall (Figure 7.12). A door socket on the southern side of the doorway indicates that room 50 was equipped with a door that could seal it off from the main reception area (Figure 7.24).

It would appear from the placement of tower 5 that the original construction also included a secondary smaller columned hall (room 6) to its east. There was, oddly, no

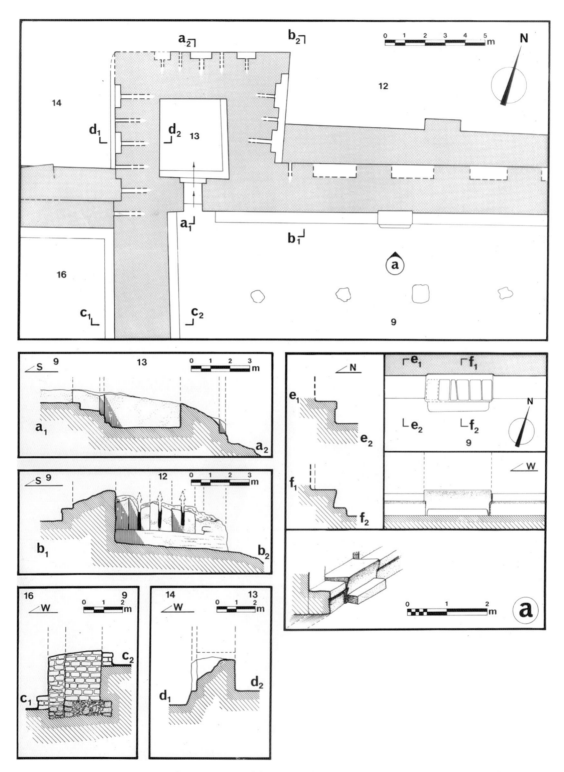

Figure 7.11. Architectural details of Godin II:2 citadel, room 9, showing north and west walls, and seat of honour

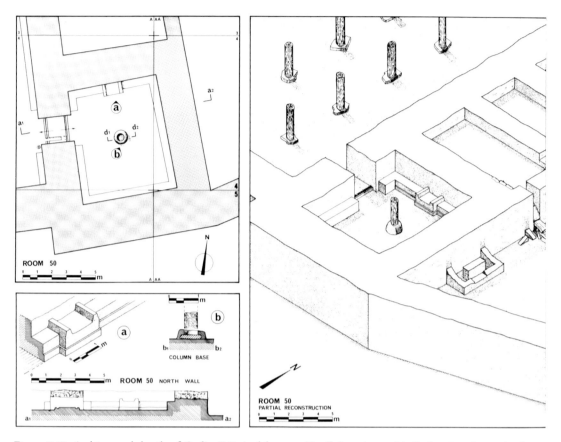

Figure 7.12. Architectural details of Godin II:2 citadel, room 50 off the columned hall, showing plastered column base and seat of honour

evidence for a doorway between the two rooms, even though the western wall of this area was relatively well preserved, so that each must have served distinct enough functions that

visitors did not pass directly from one to the other. The column bases from the western portion of this room were not recovered when the Deep Sounding was sunk through its floor. Six column bases were recovered in the 1973 season in the eastern half of the room, four in a southern row of columns and two to their north. Two of the column bases in the southern row were found under a phase II:1 wall; it is clear that all of these columns must have been

Figure 7.13. Single-columned room 50 off the columned hall with intact column base

removed, and the roof allowed to collapse, before the phase II:1 "squatter" walls were built in the ruins of this room.

The first extension to be built on the two columned halls was the northern row of magazines (storage rooms) 19–26, and tower 17, which formed the new corner of the citadel. The walls of these magazines were very thick and preserved to a surprising height. The daily logs recounting the first excavation of this area in 1967 reveal the excavator's surprise and dismay as day after day he expects to discover the floor of the room only to find that he was still digging through mud-brick debris. In the end it turned out that the walls were pre-served to more than 3 metres high in some places, much higher than any of the other extant walls of the citadel (Figures 7.15 and 7.25). This can happen when a second storey collapses and the debris of that collapse essentially protects the lower walls from subsequent water and wind erosion. It is, therefore, not unreasonable to suggest that there may have been a second storey above the North Magazines. There is one major problem with this suggestion: there is no apparent place for a staircase at this stage of construc-

Figure 7.14. Stairs in room 41 with multiple thick plaster layers

tion. Later, a staircase was added in room 41, which most probably led to a second storey or roof, but judging from the placement of arrowslots in the south wall of the North Magazines and the west wall of the South Magazines, that staircase could have been built only after the magazines were completed. Access to an upper storey does not appear to be an integral part of the plan of the magazines. It is possible that in the general area of room 41 there was always a staircase that originally led off an external courtyard, and that it was closed in and rebuilt when the more elaborate entranceway and kitchens of rooms 40–49 were built. The staircase that was eventually built was itself refurbished and replastered several times during the course of occupation (Figures 7.14 and 7.16) .

Sometime after the North Magazines were built, the Godin *bēl āli* apparently felt the need for more storage space (and which one of us hasn't shared that experience), and he ordered the construction of the south bank of magazines. The South Magazines were not as well preserved as the northern bank since the mound slopes down sharply at this point and the erosion was therefore more pronounced. It is possible that the Souh Magazines also

Figure 7.15. View of the North and South Magazines

at some point supported a second storey.

The final major construction project to be undertaken by the reigning Godin *bēl āli* was the enclosing of the large courtyard, which then lay between the south bank of magazines and the two columned halls. A massive southern wall was built to join up the two wings of the ever-expanding citadel palace, thereby either enclosing the stairway-entrance-way (if that already existed) or becoming the defining wall for this area. The bricks of the southern wall and those of the stairway complex were not bonded, but because of the very poor preservation in this area it was not possible to find out which was built first (Figure 7.16). Again, because the southern wall was preserved to only a few courses high, below the level of a door sill, the location of the doorway could no longer be determined, but it is probable that a door led through this wall into the stairway area. The stairway was set on a massive brick platform. A ramp (room 43) ran along the east side of this platform and towards the entrance to room 6 following the slope of the mound. To the west through corridor 41, a set of stairs, six of which were still intact, ran up the platform and from there undoubtedly turned to climb again to the roof or second storey (Figure 7.14).

The remaining area (rooms 44–49) became what seems to have been a large kitchen (room 46) with some surrounding, service-related rooms. The roof of this room was probably supported by four columns placed in a square in its approximate centre. These column

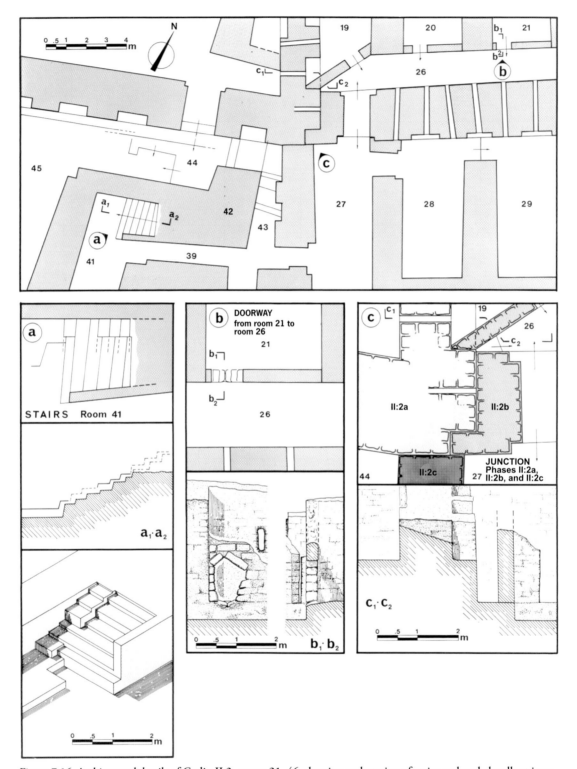

Figure 7.16. Architectural details of Godin II:2, rooms 21–46, showing replastering of stairs, unbonded walls at junction of phases II:2a–c, and arched doorway in North Magazine

bases, which were apparently found at the very end of the 1973 season, just when the rush was on to finish excavating the Period VI oval compound, are not mentioned in field notes, but they are included in the final plans for that season, and one must assume that they became visible only in final cleaning operations.

Four very large hearths were found in room 46, two along the western wall and two against the northern wall. Three of these hearths (the two on the western wall and one on the northern wall) were oddly constructed with a little mud-brick wall at their centre (Figure 7.17). These may have been supports for an iron grate on which to place pots, or perhaps the central support for a spit to roast the young sheep and pigs whose bones were found in a kitchen refuse heap. The fourth hearth, in the northeast corner of the room, had a covered mud-plaster firebox with a pot-sized hole at the top rather like an old cast-iron stove. A stone had been carefully placed to block this hole at some point, and a carbon sample was recovered from the sealed firebox (see "The Dating of Godin Period II," p. 343). It is tempting to think

of these differently shaped hearths as serving different functions in the cooking process, like a modern restaurant kitchen with a roasting oven and bread oven. It is possible however that they were never in use at the same time, and that when one got old beyond repair a new one was built. Three superimposed floors were found in this room, but it was impossible to determine if any of the hearths was associated specifically with one or more of these floors.

Figure 7.17. Large hearth in room 46 with mud-brick support

In room 49 an odd deposit was found of some seventy large rocks lining a shallow depression in the floor. Beside this depression was a circular pot stand made out of ceramic sherds cemented together with mud plaster. A large drain led out of room 49, through the centre of room 46 and out through the southern wall. This was obviously an installation for liquid processing or washing of some sort, but whether it was for animal carcasses, laundry, or the *bēl āli*'s bath there is no way of knowing.

More minor additions were made to the citadel through time, although it is impossible to determine during which sub-phase each renovation was made. These include the addition of room 33 at the eastern end of the magazines, the construction of the southern tower (rooms 36 and 37), and the addition of a third small columned hall to the west of the building.

Godin Phase II:1

After the citadel was abandoned, the valuable wooden columns stripped out for use else-where, and the roof fallen in, some farmers or shepherds took advantage of the protection from the wind provided by the still massive wall stubs and built a series of small houses and courtyards in the ruins of the once-grand palace, primarily in the area of the previ-ous small columned room 6 (Figure 7.18). For many years the excavators called these poorly defined houses the "squatter" occupation of Godin, but because that term conjures up images of non-rent-paying opportunists, we prefer the more neutral, if less evocative, term phase II:1. The walls of this phase were excavated primarily in the 1967 season as the beginning of the Deep Sounding. The excavators had not yet realized that this area had a later "squatter" occupation and were looking for the kind of substantial architecture that they were uncovering in the rest of the phase II building. There is no doubt that some of the walls and floors of Period II:1 were missed, and since the artifacts recovered were all lumped together with the same stratum designation as the rest of the Period II finds (strata 3 and 4), it is almost impossible to completely sort out the phase II:1 occupation of this area. Walls seem to end abruptly and rooms are not connected in any logical fashion, but it is probable that these walls are simply all that is left of some modest houses, more or less equivalent to the houses found in the Period III village.

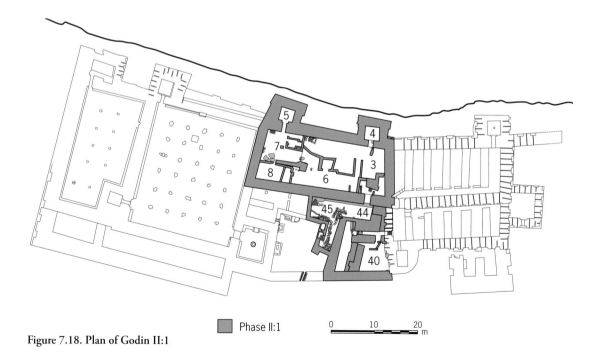

Phase II:1

Figure 7.18. Plan of Godin II:1

The phase II:1 occupation is concentrated in the area over room 6, but a large hearth and some stone walls that seem to run over mud-brick debris in rooms 44 and 45 also probably belong to this period. It is more doubtful whether the curtain walls and the animal manger built into a niche in the east wall of room 40 belong to this phase, or to the last occupation of phase II:2. A careful blocking of ramp 43 and stairway 42, however, is executed in a fashion that seems more consistent with the citadel phase than with phase II:1. Perhaps in the last days of that occupation the top floor to which these stairs led had become dangerous or simply unused, and it was decided to seal off access to it.

Construction Techniques in the Godin Period II Citadel

The citadel of the Godin *bēl āli* was built and rebuilt over the course of perhaps a century or more, yet the basic construction techniques don't seem to have changed very much through time. The basic building material of the Godin citadel, as indeed of most Near Eastern architecture, was mud-brick. These bricks were made of mud mixed with straw, placed in wooden moulds, and left to dry in the sun. At Godin, the mud for the bricks was dug up from the mound itself, and as a result many pottery sherds and even some larger objects from earlier occupations of the mound were incorporated into the bricks, presumably without compromising their structural integrity. In fact, up to 90 percent of the ceramic sherds from the eroded mud-brick debris of the citadel actually bore the very distinctive painted decoration of the earlier Godin Period III occupation. Some of the more ubiquitous small finds, such as animal figurines or spindle whorls that were assigned to Period II, might also come, instead, from the eroded mud of the bricks.

The bricks at Godin were quite variable in size, ranging from about 50 × 40 × 10 centimetres to 36 × 30 × 15 centimetres, but most measuring around 45 × 30 × 12 centimetres. In the outside fortification wall, the larger bricks tended to be laid as stretchers (i.e., parallel to the wall face), and the smaller as headers (perpendicular to the wall face), but this pattern was not always used for the narrower, internal walls. This variability is surprising, considering that the bricks were mould-made, and is probably a reflection of the Godin builders' decidedly improvisational attitude towards construction. When the builders needed a larger brick to create the throne seat in the main columned hall, for instance, they apparently set up a mould for a brick measuring 62 × 41 × 18 centimetres to suit the space, rather than joining two bricks with plaster. Yet when they were building the south wall of room 6, they used bricks of a number of different dimensions and then used plaster to make up the difference, as if it was only the final appearance that really mattered. In any event, all bench and wall surfaces would have been covered with a thick layer of lime plaster to protect the exterior surfaces from rain, and to provide an overall finished look to all the interior rooms. At Godin, white (and sometimes red) plaster seems to have cured, or at least covered, a thousand ills.

The most astonishing use of plaster to hide a construction flaw in the Godin II citadel was its application to terraced Period III debris, creating what must have been an awfully precarious base for some of the main citadel walls. The builders at Godin faced a serious problem when they decided to construct their large citadel on the very top of the then abandoned 3,500-year-old archaeological mound. If they wanted to lay out a building of any size they would need to contend with the slope of the mound, which tapered off sharply on all sides. Instead of following the logical, if labour-intensive, procedure of level-ling the whole area and building on the level surface, the builders essentially carried out their own excavations of the Period III village ruins. The floor of the main columned hall on the western end of the building was actually terraced into the earlier mound, the edge of that excavation straightened (like a good archaeologist's balk), and the upper portion of the eastern wall of room 9 built on top of this debris base. A thick layer of plaster and a row of benches masked the bizarre wall base for the casual observer, but one can't help wonder-ing if the Godin *bēl āli* himself knew about the time-saving device used by his contractor.

When it came time to build the North and South Magazines, where admittedly a level floor was not as critical, the builders (possibly representing a whole new generation of workmen) decided simply to follow the slope of the mound by founding each north-south wall on a lower level. In the North Magazine corridor (room 26) the earth floor ramped

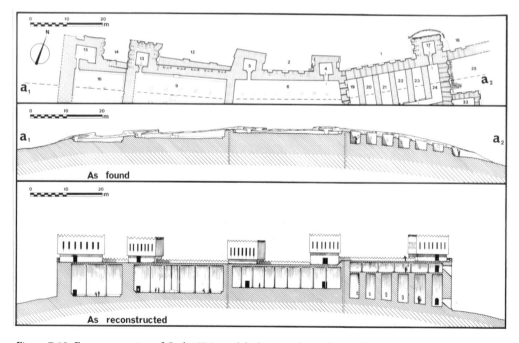

Figure 7.19. East-west section of Godin II:2 citadel, showing slope of mound

down sharply, but in the southern corridor more care was taken and a mud-brick paving was built, complete with several steps along the course of the corridor.

In most cases the walls of the Godin citadel were built without a stone foundation or even much of a foundation trench at all. The bases of the mud-brick walls were normally no more than a few courses below the interior floor. These shallow foundations were trenched directly into the Period III ruins that formed the mound by the time the citadel was built, and in most cases (the notable exceptions being the platforms for the citadel towers) no attempt seems to have been made to consolidate in any significant way the eroded Period III mud-brick. Occasionally, the builders seem to have tried to exploit the earlier structures, which may have still been partially exposed when the builders arrived at the site. The west wall of the large columned hall (room 9) was built directly over a stone wall of Period III—thereby creating a great deal of confusion for the excavator, who originally thought he was dealing with a massive stone foundation to the Period II wall, only to discover that a Period III floor ran up against it (Figure 7.11, bottom left).

The only exception to this rather unsound approach to foundations was the wide exterior fortification walls (including the south wall of the North Magazines and others that had

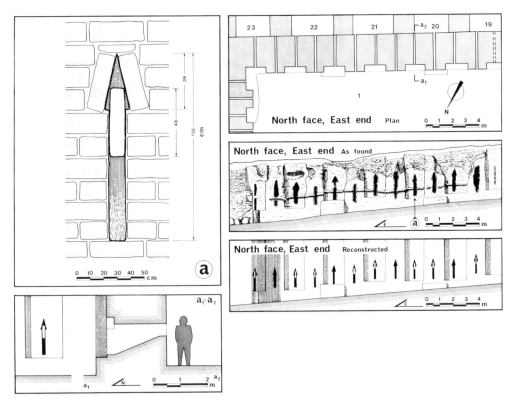

Figure 7.20. Architectural details of Godin II:2 citadel exterior fortification wall, showing wall socle and arrowslots

originally been intended as exterior walls) and the towers along the northern wall. In some places the exterior walls were found to have one or two courses of stones underlying the first mud-brick course of the wall below the floor level. On top of this rather flimsy stone foundation rose a 1-metre solid mud-brick socle (wall base), and above this the wall was laid with alternating recesses and buttresses ranging from 1.2 to 1.5 metres wide. Each buttress and recess was pierced by an arrowslot about 1.2 metres high and 20 centimetres wide.

Figure 7.21. Arrowslots showing the rebuilding of tower 17

Towers 5, 4, and 17 were each founded on a small mud-brick platform, which for towers 4 and 17 extended beyond the line of the wall itself. These platforms were only a few courses thick, but were apparently considered a wise precaution, given the weight of the mud-brick superstructure of the watchtowers. As it turned out, the platforms were apparently not a sufficient safeguard against earth shifting, because all three towers toppled down at some point, probably destroyed by a single earthquake. Each was rebuilt with the upper walls at a slightly different angle and, in the case of tower 17, clearly on top of an earlier wall (Figure 7.21). Towers 4 and 17 were further strengthened by the addition of a stone facing against the northern face of their protruding platforms, presumably to prevent the face from crumbling and dropping over the edge of the cliff.

We have almost no evidence at all for the uppermost levels of the Godin citadel walls, and even less for the techniques that may have been used to roof the building. We can certainly assume that the columned halls and rooms 44–50 were roofed with wooden beams extending between either parallel walls or columns, reed matting placed over these roofing timbers, and a layer of mud plaster applied for sealant and waterproofing. Judging from the identified wood at the site, the columns and roofing beams were almost certainly made of poplar, a fast-growing tree, whose trunks are tall and straight (see "Ancient Agricultural Landscape at Godin," p. 59). Poplar is fairly easy to grow and given the quantities of the wood at the site, it is very likely that there was a poplar plantation somewhere in the vicinity of Godin, perhaps planted by the Godin *bēl āli* himself. Traces of plaster with reed matting impressions from a collapsed ceiling, found in the debris in rooms 46 and 50, are almost certainly the remains of such a roofing system. The roofing of the towers and magazines may also have been made of matting over wooden roof beams, but it is possible that they were instead vaulted with mud-brick vaulting struts using a technique that seems to have been perfected by the Medes at the neighbouring site of Nush-i Jan.

Nush-i Jan is one of those rare archaeological marvels: a site where preservation is so complete that even upper storeys were preserved almost intact. Before it was abandoned, the temple and some of the surrounding buildings were carefully filled to their roofs with stone or brick, effectively sealing them off from decay. When David Stronach and his team began excavations at Nush, their excitement grew as they realized that instead of coming down on the eroded remains of the bottom portion of walls as one normally would, they were in fact recovering the tops of intact walls, which in the case of the central temple, reached more than 8 metres in height.

As described by Stronach and Roaf in 2008, the high quality of construction at Nush-i Jan, remarkably preserved by the careful filling, was apparent from the start of excavations. Unlike at Godin, which Cuyler once described as built by "a gang of drunken bricklayers," the mud-bricks at Nush were meticulously laid and the walls built with a carefully planned gradual "batter" (sloping out from top to bottom) that lightened the load for the wall bases and allowed water to drain away more efficiently. The architects of Nush-i Jan appear to have been both conscientious and imaginative; the buildings (two temples, a columned hall, a "fort," and some magazines) were built with diverse plans and elaborate decorative detail such as might be expected from a centrally planned and executed project. One of the most impressive engineering accomplishments of the site was the use of curved mud-brick struts to create vaulted roofs that in one case survived more or less intact. The struts were considerably larger than normal bricks, measuring up to 1.4 metres long. They were made in a distinctive, curved mould out of fine clay mixed with a lot of straw temper. The curved, or angled, struts were placed in pairs against ledges built along opposing walls so that each pair meeting in the centre created an arch. Placed in a row and reinforced by packing stones, bricks, and plaster, they built up a true vault, strong enough to support an upper storey. The vaulting struts at Nush-i Jan are the oldest yet discovered, but the builders of Nush used them with such expertise and assurance that moulded vaulting struts couldn't have been a complete innovation at the site. Even the most skilled workmen would hardly have risked their reputations (and possibly their lives) by experimenting with a new form of roof in a temple with a large congregation that might be crushed by a falling ceiling.

The builders of the Godin citadel seem to have been considerably less skilled in their craft than the construction engineers at Nush-i Jan; or at least this secular project was one that didn't require the same level of sophistication in design. Nonetheless, the pattern of the buttressed mud-brick walls and arrowslots, the size of the bricks, and the overall design of the columned hall, were all so similar to the architectural style at Nush-i Jan that they must have shared the same architectural technology. The magazines at Nush, which were of the same general proportions as those at Godin, were all vaulted with moulded struts,

Figure 7.22. Vaulted doorway into room 20 of the North Magazines

and it seems likely that the Godin magazines were also roofed in this way. No moulded struts were specifically identified at Godin, but, although well preserved, the walls of the magazines at Godin did not stand high enough for the remains of vaulting to be easily recognized. Since the vaulting struts at the magazines at Nush had not yet been uncovered in 1967 when the magazines at Godin were first excavated, and therefore nobody knew of the existence of such a technique, the excavators at Godin did not know to look for them in the mud-brick debris either. David Stronach, the director of the dig at Nush-i Jan, who has a sharp eye and keen memory for architectural detail, does recall visiting Godin in 1973. On the lookout for vaulting, he remembers particularly noticing, and discussing with Cuyler, the beginnings of a ledge on the upper part of one of the North Magazine walls that was very similar to the ledge that supported the vaults at Nush-i Jan.

With the rush and excitement of excavation of the Period VI oval compound and tablets that marked the end of that season's excavation at Godin, the recording of the detail of the vault must have fallen by the wayside, and no photographs can be found to testify to that ledge.

The existence of mud-brick vaults at Godin is one of the many details that Cuyler Young's untimely death will force us to leave open-ended. One low arched doorway into one of the North Magazines (room 20) was preserved intact (Figures 7.16 and 7.22). Two long bricks were used to create this arch, a method that was also found at Nush-i Jan.

In addition to roofing, wood was used for a lot of the architectural detail in the citadel. Although the wood itself does not preserve, the channel left by a piece of wood's organic decay can often be detected during excavation, particularly when, as at Godin, the wood was embedded in mud-brick.

All the columns at Godin would have been made of wood, almost certainly the poplar wood that was found so frequently in the charcoal analysis (see "Ancient Agricultural Landscape at Godin," p. 59). The columns were placed on large, irregular stones, a circle of mud-brick was set around them with stones filling in the gaps between them, and a thick layer of mud-plaster was then applied to consolidate and seal the support. The original stones, set into the mud-brick floor, were thereby invisible when the building was in use. In the main, large columned hall, room 9, either the excavators missed the column base surrounds or they had been destroyed when the columns were removed after the site was abandoned. In the small adjoining room 50, however, a complete base with its surround was found in 1973. Very similar bases were found at Nush-i Jan (Figure 7.23), so we can be pretty sure that all the column bases at Godin were made in this way. A hollow in the middle of the feature in room 50, which is clearly where the wooden column itself actually stood, is 50 centimetres in diameter, so we can assume that the columns themselves were of this general width (see Figures 7.12 and 7.13).

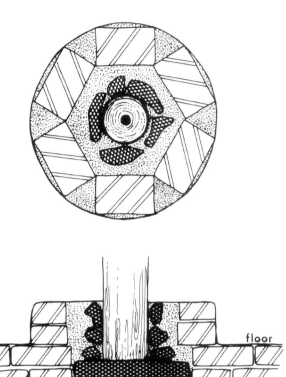

Figure 7.23. Column base from Tepe Nush-i Jan

The columns were removed after the site was abandoned. Wood is a valuable resource in this area, and the sturdy, soaring columns of the great columned hall of Godin must have been known throughout the countryside. We know that the columns were gone by the time the pastoralists of

Figure 7.24 Door socket

phase II:2 built their scrappy walls in room 6, because in some cases these walls were built directly over the then useless column bases.

Many of the smaller rooms of the citadel would have had wooden doors to seal them off from onlookers and the cold. The remains of the frame for one such door were found at the entranceway to room 50, the room with the single column just off the main columned hall. A 20-centimetre-wide channel filled with the dark, soft, organic fill of wood decay ran across the front and side of the doorway and was almost certainly the remains of a door frame. A door socket that was found set into the floor on the southern side of the doorway still bears the mark of the wooden pivot post as it swivelled to allow the door to open and close (Figure 7.24). Another door socket was found in the debris over room 6, and it is likely that there were several doors when the citadel was in use.

The Artifacts of the Godin Period II Citadel

The *bēl āli* and his family who received their guests in the Godin II citadel were undoubtedly the richest inhabitants of Godin during the entire 4,000 years of the site's occupation, but virtually no complete objects were recovered from the excavation as material testimony to that wealth. Period II has the fewest registered objects of any of the main periods of occupation at the site, and those that were found can almost all be assigned to the secondary occupation of Phase II:1. These consist of nothing more than a few grindstones, pestles, and spindle whorls, the day-to-day refuse of the shepherd/farmers who must have lived in these small shelters in the lee of the old ruin. From the primary occupation of the citadel, beyond a few broken bronze bracelets, a fibula, and a needle that were discarded in the garbage heaps, and a few beads that got lost and rolled into a crack in the floor, the building was completely cleaned of anything remotely valuable before it was deserted. All that was left was garbage by anyone's estimation. The analysis of the Godin Period II material rests solely on trying to understand how and why this garbage accumulated, but with a little ingenuity and a lot of statistics we can link these broken bits of pottery and piles of bone to the living people that produced them.

The bulk of the Godin II garbage comes from three major deposits. The largest of the phase II:2 refuse deposits lay piled in a corner in the back of the North Magazine corridor (room 26, see Figure 7.25). One portion of it was first excavated in 1969 by Lou Levine (labelled EE1 lot 2). He recalled that afternoon in an interview in 2006: "I knew right away that I was into something different here. Instead of the mud-brick debris that we had been digging through everywhere else, this was thick, dark organic dirt, and the sherds had a weird greenish stuff on them. You could smell that this was a different kind of deposit." The deposit ran up against the east wall of the magazines and was clearly deposited in layers (although unfortunately it wasn't recorded in layers so we can't separate them now). It seemed as though somebody had thrown consecutive loads of garbage into the corner of the room as they cleaned. In 1973, when all site supervisors were summoned to the

Deep Sounding to try to reach the Period VI:1 oval compound, Cuyler asked the representative from the Iranian Archaeological Service to clear out the back magazine, thinking that there would be little there. As it turns out the garbage heap that Lou had found in 1969 apparently continued into room 24 and even reached tower 17. No lot sheets or daily logs were made of this opportunistic excavation and we therefore have no details about what the deposit looked like in this area. The artifacts, bone, and charcoal were collected however (labelled Magazine 6 and, mistakenly, Tower 5). A number of joins between the sherds of these 1973 lots and the 1969 lots indicate that it was indeed all part of the same deposit.

This heap of organic dirt contained about 200 rim-sherds (the body-sherds were discarded), five beads, a broken fibula (brooch), a quantity of charred wood, a few grape and wild herb seeds, and more

Figure 7.25. Magazine corridor (room 26) looking towards east wall against which garbage was piled

than 500 animal bones. Because of its organic component, Cuyler and Lou originally suggested that it had been used as a latrine (and the pottery sherds as toilet paper), but the large quantity of animal bone here—the largest concentration in Period II—certainly suggests another source. The animal bone consists of young sheep, goat, cattle, pig, and a few bones of bird and hare, all tasty sources of meat. No remains of older, tougher animals could be identified and although there is quite a bit of horse or donkey bone elsewhere in Period II deposits, not a single piece of equid was found here (see "Summary of the Faunal Remains from Godin Period II," p. 324. Presumably the *bēl āli* and his followers weren't eating their precious horses.

Summary of the Faunal Remains from Godin Period II
Pam J. Crabtree

The collection of animal bone from Godin Period II included only 944 animal bones and fragments. The assemblage is considerably smaller than the faunal collections that were recovered from Periods III, IV, and VI. As a result it is impossible to construct detailed age profiles for the cattle, sheep, and goats. However, the faunal remains can tell us something about the nature of feasting that took place at Godin during phase II:2. The identified bones included domestic cattle (*Bos taurus*, 58 fragments), sheep (*Ovis aries*, 38 fragments), goat (*Capra hircus*, 21 fragments), sheep/goat (171 fragments), pig (*Sus scrofa*, 58 fragments), equid (*Equus* sp., 28 fragments), red deer (*Cervus elaphus*, 2 fragments), and hare (*Lepus capensis*, 1 fragment). Species ratios based on fragments counts (or NISP) indicate that the Period II assemblage as a whole included 15.5 percent cattle, 61.5 percent caprines (sheep and goats), 15.5 percent pigs, and 7.5 percent equids. The proportions in the two phases of the period are presented in Figures 7.26 and 7.27.

The striking difference in phase II:2, both in terms of the earlier levels at the site and of the later phase II:1, is the increased number of pigs. This may be related to their use in feasting. Sheep, goats, cattle, and equids can be used for a variety of non-food products including wool, hair, traction, and transport. Cattle, sheep, and goats can also be used for dairy production. Pigs, on the other hand, are useful primarily only as sources of meat. They can be expensive to keep, since, as omnivores, they compete for humans with food, whereas the other domesticated animals browse on plants that cannot be eaten by humans. The use of the site for feasting by high-status individuals during phase II:2 may have increased the demand for pork.

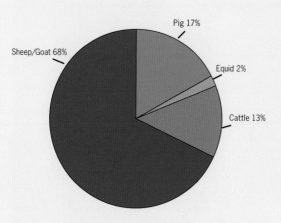

Figure 7.26. Proportions of species in phase II:2

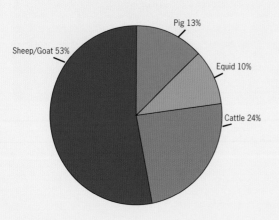

Figure 7.27. Proportions of species in phase II:1

The Period II faunal sample is too small to allow for the construction of detailed mortality profiles. Four of the five ageable caprine mandibles came from juvenile individuals, and it is likely that young sheep and goats would have been chosen for feasts. There are only two mandibles with teeth from Godin II, and both are incomplete. The sample of post-cranial cattle bones is small, but it does include a number of juvenile bones. While the samples are quite small, both the cattle and the caprines appear to be younger than the animals recovered from Godin Periods III, IV, and VI.

Additional data on the animal bone of Godin are available in the Godin Web archive at https://tspace.library.utoronto.ca.

Studies of garbage disposal in modern groups have shown that the closer material is to its place of use, the less chance it has to break and the more complete it will be. In other words, a first-time garbage deposit (such as a kitchen garbage can) will contain bigger pieces than a secondary deposit (such as the town dump). This doesn't seem like earth-shattering news to most of us, but it has become a very important principle in archaeological studies of deposition because it offers a big clue about the source of secondary deposits (see Chapter 2 for a discussion of the nature of deposits). Both the average preservation (27 percent) and average size (15 centimetres) of the sherds (as estimated from the preserved rim diameter of the vessel) from this deposit are significantly larger (Student's T, p. = .025) than for any of the other lots from all of Period II (Figures 7.28 and 7.29).

Clearly the source of this garbage was different from that of any other lot in the building. It looks as though this in-house dump accumulated in a series of single-

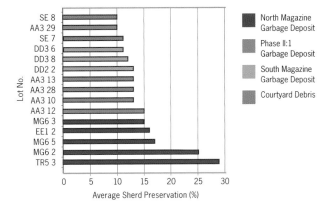

Figure 7.28. Average sherd preservation by lot, estimated from preserved rim diameter

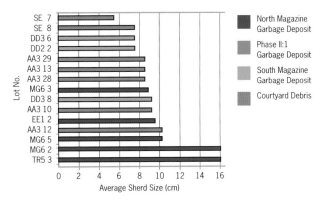

Figure 7.29. Average sherd size by lot, estimated from preserved rim diameter

Figure 7.30. Jars, bowls, and cooking pots of Godin II

episode refuse deposits that were the result of food production and consumption on a fairly large scale, rather than the long-term slow accumulation of a typical village garbage heap. The sherds came from pots and dishes that were used for a variety of household tasks including storing, cooking, eating, and drinking, but all related directly to the making or eating of food.

There were no craft tools such as spindle whorls or awls, which typically occur in the village refuse of Godin Periods III or IV, or in the debris of the farmer/pastoralist houses of phase II:1; there were only these kitchen-related artifacts. If the Godin *bēl āli* and his followers had stayed in the building, it is more than likely that this garbage heap would have been carted off and thrown over the edge of the cliff. Fortunately, they moved on before somebody decided to do a thorough spring cleaning.

In the back tower of the South Magazines (tower 34) a similar deposit was found, but here the sherds were smaller and less well preserved, and there were only two very small fragments of animal bone. Excavation notes describe the dirt matrix of this large pile of sherds as either "loose wash" or "striated occupational trash" but don't mention an organic component like that found in the North Magazine dump. The striking thing about the South Magazine deposit was that it contained the largest proportion of pieces of the distinctive thin-walled bowls and serving vessels that were one of the hallmarks of the late Iron Age pottery assemblage at Godin. The red-brown fabric (or ware) of these vessels can be almost as thin as porcelain and must have been produced by a potter with a lot of skill at the potting wheel. The proportion of bowls was much higher here than in the North Magazine dump (Figures 7.31 and 7.33), but some jars and cooking pots as well as a distinctive tab-handled tankard were discarded here as well (Figure 7.32).

The mean size of sherds in this lot (DD3 6) was not significantly different than for sherds in general at the site (Figure 7.29) (although it was in the smaller range at 7.5 cm), but a closer look at the distribution around this mean indicated that this too was not a typical dump. The *kurtosis*, a measure of the spread of a distribution around a mean, and the *skew*, a measure of the proximity of the mean to the centre of the distribution curve, were both significantly higher here than in any of the other lots. These measures indicate

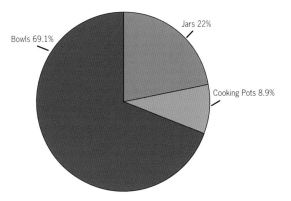

Figure 7.31. Functional types in phase II:2 North Magazine garbage deposit

that although there were some larger sherds (and in fact there were a few nearly complete bowls) that increased the calculation of mean size, many of the sherds were in the very small end of the distribution. You would expect that fine ware would break into smaller pieces, and this is in fact what I assumed when I first noticed this distinctive distribution, but the small sherds in this lot were not made only in the characteristic Godin II fine ware; they also came from some sturdier cooking pots and jars. Again, studies of garbage

disposal in contemporary societies found that sweeping debris could create just this kind of distribution: a few large pieces of broken pots and many smaller pieces of shatter. Amazingly, two of the sherds from this clearly odd lot joined with sherds from the tower 17 (labelled tower 5) portion of the North Magazine dump, tucked into the backmost recess of the North Magazines. The lots were more than 40 metres apart and were excavated in two different field seasons—by the time the tower 17 sherds came out of the ground the South Magazine sherds were already back in Toronto—so there is no possibility that either rodent activity or a labelling mistake in the sherd yard created this match. Some of the sherds in these two isolated deposits must have been put there within days or even hours

Figure 7.32. Finely made "tankard" found in South Magazine deposit

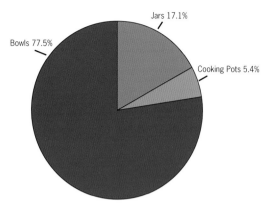

Figure 7.33. Functional types in phase II:2 South Magazine garbage deposit

Bowls 77.5%

Jars 17.1%

Cooking Pots 5.4%

of each other; one servant may have cleaned the kitchen while another swept up the dining hall, each throwing the remains in an out-of-the-way, unoccupied spot in an empty tower.

The largest single collection of pottery in Godin Period II was found over the course of several seasons of excavation and was therefore labelled with a large number of separate lot names (AA3 10, 11, 17, 19, 25 28, 34, and A3 2 and 5), but all these lots clearly belong to one major deposit. Unlike the clearly defined deposits in the North and South Magazines, this large collection of ceramic sherds was widely dispersed in debris over rooms 46–49 (see plan of citadel, Figure 7.7). Each of the excavators who dug in this area described the deposit slightly differently ("soft bricky wash," "greyish ashy fill," or "bricky wash with many reed inclusions"), but all agreed that they were finding more pottery than they had anywhere else in Period II. Each also described a clear sequence: this ashy fill with a lot of sherds, a hard layer of eroded mud-brick, and then the floor of the citadel room. One excavator suggested that these sherds might have fallen from a second-storey pottery storage area when the roof collapsed, since they seemed to be mixed into a reedy matrix that might be roofing material. Although this did seem a logical explanation, these sherds are not any better preserved than the rest of the material at the site (Figure 7.28), and although a number of people worked through the material back in the lab in Toronto, very few joins could be made and only one complete pot rim could be reconstructed. This was clearly garbage like the rest of the material from Godin Period II.

In one sketch in one excavator's field notes, this ashy, reedy, bricky, washy fill clearly runs over the stub of the north wall of room 46, and therein lies the clue to the explanation for this deposit. It must have been formed *after* the building was abandoned and the main walls had partially collapsed. This was the vacant lot into which the phase II:1 villagers, living in the ruins of rooms 6 and 45, tossed their household rubbish.

In addition to the 468 pieces of broken pottery, this deposit contained a lot of bones, some spindle whorls, an animal figurine, a carnelian bead, and a fibula. Unlike in the North Magazine dump, the bone in this lot included some animals that wouldn't typically be eaten, including horse or donkey and dog. Broken jars, bowls, and cooking pots were thrown here in about the same proportions as in the North Magazine dump, but cooking pots formed a higher percentage of the total in this phase II:1 deposit than in either of the phase II:2 garbage deposits (Figures 7.31, 7.33, and 7.34).

The larger variety of artifacts found here, and the fact that they are more widely dispersed, suggests that this was an all-purpose, slowly accumulating village rubbish heap.

The final large collection of broken pottery from Godin Period II reflects yet another way that sherds can be deposited in an archaeological site. In 1971 Cuyler Young sent one young student to explore the southeast tower (rooms 36 and 37). In an attempt to find the foundations for these very thick exterior walls, the excavator opened up a small

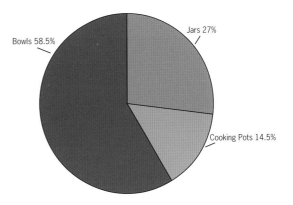

Figure 7.34. Functional types in phase II:1 garbage deposit

test trench running all along the base of the southern face of the exterior wall. In that trench, dug into what must have been the large open courtyard in front of the building, he found seventy very small sherds incorporated in a series of hard compacted surfaces. The average size of these seventy sherds is significantly smaller than any of the other collections of sherds from the site (Figure 7.29). The exterior courtyard in front of this huge building must have been the site of a lot of activity over the hundred or so years that the citadel was in use. Horses, donkeys, dogs, carts, and people would probably have congregated there on a daily basis. Often these kinds of exterior spaces were used as places to throw trash, but apparently the Godin *bēl āli* was fairly meticulous about ordering this area to be kept clean. Any large pieces of garbage were removed, but the small sherds recovered in these test trenches must have gotten trampled into the dirt and ignored.

Although these tiny, trampled sherds might seem insignificant, in fact they are our only piece of evidence for what the pottery used in the citadel might have looked like in the early days of its occupation. The sequence of architectural additions in this elaborate building suggests that it was occupied over a considerable period of time, but almost all the pottery recovered from the building, including the large dumps in the magazines, must belong only to the very latest stage of occupation. It is unlikely that even the most careless of housekeepers would allow a refuse heap to remain in that spot for very long. The ceramic sherds embedded in the dirt floor of the courtyard, however, probably accumulated over the entire span of the long life of the building, and although they may also include later material, some of these pots were probably broken soon after the Godin *bēl āli* built his first columned hall.

The North Magazine kitchen dump, the South Magazine fine-ware deposit, the phase II:1 rubbish heap, and the courtyard floor make up a little less than half of the total number of diagnostic sherds at Godin. The remaining deposits are less well defined but some can be assigned to one or the other of the phases at the site. We can assume that since the roof had collapsed in room 6 before the phase II:1 villagers built their little houses in the ruins of rooms 6 and 44–45, the rest of the building was also uninhabitable by that time. In that case, any material that was clearly on or near the original citadel floor must belong to phase II:2. Artifacts lying over this roof collapse probably were thrown there by the people living in the small houses in room 6, but in all likelihood many of these were still lying about the site from the citadel occupation. When Cuyler Young first visited Godin in 1961, some 2,500 years after it had been abandoned, he could determine all of the cultural periods through which the site had been occupied just by picking up the sherds on the surface. When the shepherd/farmers decided to set up house in the old citadel ruins, they would have been surrounded by the remains of the earlier period, and their garbage must have included a lot of the earlier sherds.

This "close reading" of the four largest deposits of artifacts from Godin, in addition to being an interesting excursion into other people's garbage, is the backdrop for understanding what was really going on at the site.

Ceramic Style at Godin Period II

When Carol Kramer and her fellow ethnoarchaeologists studied how contemporary societies made, decorated, and used pottery, they found that there was no easy way to sort out which aspects of ceramic form were influenced by the intended utilitarian function of the pot, and which by the demands of cultural identity (e.g., craft groups, ethnicity, gender, political affiliations, etc.). As discussed in Chapter 2 of this volume, ethnoarchaeologists realized that these two forces operated in tandem and mutually reinforced each other, so that the shape and decoration of the pottery reflected many cultural factors simultaneously. This complex interrelation between ceramic style and function is demonstrated by a close look at the pottery from Godin Period II.

The pottery assemblage from Godin II is remarkable in that it contains a huge variety of types. Many different analysts have tried to sort the sherds from Godin II into type groups, but it has been a challenge for all of us. One research assistant, trying to be as careful as possible, actually managed to identify more than 1,600 types for these 2,312 sherds, so that on average there were fewer than two sherds for each type. Obviously this kind of detail can't get us very far in comparing patterns from phase to phase or site to site, but it does show how difficult the task of placing this pottery into a coherent framework is. The reasons for this unusual variability are not clear, but it may have something to do with the long period of time over which the site was occupied. It is possible that even in the

North Magazine garbage deposit, some of the sherds are from the earlier years of occupation of the citadel. This is not strictly speaking a Median or Iron III phenomenon because at neighbouring Nush-i Jan there are far fewer types, but since the source of the ceramic sherds there are very different (the bulk of the published pottery from the site comes from a single, well-preserved living floor) it could be a result of how the sherds came into the archaeological record, rather than any true cultural patterning at work.

In spite of the variety of types, all the pottery from this period is wheel-made and obviously produced by skilled craftspeople. The ware is hard, the firing is even, and the rims are straight. There is no sign of pottery production at Godin itself, and the Godin *bēl āli* presumably obtained his pots from full-time, specialist potters living elsewhere in the valley.

Since there is no decoration on pottery from this period, the only way to put these sherds into groups is by ware (the fabric and firing of the vessel) and shape. When I set out to create a typology of the Godin II ceramics, I first divided the shapes into the most basic categories (bowls, jars, and cooking pots) and then used the shape of the rim to create types. I deliberately did not take the diameter of the vessel into account in forming these rim types because I wanted to see if there was a separate association between the shape of the rim and the diameter of the vessel. If there was, this would indicate that potters made choices about how to form the vessel based on its intended size, and that these size categories therefore reflected something different about the culture than would the same form made in a range of sizes. I also did not consider the ware of the rim when constructing these rim types, because I again planned to conduct a separate analysis based on ware type and wanted to see how the two would intersect.

The distribution of rim types is significantly (chi-square, p. = .01) different between phase II:1 and phase II:2. Most rim types occur in both phases, albeit in different proportions, but a few, most notably rim types 1, 76, and 93, occur only in one phase (for illustrations of all types see Figures 7.53–7.60). A separate analysis revealed that, unlike functional types, which differed significantly between deposits as well as between phases, there was no significant difference in the distribution of rim types between lots in the same phase. These rim types must be reflecting a change in the way potters made their wares between the last occupation of the citadel and the re-occupation by farmers in phase II:1.

Some of these changes are quite subtle and most new forms appear to be related to the older ones. Jar-rim type 1 shares the same diameter and general form as jar-rim type 6 and really seems to replace that type in phase II:1. Rim type 1 is very distinctive. Its rim was clearly sharply folded by the potter when the clay was still wet, such that a gap still often can be seen between the side of the rim and the vessel wall. In fact, it came to be named rim type 1 because these rims were so identifiable amidst the rest of the pile of jar rims that

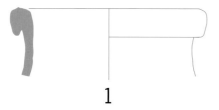

Figure 7.35. Jar-rim type 1

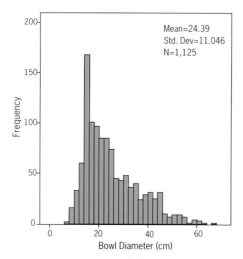

Figure 7.36. Histogram of all bowl diameters

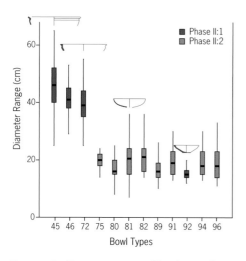

Figure 7.37. Diameter ranges of bowl types for
types with more than 15 sherds

I quickly pulled them out first. It was only after another year when the typology was finished, the lot sequences sorted out, and the data tabulated that I realized that these rims were found exclusively in phase II:1 lots. Similar small changes in form are seen in rim types 9, 22, and 35, which seem to be variants on the earlier jar-rim types.

It is impossible to guess why the generations of potters who supplied Godin during the two phases at the site started making their storage jars with a more folded rim in the later phase. Ethnoarchaeology has not really provided us with a good explanation for this kind of subtle shift, partly because ethnographers usually study pottery-making over too brief a span of time to detect this kind of change. The changes may be related to generational replacements in a single pottery-making tradition; younger craftspeople working within a tradition can use subtle differences in form to distinguish themselves from their teachers. But this rim type does also appear at other fairly distant sites that were probably not being supplied by exactly the same potting community, so it is possible that something more complex about pottery manufacturing, cultural identity, or food storage and transportation was also in operation.

During the glory years of the Godin Period II citadel, the Godin *bēl āli* and his guests were served food and wine in an elaborate set of dishes. The farmers who built their houses in the ruins of this palace ate their meals of stew out of a much simpler range of vessels. The pattern of rim-type distributions of bowls in the two phases at Godin is in large part a reflection of these changes. When I constructed my typology for the rim sherds at Godin, I deliberately did not include vessel diameter as a variable, so that I could see if the size of vessels was related to their formal type. An overall plotting of the distribution of bowl diameters at the site had not revealed an obvious split into large and small bowls (Figure 7.36).

By combining bowl-rim type with bowl diameters it became clear that there was indeed such a division, but that it was expressed very differently in the two phases of the site.

In phase II:1 (the farmer/shepherds) there is clearly a set of large-bowl types that are defined by their diameter and shape of their rim (Figure 7.37). In phase II:2 (the citadel), there are fewer of these very large bowls, but the smaller bowl-rim types were made in a much wider range of sizes. The simple, rounded-rim bowls of the citadel phase (type 81), made in a very large range of sizes, seem to get replaced in the simpler kitchens of the farmers by bowl-type 92 (Figure 7.38), which are made in the narrowest range of diameters of any of the bowl types at the site (12–17 cm). This bowl-type is indeed so standardized in ware, shape, and size that when the bowl sherds are all spread out on a table, as with jar-rim type 1, this type is easily pulled out as unique. A large part of this distinction is directly related to the quality of the ceramics from each period.

The distinctive fine wares of the late Iron Age in Iran were made by specialized potters working with a very sophisticated technology. The extremely finely burnished red-brown ware of these bowls and their angular form, suggest that they were sometimes made in direct imitation of metal bowls. These fine-ware bowls must have been a marker of status in some sense, but the true sign of wealth for the inhabitants of the citadel would have been the gold, silver, or bronze bowls, which they took with them when they left the site. Not surprisingly, the *bēl āli* and his followers used many more

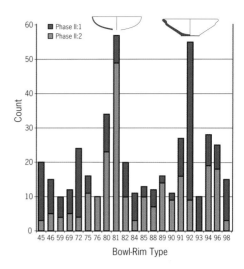

Figure 7.38. Counts of bowl types by phase for types with more than 10 sherds

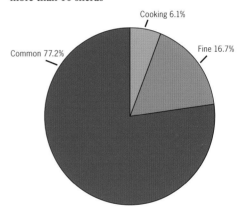

Figure 7.39. Ware types in phase II:2

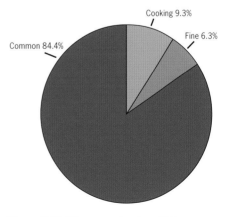

Figure 7.40. Ware types in phase II:1

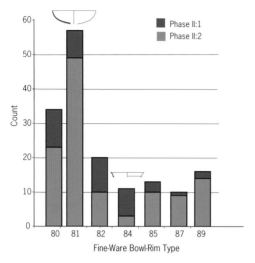

Figure 7.41. Fine-ware bowl-rim types by phase for types with more than 10 sherds

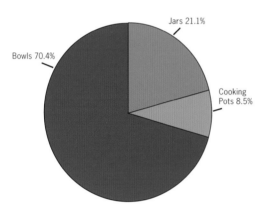

Figure 7.42. Functional types in phase II:2

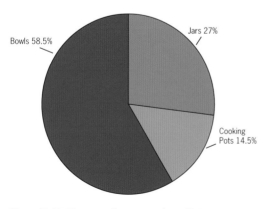

Figure 7.43. Functional types in phase II:11

fine-ware bowls than did the phase II:1 farmers (Figures 7.39, 7.40). What is surprising is that these farmer/shepherds used any at all. Yet fine-ware sherds do occur in the phase II:1 deposits, albeit in smaller numbers (Figure 7.40).

What is even more striking is that one bowl-rim type (type 84) that is almost always made in the classic Godin fine ware, appears almost exclusively in the phase II:1 deposits. In the citadel phase (phase II:2), fine wares come in a much larger variety of forms, and many more bowl types are found in both fine and common ware (Figure 7.41).

In terms of the overall proportion of functional types in both phases, the pottery collection used by the Median *bēl āli* and his guests is, surprisingly, not all that different from the dishes of the simple village houses of the phase II:1 pastoralists (Figures 7.42 and 7.43).

The basic tasks of storing, cooking, and eating demand the same repertoire of shapes. In fact, the proportion of functional forms was more different between deposits in phase II:2 (sweeping debris, courtyard trample, and kitchen refuse) than it was between phases. Only the proportion of cooking pots is consistently higher in the later phase in deposits of all types. When we factor in style and ware, however, it turns out that no matter how the deposit accumulated, the phase II:1 villagers left behind many more large, coarse-ware bowls, predominately one type of common-ware, small bowl in a very restricted range of sizes, and predominantly one type of fine-ware drinking bowl.

The dishes of the Godin *bēl āli* came, instead, in a variety of types in all wares, and

Figure 7.44. Boxes of Godin II bowl sherds in storage at the ROM

in a wide range of sizes for each type. The fine-ware drinking bowls from this period are both numerous and diverse. The relative paucity of cooking pots is striking, considering the amount of eating that seems to have occurred in the palace-citadel. The large pile of bones found in the North Magazine dump, however, all belonged to younger animals, so that roast suckling pig and lamb may have been preferred to the goat stew of the simpler shepherds, and would not have required as many stewing pots.

Xenophon describes a Median dinner, served to the great Persian king Cyrus when he was a young prince, by his Median grandfather Astyages:

Figure 7.45. Godin II drinking bowl

And then again, when Astyages dined with his daughter and Cyrus, he set before him dainty side-dishes and all sorts of sauces and meats, for he wished the boy to enjoy his dinner as much as possible, in order that he might be less likely to feel homesick. And Cyrus, they say, observed: "How much trouble you have at your dinner, grandfather, if you have to reach out your hands to all these dishes and taste of all these different kinds of food!" (Xenophon, *Cyropaedia* I.3.4)

The point of this passage is to contrast Median decadence with Persian abstemiousness for a Greek audience almost 200 years after Cyrus' death, but looking at the piles and piles of fine-ware sherds in the storage rooms of the ROM, one can't help picturing the Godin *bēl āli* reaching out his hands to all these dishes and setting before his guests all these different kinds of food.

The Function of the Godin Period II Citadel

The Godin Period II citadel was an imposing edifice. The massive walls loomed above the valley floor, and the whole building must have been a potent visual symbol of the Godin *bēl āli*'s dominance over the surrounding countryside. In the Assyrian reliefs depicting campaigns in Media, we see many of the same buttressed walls, towers, and arrowslots, with "madaaya dannu" (mighty Medes) shooting fearlessly from their midst. One relief specifically labelled Ḫarḫar (the town that Sargon renamed Kār Šarrukin) shows a columned structure inserted into the middle of the fort (Figure 7.47). It is possible that this was the Assyrian artist's attempt at rendering the most distinctive aspect of a Median citadel, its central columned hall.

If the exterior of the citadel was built for defence, the artifacts and interior architecture reflect quite another set of concerns. It was the grand columned hall that defined the building to a visitor once he was allowed past the walls, and not any military agenda. Whatever the aim was at the time the citadel was built, over the years even the exterior walls lost their defensive capabilities. Not only were the arrowslots allowed to fill up with debris, but when the North Magazines were built, no attempt at all was made to keep the cross walls out of the way of the arrowslots. The builders of the secondary wall set up against the north wall of the columned hall were also clearly unconcerned with preserving the original defensive nature of the building, since that wall blocks all the arrowslots in the largest expanse of wall in the building.

Even from the beginning, the layout and structure of the interior was not designed with a military function in mind. Here we find no guards' quarters, no barracks, and no weapons rooms. Instead, there are three columned halls, a huge kitchen with three hearths

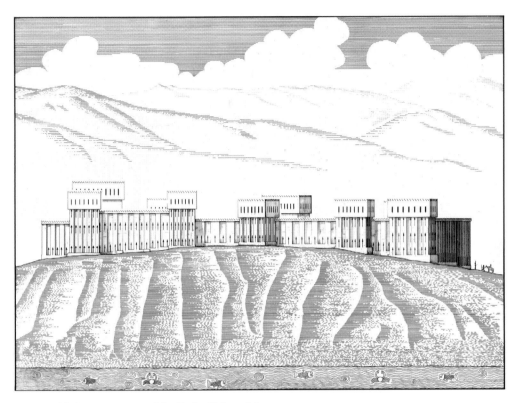

Figure 7.46. Reconstruction of the Godin II:2 citadel

Figure 7.47. Assyrian attack on the Median city of Ḥarḥar, with a columned structure in the centre of the city, from carved relief in the palace of Sargon at Khorsabad

large enough for roasting a whole lamb, and the discarded remains of many feasts. The large columned hall (room 9) at Godin was used as an assembly room for a single, powerful figure to receive his subjects. The design of this hall at Godin and halls at a few other sites of the Iron III period almost certainly served as the model for the numerous well-known columned halls of the Achaemenid Persians.

The largest and best preserved columned hall is the later Apadana of Darius (522–486 BC) at the Persian capital of Persepolis. Its soaring columns, monstrous animal capitals, and flowering bases have been the symbol of Persian majesty for thousands of years. Since its destruction by Alexander the Great in 330 BC, the ruins of this once great building have stood as a death's-head reminder of the transient nature of power. Historical sources and images in the stone reliefs that decorate the ceremonial stairway leading to the room make it clear that this hall was a ritual throneroom of the Persian king. Sitting on a high throne on a dais in the rear of the hall, Darius would receive the emissaries from all over his vast empire, each presenting the valuable resource of his home country. For many years the antecedents for this building were a mystery to architectural historians. It was completely different in design from the long, narrow thronerooms of the Neo-Assyrian and Babylonian kings who were the immediate predecessors to the Persians, and even though the construction of the columns borrowed some technical elements from early-classical Greek architecture, the layout of the building was entirely foreign to the Greek tradition.

Figure 7.48. Arrowslots in north wall of citadel showing the successively higher lines of plastering

Figure 7.49. Reconstruction of the interior of the Godin II:2 columned hall (room 9)

Some art historians argued that its form was derived from the tents of the nomadic herdsmen from whom the Persians were thought to have descended. The most authoritative statement on the subject came from Henri Frankfort in his definitive treatise, *The Art and Architecture of the Ancient Orient,* published in 1954: "Much has been written on the origin of the Achaemenian pillared halls, but to little purpose. They have been derived from Median architecture, of which nothing remains." The 1960s excavations of the Median columned halls at Godin and Nush-i Jan provided that missing link.

The columned hall of Godin is many times smaller than that of Darius; the whole Godin building would fit into the Apadana at Persepolis several times over. But there can be little doubt that the room was a reception hall like the Apadana. The plastered seat at the rear of the hall was clearly a seat of honour, and the benches that ran all along the sides must have been intended for waiting suppliants.

Much to many people's surprise, in the past few years similar Iron-Age columned halls, although on an even smaller scale, were excavated by Peter Magee and Remy Boucharlat at the sites of Muweilah and Rumeilah on the Oman Peninsula in Arabia, some 1,500 kilometres away. There is no reason to believe that there was direct contact between central western Iran and Arabia at this time; the idea of these halls probably came to Arabia via southwestern Iran where the Persians first made their home, although no columned halls of this early date have yet been excavated in that area. In Arabia the halls are the largest

Figure 7.50. The tomb of Darius at Naqsh-i Rustam, showing subjects as columns supporting the king's throne

structure in a village of houses, rather than free-standing citadels. At both of these sites, however, proportions of the pottery types found in these buildings is different than that in the rest of the town and, as at Godin, seem to be closely associated with eating and drinking on a large scale.

The social and ritual function of feasting has received a lot of attention in anthropological and archaeological literature in the past few years, in part because it leaves a fairly clear trace in the archaeological record. Feasting is used by many different types of cultures in the promotion of a wide array of social, cultural, and ritual networks. People in power use feasts to cement social relationships, to identify themselves as providers, and to promote ritual identities. The Godin *bēl āli* probably used his supplies of sheep, goat, and pig to fulfill all these functions. The columned hall was a meeting place as well as a place to hold court, and it may be that it was this role that promoted the development of this unique architectural form.

Columns had been used throughout the Near East in a variety of ways for the previous 3,000 years. They held up balconies, fronted temples, and formed porticoes around buildings. They were rarely used in interior spaces, however, and never in thronerooms, which

Figure 7.51. Workers standing in for columns in the Godin II:2 columned hall (room 9)

were always long and narrow so that the axis of attention was focused on the king. At the ninth-century site of Hasanlu in northern Iran, columns were used in interior reception rooms, but here they were placed in two rows to form an aisle running up the middle of the room with the seat of honour at its end. Again, the structure of the architecture created a space that led any person entering the building either toward or away from the central figure. No culture in the Near East had ever before built their reception rooms as one large enclosed space with multiple rows of evenly spaced columns supporting a roof. In fact the design is relatively rare in the history of world architecture, which is pretty surprising given how simple it is both conceptually and technically.

The reason why this form seems to be avoided in most architectural traditions may be exactly why it was adopted by Iron Age chieftains. Architectural structures (walls, piers, arches, etc.) are usually designed to define and shape people's experience of an interior space. Normally the architectural elements themselves are used mostly to draw attention to the spaces that they create. The piers in a cathedral, for instance, divide the central nave with its altar from the side aisles and draw the visitor's eye upwards to the soaring vaults above. The evenly spaced columns of the Iron Age columned halls, however, actually seem to impede this kind of division into discrete spaces. At Godin the seat of honour along the back wall and the hearth in front of it create an axis of sorts, but the layout of the columns does nothing to draw attention to this particular aisle, which is not even centrally placed. The columns draw attention to themselves instead of to the space around them or towards a particular focal point such as an altar or throne. This is an odd choice for a throneroom where the emphasis should be on a central figure.

The Medes may have adopted columned halls as their main reception rooms precisely because of the tendency of the rows of columns to negate space. The disorienting multi-axiality of the room would be a particularly effective architectural device for a structure designed explicitly for large public displays of strength in numbers. The multiplication of the columns creates a many-to-one, instead of a focused one-on-one, encounter with the central figure. If the function of these halls was ritual gathering and feasting, then it may well have been that visually emphasizing the large number of celebrants was as important as focusing on the power figure. It is interesting in this regard that a small, single-columned room opening directly off the main hall is a feature of all these sites. At Godin, room 50, which could be sealed off from the main hall by a wooden door, is elaborately outfitted with benches and a seat of honour, as if to accommodate a one-on-one meeting with the Godin *bēl āli*.

It is even possible that the columns themselves served as a metaphorical reference to the followers of the Iron Age rulers who held court in these halls. On the later Achaemenid Persian tomb of Darius at Naqsh-i Rustam, subjects of the king are shown in carved relief as if they were columns with their arms raised above their heads supporting the king on his throne dais (Figure 7.50). These figures are very clearly meant to look like the architectural columns that are also carved on the monument. In case there were any doubt as to his metaphorical meaning, Darius actually adds a textual gloss of his visual pun:

> If now thou shalt think that "How many are the countries which King Darius held?" look at the sculptures (of those) who bear the throne, then thou shalt know, then shall it become known to thee: the spear of a Persian man has gone forth far; then shall it become known to thee: a Persian man has delivered battle far indeed from Persia. (Kent, p. 138)

It is possible that this equation of columns with subjects was formed in the columned halls of the Godin *bēl āli* and his compatriots.

The Dating of Godin Period II

There are several sources of evidence for dating Godin Period II. Previously, all dating of Godin has been based on comparative ceramic chronologies. Cuyler Young's early 1960s division of the Iron Age of western Iran into four basic ceramic phases, which he called Iron I, II, III, and IV, has remained more or less unaltered. The absolute dating of these ceramic groups has remained problematic, however, even after all these years. A few key dates, such as the destruction of Hasanlu in the ninth century, bracket these periods, but by and large, sites are dated by ceramic comparisons to other sites that are themselves dated by ceramic comparisons to a third site. Often this creates a knot of circular reasoning that is very hard to untangle. The Iron III period is particularly resistant to more detailed sub-divisions because the undecorated pottery from this very long period of time is remarkably unchanging. The changes that do occur, as is evident from the sequence at Godin, are usually in small variations in rim form and in proportions of types rather than in clearly identifiable forms. So far, it has been impossible to say that the presence of a single type, or even a set of types, definitely establishes a date for a site.

I compared the ceramic types from Godin to the other main sites in western Iran to try to determine where the bulk of the parallels were to be found (the full details of this study are published in Gopnik 2003 and the parallels are listed in the description of the pottery plates.) The following comparative chronological chart summarizes these findings.

Radiocarbon analysis can provide a greater degree of accuracy for absolute dating, but it too is subject to error and interpretation. Although most of the best carbon samples from Period II were among the "best 100 samples" that disappeared in the 1980s (see "Archaeological Dating at Godin," p. 36), a limited number of samples had been run in the late 1960s at the University of Pennsylvania, and some charcoal that duplicated other samples, or was not from the best contexts, remained in storage at the ROM. We submitted those stored samples for analysis to the BetaAnalytic laboratories in Florida. Both the earlier Penn results and the newly run dates are plotted below.

The samples fall into two stratigraphic groups: the first is charcoal and charred grain from poorly understood floors recovered in 1967 during the removal of tower 5 to start the Deep Sounding, and in 1969 below the North Magazine. Both of these floors pre-date the building of the citadel and are the only evidence for any post-III but pre-II occupation at the site. The samples that were run at Penn in the 1960s (sample numbers Penn 1470–72) were all from the same exact deposit: a pile of burnt barley beneath tower 5. Two of these dates match well with each other and with the newly run pre-II date (sample Beta 236032). Penn 1472 is clearly aberrant, and may have been either mislabelled or contaminated. Bayesian statistics (using the OxCal modelling program developed by Bronk Ramsey) indicate that if

Table 7.1. Relative chronology of Iron III, western Iran. Shaded bars represent revised dates based on new radiocarbon dates from Godin II.

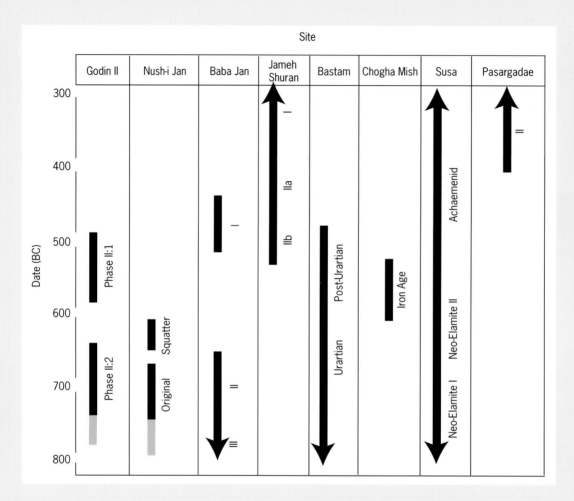

the sample Penn 1472 is eliminated, these dates can be combined with a 95 percent probability of acceptance to a range of 908–812 BC. The second set of samples was found in the citadel itself. Beta 231141 was a large chunk of charcoal removed from the northern hearth in room 46. This hearth had a covered firebox with a hole in the top on which a stone had been carefully placed, effectively sealing its contents. This sample was dated to 820–760 BC, considerably earlier than the mid-seventh-century date that had previously been suggested for the main occupation of the Godin citadel. Five more samples were recovered from the large garbage deposit that accumulated in the North Magazine corridor, Magazine 6, and tower 17. Although there is some variation in the range of these dates, OxCal modelling indicates that these dates can be combined with a 95 percent probability of acceptance to a range of

Table 7.2. Radiocarbon dates for Godin II

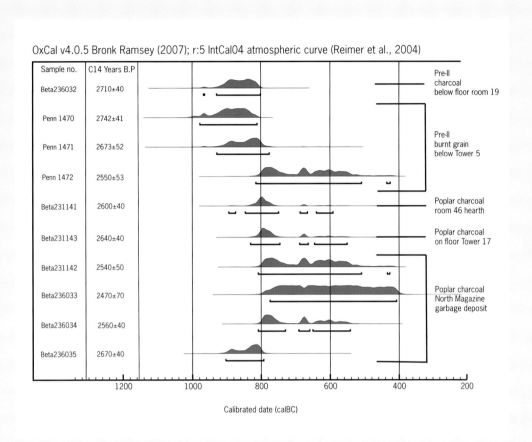

OxCal v4.0.5 Bronk Ramsey (2007); r:5 IntCal04 atmospheric curve (Reimer et al., 2004)

Sample no.	C14 Years B.P
Beta236032	2710±40
Penn 1470	2742±41
Penn 1471	2673±52
Penn 1472	2550±53
Beta231141	2600±40
Beta231143	2640±40
Beta231142	2540±50
Beta236033	2470±70
Beta236034	2560±40
Beta236035	2670±40

Pre-II charcoal below floor room 19

Pre-II burnt grain below Tower 5

Poplar charcoal room 46 hearth

Poplar charcoal on floor Tower 17

Poplar charcoal North Magazine garbage deposit

Calibrated date (calBC)

806–674 BC. All these samples are from cooking-hearth remains and should therefore date the occupation itself rather than the construction of the building. They probably accumulated over a span of not more than a few years, since it seems unlikely that this garbage heap would have been allowed to fester in the back corridor for much longer than that. It is possible that there is some "old wood" effect here; wood can be stored for a long time and the inner core of the tree dates to the time it was grown rather than to the time that the tree was cut. But poplars are quick-growing and have a limited life span, and firewood is not usually stored for extended periods, so that this effect is probably not too marked. It seems probable then that the citadel was built sometime during the ninth to eighth centuries BC, exactly when we begin to see the rising power of the Median *bēl āli* in the Neo-Assyrian texts, and may have been abandoned sometime before 650 BC, perhaps as the result of Median consolidation at Ecbatana, but more likely simply because of this particular *bēl āli's* decline.

The Abandonment of the Godin Period II Citadel

After many years, perhaps successive generations, of dominion over the Kangavar Valley, the Godin *bēl āli* decided to pack his things and abandon the citadel forever. If we could date this abandonment more precisely we would have a much better basis for reconstructing the causes that might have led to the end of his rule. From contemporary historical sources (the Babylonian Chronicles) we know that in 612 BC a coalition of Babylonian and Median forces besieged, captured, and sacked the Assyrian capital at Nineveh, bringing an end to the Assyrian Empire. The mustering of an army large enough to defeat the Assyrians doesn't seem consistent with the picture of the Medes as competing, small local powers, the *bēl āli* of the Assyrian sources. Scholars have assumed that Herodotus's account of the consolidation of the Median local rulers into a single state by Deioces must have occurred sometime before the invasion of Assyria. According to Herodotus, Deioces came to the throne around 700 BC, but Herodotus was writing more than 200 years after the events, and it is unlikely that he would get the dates right. The annals of Esarhaddon in which three Median *bēl āli* bring lapis lazuli to the Assyrian king to request his aid, "because of the other chieftains [*bēl āli*] who had raised their hands against them," can be dated to 672 BC, so we know that at the beginning of the seventh century the Median *bēl āli* were still squabbling local leaders rather than a unified force. We also know that by 614 BC they were fighting under a king Cyaxeres (Umakištar in the Babylonian sources), which leaves some fifty years for the unification described by Herodotus to take place.

If the Median Empire was once defeated at the hands of the great Persian King Cyrus in the mid-sixth century BC, it was brought down again by a group of university professors at a conference in Padua, Italy, in 2001 AD. At this exclusive meeting of archaeologists and historians in a charming university town, lunches of pasta and wine were followed by afternoons in which speaker after speaker argued that we have no evidence at all for any Median Empire or even for any Median state. The whole story, they suggested, may have been a mere invention on the part of Herodotus in order to create a contrast between the development of kingship in different traditions. The destruction of the Assyrian capital of Nineveh by the Medes was a transient and opportunistic confederacy of local powers, like the Godin *bēl āli,* who as soon as the deed was done, retreated back to the mountains. The Italian historian Mario Liverani summarized this position in 2003: "We get the impression of a people interested in destruction and booty, but not in territorial gains or even in a rationally planned military strategy, and we suspect that the leader of the Median army, Cyaxeres, did not have sufficient authority to keep his troops fighting after the enthusiastic moment of storming." The abandonment of Godin and Nush-i Jan, the only two archaeological sites that could confidently be called Median, were cited as evidence that Median power had contracted rather than expanded in the early sixth century BC when the Median Empire was supposed to have been at its peak.

It is possible that the abandonment of Godin was involved in a retraction of these local Median powers, but it is equally possible that Herodotus's story has some basis in historical reality. If Median power really was consolidated, and the centre of power moved from the local to the regional level at Ecbatana (Hamadan), east of Godin, as Herodotus claims, then we would expect just such a gradual, peaceful abandonment of sites during the mid to late seventh century as the local *bēl āli* move east to Ecbatana to take their place in the new Median court. The new radiocarbon dates for Godin II may confirm this view of history by pushing back the dates of the abandonment of Godin to the mid-seventh century. The overburden of later occupation at Hamadan may prevent us from ever discovering the short-lived Median capital, and the difficulty of sorting out the exact dates of the Iron III ceramic assemblages in western Iran may mean that we wouldn't even recognize it as Median, rather than Achaemenid Persian, if we did find it.

While it is possible that the abandonment of Godin is explained by a traditional history of kings and battles, the archaeological evidence gives us the power to move beyond those narratives. The excavations at Godin remove the distorting lens of Assyrian, Greek, and modern interpretations of Median culture. The claim that the Medes were incapable of organizing an orchestrated campaign against their Assyrian conquerors reduces the description of the Median *bēl āli* to the "barbarian" mountain dwellers promoted by Assyrian ideology. This is not the picture we get from the columned hall of Godin or the elaborate temple at Nush-i Jan; the architecture at Godin and Nush-i Jan certainly reflects a culture capable of "rational planning" at many levels. Anthropologists and historians have begun, increasingly, to question the notion of a single evolutionary pathway to complexity in which tribes become chiefdoms, and they in turn become states and empires. If the Median *bēl āli* can be characterized as "chiefs," the current anthropological studies of this form of social organization suggest that chiefdoms display many forms of complexity that do not necessarily mirror the Western view of a hierarchical power structure. It may not be surprising that we don't have the same kinds of evidence for the Median Empire that we do for the Assyrians or later Achaemenid Persians. The complex social and political structure centred on the figure of the *bēl āli* may be as impenetrable to us as it was to the Medes' Neo-Assyrian overlords. At least the discarded bits and pieces of life on the High Road of central western Iran give the Godin *bēl āli* a chance to speak to us directly of his experience.

Metallurgy in Godin Period II: The Appearance of Iron at Godin

Lesley D. Frame

The most notable aspect of metallurgy during Godin Period II is the appearance of iron implements. Almost all weapons and tools found in Godin II were made of iron, although arrowheads continued to be made of bronze. Most tools benefited from the superior strength, hardness, and edge-retention of iron over bronze. Arrowheads, however, require high toughness for shock absorption so that they do not shatter after a single impact, and this is more easily achieved with copper alloys such as bronze than with iron. Decorative items such as pins, needles, and jewellery all continue to be made of copper-base alloys. There is no evidence for metallurgical processing at Godin Tepe during Period II.

Additional data on the metallurgy of Godin are available in the Godin Web archive at https://tspace.library.utoronto.ca.

Figure 7.52. Metal artifacts from Godin Period II

Godin Period II Pottery Typology

Sources for Pottery Catalogue Parallels

Baba Jan. Goff, B. "Excavations at Baba Jan: The Architecture and Pottery of Level I." *Iran* 22 (1985): 1–20.

Bastam. Kroll, S. "Die urartaischer Keramik aus Bastam." *In* W. Kleiss (ed.), *Bastam I*, 203–220. Berlin: Gebr. Mann Verlag, 1979.

Choga Mish. Delougaz, Pinhas, Helene J. Kantor, and Abbas Alizadeh. *Chogha Mish.* The University of Chicago Oriental Institute Publications, vol. 101. Chicago: Oriental Institute of the University of Chicago, 1996.

Jameh Shuran. Unpublished pottery typology from Jameh Shuran, Iran, by L. D. Levine.

Kroll. Kroll, S. *Keramik Urartaischer Festungen in Iran.* Berlin: Dietrich Reimer, 1976.

Nush-i Jan. Unpublished pottery typology from Nush-i Jan, by Ruth Stronach.

Pasargadae. Stronach, D. *Pasargadae.* Oxford: Clarendon Press, 1978.

Susa VRII. Miroschedji, P. de. "Fouilles du chantier Ville Royale II à Suse." *Cahiers de la D.A.F.I.* 12 (1981): 9–136. Miroschedji, P. de. "Fouilles du chantier Ville Royale II à Suse: niveaux d'époques Achéménide, Seleucide, Parthe et Islamique." *Cahiers de la D.A.F.I.* 15 (1987): 11–121.

Sources for Quotations

ARAB 2. Luckenbill, D. D. *Ancient Records of Assyria and Babylonia*, vol. 2. London: Histories and Mysteries of Man Ltd., 1989.

Grayson. Grayson, A. Kirk. *Assyrian Rulers of the Early First Millennium BC II (858–745 BC).* Toronto: University of Toronto Press, 1991.

Herodotus. Godley, A. D. *Herodotus, with an English Translation.* Cambridge: Harvard University Press, 1920.

Kent. Kent R. G., *Old Persian Grammar, Texts, Lexicon.* New Haven: American Oriental Society, 1950.

SAA I. Parpola, S. *The Correspondence of Sargon II, Part I. State Archives of Assyria I.* Helsinki: Helsinki University Press, 1987.

SAA II. Parpola, S., and K. Watanabe. *Neo-Assyrian Treaties and Loyalty Oaths. State Archives of Assyria II.* Helsinki: Helsinki University Press, 1988.

SAA XV. Fuchs, A., and S. Parpola. *The Correspondence of Sargon II, Part III. State Archives of Assyria XV.* Helsinki: Helsinki University Press, 2001.

Xenophon, *Cyropaedia.* Miller, W., ed. Xenophon in Seven Volumes. Cambridge: Harvard University Press, 1914.

Table 7.3. Catalogue of pottery types

TYPE	NUMBER OF SHERDS				PARALLELS	
	Phase II:1 Lots	Phase II:2 Lots	Mixed Lots	Courtyard Debris Lots	Site and Phase/Stratum	Figure Number in Source
Jar Types (1–41)						
1	19	0	5	0	Jameh Shuran I, IIa, IIb Susa VRII 5-4 Pasargadae	16: 9 117: 8, 10; 118: 15
206	3	6	1	0	Bastam Kroll	9: 21 type 58
4	2	3	8	4	Baba Jan I Nush-i Jan Jameh Shuran IIa, IIb Pasargadae Chogha Mish	5: 2, 6 117: 23 75: BB
6	3	7	6	1	Baba Jan I Nush-i Jan Jameh Shuran IIb Susa VRII 5-4 Chogha Mish	5: 1, 13 15: 2 75: Y
7	7	5	8	5	Baba Jan I Jameh Shuran IIb Kroll (8-7c.) Chogha Mish	5: 4 type 49 75: W
9	8	1	13	6	Jameh Shuran IIa, IIb Susa VRII 4 Pasargadae	14: 10 119: 24, 25
10	3	3	5	2	Jameh Shuran IIa, IIb Susa VRII 5-4 Bastam	15: 10 9: 2
11	3	8	4	0	Bastam	9: 10
12	5	1	4	2 0	Nush-i Jan Jameh Shuran IIa, IIb	
14	4	5	5	0	Kroll Chogha Mish	type 57 75: V
18	8	4	11	3	Baba Jan I Nush-i Jan Jameh Shuran IIa Pasargadae Chogha Mish	7: 7 120: 7 75: CC
22	11	6	12	4	Baba Jan I Nush-i Jan Jameh Shuran IIa	5: 9, 11
24	7	14	20	5	Baba Jan I Nush-i Jan Jameh Shuran I, IIa Kroll Chogha Mish	6: 24 type 83a 75: B
26	7	1	3	1	Bastam	9: 12
27	0	3	8	3		
28	6	10	5	4	Nush-i Jan Chogha Mish	75: G
30	4	6	8	1	Baba Jan I Nush-i Jan Pasargadae Bastam	5: 10 117: 4 9: 3
32	7	3	3	1	Baba Jan I	5: 19, 27

Table 7.3. Catalogue of pottery types (*continued*)

TYPE	NUMBER OF SHERDS				PARALLELS	
	Phase II:1 Lots	Phase II:2 Lots	Mixed Lots	Courtyard Debris Lots	Site and Phase/Stratum	Figure Number in Source
33	3	1	8	2	Baba Jan I Nush-i Jan	5: 22
35	11	4	10	3	Baba Jan I Nush-i Jan Jameh Shuran IIa Susa VRII 5-4	5: 17, 18 14: 4; 16: 2, 3
41	3	6	5	3		
Large Bowl Types (45–72)						
45	17	3	15	4	Baba Jan I Jameh Shuran I	2: 23
46	10	5	14	1	Baba Jan I	3: 12, 13; 4: 21
47	8	1	5	1	Baba Jan I	3: 7, 11
48	7	0	8	4		
50	0	6	6	5	Baba Jan I Nush-i Jan Chogha Mish	4: 11, 12, 13 75: S
52	6	6	7	2	Baba Jan I Jameh Shuran I, IIb	3: 5, 9
55	4	0	7	2	Jameh Shuran I	
57	7	1	7	1	Baba Jan I Pasargadae	3: 21 111: 19
59	6	4	14	4	Jameh Shuran IIa Pasargadae	 111: 20
60	3	6	8	3	Nush-i Jan Jameh Shuran IIb Bastam	 6: 13
69	7	5	13	9	Nush-i Jan Bastam Kroll (7c.)	 6: 12 type 32
70	2	3	9	5	Nush-i Jan Jameh Shuran I Pasargadae Bastam Kroll (7c.)	 108: 12 6: 5 type 42
71	3	1	13	5	Nush-i Jan Jameh Shuran I Kroll (8-7c.)	 type 29
72	20	4	14	2	Baba Jan I Jameh Shuran IIa Kroll (ach.) Chogha Mish	4: 17 type 27 75: R
Small Bowl Types (75–109)						
75	5	11	9	3	Baba Jan I Jameh Shuran I	2: 3, 6, 9
76	0	10	26	13	Baba Jan I Nush-i Jan Jameh Shuran I, IIa Bastam Kroll (ur-ac)	4: 1 4: 37 type 26

Table 7.3. Catalogue of pottery types (*continued*)

TYPE	NUMBER OF SHERDS				PARALLELS	
	Phase II:1 Lots	Phase II:2 Lots	Mixed Lots	Courtyard Debris Lots	Site and Phase/Stratum	Figure Number in Source
78	1	2	8	3	Nush-i Jan Jameh Shuran I	
79	4	3	15	9	Baba Jan I Nush-i Jan Jameh Shuran I Bastam Kroll (7c.)	2: 11; 3: 10 4: 20 type 33
80	11	23	20	7	Pasargadae Bastam	110: 10 4: 5
81	8	49	37	18	Baba Jan I Nush-i Jan Jameh Shuran I, IIa Susa VRII 5-4 Pasargadae Kroll (ur-ac) Chogha Mish	2: 19-21; 4: 3-4 7: 16 110: 6, 9 type 2a, 3, 8 73: I
82	10	10	18	5	Nush-i Jan Jameh Shuran IIa	
84	8	3	9	2	Baba Jan I Susa VRII 5-4 Pasargadae Kroll (ach.) Chogha Mish	2: 51 7: 8 106: 9, 12, 17 type 11 74: F
85	3	10	17	4	Baba Jan I Nush-i Jan Kroll (ac-pa)	2: 17 type 22
87	1	9	5	2	Jameh Shuran IIa, IIb	
88	5	7	10	3	Nush-i Jan Jameh Shuran IIa, IIb Pasargadae Bastam Kroll (8-7c+) Chogha Mish	 107: 6 4: 15, 41 type 23 73: L
89	2	14	31	12	Baba Jan I Jameh Shuran I Susa VRII 5-4 Pasargadae Chogha Mish	3: 16 8: 8 108: 2 74: H
90	2	9	12	3	Baba Jan I Nush-i Jan Jameh Shuran I Bastam Chogha Mish	3: 17 5: 8 74: C
91	11	16	33	12	Baba Jan I Nush-i Jan Jameh Shuran I Susa VRII 5-4	2: 7, 18, 22, 16 8: 9
92	46	9	25	3	Jameh Shuran I, IIa, IIb Susa VRII 5-4 Pasargadae Kroll (7c.+)	 8: 5, 6 108: 11; 110: 13 type 5b
93	10	0	10	1	Jameh Shuran IIb Pasargadae	 107: 14
94	9	19	18	4	Baba Jan I Nush-i Jan Chogha Mish	2: 31; 4: 16 73: K ; 75: B

Table 7.3. Catalogue of pottery types (*continued*)

TYPE	NUMBER OF SHERDS				PARALLELS	
	Phase II:1 Lots	Phase II:2 Lots	Mixed Lots	Courtyard Debris Lots	Site and Phase/Stratum	Figure Number in Source
95	0	4	7	3	Nush-i Jan Chogha Mish	 73: J
96	7	18	12	2	Nush-i Jan Pasargadae Chogha Mish	 107: 2 74: I
97	6	4	4	0	Baba Jan I	2: 2
98	12	3	7	2	Baba Jan I Jameh Shuran I Susa VRII 5-4 Pasargadae Kroll (8c.) Chogha Mish	2: 25 7: 14 107: 4; 108: 3 type 12 74: G
103	2	6	16	4	Baba Jan I Jameh Shuran IIa Susa VRII 5-4	2: 8 9: 4
104	0	5	8	4	Baba Jan I Bastam Kroll (me-ac)	2: 12 5: 11 type 14
105	1	6	9	7	Baba Jan I Susa VRII 5-4	2: 15 9: 1
106	0	3	9	3		
108	3	0	8	4	Nush-i Jan Chogha Mish	 73: A, G
109	8	10	29	14	Nush-i Jan Bastam	 4: 36
Cooking-pot Types (112–122)						
112	6	3	5	4		
113	8	5	5	0		
114	8	1	5	2	Baba Jan I	5: 29
115	8	4	14	3		
117	14	3	5	2	Baba Jan I	4: 35
118	4	5	6	3		
119	6	0	5	1		
120	5	0	6	4		
121	3	7	13	1		
122	8	11	11	3		

Note: Additional pottery figures are available in the Godin Web archive at https://tspace.library.utoronto.ca.

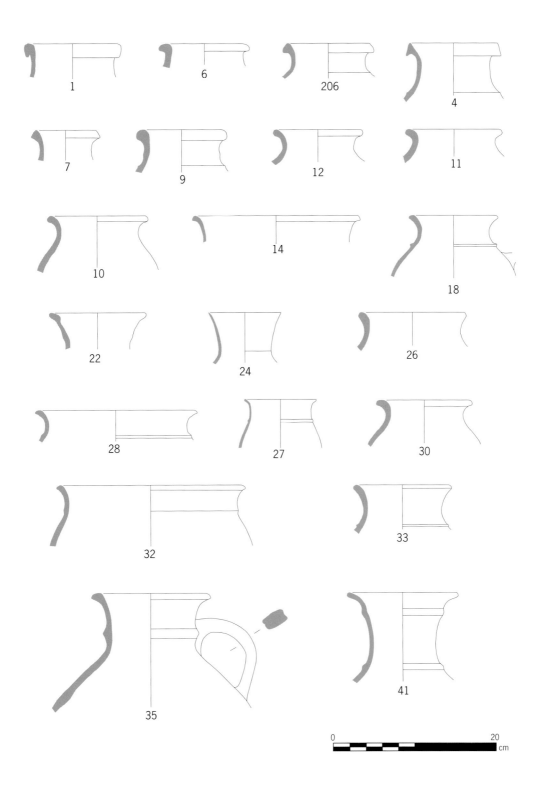

Figure 7.53. Jar types 1–41

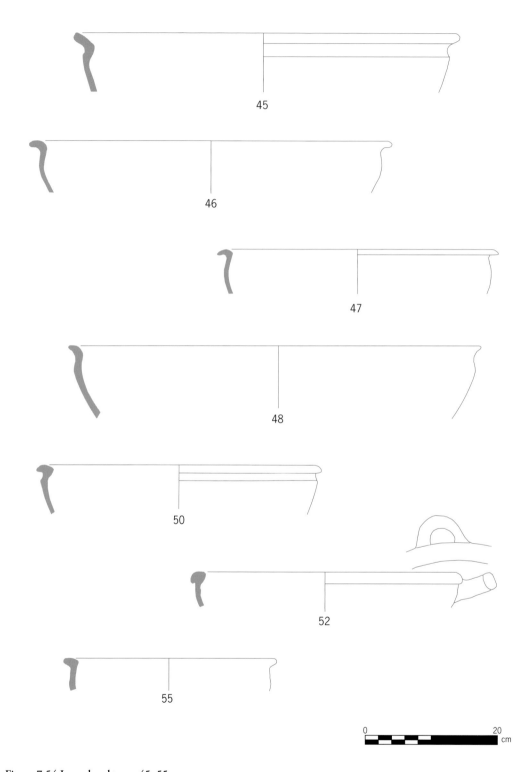

Figure 7.54 Large bowl types 45–55

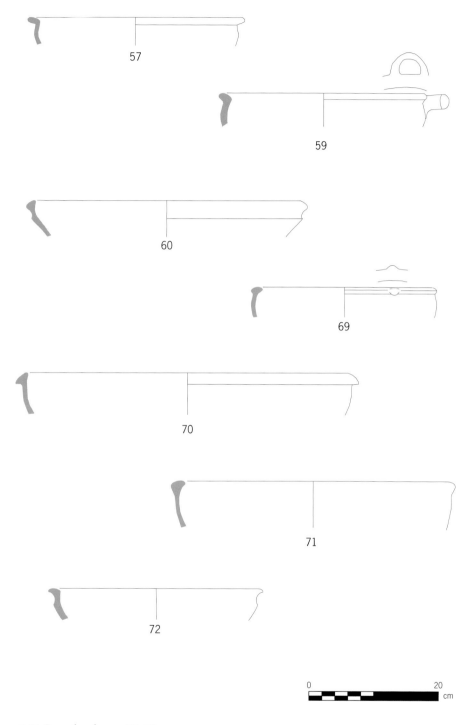

57

59

60

69

70

71

72

0   20
     cm

Figure 7.55. Large bowl types 57–72

Figure 7.56. Small bowl types 75–89

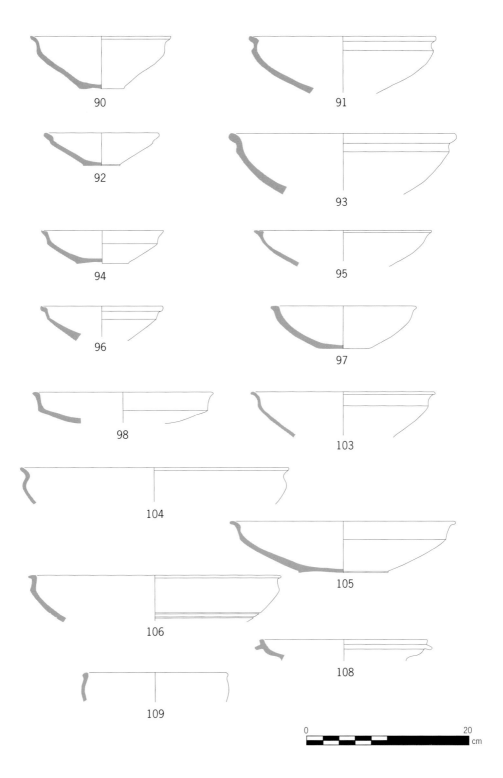

Figure 7.57. Small bowl types 90–109

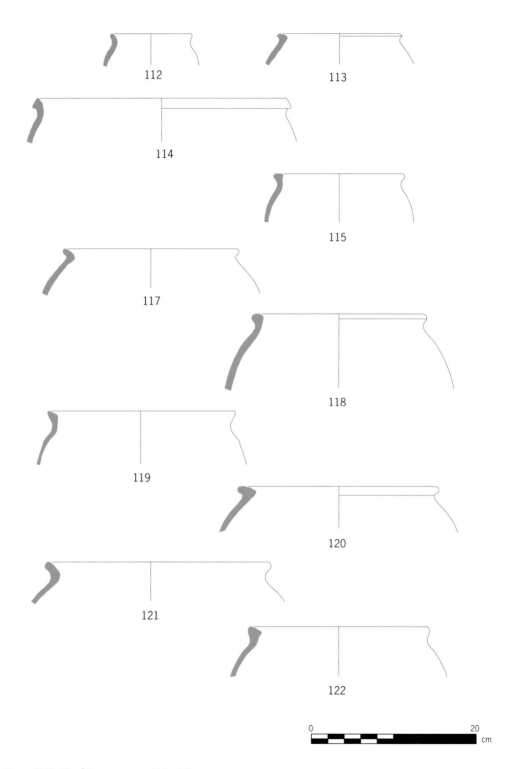

Figure 7.58. Cooking-pot types 112–122

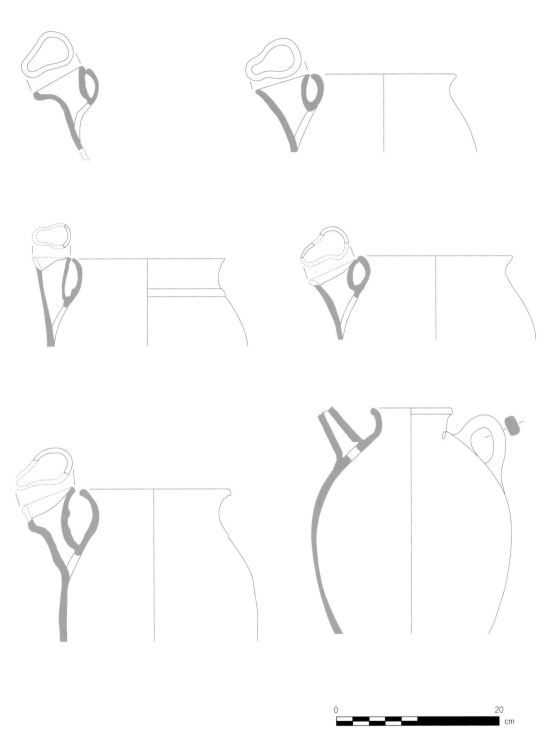

Figure 7.59. Spouted vessels

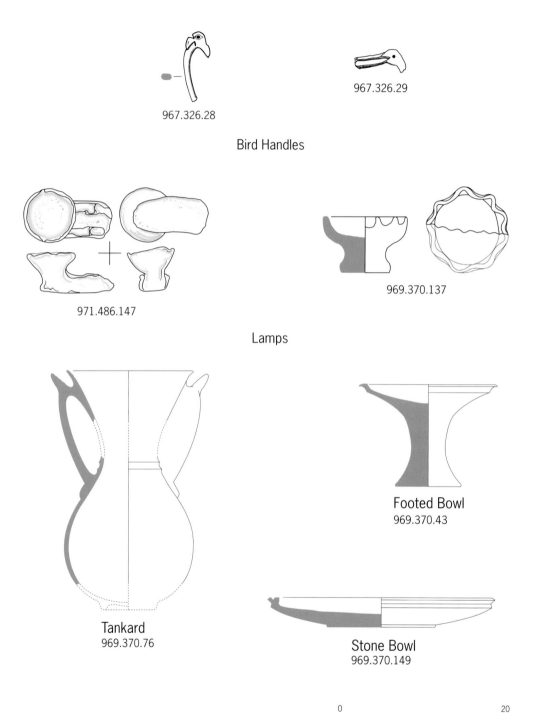

Bird Handles

Lamps

971.486.147

969.370.137

Tankard
969.370.76

Footed Bowl
969.370.43

Stone Bowl
969.370.149

0   20
                      cm

Figure 7.60. Miscellaneous forms

Further Reading

Note: Additional references are available in the Godin Web archive at https://tspace.library.utoronto.ca.

Boessneck J., H. H. Müller, and M. Teichert. "Osteologiche Unterscheidungsmerkmale Zwischen Schaf (Ovis Aries Linné) und Ziege (Capra Hircus Linné)." *Kühn-Archiv* 78/1–2 (1964): 5–129.

Boucharlat, R., and P. Lombard. "Le Bâtiment G de Rumeilah (Oasis d'Al Ain). Remarques sur les salles à poteaux de l'âge du fer en péninsule d'Oman." *Iranica Antiqua* 36 (2001): 213–238.

Bradley, R., and M. Fulford. "Sherd Size in the Analysis of Occupational Debris." *Bulletin of the Institute of Archaeology* 17 (1980): 85–94.

Bray, T. L. "The Commensal Politics of Early States and Empires." In *The Archaeology of Food and Feasting in Early States and Empires,* edited by T. L. Bray, 1–16. New York: Plenum Press, 2003.

Bronk Ramsey, C. "Development of the Radiocarbon Calibration Program Oxcal." *Radiocarbon* 43 (2001): 355–363.

———. "Comment on 'The Use of Bayesian Statistics for 14C Dates of Chronologically Ordered Samples: A Critical Analysis.'" *Radiocarbon* 42 (2000): 199–202.

Brown, S. "Media and Secondary State Formation in the Neo-Assyrian Zagros: An Anthropological Approach to an Assyriological Problem." *Journal of Cuneiform Studies* 38 (1986): 107–119.

———. "Kinship to Kingship. Archaeological and Historical Studies in the Neo-Assyrian Zagros." PhD diss., University of Toronto, 1980.

Collon, D. "Mesopotamian Columns." *The Journal of the Ancient Near Eastern Society of Columbia University* 2 (1969): 1–18.

Dietler, M., and B. Hayden. "Digesting the Feast—Good to Eat, Good to Drink, Good to Think: An Introduction." In *Feasts: Archaeological and Ethnographic Perspectives on Food, Politics, and Power*, edited by M. Dietler and B. Hayden, 1–23. Washington: Smithsonian Institution, 2001.

Frankfort, H. *The Art and Architecture of the Ancient Orient.* New Haven: Yale University Press, 1970.

Gifford-Gonzales, D. D., B. Damrosch, J. Pryor, and R. L. Thunen. "The Third Dimension in Site Structure: An Experiment in Trampling with Vertical Dispersion." *American Antiquity* 50 (1985): 803–818.

Gopnik, H. "Why Columned Halls?" In *The World of Achaemenid Persia,* edited by S. Simpson, 195–206. London: British Museum Press, 2010.

———. "The Shape of Sherds: Function and Style at Godin II." *Iranica Antiqua* 40 (2005): 249–270.

———. "The Ceramics from Godin II in the Late 7th to Early 5th Centuries BC." In *Continuity of Empire (?) Assyria, Media, Persia,* edited by G. B. Lanfranchi et al., 249–267. Padova: S.A.R.G.O.N. Editrice e Libreria, 2003.

———. "The Ceramics of Godin II: Ceramic Variability in the Archaeological Record." PhD diss., University of Toronto, 2000.

Grayson, A. Kirk. *Assyrian Royal Inscriptions. Vol. 2: From Tiglath-Pileser I to Ashur-Nasir-Apli II.* Wiesbaden: Otto Harrassowitz, 1976.

Gunter, A. "Representations of Urartian and Western Iranian Fortress Architecture in the Assyrian Reliefs." *Iran* 20 (1982): 103–111.

Hayden, B., and A. Cannon. "Where the Garbage Goes: Refuse Disposal in the Maya Highlands." *Journal of Anthropological Archaeology* 2 (1983): 117–163.

Huff, D. "From Median to Achaemenian Palace Architecture." *Iranica Antiqua* 40 (2005): 371–396.

Lanfranchi, G. "The Assyrian Expansion in the Zagros and the Local Ruling Elites." In *Continuity of Empire (?) Assyria, Media, Persia,* edited by G. Lanfranchi et al., 79–118. Padova: S.A.R.G.O.N. Editrice e Libreria, 2003.

Larsen, M. T. *The Conquest of Assyria: Excavations in an Antique Land 1840–1860.* New York: Routledge, 1994.

Levine, L. D. *Two Neo-Assyrian Stelae from Iran.* Toronto: Royal Ontario Museum, 1972.

Liverani, M. "The Rise and Fall of Media." In *Continuity of Empire (?) Assyria, Media, Persia,* edited by

G. Lanfranchi et al., 1–12. Padova: S.A.R.G.O.N. Editrice e Libreria, 2003.

———. "The Medes at Esarhaddon's Court." *Journal of Cuneiform Studies* 47 (1995): 57–62.

Magee, P. "Excavations at the Iron Age Settlement of Muweilah 1997–2000." *Proceedings of the Seminar for Arabian Studies* 31 (2001): 115–130.

Majizadeh, Y. "Excavations at Ozbaki: Second Preliminary Report 1999." *Iranian Journal of Archaeology and History* 14 (2001): 38–49.

———. "Excavations at Ozbaki: First Preliminary Report 1998." *Iranian Journal of Archaeology and History* 13 (2000): 57–81.

McIntosh, S. Keech. "Pathways to Complexity: An African Perspective." In *Beyond Chiefdoms: Pathways to Complexity in Africa*, edited by S. K. McIntosh, 1–30. Cambridge: Cambridge University Press, 1999.

Oates, D. "Innovations in Mud-Brick: Decorative and Structural Techniques in Ancient Mesopotamia." *World Archaeology* 21 (1990): 388–406.

Parpola, S. "Sakas, India Gobryas and the Median Royal Court." In *Continuity of Empire (?) Assyria, Media, Persia,* edited by G. Lanfranchi et al., 339–350. Padova: S.A.R.G.O.N. Editrice e Libreria, 2003.

Radner, K. "An Assyrian View on the Medes." In *Continuity of Empire (?) Assyria, Media, Persia,* edited by G. Lanfranchi et al., 37–64. Padova: S.A.R.G.O.N. Editrice e Libreria, 2003.

Rollinger, R. "The Western Expansion of the Median 'Empire': A Re-Examination." In *Continuity of Empire (?) Assyria, Media, Persia,* edited by G. Lanfranchi et al., 289–319. Padova: S.A.R.G.O.N. Editrice e Libreria, 2003.

Root, M. *The King and Kingship in Achaemenid Art.* Leiden: E.J. Brill, 1979.

Stark, M. T. "Current Issues in Ceramic Ethnoarchaeology." *Journal of Archaeological Research* 11 (2003): 193–230.

Stronach, D. "Independent Media, Archaeological Notes from the Homeland." In *Continuity of Empire (?) Assyria, Media, Persia,* edited by G. Lanfranchi et al., 233–248. Padova: S.A.R.G.O.N. Editrice e Libreria, 2003.

Stronach, D., and M. Roaf, *Nush-i Jan I: The Major Buildings of the Median Settlement.* London: British Institute of Persian Studies, 2008.

Stronach, R. "Excavations at Tepe Nush-i Jan: Part 2, Median Pottery From the Fallen Floor in the Fort." *Iran* 16 (1978): 11–24.

Venturi, R. "Complexity and Contradiction in Architecture." New York: Museum of Modern Art, 1977.

Winter, I. "The Program of the Throneroom of Assurnasirpal II at Nimrud." In *Essays on Near Eastern Art and Archaeology in Honor of C. K. Wilkinson*, edited by P. O. Harper and H. Pittman, 13–21. New York: Metropolitan Museum of Art, 1983.

Acknowledgements

This publication of Godin Tepe has been more than forty years in the making and is the product of many more people than can be named here. First and foremost we want to acknowledge the life and work of the late T. Cuyler Young, Jr., to whom this book is fondly dedicated. Cuyler's scholarship had a profound impact on our knowledge of the archaeology and history of Iran, and his excavation of Godin Tepe was one of the most significant archaeological projects in central western Iran in the past century. The authors hope that this volume and the accompanying Web archive fulfill the high standards that Cuyler would have wanted for the final publication of this important site.

All of Cuyler's work on Godin would have been impossible without the help and dedication of his wife Pam. Not only did she provide the emotional support that allowed him to go off to the field year after year knowing that their children, Kate, Bridget and Timothy, would be nurtured back at home, but Cuyler often credited Pam, an expert editor and writer, with smoothing out the rougher edges of his prose style. Pam was Cuyler's centre in the world, and his devotion to her was an inspiration to his graduate students. The Young family has continued their support of Godin with this publication, providing anecdotes and photos of the Godin years. We thank them for all they selflessly gave up of their husband and father for the sake of Godin and for all the help they have continued to give us in order to make this publication happen.

Archaeology is above all a collaborative enterprise. Each member of the Godin excavation team contributed in some way to the final product, and the authors are indebted to everyone involved in the five field seasons. Some members of the team were particularly helpful in this final push to publication and deserve special thanks: Louis Levine, Cuyler's close collaborator and associate director of the Godin excavation project, was a driving force in getting this publication project underway and generously agreed to share his memories of the excavation with the authors. Harvey Weiss, Irene Winter, and Marie-Henriette Gates, graduate-student excavation supervisors at Godin and each now a distinguished professor of archaeology, provided valuable insights and photos of the excavation units that they had supervised all those years ago. Claus Breede, the architect and draftsperson of the excavation project, executed many of the original drawings used in the book and provided helpful details about some of the plans. The late Carol Kramer's ethnoarchaeological studies of the villages near Godin influenced many of the arguments made in this volume. Her powerful anthropological voice is missed throughout the academic community.

We are equally indebted to the generations of researchers who recorded, classified, and analysed many of the artifacts that were brought back from the site. Special thanks are due to Allan Gilbert who did the original analysis of Godin bone and passed much of this material on to Pam Crabtree at NYU. The late Seanna Henrickson was responsible for the analysis of the earliest periods from Godin and neighbouring Seh Gabi, and her work is the basis for much of the analysis of those periods presented in Chapter 4 of this volume. Seanna's perpetual good humour in the face of piles and piles of sherds was an inspiration to Hilary Gopnik as a young graduate student, and her presence was sorely missed throughout this publication process.

When this publication project got underway three years ago a new collaborative team was corralled into the Godin fold. Angelica Magsisi was hired to create illustrations of Godin artifacts, but her dedication and remarkable work ethic transformed her into supervisor, researcher, archivist, and all around go-to person for the project. Her talent and accomplishments in illustration can be seen in the volume; our gratitude to her for her invaluable organizational contributions can be expressed only feebly here. Steve Batiuk helped honour Cuyler's memory by producing all of the excellent maps in the volume. He little knew how much time he would spend on this demanding task when he began it, but his cheerfulness with the authors' unending dithering went well beyond what could be expected from such an altruistic offer of help. We cannot thank him enough. Julie Kim, an architect, skillfully produced the isometric reconstructions of the plans for all periods. The University of Toronto work study program provided a number of able student research assistants to the project.

The authors were fortunate in the exceptional group of professionals who completed the more specialized analyses of the Godin artifacts. Naomi Miller, of the University of Pennsylvania Museum's MASCA division, undertook the identification of charcoal specimens and the analysis of charred seeds. Pam Crabtree of New York University took on the identification and analysis of the thousands of animal bone fragments. William Hallo, professor emeritus at Yale University, had already begun a study of the tablets from Godin and he agreed to include it in this publication. Holly Pittman from the University of Pennsylvania, who had been associated with Cuyler and the Godin project for a very long time, also agreed to include her work on the seals and sealing from Godin Period VI. James Blackman at the Smithsonian Institution was asked to extend his INAA analysis of the pottery from the site. And Vince Pigott suggested that we ask Lesley Frame, a graduate student at the University of Arizona, to analyse the metal from Godin. This talented group produced interesting and novel analyses, and the authors thank them for their invaluable contributions to the publication.

The World Cultures department at the Royal Ontario Museum was a sponsor and host of the Godin project from the beginning and has provided support for this publication.

This volume would never have happened without the inspiration of Lisa Golombek who, as the chair of the ROM publications committee, insisted that the publication of Godin become a reality even after all these years. We are deeply grateful for the many, many hours collections manager Bill Pratt spent sifting and recording the Godin material and supervising our research assistants with unstinting patience. This project would have been quite simply impossible without him. Ed Keall, a devoted step-father to Godin over many years, advised us about plans, maps, and illustrations. The department chair, Krzysztof Grzymski, ensured that we had space and computers available for our project team. Peter Kaellgren and Chen Shen, as members of the ROM publication committee, ably guided the manuscript through the review process. Conservator Susan Stock helped metallurgist Lesley Frame to collect samples for her analysis. Clemens Reichel contributed to our final push to press and in mounting the Web archive. Finally, Dan Rahimi not only generously opened his home to Mitchell Rothman during his visits to the Godin Period IV collections at the ROM, but was a guiding light throughout the publication project. In spite of his very busy schedule, Dan cheerfully found time to sort through the Godin lithics and provided advice to our illustrator about how to draw them. The authors thank him deeply for his many contributions.

The Royal Ontario Museum publications department was a driving force behind the Godin publication project from its inception. Our managing editor Glen Ellis promoted the book through every step of the project, made sure that we had the funds and people in place to get the job done, and provided valuable advice about content and design. Designer Tara Winterhalt's unbeatable eye ensured that the colour and layout design highlighted the best of the Godin collection. When maternity leave prevented Tara's continuing with the project, Mia Ijacic took over and ably completed the book's final layout. Brian Boyle has photographed the Godin artifacts since they were excavated; we are proud to have his excellent photographs grace these pages. Andrea Gallagher's heroic last-minute copyediting of the final manuscript smoothed the rougher edges of the authors' prose and marshalled every comma into its proper place.

We would like to thank our many colleagues, too numerous to name here, who have contributed to our knowledge of the long period of history and archaeology of Iran that are spanned by the occupation of Godin. A number of these scholars have made specific contributions to this volume. David Stronach has been a fundamental part of the Godin story since Cuyler first saw the site in the early 1960s. As one of Cuyler's closest friends and colleagues, and as a mentor to Cuyler's graduate students, David's deep knowledge of Iranian archaeology were always a part of any discussion of the site. His inspiration, advice, encouragement, and criticism have made this volume a much better work. Tony

Sagona read early drafts of Chapter 5 and made many useful suggestions. Henry Wright's thorough editorial comments on Chapters 3, 4, and 5 were invaluable to the final volume. Thanks also to Lily Niakan and the Iranian Cultural Heritage Organization Archaeological Research Center for generously providing photographs of the Godin artifacts housed in Iran, and to Norm Badler for his help in organizing the Godin Period VI spreadsheets.

The original excavations at Godin were funded by the Social Sciences and Humanities Research Council of Canada, the University of Toronto, and the Royal Ontario Museum. Funds for this publication project were provided by the Shelby White–Leon Levy Program for Archaeological Publications and the Louise Hawley Stone Publications Fund. We thank all these organizations for their generous support.

Finally the authors would like to offer their own personal thanks.

Hilary Gopnik: After fifty years of university teaching and with six literary kids, my parents Irwin and Myrna probably hold some kind of record for being thanked in acknowledgements pages. Still, the inspiration they have provided remains understated. Their insistence that an argument had to be supported by the data at hand (claiming that you hadn't crossed the street when you were standing on the other side just wouldn't wash), but that it was also always worth telling your story well (especially if you wanted to be heard over five other know-it-all voices at the dinner table) has served me well through the writing of this book. Their love, support, patience, and guidance have been the too often unacknowledged presence behind all of our work. We are lucky to have acknowledgment pages to express our thanks. Thanks also to those know-it-all siblings Alison, Adam, Morgan, Blake, and Melissa who fortunately really do know an awful lot and who have given me so much academic, literary, and managerial advice throughout this project. Shannon McManus and Paul Bilodeau gave me a home away from home in Toronto and were always ready with a glass of wine, a good meal, and cheery commiseration after a hard day wrestling with old field notes and new research assistants. Paul served as a "non-expert" reader of the manuscript and gave some very expert editing suggestions about how to make the text more accessible. My frequent trips away from home would have been dreary without their company, and I am deeply grateful for it. Between my graduate work and this project, my daughters Zoe, Oona, and Ayala have spent all their lives with Godin Tepe as the Scrooge-like spectre who delayed trips to the park or made me take a computer on vacations. Yet their spirits seem to harbour no resentment, and they were ready to read drafts and offer support in the best Gopnik-McManus tradition of working together to get the show up and running. It seems redundant to thank them because they know they are at the very centre of my soul. Finally and most profoundly I want to thank my husband-as-protagonist, Donald McManus. Donald read and gave advice on every word and picture in this volume, and it's hard to know where my words end and his begin. Most importantly, he was always there to encourage me to work when I should and to discourage me from working when there were more important things to do. I might have gotten this book done faster without him, but there wouldn't have been nearly as much joy along the way.

Mitchell Rothman: Thanks to my wife, Leslie Simon, and daughter, Dena Rothman, for tolerating my hours and hours in the study working on this volume, and for their many subtle encouragements of my work. Thanks to my ninety-five-year-old father, Carl, always ready to give support and praise, even as he faces an uncertain future. My appreciation goes to the Faculty Affairs Committee and President of Widener University for granting me a semester sabbatical to work on Godin. I want to thank Lisa Cooper, who on a hot day in Birecik, Turkey, suggested that I call Cuyler to ask about helping in the final publication of Godin Tepe. Many other teachers and colleagues played some role in helping me think through the myriad of issues on the fourth and third millennia in Mesopotamia and beyond before I could reach my own interpretations. Among them are Henry Wright, Guillermo Algaze, Gil Stein, Marcella Frangipane, Glenn Schwartz, and Tony Sagona. There are many more too numerous to list here. To all, many thanks.

Index

Arnold, James, 36
Arslantepe, 96, 120, 157–58, 195
artemesia, 55
artifacts
    apportioning of, 11
    from Brick Kiln Cut, 107–9
    carnelian shell and lapis lazuli found at Godin,
        photo of, *64*
    and field records taken from Godin, list of, 18
    from oval compound, 98–104, 105, 106
    See also artifactual remains of; burials, artifacts found in;
        metallurgy; pottery; seals and sealings; tablets
artifactual remains of Period II
    animal-bone remains, 313, 323–25
    beads, carnelian and ivory, 299
    deposition of, 329–30
    lack of complete objects recovered, 322
    phase 1, secondary occupation
        grindstones, 322
        pestles, 322
        spindle whorls, 322
    phase 2, primary occupation
        beads, small quantity of, 323
        bronze bracelets, 322
        fibula (brooch), 322, 323
        needle, 322
    weapons and tools, metal, 348
    See also metallurgy; pottery
artifactual remains of Period III
    andirons, 218, 231, 232, 233
    animal-bone remains, 223
    beads, carnelian, shell and lapis lazuli, 299, 300
    blade cores, 222
    bone tools, 224
    bronze items, 226, 227
    ceramic tray, 218
    charcoal, 215
    clay pellets, 223
    figurines, 225, 226, 230–31
    flint blades for sickles, 222
    grinding stones, 222
    human skeletons, 215, 216, 235
    loomweights, 225
    moulds, metallurgical, 226
    pins, decorative, 229
    stone tools, *222*
    tuyere fragment, 228–29
    See also metallurgy; pottery
artifactual remains of Period IV
    andirons, 186
    animal-bone remains, 175–78, 184, 186
    beads, 179
    blade cores, 175, 182, 184
    bone tools, *177*
    braziers, 182
    crucibles, 175, *176*, 182, 186
    distributions of, over site, *181, 182, 183, 185, 187, 188*
    figurines, 180, 186
    flints, *175*
    food preparation tools and vessels, 186, 189

grinding stones, 175, 177
    pottery-making tools, 174
    spindle whorls, 179, 182, 186
    stone tools, 174, *175, 176*, 182
    wool and leather-craft tools, 179
    See also metallurgy; pottery
artifactual remains of Period VI
    animal-bone remains, 60, 103, 108–9
    beads, 101, 103
    bone tools, 101, 103
    ceramics used in metallurgy, *105*
    distribution over site, *97*
    figurines, *103*
    grain, 99
    lithic cores, 101
    lithic flakes, 103, 104
    sickles, 103
    sling balls, 99–100
    spindle whorls, stone, 101, *103*
    stone quern, 101
    stone tools, blades and flakes, *102*, 104
    weapons, 99
    See also metallurgy; pottery; seals and sealings; tablets
Ashurnasirpal II, 285
Assyrian depictions of conquered lands, 303, 336, 337
Assyrian Empire
    adê (loyalty oath) tablets, 300–301
    administrative control over Medes in Zagros Mountain
        region, 301–2
    divide and conquer policy, 300, 301
    ideology of, 298–99
    overthrow of, by the Medes and Babylonians, 302, 346
    rise and expansion of, 286
    Sargon's military campaigns against the Medes, 290, 291
    trade, control of, along the High Road, 298, 299
    trade networks, 298, 299, 300
    tribute demanded from the Medes, 298
    violent nature of, 286
    vs state of Urartu, 24, 289
"Avenue Road," 211, 218, 273, 277
awls and burins, 179

B

Baba Dervish, 195
Badler, Virginia, xiii , 81
Batiuk,Stephen, 195
beads. *See* jewellery
bēl āli
    relationship with Assyrian rulers, 300
    translations of term, 297
    use of term, 295
    wealth of, 298
beveled-rim bowls, 44, 88–89
    See also pottery
Blackman, James, 244
Boucharlat, Remy, 339
Breede, Claus, 16
Brick Kiln Cut, *31, 32*, 95, 107–9, 162–63, *165*, 182
British Institute of Persian Studies, 10

Bronze Age. *See* Godin Period III
burial grounds, 221
burials, artifacts found in Period III, 229, 232, 235, 266
as primary deposits, 24–25
valuable nature of, 299

C

carbon-14 dating
    discussion of, 36–37, 84
    Period II, 343–45
    Period IV, 163, *166*
    Period VI, 84–85
    See also chronology; dating
ceramic objects
    figurines, *103*, 180, 186, *225*, 226, 230–31
    moulds, metallurgical, 226
    tray from Period III structure, 218
    used in metallurgy, *105*
Chalcolithic periods in Zagros Mountains
    Early and Middle
        earliest occupation in, 73
        population growth and decline, 75–77
        settlement sites, *74*, 75
    Late
        political change in, 77–78
        seals and sealings, 77, 79
        sites, *83*
        trade, complex network of, 79–81
        trade routes during, 77
    See also Godin Period VI, VII; pottery
charcoal
    artifactual remains of Period III, 215
    dating of, Godin Period II, 343
    lost samples of, 58
chronology
    change in nomenclature for Uruk-Warka period, 69
    comparative ceramic
        development of, for western Iran, 39–40
        of Period II pottery, *344*
        of Period III pottery, 12, 15, 270
        of Period IV pottery, 163–67
        of Period VI pottery, 90–92
    of Early Transcaucasian Culture, *144*
    of Greater Mesopotamia from Neolithic to end of
        Chalcolithic Age, *70*
    See also dating
citadel of Godin. *See* Godin Period II
clay balls, 99–100
columned halls in Arabia during Iron Age, 339–40
Crabtree, Pam, 60, 61, 109
cultural periods at Godin, 2–3, 22
See also specific periods

D

dating
    carbon-14, 36–37, 84
    Early Transcaucasian Culture (ETC), 143–44
    Period II, 343–45, 347
    Period III, 210

Period IV, 160–67
Period VI, 82–85
relative, 36, 39, 84
See also chronology
Dawkins, Richard, 44
Deep Sounding
    excavation of, 2, 13–14, 16
    Period III
        phase 3, 216
        phases of, exposed, 210, 211
        village architecture, 15
    Period IV, 182
    stratigraphic section of, *31, 32*
    superimposed layers of architecture in, *27*
Dur-Šarrukin (Khorsabad), 290–91
Dyson, Robert, 7, 8, 24, 28

E

Early Neolithic societies, 71–73
Early Transcaucasian Culture (ETC)
    ceramics, in Amuq valley, 158
    dating, 143–44
    economic strategies of, 154–55, 159
    expansion, vs Uruk expansion, 142
    geographic origins of, 141
    house types, description of, 152, *153*, 154
    ideological (ritual) elements of, 149–52
    migration
        to Godin in Period IV, 195–97, 272
        map of sites, *140*
        models of, 156–60
        in Muş Province, 157, 158
    Norşuntepe, 151, 154, 197
    social organization, 150–51
    trade routes, 195
    See also Godin Period IV; pottery
Edens, Christopher, 174
Elam, 278, 279
Elamite confederation, 279
Elar, 195
environments, natural
    altered by human beings, 55, 57
    and culture, 56
    impact of, on Godin cultures, 49
    study of ancient, 54
Esarhaddon, 300–301
Esarhaddon, annals of, 299, 346
Eshnunna state, 279–80
ethnicity, 155–56, 159
ethnoarchaeological studies of Zagros village societies, 221
ethnoarchaeology, 40–41, 43
ethnographic accounts of pottery production, 241–42,
    245, 246
excavations
    of burials, 25, 221
    of Deep Sounding, 2, 13–14, 16
    details of, 18
    grid system, 28
    at Hasanlu, 8
    impact on stratigraphic record, 31–34

grid system of excavation, 28

H

Habuba Kabira, 95–96
Haftavan Tepe, 11
Hamlin, Christopher, 14
Hasanlu, 5, 8, 24
hearths
    Godin Period II, 313
    Godin Period III ("kursi"), 218, 220, 224
    Godin Period IV, 173, 186, 189
    Godin Period VI, 94
    as shrines, 151
Henrickson, Elizabeth, 173
Henrickson, Robert, xiv, 18, 168–69
Herodotus, 285, 296, 303, 346
highland societies
    agricultural practices, 57–58
    political organization in, vs lowland societies, 78–79
    polities, banding together, 277–78, 302, 346
    relations with lowland societies, 69, 268, 275–76, 277, 295–96, 297–98, 347
    and trade with urban centres of Mesopotamia, 63–64, 119, 273–74, 279–80, 300–301
highlands of central Iran, natural resources of, 63–64
High Road, 62–63, 195, 269, 298
historical geography, 269
house construction, 152, 153, 210, 236
    See also Godin Period II; mud-bricks
human remains, 215, 216, 235

I

intellectual culture, bias of, 297
Iranian and United States relations, 8
Iranian Archaeological Service, 9, 11, 17, 323
Iranian archaeology, 8, 39
Iron Age citadel. See Godin Period II
Iron Age columned halls in Arabia, 339–40
Iron Age sites, 288
Islamic tea house, 2

J

Jebel Aruda, 95–96
jewellery
    Period III Bronze Age town, 299, 300
    Period II Iron Age citadel, 299, 322, 323
    Period IV, 180
    Period VI, 101, 103

K

Kangavar Valley, ancient
    climate of, 54
    farming, 1–2, 57, 58–59
    fertility of, 52
    Karkhaneh, 196, 211, 214
    and mountain culture, 119
    and other valley cultures, 56
    pastoral nomadic economic activity, 61, 77, 155,
        176–77, 183, 196
    pastoral products, 175–76
    population growth during Late Chalcolithic period,
        75–77
    rivers and aquifers in, 53
    routes from, 62–63, 195
    Seh Gabi, 69, 75, 80
    settlement in
        Period III, 210, 214, 273, 278–79
        Period IV, 196
        survey of, 110–11, 196
    social organization, 183, 184, 186, 197
    trees of, 54–55
    vs modern Kangavar environment, 55
    See also Zagros Mountains
Karkhaneh, 196, 211, 214
Khorsabad annals, 290, 295
Khorsabad (Dur-Šarrukin), 290–91
Kramer, Carol, 40–41, 42, 43, 44, 57, 224, 330

L

land tenure system in "Aliabad," 57–58
Lanfranchi, Giovanni, 295
lapis lazuli, 64, 299, 300
Late Chalcolithic (LC 1–5), 69
Lemonnier, Pierre, 42
Levine, Louis D., 11–12, 13, 24, 28, 29, 291–92, 322
Libby, Willard, 36
lithic industries at Godin, 104
Liverani, Mario, 300, 346
looms, evidence of in Period III, 225
lot system of record keeping, 28–29
Luristan, 269, 272, 277

M

Magee, Peter, 339
Malatya plain and ETC migration, 157, 158, 195
Malayer valley, 273
Mallowan, Sir Max, 13
massif funeraire, 78
Matthews, Roger, 81
McDonald, Mary, 173
Medes
    Assyrian and Greek perspectives on, 303
    Assyrian Empire, overthrow of, by, 302, 346
    Assyrian subjugation of the, 289–90
    conquest of the, by the Assyrians, 286–87, 287, 290,
        291, 293–95
    economic relationship with Assyrian Empire, 119,
        300–301
    horses of the, 289
    political organization under Assyrian rule, 295–96,
        297–98, 347
    search for sites of, 5, 9–11, 302–3
    settlement in Zagros Mountains, 286, 287, 289, 302
    trade in lapis lazuli, 299
Median cities, depiction of, by Assyrians, 303, 346
Median dinner, description of, as told by Xenophon, 336
Median Empire, existence of, 346–47

Median history
    Assyrians as sources of
        Khorsabad annals, 290, 291
        Najafehabad stele, 293–95
        Obelisk of Shalmaneser III, 286–87
    Greeks as sources of
        Herodotus, 285, 296–97
Mesopotamia
    Akkadian state, 275, 276, 277
    cultures, nature of, 144
    Early and Middle Chalcolithic sites in Greater, *74*
    Eshnunna state, 279–80
    Isin-Larsa period, 279
    Khorsabad (Dur-Šarrukin), 290–91
    land ownership and use in southern, 57
    resources, need for, 77
    scarlet ware of Early Dynastic I, 272
    societies of, 50, 139, 141
    as sources of written history, 268, 269
    Sukkalmah, 280
    Susa, 78, 79, 114, 228, 250, 251
    Urartu, state of, 24, 289
    Ur III dynasty, 275–76, 277, 278, 279
    Uruk Warka period, 2, 16, 69, 79, 96
Mesopotamian archaeological periodization, 39
metallurgy
    Period II, 348
    Period III, 226, *227*, 228–30
    Period IV, 175, 176, 182, 186
    Period VI, 105
Miller, Naomi, 54, 58, 59
mud-brick houses, life of, 236
mud bricks
    erosion of, 26–27
    fabrication of, 223, 315
    vaults, 320

N

Najafehabad stele
    discovery of, by Cuyler Young and Louis Levine, 291–92
    translation of, 293–95
    unearthing of, 293
Neo-Assyrian Empire, 3
Neolithic Period, 75
    See also Early Neolithic societies
Neolithic Revolution, 71
Neutron Activation Analysis, 111–12
New Archaeology, 7
nomadism and pastoralism, 61
    of ETC populations, 155
    Godin Period IV, 176–77, 183, 196
    nature of, 61
    and population fluctuations, 77
    See also agricultural practices
Norşuntepe, 151, 154, 197
Nush-i Jan, 10–11, 15, 303, 319–20, 331

O

object cards, *29*

objects. *See* artifactual remains
Operation EEE, 235, 238
Operation F, 182
Operation O, 226
Operations A and B, 12, 13, 28, 73, 82
Operation XYZ, 73
    oval compound
    architecture of
        common features (niches and hearths), 94
        description of, 92–93
        function of site's buildings, 95, 97–99, 101, 103–5, 107
        sequence of construction, 93–94
    artifacts found at, 98–104, *105, 106*
    dating of, 82–85
    discovery of, 2
    excavations of, 17–18, 82
    faunal analysis, 60, 103, 108–9, 176
    metallurgy, 105
    photo of, *68*
    plans of, *84, 93, 94*
    primary deposits, 24
    sealings found at, 11, *98*, 113–15, 134–35
    tablets found at, 16, 98, 116, *117–18*, 134–35
    See also Godin Period VI

P

pastoralism and nomadism
    of ETC populations, 155
    Godin Period IV, 176–77, 183, 196
    nature of, 61
    and population fluctuations, 77
    See also agricultural practices
Persian Empire, 302, 303, 338
Petrie, Sir Flinders, 21, 38
plans, key to, xi
population size, Periods III, IV, VI, 197
post-structuralist anthropology, 297
pottery
    change, Petrie's illustration of, 38
    of Early Transcaucasian Culture (ETC)
        ceramics, spread of, 156–60
        designs of Period IV, 149
        as identifying element of, 141–42
        merging with Late Chalcolithic style, 148
        style periods, 147
        styles of, 145–49, 272
        style zones, *146, 147, 148, 149*
        traditions, 75, *76*
        types, 86, 123–33
    of Godin Period II
        bowls, photo of, 335
        bowl sherds from, photo of, 291
        broken, found in phase II:1 rubbish heap, 328
        chronology, comparative ceramic, *344*
        fine ware found in South Magazine deposit, 326–27
        fine ware (red-brown ware) of late Iron Age, 333–34
        functional types found in North Magazine deposit, *327*
        jars, bowls, and cooking pots, photo of, *326*

manufacture of, 331

sherds assemblage, 323, 325, 328, *335*

sherds found on courtyard floor, 329

"tankard," photo of, *327*

types, difficulty in sorting, 330–31

typology: bowl diameters by type for each phase, *332,
333*; counts of bowl types by phase, *333*; creation
of, 331; functional types in each phase, 334; large
range of sizes and types, 334–35; rim types, distribution of, between phases, 331–32

of Godin Period III

chronology of, and related sites, 12, 15, 270

dating of, 251, 264, 266

decorative designs, animal motifs in, 231–32, *234,
236*

distribution of, by phase, 246

distribution of, geographic, 259, 262, 266, 273, 276

end of, tradition, 280

grave goods, 235, 238

grey ware, Isin-Larsa, 262, 278, 279

jar, as work of art, 21, *22*

painted buff-ware: from burial site, 238; clay preparation, 243; decorative repertoire of, 45; decorative
style of, 242, *256*; large vessels, 241; medium
vessels, 240–41; oversized vessels, 241–42; paste
and production sequence, 244–45; photos of, 237,
238, *239–40, 276*; small vessels, 239–40

production: organization of, 242–43; and paste
characterization, 243–44; specialization of, 243

red-slipped ware, *237*, 238, 243, 244, 245

styles and types: phase 1, *265*, 266; phase 2, 260,
261, 262, 263, 264, 266; phase 2, post, *263*,
264–66, 280; phase 3, 215, *222*, 259; phase 4,
256, 257, 258, 259; phase 5, *252, 253, 254*, 255;
phase 6, *247, 248, 249*, 250–51, 255, *271*

theriomorphic (animal-shaped) vessels, 230

vessels found in phase 3 occupation, 215, 222

wares vs Chalcolithic wares, 243

xeroradiographs of, *238, 239*, 240, 241

of Godin Period IV

assemblage, 167–68

beaker or cup, typical, photo of, *172*

bichrome firing colour, photo of, *169*

bowl handles, photo of, *170*

chronology, comparative ceramic of, 163–67

colours of, photo of, *168*

designs; comparisons with other ETC sites, 193, *194*;
and cultural identity, 189, 192, 277; distribution
of, *191*, 192–93; incised designs, *190, 191, 195*

functions, 173–74

grog inclusions in, photo of, *169*

inturned-rim bowls, photo of, *88*

jar, red-slipped, photo of, *88*

jar, typical, *172*

limited nature of, 149

at Pulur, *151*, 173, 193

storage jars, photos of, 172

types: comparison with other ETC sites, *194*;
by phase, *166*, 167–68

typology: bowls, 170–71; categories, 170; cooking
pots, 171; jars, storage jars, and cups, 171–72;

lids, 172; trays, 171

of Godin Period VI

assemblage of, 85–86

beveled-rim bowls, 44, *89*

chemical analysis of, 106

chronology, comparative ceramic, 90–92

comparanda, *122*

manufacture of, 86–90, 168–70

painted pot, photo of, *79*

wine jar, photo of, *106*

of Godin Periods VI–VII

development and change in, 89–90

types, *86, 121–33*

Uruk, *88, 89*, 91

of Godin Period XI, pre-, 75, 76

production, ethnographic accounts of, 241–42, 245,
246

stylistic changes in

of each cultural period, 44–45

over time and space, 39, 40

Pottery Typology catalogues

Period II, *349–62*

Period IV, *199–204*

Periods VI–VII, *121–33*

Potts, Dan, 269

Proto-Elamite cultural unit, 114, 197

Pulur

building types, 152, 184

pottery comparison to Godin Tepe, 193

ritual at, 151, 162

Q

qanat, 58

R

radiocarbon dating

discussion of, 36–37, 84

for Period II, 343–45

for Period IV, 163, 166

for Period VI, 84–85

See also chronology; dating

Radner, Karen, 295

record-keeping techniques, changes in, 28–29

relative dating, 36, 39, 84

See also dating

ritual

evidence of, at ETC sites, 150–52

evidence of, at Godin Period III, 230–32, 235

and feasting, 340

ideological elements of, 149–52

at Pulur, 151, 162

Roaf, Michael, 319

Rothman, Mitchell, xiii

Royal Cemetery of Ur, 274

Royal Ontario Museum (ROM),

carbon samples stored at, 58

Cuyler Young as director of, 9, 19

Godin artifacts and field records housed at, 18

Period IV pottery housed at, 167–68

Y

Yanik Tepe, 193, 195
Young, T. Cuyler, Jr.
    at age 11, photo of, 7
    carbon samples sent for analysis, 36–37
    and ceramic chronology for western Iran, 8, 39
    childhood and teen years, 6
    David Stronach, relationship with, 10
    examining pottery, photo of, *10*
    excavation data, goals for, 18
    father, relationship with, 7
    Hasanlu, role as field director at, 5, 8, 24
    Louis Levine, relationship with, 11–12
    with Louis Levine, photo of, *12*
    Middle Eastern research and significance of Godin VI,
      81
    Najafehabad stele, discovery of, 291–92
    publishing intentions, 19, xiii
    quotation on Godin, 5
    and record keeping at Godin Tepe, 28–29
    Royal Ontario Museum, role as director of, 19
    site search, 5, 9–11, 14–15, 302–3
    as a young man, 7–8
Young, T. Cuyler, Sr., 6

Z

Zagros Mountains
    agricultural practices in Luristan, 269
    artemesia, 55
    Early Neolithic in, 71
    geographic location of Period III sites, 267, 268
    geology of, 50–51
    Medes, settlement of, in, 286, 287, 289, 302
    migration of ETC peoples into, 195–97, 272
    natural resources of, 63–64
    physiographic zones of, and occupation by ethnic
      groups, 56
    rivers and aquifers, 53
    settlement patterns of Period III, 211, 213–14, 215,
      221, 278–79
    temperature and rainfall, 53–54
    topography
      and geographical zones, 268
      and traditional tribal and ethnic areas, 269
    trade routes, 1, 62–63, 77, 195, 268–69, 273, 280
    transportation challenges in, 62
    village societies in, ethnoarchaeological studies of, 221
    See also Chalcolithic periods in Zagros Mountains;
      Kangavar Valley, ancient
zooarchaeology, 60–61